MORE PRAISE FOR *ALL UNDER*

"Zhao's fresh ideas, arguments, and methods are important and well done."
  —Stephen C. Angle, Wesleyan University

"This book allows Western readers to participate in important current
discussions in China about globalization and world order."
  —Fred Dallmayr, University of Notre Dame

All under Heaven

GREAT TRANSFORMATIONS

Craig Calhoun and Nils Gilman, Series Editors

All under Heaven

THE *TIANXIA* SYSTEM FOR A POSSIBLE
WORLD ORDER

Zhao Tingyang

Translated by Joseph E. Harroff

*with a new foreword
by Odd Arne Westad*

UNIVERSITY OF CALIFORNIA PRESS

B Berggruen
Institute

University of California Press
Oakland, California

© 2016 by Zhao Tingyang, English edition © 2021 by University of
California Press, by arrangement with Zhao Tingyang c/o CITIC Press
Corporation. All rights reserved.

Library of Congress Cataloging-in-Publication Data

Names: Zhao, Tingyang, author. | Harroff, Joseph E., translator. |
   Westad, Odd Arne, writer of foreword.
Title: All under heaven : the Tianxia system for a possible world order /
   Zhao Tingyang; translated by Joseph E. Harroff; with a new foreword
   by Odd Arne Westad. Other titles: Tian xia de dang dai xing. English |
   Great transformations ; 3.
Identifiers: LCCN 2020047088 (print) | LCCN 2020047089 (ebook) |
   ISBN 9780520325005 (cloth) | ISBN 9780520325029 (paperback) |
   ISBN 9780520974210 (epub)
Subjects: LCSH: Political science—China—Philosophy. | Cosmology,
   Chinese.
Classification: LCC JA84.C6 Z488 2021 (print) | LCC JA84.C6 (ebook) |
   DDC 320.01—dc23
LC record available at https://lccn.loc.gov/2020047088
LC ebook record available at https://lccn.loc.gov/2020047089

Manufactured in the United States of America

30 29 28 27 26 25 24 23 22 21
10 9 8 7 6 5 4 3 2 1

Contents

Foreword to the Chinese Edition

Tianxia (All under Heaven) is a concept with much spiritual vitality. It involves a spiritually vitalizing relationality among persons and a spiritually vitalizing relationship between the ways of humanity and the ways of *tian* (conventionally translated "Heaven"). As the spirit of *tianxia* amounts to *tian* itself, it is difficult to describe. Thus the ink spilled on the topic of [what *tian* is] will be limited. *Tianxia*, though, is an ideal concerned with achieving cosmopolitical order. This book attempts to use a realist method to approach the idealism of *tianxia* narratively and give expression to the distance between the ways of *tianxia* (*tianxiazhidao* 天下之道) and the instrumentality of *tianxia* (*tianxiazhiqi* 天下之器). The conceptual capaciousness opened up is the space between ideals and reality, and between the past and the future. *Tianxia* is also a methodology, and I attempt to explain how *tianxia* as a concept can be used to understand the theoretical spaces of history, social institutions, and political order to the extent of redefining the concept of political order.

Because this concept is so fecund, the problems that *tianxia* as a political concept can open up are manifold. Therefore I needed to discover a method for getting as close to this concept as possible. The method this book employs can be referred to as a "synthetic text" approach. Things and

events are originally complete wholes, but when we attempt to comprehend things in their microcomplexity, we invariably analyze things into
a plurality of aspects. It is for this reason that fields like political science,
economics, ethics, aesthetics, sociology, history, and so forth all take on a
complete body of one thing and split it into many subfields with aspects
appropriate to their different disciplines. Each discipline raises its own
particular questions about the subject under scrutiny. However, one discipline is not necessarily able to answer all of the questions that it has posed
for itself because the answers to the questions quite possibly belong to the
domain of discourse of other disciplines. Although this might not always
be the case, it in fact often occurs this way.

For example, some political problems require economic solutions, and
some economic problems require political answers; some ethical solutions
are political problems, and some political institutions rely upon ethics;
some reasons for political decisions have to do with history, and some
historical narratives are really theological.[1] The so-called synthetic textual method is an attempt to return to the wholeness of things to allow
for all of the various questions to be asked of each other, and the knowledge domains of all the disciplines to be brought to bear on the explanation. The synthetic textual method is philosophical, and with respect
to its research into *tianxia* this philosophy returns us to the wholeness
of things. This means that the emergent problems and relevant answers
might be simultaneously historical, political, economic, game theoretic,
or theological. I hope that this method of synthetic textualism is up to the
task of appreciating the fecundity of *tianxia* as a concept.

The *tianxia* concept itself involves a profound affective dimension, as
it carries with it the entirety of Chinese history—its traditions, its experience, and its spirit. With respect to a philosophical account of *tianxia*,
I am attempting to limit myself to a rational explanation, avoiding as
much as possible the affective narrative and the hitherto prevailing values
entailed therein. It is only with such an aspiration aimed at providing an
unbiased account that there can be an approximation of truly universal
validity. By way of illustration, in the historical construction of the *tianxia*
concept, the efforts of the Confucian tradition are readily apparent, but
this doesn't mean that the Confucian construction is the whole story.
One weakness in Confucianism is the difficulty it has with the so-called

"stranger problem."[2] At different times Confucian scholars have attempted to engage in apologetics regarding this question, but from my viewpoint their often sentimental argumentation has not been effective in getting at the real problem.

Here I want to revisit the so-called "no position" or "view from nowhere" analysis. A "no position" analysis can be defined as taking any value-laden interpretation, judgment, or narrative and limiting it to a "nonaffective" existential analysis—and then asking "Can some existent according to its own mode of existing continue to thrive?" In other words, such a theoretical orientation, setting aside affects, emotions, and values as so many axiological addendums to experience, only considers whether or not the logic of practice surrounding something is sustainable, and whether it can be sustained further in the long term. This is a presuppositional problem. Since existence precedes values, only when something has the capacity for existence can it hope to achieve a better existence. Just as rationality doesn't refute affective reasons, affect doesn't refute rational reasons. I believe that most persons would maintain that peace is better than war, but a certain ethical scandal persists despite this fact. Except for speaking in the interest of a nonsensical political correctness, throughout the ages not a single ethical philosopher has been able to offer a knockdown rational argument, one with necessary and sufficient conditions, for refuting the thesis that the strong should devour the weak. Therefore, in attempting to prove that the logic of hegemony rests on a fallacy, one cannot use ethical theory alone. By appealing to game theory, however, one might be able to argue that hegemonic logic is incapable of sustaining itself in the long run because of the game theoretic problem of vengeance and its leading to the "tragedy of imitation."

Moreover, in terms of choosing to make use of certain historical materials, my criterion is based on the following. In the time before the written text, we should use the standards provided by archeological evidence; and after the appearance of texts, what is important is the text setting an "established mode of thinking" for historical persons as such thinking comes to have a pervasive influence. For example, regarding the description of *tianxia* in the Zhou dynasty, of course, the documents produced during the dynasty itself should be the primary sources, but that does not mean we should exclude Qin and Han period textual sources. Even if we can ascertain that certain passages regarding the Zhou are actually Qin-Han apocrypha, because those Qin-Han documents narrating Zhou stories have already been incorporated into the sedimented imagination of the people, they have come to have a real function as part of the collective imaginary.

My earliest research into the *tianxia* system is collected in the *Tianxia System* (2005).[3] After its publication it happily received a lot of scholarly attention, criticism, and debate. But *Tianxia System* was only an initial foray into the research field of a *tianxia* institutional order. A decade having past between the publication of *Tianxia System* and this *Tianxia System as a Possible World*, important differences have emerged regarding the questions, problems, arguments, and narratives, but still the basic outlook has remained consistent. Moreover, *Tianxia System* was compiled by translating and editing two English language essays that I had originally written five years earlier. Because of the limits of expressing such things in English, a lot of ancient materials difficult to translate into English were ignored. This present book is in some degree a correction of the aforementioned deficiencies, but it still has failed to reference a lot of related historical materials. After all, this book is not the work of an intellectual historian, so here at the outset I politely ask for forgiveness from the historians.

My ongoing research on the *tianxia* order has received support from many friends and readers who have provided helpful criticism and constructive ideas. Let me first thank Alain le Pichon who in 2000 supported me in writing the two English essays on the concept of *tianxia*. Also, Qin Yaqing, Tang Yijie, Yue Daiyun, Tong Shijun, Huang Ping, Wang Mingming, William Callahan, Fred Dallmayr, Luca M. Scarantino, and Peter J. Katzenstein—all of whom urged me to research the *tianxia* system, offering many important suggestions along the way. I also want to thank Stephen C. Angle, Regis Debray, Prasenjit Duara, Gan Chunsong, Zhang Feng, Xu Xin, Wang Yiwei, Gao Shangtao, Zhong Fangyin, Elena Barabantseva, Anthony Carty, Sundeep Waslekar, Nicole Lapierre, Liu Qing, Bai Tongdong, Zhou Chicheng, Zhou Lian, Sun Shu, Zhang Shuguang, Xu Jianxin, and Jiang Xiyuan—who all offered critical commentary that caused me to think deeper about many difficult problems in the *tianxia* system of thinking.

I would also like to express my sincerest gratitude to several friends who helped me through many critical conversations on the subject matter: Jean-Paul Tchang, Hans Boller, Elizabeth Perry, Rainer Forst, Joshua Ramo, Francesco Sisci, Zhang Yuyan, Han Dongyu, Ci Xuwei, Lu Xiang, Li He, Cheng Guangyun, Zhang Dun, Guan Kai, Zhao Tao, Lu Ding, Qiao Liang, Wang Xianghui, Pan Wei, Yan Xuetong, Yuan Zhengqing, Sheng Hong, Zhao Quansheng, Shen Wenjing, Wang Jianyu, Enno Rudolph, Philippe Brunozzi, Daniel Binswanger, Evgeny Grachikov, Joël Thoraval, Michael Pillsbury, Iain Johnston, Jean-Marc Coicaud, In-suk Cha, Moon Chung-in, Han Sang-jin, Mark Siemons, and John G. Blair. Among these friends, Zhang Wanjia (Jean-Paul Tchang) gave me clear guidance and incomparable assistance on some complex problems in global finance. Hans Boller believed that relational reasoning is a concept of reasoning that addresses the deficiencies of the modern individualistic understanding of rationality. Constructively he suggested that I provide a clearer definition and theoretical treatment of relational reason. Lu Xiang and Guan Kai offered critical suggestions to expand the treatment on the theoretical relationship between *tianxia* and China. Because China is an unavoidable question, I herein have devoted an entire chapter to discussing "What Is China?" I have submitted the very idea of Chinese historicity to philosophical explanation while also historicizing our understanding of the *tianxia* concept. Even so, this book can only partially address all the stimulating questions and criticisms offered by my friends.

Finally, I would like to thank the CITIC Press and Li Nan and Wang Wenting, who prepared this book so perfectly for publication.

Zhao Tingyang 赵汀阳
2015 年 *8* 月 *18* 日

Foreword to the English Edition

I am delighted that this book has been translated into English and is being published in the United States, making it now available to the largest population of readers in the world. As this world in our own historical moment is suffering from a global pandemic and the economic and political turbulence that has followed in its wake, I hope the positive message of this book is meaningful and will prove useful. This book is a deliberate analysis of the future possibility of a *tianxia* "All under Heaven" system as a philosophy of world order. Doing philosophy is rather strange in the sense that philosophers create more problems than they solve. Actually it is precisely because none of the basic philosophical problems have thus far been resolved that philosophers have a good reason or perhaps an excuse to continue their investigations.

Many readers of this work have repeatedly asked me three questions. Who will lead this *tianxia* world? Is this a Chinese ambition or even a Chinese threat to the rest of the world? And what will be the concrete institutional arrangement of a *tianxia* world? In response, I feel obliged to explain the methodology applied in my investigation of a *tianxia* system. My approach has been one of "taking no sides" (*wulichang* 无立场). That is, I assume the perspective of an extraterrestrial anthropologist who comes to Earth and does anthropological fieldwork on our planet. The horizon of such an investigator must quite reasonably be the world as a whole rather than any particular nation. I try in this way to present a theory of *tianxia* that is meant to speak to the world in general and to go beyond any particular population or nation-state.

My reinvention of the ancient concept of *tianxia*, literally "All under Heaven," connotes a system for world order that is both of and for all of the world's peoples. The concept of *tianxia* was the political starting point of China some three thousand year ago and stands in contrast to the Greek *polis* as the political starting point of European culture. It suggests that the Chinese political thinking of this era had in a quite unusual way begun from a sense of "world" rather than of "state." It developed into a concept of "world governance" that proved to be too early for its own time, but at the same time, might have some relevance for the modern world. Indeed, it is because the Chinese *tianxia* system ended in 221 BCE that I have not had recourse to discuss much of post-*tianxia* China and have had very little to say about China's "tributary system" in the sixteenth through the nineteenth centuries that seems to interest Western scholars so much. Just to be clear, the tributary system provides some explanation about post-*tianxia* imperial China but definitely not about the *tianxia* system itself. My real interest has been in discovering the best possible implications of our historical resources, and to think through the most meaningful possibilities they might imply for our future world, with little interest at all in ancient relics that are of no more use today. In short, I revisit the wisdom of the tradition rather than its tombs.

There have been two triggers for my reinvention of *tianxia*. The first has been my long time trust in the Kantian search for peace that has been challenged in our time by Huntington's clashes of civilizations. This tension exposes a larger problem beyond the Kantian notion of peace with respect to issues of shared values, religious beliefs, and the political regimes defining of nations. The second trigger has been the utter failure of international politics. As it stands, it is and continues to be an ineffective game that brings with it the hostile strategies of deterrence, sanction, interference, the balancing of powers, cold wars, and even war itself—all of which only serve to make the world even worse off than it was.

Contrary to much popular yet misleading thinking, the concept of the political when it works does not mean the *recognition of an enemy*, and the concept of war cannot be defined as the *continuation of politics by other means*. In fact, the event of war is the precise proof of the failure of politics. Instead the political should be understood as the art of *changing hostility into hospitality*. Politics does not make any sense if it offers no change to a hostile situation. My effort has been to trace back to an understanding of the ancient concept of *tianxia*, rethinking its ambition to formulate an all-inclusive world system under a world constitution that would ensure world peace.

Up until now, the world has remained a nonworld in its "original state" not far from the Hobbesian state of nature, full of conflicts and hostilities that portend ominous clashes of civilizations. The anarchy that prevails in the world today is wholly at odds with the notion of a world of well-organized states. It is a failed world that is lacking in world-ness. The *tianxia* system is meant to address the world-size problems of a global time, including those of technologies, economies, climate, and indeed of civilization itself.

A *tianxia* system is to be established on the basis of three *constitutional* concepts: (1) the *internalization of the world*, inclusive of all nations in a shared system that constitutes a world with no negative externalities; (2) a *relational rationality* that gives priority to minimizing mutual hostility over the maximizing of exclusive interests and stands in contrast to individual rationality and its pursuit of the maximization of self-interest; and (3) *Confucian improvement* requiring *one improves if-and-only-if all others improve*. It is a nonexclusive improvement for all and is thus more compelling than Pareto's improvement. In other words, Confucian improvement is Pareto's improvement not for one person but for everyone.

There is obviously a distance between concepts and their practice. I have been trying to develop some practical ideas for a *tianxia* system in recent years following the publication of the Chinese edition of this book in 2016. In this English edition I have included the sketch of an argument for a "smart democracy" that might serve as a practical choice for a possible *tianxia*. This smart democracy suggests a knowledge-weighted democracy and is thus different from the modern notion of democracy. It anticipates a democracy designed to become institutionally intelligent, as if it were "automatically" smart by itself, free of the democratic mistakes made by collective irrational choices.

I want to take advantage of this opportunity to express my sincere gratitude to the Berggruen Institute for its support of the translation of my book, and to the University of California Press for its professional editing and printing. I am mostly grateful to my good friend Roger T. Ames, whose support for me and my work goes beyond any expression of gratitude. I want to thank Joseph E. Harroff for a translation that is at once lucid and beautiful, and also Odd Arne Westad for his fine new foreword. This publication would not have been possible without the strong Berggruen leadership provided by Song Bing and Nils Gilman, and their incredible staff, Li Xiaojiao and Shelley Hu.

Zhao Tingyang 赵汀阳
2020 年 11 月 1 日

New Foreword

ZHAO TINGYANG AND THE *TIANXIA* WORLD

Odd Arne Westad

Tianxia is a Chinese term that literally means "All under Heaven." In ancient Chinese philosophy and political theory it came to signify the realm of humans (as opposed to the possible realms of spirits, immortals, or gods).[1] Very often it was used to signify the world as it was known to the Chinese and sometimes the territory that was ruled, or in theory should be ruled, by one of the Chinese states. In its origin, *tianxia* is a complex, composite, and contested term. Many Chinese thinkers have tried to simplify or universalize it. In the *Analects*, Confucius used *tianxia* to claim universal morals but also to argue for global human capacities: "To be able to practice five things everywhere under heaven constitutes perfect virtue[:].... Gravity, generosity of soul, sincerity, earnestness, and kindness."[2]

This book presents the views of Zhao Tingyang, a distinguished Chinese political philosopher who is now a professor at the Chinese Academy of Social Sciences. Zhao has for some time been preoccupied with finding ways in which Chinese thinking, and especially terms and practices that come out of Chinese antiquity, can be helpful in overcoming what he sees as today's decaying and unjust global order. Professor Zhao puts the concept of *tianxia* at the center of these efforts. "*Tianxia*," says Zhao, "is an ideal concerned with achieving cosmopolitical order." But although he is inspired by the Chinese past, Zhao is very careful in not presenting his version of "under heaven" as a direct transposition from what existed three thousand years ago. His *tianxia* is characterized by its utility for contemporary conditions, in which "we must go above and beyond the nation state as a horizon for understanding world politics. We need to take *the world* as a measure for defining political order and political legitimacy."[3]

Zhao's ideas are, very understandably, seen as significant within China and abroad. He has been lauded by many, both for taking on a number of challenges with regard to how to critique today's international system and for his knowledge of Chinese political theory from the pre- and early Confucian era and from later periods. First and foremost, Zhao has been praised for his attempts at applying some of these concepts toward a reconceptualization of our thinking about international relations today. In a world that is in desperate need for theory that is not originating from the same predominant Western sources, Zhao's work is both important and refreshing. Alongside a number of other Chinese political theorists of the global and international, such as Qin Yaqing and Yan Xuetong, Zhao has provided a body of work that set pathways for other scholars, inside and outside of China, to engage with and critique.[4]

A main strength of Zhao's work lies in his invitation to take the principle of one world as the starting point for global thinking. "In the political sense *tianxia* refers to a world political order," Zhao says. "A *tianxia* system has only internality and no externality. This also cancels out the semantic value of 'foreigner' and 'enemy' within political discourse." Correctly, he complains, "the current world is actually still functioning as a 'nonworld'; it is only a geographic category of existence and not a political one. The most important future political problem will be how to create a world, which would be to complete the process of world internalization."

Zhao insists that such a world order would have to be pluralistic. "Simply put," he argues, "what the *tianxia* system anticipates is a world order based on the principle of coexistence," in which "any political entity maintaining externality must become a problem of reconciliation and not an object to be conquered or colonized." It is hard not to welcome such a pluralistic and heterogeneous approach to what future world orders may consist of, especially given how often the West has misused its own values and its own patterns of law and institutions to gain control over others. Zhao's views on pluralism, theoretical as well as political, is one of the main aspects of his philosophical approach.

One must also welcome his willingness to take the past seriously, both as inspiration and to understand long-lasting practices. Zhao's views are (mainly) limited to the Chinese past, although this is understandable, both given his own background and the significance of China on a global scale (which Zhao, again understandably, presupposes without investigating much further). The weight of the past is perhaps more visible in Chinese discourses than in any other cultural and philosophical tradition I know, and Zhao is entirely correct in taking it as the starting point for his investigations, without feeling constrained by it. Zhao is an innovator as much as a continuator of the past, in the best tradition of Chinese thinking.

Zhao is particularly insistent that a major objective of any kind of thinking about international orders must focus on the need to avoid war. "To say that war is politics continued by other means (the viewpoint of Clausewitz) is not as good as saying that war is a failure of the political," Zhao contends. Any war is a setback, and war between "leading countries" (which Zhao uses instead of "great powers") will mean that the world itself is under threat. Any kind of system that prevents wars has a positive value in it, in Zhao's view. Part of the purpose of establishing a *tianxia* that states voluntarily participate in and which helps resolve common problems is to preserve the peace and over time remove war as an instrument of international relations.

A final strength of Zhao's political philosophy is his emphasis on the preservation of the global commons. Part of the argument for an expanding *tianxia* is that previous systems have led to unacceptable levels of environmental damage of what is not governed by individual states. The United Nations is not capable of rising to the occasion, and a new system is needed in which decisions can be made and implemented on a global scale. And such a system can only be put into action when all people, not just Westerners, feel that their interests and values are looked after within *one* world.

Other aspects of Zhao's views have led to criticism. His emphasis on the role of states over the role of nonstate groups and individuals is one of these. When Zhao speaks of compatibility, he often speaks of "compatibility of countries."[5] When he, with reason, criticizes "the ideology of hegemonic nation-states where other nation-states and even the high seas are just territories to be dominated," it is injustice among states that preoccupies him. He echoes Mao Zedong's "three worlds" theory in saying that "the interests of the peoples of Europe and America and the interests of the people in the rest of the world are not coincident," but Zhao's reflections on this incompatibility is always kept at the state level.[6] The problem with this is that it is hard to imagine how states, who (therefore) have their own narrow interests to look after, can move to the next level of cherishing the *tianxia* without being in some way forced to do so. There seems to be little in the idea of state sovereignty (which Zhao at least accepts and sometimes comes close to seeing as a positive) that will produce a *tianxia*.

There is, of course, the possibility that today's rising states outside Europe and North America will be different in their approach than the European-origin states have been. "What is most perplexing," Zhao asks somewhat rhetorically, "is why global justice remains such an unrealizable possibility?" He answers immediately: "The reason is not particularly mysterious or profound. It is just because hegemonic nation-states still hold a pronounced strategic advantage, and they use every possible way to preserve this advantage." All of which is true, although it slightly contradicts Zhao own emphasis on states, unless of course there are states that in their nature are different from the United States and its European predecessors.

Although he never states it plainly, it is Zhao's view that China is different from such hegemonic practices today and will remain different in the future. China is not and will not be imperialist; it will not be like the United States, which "carried out some institutional renovations within imperialism, turning modern imperialism into a globalizing imperialism." China will help build a *tianxia*, because "the *tianxia* concept itself carries a very heavy affective dimension, and carries with it the entirety of Chinese history, its traditions, its experience, and its spirit." Zhao declares, "China is a 'world-pattern state' that takes *tianxia* to be internal to its structure."

Since, as Zhao correctly notes, we cannot say much for certain about the future, this is an argument that is based on a view of China's past and present. And it is here that the *tianxia* concept becomes most problematic. In Chinese antiquity "the Zhou dynasty *tianxia* system as an 'earth web' has an ancestral state at its center serving to oversee and protect the world," Zhao contends. This was a stable and beneficial system for a long time, and "the decline of the Zhou dynasty was very likely a result of being unable to live up to its own high standards of moral governance." The problem with all of this is of course that historically it is as, if not more, likely that the Zhou collapse came because others would no longer be ruled by the Zhou. There is no evidence that the Zhou state, or later Chinese states or empires, were as inclusive or harmonious as Zhao claims them to have been.

As some of Zhao's critics have noted, this becomes especially problematic when there is no attention to Chinese expansion, predomination, and hegemony in the past. Zhao's understanding of the Chinese past can sometimes seem a bit naïve, as when he asserts that "the distinction between 'civilized' [*hua* 华, also meaning Chinese] and 'barbarian' (*yi* 夷) was merely a way of referring to differences of natural geography, life styles, and cultural customs. As such, this was a 'descriptive' conceptual cluster without any racist or ethnocentric prejudice involved." This flies in the face of very durable traditions of Chinese exceptionalism and preoccupations with race, some of which Zhao must be aware of.

Zhao also seems to think that today's China has got its present geographical shape "as the central plain cultures continually expanded and radiated outward into the periphery," and worse, that "the 'Hanification' of China has an inherent connection with the spiritual attraction of Han culture." In reality, much of the expansion of China, as with all empires, happened through conquest and subordination. Ask today's indigenous populations in Tibet, Xinjiang, and Mongolia. When Zhao, quoting Wang Tongling, claims "that no matter who held political leadership in China, political power and the ruling class was always open to all ethnicities," then it is correct to note that there are examples of openness and examples of closedness in Chinese history. Today's ruling Politburo of the Chinese Communist Party has no member who is not Han Chinese.

Given the problems China is facing in terms of governance, some of Zhao's critique of democracy elsewhere rings a bit hollow. He is undoubtedly right that "many factors can mislead democracy into a distorted expression of the people's shared aspirations. For example, manipulation by wealthy interests, propaganda, speculation, passion, ignorance, fake news, and so on can all mislead popular opinion." But Zhao's main point is that Chinese traditions can lead the world toward a better future. And given the state of pluralism in China itself today, this does not seem like a safe bet. As long as political dissidents, trade union activists, and minority right advocates can be arrested and kept in prison simply for expressing their views, China will not seem a guarantor for "expansive harmony" in the world. Zhao is of course aware of this, and we can assume the reasons why he cannot openly critique it. But the sorry state of affairs of justice within China does present problems for his overall theory, too.

The biggest challenge for the *tianxia* concept in the future is, as in so many other cases, about who will call the shots. Zhao wants to see a more inclusive and just world, with effective governance of expanding global commons. It is hard not to agree with such a vision. But it is also hard to see who will lead us toward it. China has rich traditions of governance and political thought, and Zhao Tingyang does us all a favor in explaining them and setting out agendas for how they may be of use in the future. Just like China will learn from the rest of the world, the world will learn from China. Whatever we think of the *tianxia* concept, we know that there will be more Chinese involved in debates about global governance in the years to come. And, for most of them, the traditions that Zhao draws from will be central to their thinking. By reading his work, we will all be better prepared for joining in the multifaceted dialogues that are certain to come.

Translator's Preface

Tianxia 天下 is a vital concept swirling around in the centripetal and centrifugal flows animating the many imagined geographies of an ongoing ethical-political narrative with China (*Zhongguo* 中国) as political center of a humanistic and harmonious cosmopolitan ideal resulting from the aesthetic-religious achievement of a ritualized civilizational and refined cultural elegance. Zhao Tingyang creatively reimagines and redeploys this archaic Zhou dynasty invention at the heart of a political culture seeking to noncoercively realize harmonious interstate and interpersonal relations within a shared aesthetic-religious project of a ritually enacted community of interpretation involving a convivial musical flourishing with the world as subject—this is what I take to be the real gist of the so-called "institutions of ritual and music" (*liyue zhidu* 礼乐制度) of Confucian political ethics. *Tianxia*, in Zhao's political philosophy, as "All under Heaven" serves as an all-encompassing ethical-political and aesthetic-religious ideal that seeks to imagine the world itself as a political subject, departing from the de facto inheritance of a Western imperialist imagined geography that can at most hope to achieve world "peace" as a mere absence of hot war due to hegemonic means of strategic deterrence, or by what often amounts to the very same thing just repackaged under a different name, contractually determined international agreements, treaties, and sanctions.

Zhao is bold enough to imagine a possible world wherein there is "no outside" and the interests of all peoples, and indeed the interests of all the myriad things (*wanwu* 万物), operate as an unsummed ecological totality and are included within a theory of the political that starts with the basic political units of *the world* (*tianxia* as a political subject) and a *relational reasoning* (wherein any negotiated ameliorative courses of action have to be realized relationally and noncoercively in cooperative deliberations or not at all). The move to relational reasoning and an all-encompassing cosmopolitan vision should be a most welcome theoretical offering for those of us who have grown increasingly exhausted and exasperated by the all-too-pervasive appeals still being made by those in the highest positions of power to an atomizing and alienating political logic that presupposes as basic units discrete and self-sufficient foundational individuals and exclusively sovereign nation-states. Indeed, the apotheosis of such atomistic and foundationally individualistic political reasoning can be laid bare by the increasingly stark contrast that has arisen between the "foreign" policies of the United States and the People's Republic of China. As I wrote this preface, the occupant of the White House was making blustering proclamations as part of the shortest speech a US president has ever given on the floor of the meeting of the UN General Assembly. And without any scientific backing or even reasonable suspicions regarding the causal origins of a global pandemic that has radically altered social and political life around the globe with no regard for discrete territorial boundaries or international treaties, Trump was threatening China and claiming that China be held solely accountable for all of the global predicaments ushered in as a result of the ongoing pandemic.

Such shameless Sinophobic fear-mongering and alarmist conspiracy theory is part of a cynical but concerted strategy to return the United States and China to a Cold War dynamic most profitable for the military-corporate-industrial complexes animating the fantasies of those still part of hegemonic political cultures aimed at imperialist domination of the entire world. We need only witness the US State Department's recent decision to close the oldest Chinese diplomatic consulate in Houston, again under the pretense of totally unsubstantiated claims about purported espionage (ostensibly having to do with a capitalist-imperialist race to develop a marketable vaccine for Covid-19/Sars-2). In stark contrast, the rhetoric coming from the leaders of the People's Republic of China have in recent times consistently called for more forms of global cooperation to address world-scale problems such as pandemics and anthropogenic climate chaos. A key component of President Xi Jinping's address to the aforementioned UN General Assembly was a pledge to make China "carbon neutral" by the year 2060 and a critique of American "obstructionism" occurring via organizations like the WTO, IMF and other international bodies seeking to stymie China's attempts at developing new and affordable technologies as part of a "green revolution." As anyone paying attention to the weather (let alone the science!) knows, such a world economic and geopolitical revolution stands before us as a most urgent task for the sake of ensuring the sustainable development and even the mere survival of human societies on this planet in the near future.

Moreover, this stark contrast in rhetoric and operative political logics is evenly matched in terms of actual policies and conduct. To cite just one shockingly illustrative example, on March 12, 2020, on the very same day that China sent a major shipment of various supplies to Iraq to be used in battling the spread of a global pandemic (personal protective equipment, ventilators, test kits, medicines, and other humanitarian supplies), the United States fired twelve missiles on five different sites that were never even verified to be part of arms storage facilities of an Iranian-supported militia. Even if these sites were part of an Iranian intervention in Iraqi national politics, what about the so-called "sovereignty" of independent nation-states, as presumably no one from the Pentagon bothered to ask the Iraqi legislative council if they wanted bombs dropped on their land and people?

So there we have it: either bombs or medicine *sans frontiers*. That is, *either* we can carry on with the insanity and "business as usual" of a "might makes right" dystopian "failed world" with an increasingly alarming number of "failed" states emerging with authoritarian heads of state harboring in their historical-institutional "genes" as it were ambitions of a totalizing imperialist hegemony, *or* we can dare to imagine another possible world wherein truly all-encompassing ideals are operative in working together to cultivate shared deliberative spaces requiring guidance by so much more than mere instrumental reason as such cosmopolitical thinking requires deeply embodied cultural values to be appreciated within a framework of a ritually constituted community of interpretation. This is necessary in order to realize concrete policy proposals and new "game rules" for a truly global, cosmopolitan body politic together or not at all. Zhao's method of creatively reanimating the Chinese past to realize new possibilities of the world political (*wengu er zhixin* 温故而知新) is a great resource to be consulting to be sure as we find our political hopes and moral imaginations aligning with the latter half of the aforementioned ethically and politically exclusive disjunction.

It is with a great sense of honor and ethical urgency that I approached this translation project. A significant challenge in translating a work like this was the result of a feature that is simultaneously a great theoretical strength within Zhao's vision of the possibilities of a new conception of the world political—namely, the frequent linguistic and philosophical shifts occurring between two distinct registers of Chinese writing. Zhao's frequent redeployment of classical Chinese texts and concepts had me striving to balance fidelity to the original source material while also attempting to provide a faithful rendering of Zhao's creative resourcing of the historical writings relating to *tianxia* 天下. Moreover, not all of the writings that Zhao deploys are easily identified as proprietarily Confucian, as many Daoist, Mohist, Legalist, and other historic designators of philosophical schools vying to be heard by those in positions of power to influence statecraft in the complex and pluralistic political history of China also are frequently referenced.

Thus I had to make sure that any translations of primary sources (across distinctive philosophical schools in early China) received at a minimum an approximately similar amount of careful harmonizing as they did in Zhao's theoretical treatment. For these reasons, it had to be the case that all translations within are my own unless otherwise noted. Whenever possible I have provided cross-references, usually citing James Legge as my "crib." Legge's corpus is always a good place to start in checking on the veracity of translations, for even when he has mistranslated, it is often still quite illuminating. We can sometimes detect how his Presbyterian sensibilities and/or Victorian-era orientalist hubris might have gotten in the way of his better judgment as a masterful philosophical translator. In any event, having an external citation to cross-reference is important in that it will provide those interested readers who aren't necessarily trained in Sinology a place to go for acquiring further historical-philosophical context.

A great joy of translating this work was of course developing a new philosophical friendship with a luminary political theorist in contemporary China. It was a wonderful experience to have the pleasure of conversing with Professor Zhao as a frequent interlocutor whenever I came to passages that I was having difficulty with or just in seeking stylistic advice on how to best "English" his prose. The appendix on "Jizi's Lost Democracy" was written in English by Professor Zhao, and I learned a lot from this in terms of how to be optimal in translating his thinking to an English reading audience, and from his many other published works in both English and in Chinese.

The other luminary interlocutor who must be spotlighted here is Roger T. Ames, as he was the creative catalyst for this entire translation project in so many ways. It was originally Professor Ames's suggestion that I work on this project, and anyone familiar with his voluminous and path-blazing philosophical translation work will surely perceive his profound influence throughout these pages. This is for two important reasons. First, as my teacher I owe Dr. Ames an infinite debt for the creative philosophical vision and methods that I learned from him, part of which requires always imaginatively striving to be engaging in responsible cross-cultural hermeneutics by productively foregrounding the unique and culturally specific philosophical grammars at play in any work of philosophical translation. Such translingual contextualizing is to be done with the aim of better "appreciating" the differences. After all, as I've heard him say many a time, and each time with a novel and deeper appreciation on my part, the "only thing worse than making generalizations," in approaching unfamiliar philosophical texts and traditions is "failing to make any generalizations at all." This maxim should be action-guiding because as Roger has consistently shown, what such failures really amount to are failures of imagination, and absent such failures we could otherwise be letting inter-cultural interpreters be more effectively putting their received prejudice at risk, thereby "anticipating" very different possible philosophical grammars as part of working (i.e., nonfinal) vocabularies as translational ends-in-view.

Another major reason that those familiar with Professor Ames's expansive corpus will detect his significant influence here is that at a critical juncture in the process of this collaborative translation project, he generously shared of his precious time and energy to carefully pore over a rather rough first draft in its entirety, making substantial changes throughout. The final product is surely a quantum improvement as a result. But in appropriate deference and reverence to my teacher, it should be related that any errors or infelicities in this translation are entirely of my own doing.

I would be sorely remiss if I didn't extend my heartfelt thanks to the creative community of the Peking University Berggruen Research Center, for without their generous support and assistance I could not have possibly completed this translation. The director, Song Bing, offered supportive advice and solid leadership throughout the entire process. Xiaojiao Li, Jennifer Bourne, and Shelly Hu all made sure in their own uniquely caring ways that the manuscript installments arrived in due course by checking in on my (sometimes slow) progress, offering critical suggestions for improvement and always offering kind words of encouragement. The Berggruen Institute, as a nonpartisan thinktank aimed at supporting intellectual and cultural spaces for more optimally engaging world issues on a truly world scale, is a result of the bold and creative vision of its founder Nicolas Berggruen. For the philosophical philanthropy coming from the Institute, which is aimed ultimately at ensuring that a sustainable and convivial cosmopolitan future be at all possible, we should all be most grateful.

Finally, for making sure that the manuscript arrived to press in a presentable fashion, I would like to extend my gratitude to Craig Calhoun and Nils Gilman, both respected scholars serving in leadership roles within the Berggruen Institute, for their careful editorial comments and patience in seeing this vital project to press. And in the final stages of copy-editing and formatting let me take this opportunity to thank David Peattie and Francisco Reinking for their careful editorial work and attention to detail. As a truly team project this has become a very elegant book. This was indeed a collaborative project in a profound sense, and it was made infinitely more optimal due to the exemplary and graceful "relational reasoning" that I discovered in the many heartminds mentioned here.

Joseph E. Harroff
Philadelphia, Pennsylvania
Autumn 2020

Introduction

WORLD AS POLITICAL SUBJECT

China is a story, but *tianxia* is a theory.

Globalization has entered into every aspect of all things. There is no outside of the globalization process to which one could escape. If we fail to see the nature of this new political situation, it is extremely difficult to even begin to deal with the problems of the present. This is not just a matter of political transformation but is also a total alteration of the very mode of being of the world. We can predict that the future world will need a fitting "order of being"—an order that emerges realistically from the immanent transformation of the world. This order I call the *tianxia* system. *Tianxia* is of course a concept from Chinese antiquity but is not a concept that applies only to China. The field of questions it opens up and alludes to transcends China and relates to the universal problems of the world.[1] *Tianxia* references "a cosmopolitan world." If we understand *tianxia* as a dynamic and vital process, we get the sense of "the world-ing of the world." The Zhou dynasty *tianxia* system is already long gone, but the traces of the concept have become one way of imagining future possibilities. Although the future cannot be known, still one cannot remain silent because this kind of universal and ameliorative (善意) world order is really something that merits our best imaginative efforts.

The international political concepts as defined by ethnonational systems, imperialism, and hegemonic power struggles are receding in the reality of globalization as they are losing efficacy in dealing with current situations. If globalization hadn't affected such a reversal, the ethnonational state as the defining framework for the supreme power and its related international political games would eventually become a thing of the past. But the possibility of transcending modern geopolitical "systematized power" (系统化权力) and achieving globalized governance is something looming on the future temporal horizon.

The *tianxia* conceptual imagination anticipates a world system wherein the world comes to have its own political agency.[2] This would be an "order of coexistence" wherein the whole world is the basic unit of politics. Starting from *tianxia* to comprehend the world means that we take the entire world as the thinking unit for analyzing problems that allows us to conceive of the political order as that which matches the process of globalization. The previous and current imperialistic organization of the world order is grounded in a concept of nation-state and concomitant national interests where all those wishing to preserve the imperialistic system are too lazy to carefully distinguish between what they consider to be "the rest of the world" and simply take it as other places to be conquered. The worldview of imperialism views the world as an object to be conquered, dominated, and exploited—never recognizing the world as a political agency in its own right. "Thinking of the world" and a "thinking that emerges from the world" mean totally different things and are based on wholly different conceptual grammars. To take world understanding as either the subject or object of political discourse is decisive in the "to be or not to be a world" problem of politics. The starting point of the *tianxia* method takes the world as a political agency in its own right. This is in the same vein with both Guanzi and Laozi who highlighted a method of: "taking *tianxia* as *tianxia*" (以天下为天下)[3] or "using *tianxia* to view *tianxia*"[4]—meaning that we must go above and beyond the nation-state as a horizon for understanding world politics. We need to take the world as a measure for defining political order and political legitimacy.

Taking the world as a measure for understanding the holistic political existence of the world is the "nothing outside *tianxia*" principle.[5] This principle means that *tianxia* is the most expansive limit for any political world-ing. All political existence is encompassed within *tianxia*. The "nothing outside *tianxia*" principle depends upon a metaphysical reason. Because *tian* (or "Heaven") is a holistic existence, *tianxia* (or "All under Heaven") must also be a holistic existence. The capabilities of *tianxia* and that of *tian* are mutually entailing. This is what is meant by "*Tian* provides no private canopy, and earth provides no private conveyance."[6] The "nothing outside *tianxia*" principle is an a priori presupposition that the world is a holistic political concept. Therefore a *tianxia* system has only internality (内部性) and no externality (外部性). This also cancels out the semantic value of "foreigner" and "enemy" within political discourse. No persons can be construed as unacceptable foreigners, and no specific nation-state, ethnicity, or culture can be regarded as an incommensurable enemy. Any nation-state or geographic realm yet to be included within the *tianxia* system is always welcome to become part of *tianxia*'s order of coexistence. Theoretically, the *tianxia* concept a priori encompasses the entire world; but in reality, it does not exist. Three thousand years ago the Zhou dynasty *tianxia* system, even though only realized within a finite geographic realm, was able to provide a practical example of how the *tianxia* concept might transform externality into internality. This is the most important legacy of the ancient idea of *tianxia*.

Since *tianxia* as a concept promises to transform all externality into internality, it also precludes the conceptual logic of mortal enemies, absolute otherness, aliens, and the idea of a "pagan." In this regard, it differs profoundly from any monotheistic mode of thinking. Even if Christianity in Europe has largely declined into a mere spiritual symbolism and is no longer a comprehensive way of life, the concept of "pagan" has become sedimented in cultures as a mode of thinking and still influences current political narratives. If one cannot find an alien or enemy, Western politics seems to lose its weather vane and its driving passion as a motivating raison d'être. Carl Schmitt quite profoundly interprets the foundational distinction between enemies and friends as an eternal struggle at the heart of the concept of the political.[7] No matter if it is a tension between Christianity and paganism, or an internal tension between Christian orthodoxy and heterodoxy, or Hobbes's hypothetical state of nature or Marx's theory of class struggle, or a grounding in the ethnonationalist, nation-state system of international political theory or Samuel Huntington's clash of civilizations thesis—all of these oppositional conflicts presuppose the basic distinction between friend and enemy as being at the heart of all political concepts. In contrast to all of this, what the *tianxia* concept presupposes as a precondition for any mode of existence or political method, is that alterity can be transformed into a shared order of coexistence. Even if some alterity were to resist being encompassed by a *tianxia* system, it is still the case that the *tianxia* order must seek peaceful means of coexistence. Therefore under such an order any political entity maintaining externality must become a problem for reconciliation rather than remaining an object to be conquered or colonized.

Between the two political poles of oppositional conflict and a transformative process of internalizing the external, we can see a philosophical dichotomy between two distinct concepts of the political. I have tried to argue that what the political concept of oppositional conflict expresses cannot be the true nature of the political, but rather is essentially one of enmity or war. Conflict and enmity are a basic reality of human experience. But if politics is just a matter of researching how to carry out a struggle to its final conclusion, then there is no way to ultimately resolve the problem of conflict—rather, conflicts simply continue by other means or intensify. If a theory can only make the actual situation worse, we don't need this kind of theory. The political conception of oppositional conflict merely exacerbates existing problems and has nothing to offer by way of resolution. Therefore politics grounded in oppositional conflict are an instance of a "grammatical fallacy in theorizing" if not also an "ontological fallacy" that can only bring disaster on humanity. War and conflict indicate the ineffectiveness of politics. In other words, war and conflict signal the failure of politics. If politics aren't used to construct a shared social life of humanity or used to construct a peaceful world, wherein lies its significance? A politics of mere oppositional conflict fails to respect humanity and the world. Thus what is needed is a subversion of the centrality of conflict as part of a political concept, and to replace it with coexistence as a focal point of political conceptualization. In a word, politics *must* learn to reverence the world.

THE WORST AND THE BEST OF POSSIBLE WORLDS

Without a shared social life there can be no politics. In order to analyze and unlock the genetic secrets of the political, philosophers have hypothetically posited an experimental starting point for the practice of political theory. This is the so-called "original position."[8] If an original position includes the genetic core of the concept of the political, only then can it adequately explain the secret of politics. An original situation having overarching explanatory power must also be capable of encompassing all possibilities. This is why John Rawls's "veil of ignorance" (or any similar hypothetical scenario) can't be used as a hypothetical presupposition. This is because a veil of ignorance blocks out the worst possibilities (e.g., a Hobbesian state of nature) and mitigates the enabling conditions for the emergence of the political. Using a veil of ignorance does not provide a universal theory, but at best offers a political theory limited to contractual problems.[9]

The original position of an authentically realistic and universal explanatory framework must be something akin to what Hobbes and Xunzi hypothesized. Even though the state of nature that Hobbes posited was not realistic, it still included several key enabling factors of the political: (1) the concept of the political must include the worst possibilities as part of its deliberative schema, otherwise it cannot hope to provide universal explanatory scope; (2) security is the first necessity; and (3) any alterity should not be totally trusted. Hobbes's hypothetical scenario is powerful in representing the constraints imposed of a worst possible world, but it also has a weak point in that it excludes the very genetic possibility of cooperation. If such a Hobbesian original position had been the case, humanity's evolution from conflict to cooperation would lack any necessary reason. Hobbes's Leviathan image plays the role of a method of explanation for the construction of a social order. But this hypothesis still has a significant vulnerability—namely, the Leviathan's power to construct a social order can only be realized internally. How then can this Leviathan bring about social cooperation? If according to the Hobbesian presupposition all persons are mutual enemies, how can a cooperative order of trust in the Leviathan be realized? Obviously, conflict can't spontaneously transform into cooperation unless originally there exists some sort of cooperative gene.[10] This transformative potential is what Hobbes overlooked in thinking through how conflict might transform into cooperation.

Xunzi was perhaps one of the earliest thinkers to discuss the problem of the original situation, preceding Hobbes by more than a millennium. Differing from Hobbes, though, Xunzi's original situation posits a cooperative gene by prioritizing the communal body over the individual body. Xunzi points out that in terms of the strength and capabilities of individuals, we are ever so weak, not even on par with cows or horses. But in terms of the cooperative capacities of the communal body, every person depends upon this as a precondition for their survival. Therefore cooperation must take precedence over conflict. This is what is meant by the expression "human life cannot persist without community."[11] I take this hypothetical evolution to be an ontological principle: social existence precedes individual existence. In other words, social existence is a precondition for individual existence. Xunzi analyzes the formation of political order from the perspective of economics:

> People are born with desires. When desire is frustrated, there must be seeking. Seeking without limit leads to divisions. Thus, there cannot but be competition. Competition leads to disorder, and disorder leads to poverty. The previous kings despised disorder, so they instituted the distinctions based upon ritual and propriety.[12]

Xunzi discovered a seemingly paradoxical phenomenon: that is, cooperation leads to conflict. This is simply to say that cooperation creates surplus dividends, thereby giving rise to unfair distributions which leads to conflict. In order to bring about a stable and trustworthy cooperative schema, a cooperative gene must be institutionalized. Xunzi in presupposing this cooperative gene avoids Hobbes's particular difficulty, but such a hypothesis cannot resolve all of Hobbes's problems. Although a Hobbesian framework has difficulty in accounting for the internal conditions of social cooperation, with respect to anarchic situations of nongovernmental conflict it has quite a lot of explanatory power. Therefore the Xunzian and Hobbesian perspectives can complement each other, providing a more adequate theory of the original situation as a way of addressing the problems of the political. We can call this the Xunzian-Hobbesian hypothesis: an original situation wherein a communal body realizes internal unity while at war with all external bodies.

The extensive magnitude of the political is a result of the space defined by the polar extremes of the worst and the best of all possible worlds. Hobbes already defined the worst possible world. How then are we to conceive of a best possible world? If the worst possible world defined by Hobbes is one extreme within "the set of possible worlds," it stands to reason that the other extreme must have precisely the opposite characteristics. That is, it would be a world free from insecurity, mistrust, defiance, deficiencies, and loneliness. Interestingly, a person's imagination, when directed at the best of possible worlds, is not the same as when it is directed toward the worst of possible worlds. People tend to long for the realization of a world of all good things—for example, freedom, equality, all-embracing love, justice, good will, peace, and material abundance, a world without negativity, without pressure, without class distinctions; a world wherein everyone can realize themselves as self-actualizing, a world without alienation, a world where everyone is happy. This mythologization of a world needs at the same time, though, to be reinforced by a historical myth of modern progress. The problem is that a perfect world is not a possible world. In fact, it is an impossible world. It is for this reason that the best of all possible worlds remains opaque.

Human freedom is not sufficient to transcend the natural limits of human nature. From the viewpoint of Confucius, basic human feelings are the "field of the Sage Kings" (圣王之田).[13] Only within the realm of human feelings can one engage in cultivating practices,[14] and there is no way of transcending human affect in order to construct an impossible world. Cultivating practices within the field of human affect means that human feelings set the internal boundary for cultivation, and that such practices cannot run contrary to these feelings. Confucius was not an idealist, he was a realist. His envisioned best possible world was a world of *datong* 大同 or "Expansive Harmony"—a world with the highest level of well-being, in which everyone shares in mutual appreciation, mutual trust, and mutual assistance.[15] This would be a harmonious and peaceful world in which strategies for competitive conflict have been invalidated:

The practice of the expansive way is to recognize "the world as common property" (天下为公). It is to prefer worthies and the capable [this is similar to Plato's political imagination]. It is to teach trustworthiness and cultivate harmony [this is a secure situation opposite to the Hobbesian state of nature]. Thus, persons cannot just care for their own parents, they cannot just nurture their own children. It means that the elderly reach a dignified end of life, that the youthful and vigorous have proper employment, and that the young receive proper guidance in their growth. The orphans, bereaved, disabled, and ill all receive sufficient care. The men have their distinctions and the women have refuge. Goods hate being wasted on the ground, so there is no need to store them up for oneself; strength hates to leave the body, so there is no reason to exert energy in service to oneself. Thus, deceptive schemes are not hatched [this point is so important—if a sustainable social order can be realized in which strategies for competitive struggle have been invalidated, then there is certain to be a harmonious and peaceful world], thieving, looting, and rioting will not occur. The household gates need not be locked. This is called the Expansive Harmony (*datong* 大同).[16]

Even though this best of possible worlds has never been realized, it is still realistic and not an impossible aspiration. The world of Expansive Harmony concerns itself with the criteria of security, harmony and peace, mutual trust, mutual assistance, and the material conditions for a surviving and thriving life. But it doesn't require a cultural or religious uniformity. This means that the world that Confucius envisioned recognizes a plurality of different ways of life, seeking diversity and pluralism as ideals without requiring uniformity. This calls to mind the *Focusing the Familiar* (中庸) passage:

> Just as heaven and earth do not fail in conveying anything or sheltering anything.... the myriad things are nourished together and don't harm each other. The diverse modes of proper way-making (道) proceed together without running contrary to each other.[17]

This means that a society should model its respect for diversity on the way that heaven and earth show respect for the myriad things. Here we have the positing of a metaphysical ideal: *heaven and earth are the horizonal limit concepts of all possibilities, and thus they are the ultimate axiological points of reference.* Since heaven and earth are all-inclusive, it follows that *tianxia* must embrace pluralism as a value. This is similar to how

Leibniz conceived of God's standards. Leibnizian "logic" deduces that God's standards are the very "compossibility" (共可能性) of all things.[18]

The future *tianxia* system that I am imagining would satisfy the standards of Confucian pluralism and Leibnizian compossibility. This *tianxia* system is not idealistic or utopian. It doesn't promise happiness for all, but rather hopes to vouchsafe a system of peace and security. The key of this institutionalized plan is to render strategies based in zero-sum competition and enmity null and void. More pointedly stated, a *tianxia* system aims to make any plan to annihilate an external Other null and void. Thus it can secure the conditions necessary for realizing a truly cooperative social order. Simply put, what the *tianxia* system anticipates is a world order based on a principle of coexistence.

POLITICAL UNITS

The problem of any politics hinges upon the identification of "existing political units." Political units (as systems or entities) determine the internal and external nature of political existence. They decide the scope of political problems, the calculative methods for deciding political benefits, and the general deployment of rights discourse and practice. For example, in current discourse the individual is the most basic political unit. This unit determines individual benefits and individual rights. Such a conception of individuals takes an exclusive (egoist) conception of benefits in order to calculate how to deal with any salient political problems. On many different levels, political units establish the very framework of politics and determines the space of the political. Political units decide what sorts of political actions and political problems are possible or impossible within any given emergent framework.

In the framework of traditional Chinese political philosophy political units have three levels: *tianxia*, state, and family (天下—国—家). In this framework the individual is just a biological unit, and in part a unit of economic calculation, but *not* a political unit. Therefore ancient China never produced political liberalism and individual rights as political issues.[19] Only now with modern China importing the Western concept of individualism has "the individual" become a political unit. In the political framework of *tianxia*, state, and family, *tianxia* is not only the great-est measure of any political unit, but moreover it is the ultimate principle of explanation for the entire framework. This means that *tianxia* defines political discourse and all political problems as interpreted within a con-ceptual constellation focused by *tianxia*. In such political space a political interpretation of *"tianxia*—state—family" constitutes an "inclusive order." And the ethical interpretation of "family—state—*tianxia*" is an "extend-ing order." Both of these interpretive trajectories create a mutually entail-ing hermeneutic circle.

The mainstream modern political framework follows an "individual—community—ethno-nation-state" (个人—共同体—民族国家) definitional structure. The ethno-nation-state is the largest scale of a sovereign politi-cal unit. In this model there can be no world political subject trumping the nation-state. The individual is the foundation of the modern political framework and is simultaneously the ultimate explanatory factor in any comprehensive political structure. This is precisely the opposite of the way in which "All under Heaven" serves as the ultimate factor in a *tianxia* sys-tem of political theory. The conceptual space between the political systems of "individual—community—ethno-nation-state" and the political system of *"tianxia*—state—family" creates a gear-like misalignment that might serve as a kind of structural complementarity. This kind of complemen-tarity can expand the capacity and scope of the world political and can be helpful in constructing a new concept of the political. If the level of the "individual" is missing, then the "autonomy" of all such individuals has no political safeguards. If the level of *"tianxia"* is lacking, then the insti-tutional order of the world political has no basis, and as such there is no way of transcending anarchic situations in order to achieve world peace and harmony. This is especially the case under the conditions of global-ization in which national governments and international governmental bodies are increasingly at a loss to face the challenges brought on by new powers. If a world order can't be established to meet the demands of real-izing a possible global governance, then world politics might just become powerless in exercising any control over the risky games being played by irresponsible global actors.

Modern politics gives rise to two types of political problems: namely, *national politics* and *international politics*. The characteristics, goals, and rules of national politics are already quite clearly understood. However, the characteristics, goals, and rules of international politics harbor within them profound uncertainties, even to the point of casting real doubt upon the very capability of international politics to resolve conflicts and disputes between nation-states. This is a result of the lurking suspicion that, as an existing discourse, international politics might be causing more harm than good. International politics has no distinctive aims or ideal aspirations of its own. Rather, it has only been an extension of national politics and serves only as a set of external strategies for promoting national interests. Therefore international politics are just an auxiliary of national politics. Immanuel Kant put forth a most admirable idea—he thought that war could not solve the conflict of competing interests between nation-states, and thus a proposal for perpetual peace was necessary. But at the same time, Kant thought that the "alliance of free nations" could not transcend the ethnonationalist foundations that any concept of international politics was based upon. Kant's proposal was not only unable to address what Samuel Huntington later pointed out as the problem of a "clash of civilizations," but also was even unable to secure the very possibility of a stable and trustworthy mode of realizing international alliance. Given an isomorphism holding between the sovereign nation-states seeking exclusive and optimum benefits and the optimization of private profits for individuals, even if the survival conditions for a stable and trustworthy mutual alliance aimed at shared interest are present as possibilities, it would remain impossible to realize international alliances even between relatively similar cultures.[20]

The high level of technological and economic achievements realized asymmetrically in the modern world have led to a dominating and exploitative "other world locations" ideology that is used as an imperialistic "dominating strategy" by powerful nations. An oppressive and exploitative world can only bring about temporary successes, as imperialism cannot totally eradicate resistance and cannot possibly prohibit the imitative strategies of competitors. Hence imperialism can never be a sustainable strategy for flourishing. Marx revealed to us how capitalism inevitably produces its own gravediggers, and it would seem that something similar can be said about imperialism. But the Marxian ideal of "internationalism" based on a theory of class conflict is also untenable. In the dynamic of competition set by the nation-state system, the conflicts existing between the various proletariat classes of separate nation-states actually exceeds the experienced contradictions imposed by the various capitalist classes within each nation-state. Therefore the possibility of organizing a self-conscious international proletariat is always vaguer and harder to realize than the possibility of organizing an international capitalist class. Unless the existing world order were to undergo a substantial transformation, there is no way to resolve these international contradictions. We cannot expect that current geographical politics and its concomitant "cultural hegemony" based as it is upon an international political order of domination, containment, sanctions, intervention, and war, and only a notional equality among states, to be providing effective strategies for resolving international conflicts. In fact, we should only expect that such an order will be increasing and intensifying international contradictions. And we have no grounds for hoping for the realization of cosmopolitanism or internationalism as some sort of moral utopia, since such ethical idealisms are powerless to change the self-interested choices of actors within the current paradigm of the political. Such idealisms can at best serve to make the absurdity and futility of life in the present world order all the more apparent. For before the world becomes a universal and shared world order, how can a world citizenry exist? Where could they exist? We have to imagine the future, but we can't determine it in advance.

Currently, international politics are not only powerless in resolving international conflicts, but moreover continue to research policies aimed at totally defeating enemies. This strange phenomenon is really not that peculiar. Since within the ethnonationalist system of national politics there is no optimal method for resolving conflicts, we are only left to carry out struggle to the fullest extent possible. The current strategies of international politics are not in the least bit foolish; in fact, they are all too cunning. Here is precisely the problem. Why is it that with sufficient intelligence in theory, strategies, and experience, there is still not the slightest reason to hope for conflict resolution at the international level? With the exception of those who would claim that such theoretical pessimism is just so much ado about nothing, it would seem that not a single international conflict has been meaningfully resolved. For instance, consider the Palestinian-Israel conflict, problems in the Middle East, the West and

Russia conflicts, and the various contradictions between the United States and China. Political analysts can point to all sorts of contingent reasons for why this or that political failure has occurred, and all such explanations have a certain merit, but the truly fatal reason for all international political failures is that the competitive strategies of adversarial parties are equally intelligent.

Many cunning international political strategies have already become "common knowledge," and thus the deadlock of conflict is hard to avoid. As long as competitors are not stupid, nor naively good, and are roughly equal in terms of implementing intelligent strategies, then any temporary advantages will depend entirely upon the successes or failures of the tactics and strategies of adversaries. The tactical, strategic, and theoretical level of international politics has already reached its zenith. It is not that we are waiting to develop better tactics and strategies in this paradigm, but rather no matter how intelligently we struggle using this set of tactics and strategies there will inevitably be loss and failure. This phenomenon is indicative of the limitations of the current global political order and signifies the fact that the concept of international politics is currently receding in the face of all this failure. Under the conditions of globalization, international political theory can only shrink into the finite realm of a theory of conflict and is already clearly incapable of addressing the entire range of world political problems.

Globalization changes the mode of being of the world and the ways of life afforded to humanity. And as such globalization must also alter the nature and scope of political problems. It is precisely with the advent of globalization that the limitations of international politics have become patently clear. International politics are powerless to address the new problems brought about by globalization and can't even begin to address the problems of globalization itself. The concept of shared, communal life is assumed to be merely the province of ethnonationalist nation-states and part of an internal dynamic to natural communities themselves. Moreover, the concept of a shared way of life is becoming increasingly rare as a possibility in this current world order. But, as a concept, communal life provides a way of transcending ethnonational systems and the associated problems that come with the implementation of human rights. As our contemporary world becomes ever more intimate and interdependent among nation-states, a renewed problem of world sovereignty emerges. Therefore, outside of national and international politics, it becomes obvious that we need a third kind of political concept. We can call this a "planetary politics" or a "world politics." Such a new political concept takes the whole world, understood as the optimal measure for the conditions of shared, communal life, and attempts to understand and interpret the world as a political agency. This means that the central problem of contemporary planetary politics is the "internalization of the world"—or in other words, the changing of this world into a *tianxia*.

WORLD INTERNALIZATION AND WORLD SOVEREIGNTY

Although national politics seems to flow seamlessly into the development of international politics, it is impossible for current international politics to develop into a world politics. International politics and world politics have contradictory political logics. Because of this, international politics cannot serve as a basis or conceptual foundation for world politics. This means that political theory must seek out an alternative starting point. The language games of modern politics are primarily defined by the concept of the individual and the ethno-nation-state. Modern governmental institutions take the nation-state as the largest discursive boundary. In terms of going beyond the sovereign nation-state onto the world stage, there are only war tactics and an absence of any institutional order. Therefore sovereignty and the political are limited by national boundaries. Any attempt to extend the political into the external world changes its basic character so as to become a mode of resistance or war. It is better to say that war is a failure of the political than to say that war is politics continued by other means (the viewpoint of Carl von Clausewitz); war is a wager operating outside the calculations and deliberations of the political. Just because the world has been viewed as an externally existing object, the true meaning (if only implicit) of international politics is just war in pseudo-political packaging. Such "politics" are actually the antithesis of the political. The oppositional logic of modern politics ineluctably leads to a hopeless situation—a world of conflict and chaos. No matter how excellent a nation's internal political order might be, such an order cannot avoid being threatened from an unstable world situation. Such a nation-state might even be cast into total chaos where, as a single actor, it cannot extirpate itself. But when globalization develops a politics on a world scale, current international warring strategies will no longer have purchase.

Early on some modern philosophers recognized the looming danger of modern politics. Immanuel Kant thought that international law should develop a "cosmopolitan law" wherein everyone not only has their own set of rights associated with being a citizen of a nation-state but also should be conceived of as part of a "cosmopolitan commonwealth" with the rights belonging to a world citizen. However, to reiterate, before the world becomes a world of shared coexistence, there can be no world citizenship. So currently the expression "world citizen" is a specious identity, even though an imagined "world citizen" obviously influences possible futures. Kant himself discovered that an imagined world commonwealth was unreliable (and could even lead to authoritarian despotism). What ultimately can be trusted for Kant, though, is the ideal order of a "commonwealth of autonomous sovereign nation-states." Jürgen Habermas in a similar way has recognized an imperative that the United Nations should transform international law into world law and that human rights could serve as a foundational principle for constituting world law. But such heroic efforts share a common fragility in not taking into consideration the "worst possibilities." Such perspectives cannot deal with the challenges of the deep conflicts of self-interest and culture. Moreover, there is a basic contradiction implicit in these approaches to political theory. In attempting to transcend the limitations of modern politics, they preserve the political logics of modernity. Kant's ideal could perhaps be put into practice under relatively favorable cultural conditions (like Europe) but is powerless to address adequately the political problems of the entire world—for example, civilizational clashes, global financial warfare, hegemony, and so on. Such an ideal is even powerless to secure long-term international agreements, with the current fragmenting of the European Union an illustrative example here. And the Habermasian hope for a principle of global human rights is a more contemporary and popular vision, but the concept of human rights implies all sorts of "ethical dilemmas."[21]

Since every individual's rights are absolute, then what to do about disputes between different individuals involving the violation of their rights?

And what if the human rights of one geographic region and another geographic region were to come into conflict? How do we deal with all of these sorts of intractable dilemmas? If these dilemmas can be adjudicated, it means that there is some other evaluative standard higher than human rights; and if they can't be adjudicated, it means that human rights discourse harbors an internal contradiction. Human rights is surely a great concept, but the problem lies in the fact that the theory of human rights, as it is presently conceived, harbors many internal contradictions. As such, appeal to human rights alone is not sufficient to resolve many conflicts. Modern politics still attempts to solve problems through discursive deliberations, bargaining, and the negotiation of contracts. However, not only is it the case that international contractual agreements can't be relied upon, but more important, what do we do about the conflicts of interests and rights arising from the inability to enter into shared deliberations, intolerance, and a failure to reach contractual agreements, in addition to profound cultural and religious differences? Although Samuel Huntington's analysis of geopolitical power formations includes many mistaken judgments, the basic problems he raises are compelling. The theoretical positions propounded from Kant to Rawls and Habermas cannot adequately address the problems of civilizational conflict as diagnosed by Huntington.

The basic spirit of modern politics is "division." Modern political discourse is obsessed with drawing all sorts of "borders." Individual rights are a boundary for individuals and sovereignty is a boundary for nation-states; taken together these are part of a basic logic that splits up the world. The internal contradictions of modern politics have always been hard to resolve. In order to protect all these boundary divisions, modern politics is focused on seeking out external enemies. And without the presence of a real enemy there is still a need to define an enemy. This sort of divisive politics can be seen in virtually every kind of context: from definitions of religious heterodoxy to racism; from hot to cold wars; from colonialism to human rights interventions; from economic and militarized hegemony to financial oligarchy; from technological domination to cultural imperialism—even to the point of *Star Wars* sci-fi scenarios in which we always witness the urge to seek out an enemy.

To clearly demarcate oneself from another, one need only to turn the original state of nonopposition into one of oppositional conflict. This kind of politics is unable to conceive the internalization of the world as a root political problem and as such remains unable to understand the world as a political subject. It is also unable to define world interests and is even more incapable of realizing that the world is in dire need of *world sovereignty*. Therefore, when divisive politics encounters difficulties based in oppositional conflict, the only responses it can come up with are peaceable solutions in the form of "assemblies" among international alliances. However, the world within such a political dynamic cannot be assembled because all of the actors involved in oppositional conflicts cannot be made into an assemblage. Thus, with certain a priori presuppositions regarding the externality of alterity, it doesn't matter whether we follow a Hobbesian tradition that emphasizes war, a Lockean tradition that emphasizes competition, or even a Kantian tradition that seeks peaceful contracts—no matter how much we understand the dangers of conflict, all of these positions are unable to dispel such "intersubjective" tension and conflict.

A key issue here is that globalization has fundamentally changed the mode of being of the world and the basic nature of political problems. Modern politics has lost the explanatory and interpretive power to address these newly emergent political problems. Attempting to ameliorate piecemeal the operative political concepts of modernity is not a viable strategy. We can only admit that modern political philosophy merely offers an incomplete set of political theories. As long as we lack the principle of the internalization of the world, it will remain difficult (if not impossible) to explain the legitimacy of political practices outside of the realm of national politics. Political concepts as defined by modern political philosophy have many dubious points regarding the realization of a universal set of practices and modes of legitimization. For example, modern politics believes that democracy is universally effective. But if national democracy was elevated to a global democracy, it would seem that all of the developed nation-states would object. Even the lover of democracy, John Rawls, has opposed the idea of a global democracy. Justice too is accepted as a universal value, but the developed nation-states, as most supplied with capital, are the least likely to accept the terms of any global justice. Suppose that the majority of the world's population were to seek terms of free migration under the banner of world citizenship and global freedom. It seems highly unlikely that developed nation-states and those with relatively good natural conditions would agree to such terms. From this and other hypothetical examples, we can see that the values and the institutions proposed by modern political philosophy are leading to disastrous consequences. This means that modern political philosophy is far from a universally effective political theory and is rather limited as a theory of nation-states. In order to better interpret world political problems, what we need to do is to seek for a new starting point.

First, what we need is a *world-internalizing principle*. In order for a rule of a political language game[22] to be universally effective, it must have universal application to the entire world. As long as there exists a portion of uncooperative or excluded political space, such a political language game is not universally effective since there still exists a negative external aspect that cannot be incorporated—and hence is a root source of conflict. Therefore a universally effective political language game must have a fully holistic conception of the world, wherein every level of politics achieves a systematic "transitivity" and internal "coherence." This is to say that the rules of a political language game must be applicable in all places (every nation-state and geographic region) and in all relationships (relations between individuals and nation-states); and these rules cannot result in harm to any particular place or person—otherwise, there must still remain the roots of an insoluble conflict. Without a doubt, the world will always give rise to conflicts, this is a fact of life. So a totally harmonious world is an impossibility. But a political language game with universal effectiveness is able to continuously be resolving conflicts as they emerge, without thereby precluding the very possibility of conflict emergence. The *tianxia* system is a politics aiming at "compatibility" (协和). The expression "compatibility of countries" comes from the most ancient political anthology, the *Exalted Documents* (尚书).[23] Such compatibility refers to the capacity to transform enemies into friends within a pluralistically inclusive order of political security and peace. Basically, if a political order is not based on an ontological presupposition of "coexistence," there is no way to imagine within such an order of discourse the internalization of the world. According to an ontology of coexistence, if between different entities the possibility of necessary or noncontingent mutual interdependence exists, then there is always already the possibility of a virtuous circle of coexistence being realized. With regards to the internalization of the world, the stable formation of a trustworthy "coexistentiality" is key.

Confucian philosophy takes the family as a basic unit of coexistence and aims to extend an ideal type of coexistence found in family experience to every level of society, with the ultimate unit of coexistence being an all-inclusive *tianxia* family. Fei Xiaotong has questioned this seemingly romantic Confucian political ideal. As soon as family feeling is extended to strangers, the "gene" of family feeling becomes weak and too thinly dispersed, thereby losing its effectiveness as an ethically developmental root.[24] Even if family experience is the best condition for internalization, it is very difficult to achieve a robust family experience for the entire world. Thus between *tianxia*—state—family there can only be a partial affinity, not a total isomorphism. The *Laozi* proposes a more realistic methodology: "Use person to view the person, use family to view the family, use the village to view the village, use the state to view the state, use *tianxia* to view *tianxia*. How do I know that *tianxia* is like this? From *this*."[25] This means that if we want to understand "X" then we can only start from "X" itself in order to understand it. If we take up Laozi's method here, we can more reasonably interpret a principle of world internalization. "World internalization" means to take the whole world as the "all-inclusive" *tianxia*, which entails that there is "nothing outside *tianxia*."

Such an order also entails that we would no longer have externalized insurmountable or incommensurable spaces, but only processes of world internalization. And it follows that we could no longer distinguish an alien Other as being fundamentally unable to share a life of coexistence. We would no longer regard different structures of values as unacceptable forms of "paganism or heterodoxy." This would be a sustainable and universal world politics of general peace and security. Of course, there would need to be the material preconditions for any such universal cooperation. Even if the internalization of the world might not reach the Confucian ideal of "all in the four seas as one family" (四海一家), it still remains possible for the world to strive for that which is realistically achievable. To do away with exteriorization and only have a world of interiorization means that the incentives for coexistence and cooperation are always greater than the incentives for enmity and opposition. And only when the incentives for coexistence are greater than the incentives for enmity can a peaceful and secure order be sustainably realized.

In terms of trustworthiness, the global security as promised by the internalization of the world is clearly superior to the kind of security as promised by international agreements and interstate balances of power. The two primary strategies for realizing peace in international politics are in practice very unreliable:

1. *Peace brought about by hegemonic systems.* Systemic domination is unable to totally control the world. It has no way of preventing newly emergent powers from taking over or subverting its own power structure (history continues to prove this point). Moreover, the oppression and exploitation inherent to hegemonic systems always gives rise to resistance and noncooperation (wherever there is oppression there is resistance). And this gives rise to the unraveling or collapse of such systems.

2. *Using force to balance powers.* Establishing a negative balance is not a solution to conflict, but only a kind of limiting condition. Moreover, the balance of powers is always vulnerable to being quickly overturned in the midst of violent conflicts. As such, it cannot preclude the rapid escalation of competitive struggles that would result in the failure of the dominant power among the various parties involved. In addition, an always present threat of the possibility of war looms dangerously on the horizon (and history is continuously proving this point).

Even if the so-called "mutually assured destruction" mode of balancing of power were to be achieved, still there can be no way to prevent the possibility of a mutually destructive warfare (economic and financial battles, as well as cultural conflicts are also to be included here). Ultimately, such balances of power result in the degeneracy and collapse of any collective body of governance. Game theoretic thinkers have bitterly sought out the causes of the evolution of cooperation from conflict situations but have been unable to come up with any satisfactory explanations. The reason for this is that this difficulty is not an epistemological problem but rather an ontological predicament. Therefore the evolution of cooperation from conflict cannot depend solely on a rational theoretical framework but must stem from a substantial change in the ontological order. As long as the game participants are always seeking to maximize their selfish interests, and in so doing, give rise to the negative existence of political exteriority, then conflict has no way of being resolved. Only if ontological conditions are transformed can the rules of the game be changed. Only through the internalization of the world and the ontologizing of coexistence as necessary conditions can a new ontological order be realized. Only then can we possibly make progress, changing the rules of the game from conflict-based to cooperatively construed.

A major reason that the internalization of the world has for so long been ignored as an essential problem for reflection is that, prior to globalization, the relationships of mutual reliance among nation-states hadn't reached a sufficient degree of entanglement and dependency, and there still hadn't been the formation of shared world interests that transcend those of the nation-state. In other words, a world of coexistence as a political problem just didn't exist. Globalization creates a world of increasingly interconnected lives, economies, markets, finances, technologies, and cultures. Globalization situates the life of every individual person to be not only located "somewhere" but simultaneously to be located "everywhere." Even if our present has not yet reached this point, such a juncture is not far off as a future horizon. A web of interconnectedness is the prophecy of globalization. Globalization is not just some advanced stage of "communication" but is also a world currently being created by events and phenomena as a world of "trans-existence." It is for this reason I am suggesting that this is a kind of transformation of ontological significance. Given the looming global politics, we must, within the conditions set forth by an internalizing process of the world, seek to redefine the rules of the game, to reconstruct human rights discourse, to redistribute benefits and resources, and to restructure the narratives of history and knowledge production. Only in this way will the imperative of finding appropriate political principles and institutions be able to secure a communal global order of life and world political legitimacy be realized. The logic at play here is as follows: (a) globalization inevitably raises the problem of the internalization of the world, and (b) the internalization of the world requires the construction of a new *tianxia* system; therefore, (c) a new *tianxia* system definitively requires that the world become a political subject with world sovereignty.

With regard to world sovereignty, I am currently unable to envision what this would look like in terms of the concrete arrangements of rights and powers, but we can reference certain aspects of the Zhou dynasty's *tianxia* system here and its institutional arrangements to better imagine such world sovereignty. My vision of such an arrangement has at least two basic rules:

1. Although world sovereignty is greater than national sovereignty, it doesn't negate national sovereignty. Rather, it serves as a sort of external limit on any national sovereignty. Therefore world sovereignty and national sovereignty come together to form a pattern of one body. This means that the internal politics of nation-states would still fall under the auspices of national sovereignty, but that the "externalized politics" or the politics that nation-states get involved in requiring arbitration would be considered the domain of world sovereignty. Simply put, political problems internal to nation-states would be considered a matter of national sovereignty, and political problems external to nation-states would be considered the domain of world sovereignty.

2. And everything that concerns the collective fate of humanity would fall under the domain of world sovereignty. This is especially the case when it comes to the power of globalization as defined by systems of global finance, technology, the Internet. The need to employ world sovereignty for control and to achieve justice in these spheres is readily apparent. I believe that, short of the world experiencing some major aberration, the internalization of the world and world sovereignty will become the root problem for politics in the immediate future.

The current world is actually still functioning as a "nonworld"; it is only a geographic category of existence and not a political one. The most important future political problem will be how to create a world, which would be to complete the process of world internalization. When the scale of the political reaches the world as its basic political unit, the problem of the political will have reached its theoretical limit, and all of the problems of the political will appear on stage. When the internalization of the world is made an ultimate political problem, this would not mean the end of politics but rather that the internalization of the world would become the framework for including all political problems. The internalization of the world would thus become a meta-concept for reflecting on and seeking the answer to all political conundrums. The problem of the internalization of the world will clarify the fact that politics is nothing other than the communal art of living. The political is the creative art of coexistentiality for everyone involved. It is the art of transforming the spaces of conflictual competition into a world of shared coexistence. In this sense the political is the end of war. In other words, any politics that is unable to end war is not living up to the basic normative task of the political.

In reality, the transformation of the world has already happened before our political thinking has caught up. Globalization is everywhere and is every day creating the conditions for the internalization of the world. However, whether globalization is up to the task of automatically generating a rational world order is a most open question to be sure. Could such an order generated spontaneously by the processes of globalization realize political coexistence? Can it generate a shared lifeworld universally acceptable to all of humanity? These are questions that leave little room for optimism because we have to consider the worst possible worlds that globalization could generate. For example, with the advancing technologizing of the world, we are witnessing an increasing authoritarianism. Advanced technologies make it easier to establish systems of domination, management, and control over every aspect of life. Such dystopian scenarios might even result in a totalizing psychological control that would turn freedom into an empty concept. We cannot ignore the possibilities of technological authoritarianism. If the forces of advanced technological systems and global financial capitalism were to form a strategic alliance, this could possibly give rise to a historically unprecedented type of power. This would be a form of unlimited "systematized power" exerted over virtually everyone. Such a world order as defined by technology and capital might be a very efficient order, but it would certainly not be a benevolent one. To appropriate a Marxian concept, such an alliance would most certainly result in a totally "alienating" order.

The absurdity lies in the fact that globalization is produced by modernity, but modernity has no way to resolve the problems brought about by globalization. Why is modernity unable to produce its own responsible solutions to the problems wrought by globalization? A very easily overlooked factor in this predicament is that the logics of modern technology and capitalism are not in agreement with the logic of modern politics. The developmental logic of modern technology and capitalism is aimed at realizing a maximal degree of global interconnectedness, but the logic of modern politics is geared toward *dividing* the world along the lines set by hegemonic imperialism. Reality proves this point by showing how technology and capital both aim at maximizing growth and thus align as unified global forces realizing rapid development. But such development cannot keep pace with the rapid degeneration caused by the conflictual logic of modern politics. People all over the world have accepted the globalizing forces of technology and capitalist economies but at the same time resist being dominated by them.

Thus modern technology and capital have become the grave diggers for modern politics, while at the same time serving as the material foundations of a globalizing politics—that is, technology and capital are the material foundations for world internalization. If the phenomenon of conflict can produce the conditions for pluralism and compatibility, then it must also produce the conditions for coexistence. For this reason world internalization must pass through the establishment of a system of global coexistence in order to be realized. And the globalization of technology and capital will provide the necessary material preconditions for this world internalization process. However, technology and capital only seek after their own boundless expansion and have no concern for the benefit of the world. They are, as world-historical forces, even blind to the dangers of unlimited development. The most rational operations of technology and capital are, from the perspective of political goals, entirely irrational. This sort of irrationality has brought the world to the brink of disaster and despair. This is why the world needs a new sovereignty, and why the world needs to become a *tianxia*. The world needs to establish a new ontological order out of the system of international politics. In order to establish global justice, and to control the irrational development of technology and capital, the world needs to become a space for security, peace, and communally shared life.

RELATIONAL REASONING

The core political problems of modern politics involve the "distribution" of interests, power, and rights. Thus modern politics gives rise to philosophies of instrumentality based in logics of oppositional struggle. Much like

the historical positions of Legalism and Latitudinalism,[26] modern politics is based on an interpretive framework that thinks through political
control and competition to effectively realize strategies of governance. As
such, politics is considered a "technique," whereas to attempt to construct
a humane ontological order of political philosophy is a creative "way" (*dao*
道). What merits reflection here is precisely what sort of ontological order
can make an ameliorative "contribution" toward realizing a shared life. If
politics is conceived of as the art of constructing an ontological order, then
the political must be aimed at peace rather than conflict. Thus theories of
conflict are technological, whereas theories of peace are an aesthetic.

Being seeks sustainability. This is the established pattern of being itself.
Conflict is also aimed at existence, but the problem is that conflict cannot
secure sustainability. Actually, conflict inevitably leads to the conduct of
high-risk wagers, which is certainly not the root meaning of "existence."
This point is similar to Socrates's dictum that "no one errs knowingly." This
could be interpreted as meaning that as long as there is a better option—
that is, not having to face tragic situations—people are not going to be
intentionally choosing risk and struggle. In this sense, modern politics
can only be investigated as a history of errors in human conduct. Although
this sort of political investigation is certainly much needed, it cannot reach
the root source of the problem of the political. The "distribution of powers
and interests" is only a technical problem for the shared life of humanity.
Promoting the "contribution to coexistence" is actually the root source of
a shared life. It can be said that a politics that seeks enemies is actually
the antithesis of the political, while transforming enmity into friendship
is the true nature of the political. If we take all the seriously destructive
conditions resulting from enmity-based conduct and interpret everything
as "war" (including military warfare, economic warfare, financial warfare,
cultural warfare, biological warfare, and so on), then other than wars of
self-defense, all war is irrational. Obtaining victory in warfare would seem
to achieve the rationally "expected conditions." But if we were to consider
a sufficiently long-term future horizon (for instance, Fernand Braudel's
idea of the longue durée), then any form of destructive, enmity-based
oppositional conduct is ultimately an irrational mistake. What we need is
to take "futurity" into account in formulating an ontological perspective.
At least theoretically we can prove that any mode of conduct that directly

achieves its result can be called "rational," but if in the long run it proves to result in animosity, revenge, and destructive cycles of violence, then such conduct should actually be considered irrational.

We might consider here a kind of "universal imitation" thought experiment. Take, for instance, Xunzian and Hobbesian game theoretic discourse. Consider that every participant within the game theoretic discourse has individual rationality—that is, all parties are seeking the maximization of their own self-interest and all have sufficient capacities for learning from their experience. Under such conditions everyone will imitate the more intelligent beneficial tactics and strategies used by others. Moreover, as the game theoretic conditions proceed, either the effective strategies learned from imitation will be employed or newly effective defensive strategies will be used. In the multiple rounds of long-term, game-theoretic competition, those with stronger capabilities will always attempt to come up with ever more effective strategies in order to secure their existing advantages. But the superiority of any strategy is always only temporary, because the most intelligent strategies quickly become part of a stock of "common knowledge."

When such common knowledge gets imitated by everyone, the strategies quickly lose their effectiveness within game-theoretic conditions. For example, if we presuppose the existence of a limited set of strategies and tactics, then ultimately the condition of "the collective body of donkeys is weaker than the individual donkeys themselves." Or if we presuppose the existence of an unlimited set of strategies and tactics, due to the fact that the rapidity of imitation exceeds the rate of creativity (because of the relative low cost of imitation compared with creativity), the same condition of the "tragedy of the donkey commons" would occur. In any event the superiority of innovative strategies and tactics never ceases to diminish, and all sorts of formerly efficient strategies and tactics seem to always get assimilated by everyone through processes of universal imitation. Whether people employ commonly saturated knowledge or oppositional knowledge (knowing oneself and knowing one's enemy), the "tragedy of the donkey commons" phenomenon is unavoidable. Thus arrival at a stable strategy and tactical equilibrium (or stalemate) is an inevitability.

The problem is that a universally accepted stable strategy could possibly result in the benefit of all but could also possibly result in injury to all involved. Here the only objective standard is: if there is a strategy or tactic that is universally imitated and doesn't result in vengeance, then it must be a strategy or tactic of universal benefit. In other words, if a particular strategy or tactic receives universal imitation and doesn't develop a method of self-destruction upon delivery, then this strategy or tactic stands up to the test of experience and is thereby a good strategy or tactic. In contrast, if a particular strategy or tactic receives universal imitation and the result is the development of a situation in which the methods employed by others cannot secure their desired results, leading to a relapse into barbarism and disaster, this is proof that this particular strategy or tactic is bad. This is the so-called "tragedy of imitation." Thus we arrive at two theoretical inferences: (1) if a particular strategy inevitably results in vengeance, and fails to pass the imitation test, this strategy is irrational; and (2) moreover, a strategy inevitably resulting in vengeance also inevitably creates the predicament of a vicious cycle of violence. Therefore no matter if a particular kind of conduct is rational or irrational in terms of its relationship to its proximate aims, the process of universal imitation results in a cycle of "aggregation" and this results in collective irrationality. This proves that to simply satisfy conditions of individual rational conduct cannot guarantee that the conduct is universally rational. The power of future vengeance might prove that a particular course of action is irrational. Or we might say that a particular action cannot take itself as an instance to determine whether or not it is rational. Only insofar as individual rationality contributes toward collective rationality can it be deemed truly rational.

This result calls into question the modern concept of "individual rationality." Individual rationality typically means that every person should take the maximization of their own self-interest as a criterion of conduct. It is also typically thought that only with such a criterion can the cost-benefit analysis for any situation be calculated. Moreover, such a conception is taken for granted as the only possible way of making "consistent" an array of choices from a set of preferences that isn't viciously circular or contradictory. However, individual rationality is only a unilateral type of rational thinking. As such, it cannot rationally reflect upon the dynamic relationship between self and other as to whether a given action is optimal. Actually, for every action, not only is there a choice of aims, but at the same time there is an immediate choice of various possible modes of interactive relationality. The key is that the future is decided by interactive relationships. This means that conduct is in multiple aspects collaboratively determined as possible futures. Individual rationality is unable to secure futures that match with optimal outcomes for one's self. A complete reason must be able to achieve a logic with universal effectiveness in interactive situations. Or it could be said that when the interactivity of futures is considered as a component part of any calculation, and is sufficient to guarantee the maximization of security and the optimization of the accumulation of interests for all, then and only then can it be called a robust or complete reason. Individual rationality is not sufficient to guarantee peace and security—rather, it can only contribute to enmity and precariousness. It cannot increase mutual trust but instead only increases mutual suspicion. This results in the production of a kind of methodological self-destruction. Thus we have a clear reason to seek a kind of effective concept of reason in the midst of an interactive relationality.

The test of universal imitation shows that "individual rationality" is inadequate to express fully the concept of human rationality. The available strategies that pass universal imitation tests must seek a different type of reason beyond individual rationality. Otherwise people cannot make choices based on shared interest. As attested to by many historical examples, humanity has in the end maintained many forms of cooperation (Xunzi's hypothesis is correct here). Therefore entering into a total state of nature is not possible. According to the logic of individual rationality, to apply individual rationality one must choose to exclude the maximization of other's interests. This overly one-sided and superficial concept of rationality rests upon a mistaken understanding of the concept of interest. It is not the case that all interests are reducible to individual interests. Many types of interests are "accessible" to all and not just "exclusive" to individuals. Thus the set of exclusively individual interests is smaller than the set of benefits accessible to all. The correct ordering of individual interests does not necessarily reflect the correct ordering of accessible benefits. Because individual rationality exclusively focuses upon a set of possible choices determined by individual interest, it is therefore unable to address all sorts of accessible benefits by failing to recognize genuine benefits. The prisoner's dilemma, the tragedy of the commons, and the free-rider problem all reveal such shortcomings in the position of grounding choices based on individual rationality. If we want to resolve the difficulties of cooperation, we must overturn individual rationality's arbitrary rule and enter into a field of "relational reasoning."

Relational reasoning and individual rationality are not conceptually opposed to one another. Rather, relational reasoning and individual rationality are mutually complementary in constructing a complete concept of reason like the two sides of a coin. Individual rationality is competitive rationality, while relational reasoning is a shared reason. These two cooperate in constructing the balance of reason itself. For instance, if the ontological theory that "existence presupposes coexistence" is correct, then the application of relational reasoning must take precedence over individual rationality. I believe Confucius would agree with the prioritization of relational reasoning. This is because Confucius's core concept of "relational virtuosity" (*ren* 仁) is an ideal model of relational reasoning (caring/empathy/benevolence 仁爱 are only the ethical connotations of *ren* 仁, but the ontological meaning of *ren* 仁 is an intentional optimization of the relational space between at least two persons with respect to the best possible forms of coexistence).

Relational reasoning implies the prioritization of shared knowledge: (1) an awareness of the vengeance problem of imitative conduct means a prioritization of "retaliation aversion." This is a model of conduct that internalizes reflection on the horizon of futurity and intensifies its "risk aversion;" (2) thereby prioritizing reflection upon the "minimization of mutual harm" instead of "the maximization of individual interest"; and (3) furthermore, building upon the securing of the minimization of mutual harm, we take a step forward into the seeking of maximal cooperation and the minimization of conflict as the best of all possible conditions of coexistence. This is a way to enhance the interests of everyone. I am willing to accept the Hobbesian presuppositions—to be is to exist in conditions of terror; while at the same time entertaining certain Xunzian presuppositions—to be is to exist in the midst of coexistence. Based upon these two presuppositions, we can clearly see the divergent paths of individual rationality and relational reasoning. Individual rationality is primarily employed as a defensive strategy as the best strategy to protect the maximization of self-interest in conditions of exteriorized conflict. This understanding of individual rationality actually has some differences from the modern understanding. The aims of modern individual rationality are the maximization of individual interest. This positive aim is in ontological tension with the rational principle of risk aversion. If we restrict individual rationality to a "negative" means of securing self-interest, we can preserve the continuity of principles of risk aversion.

Relational reasoning, however, employs a constructive, stable, trustworthy conception of coexistence. The ideal aims of relational reasoning are to reach a stage of "Confucian amelioration" (孔子改善).[27] This means that a certain type of amelioration of interest must simultaneously entail the amelioration of the interests of all involved. We can say that the interests of person X are enhanced as x +, if and only if (iff), the interests of person Y are necessarily enhanced by y +. Thus promoting the interests x + are beneficial strategies for Y, because Y, in order to reach y +, must recognize that the promotion of x + is in their best interests, otherwise the opposite would be the case. So-called "Confucian amelioration" requires that any sort of amelioration of interests necessarily implies that relational interests of all involved simultaneously receive a "Pareto improvement." Usually Pareto improvements don't require that every individual's interests receive some sort of improvement, but rather simply requires that no one's interests are harmed. Thus Pareto improvement is insufficient to secure the trustworthiness of a relational order of coexistence, and it cannot produce universal satisfaction. However, Confucian amelioration requires a universal satisfaction of the universal amelioration of interests. Thus it is able to realize a stable and trustworthy sustainable equilibrium, and with further progress can achieve a stable and trustworthy political order.

According to what we can know from the universal test of imitation, not only can it provide a reason for effectively realizing an order of nonvengeance, but it also provides a reason for realizing an effective set of game rules. Thus the conditions of nonvengeance are preconditions of any "constitutionality." This test can determine if a kind of constitutionality, law or institution has universal effectiveness. This is to say that as long as the rules of the game share a logic of nonvengeance, they must be universally effective. And thereby such rules have constitutionality. The rules of nonvengeance mean that for any persons (including all existing and possibly future existing persons), they cannot have a rational reason to reject these rules (not considering purely affective reasons or nonrational reasons). If an institutional order can only consider a present person's interests and excludes from consideration the interests of future persons, then it is lacking in constitutionality. Although we cannot predict the collective intentionality of future persons, we can, at least logically speaking, exclude possible harm to persons from the standpoint of an institutional order.

This amounts to excluding possible harm to future persons. If we develop an institutional rationality based upon individual rationality, then we must depend upon the aggregated preferences of individuals. Thus it is difficult to avoid the predicament of collective reason conflicting with individual rationality. However, if instead we base our conception of institutional reason upon relational reasoning, then we can hope to avoid the disastrous predicament of aggregated preferences and realize a continuity of universal reason. This would be to reach a stage of rationality where there is no reason to oppose it. Here relational reasoning can be understood as a reasonable mode of self-constraint. Before the emergence of the political, in a Hobbesian state of nature for example, persons would already be using their individual rationality. It is because of their shared life though that rationality must be developed to a stage of relational reasoning. In this sense, to be effective in creating rational political conditions for a sustainable shared life, individual rationality must be transformed into collective reason to serve as an art of thinking.

However, politics must still face the manifold problems that arise from desire, spirit, and affectivity. Explaining the mind of rationality does not equate to being able to explain its affective aspect. Although a principle of rationality can explain political legitimacy conceptually, it is still the case that we need to confirm its application in actual practice. This is to say "thinking" needs the confirmation of "feelings" to be effective. Political justice implies political legitimacy because we cannot think of anything more just than justice.[28] Justice as an abstract concept belongs to philosophy, but the actual understanding of justice is always political. What people in actuality believe justice to be is the real issue. This means that as soon as the concept of justice hits the ground, we cannot avoid appealing to subjective preferences for confirmation. Objectivity is left hanging while subjectivity becomes the truly substantive basis for theorizing justice. Although justice must seek confirmation in subjective opinions, we must analyze the different possible kinds of subjective evidence for justice:

P1: An institution is legitimate if and only if (iff) all people consistently agree with the institution.

This standard is the most perfect, but it is overly stringent, since in actuality it cannot be realized. Even theoretically it would seem that there cannot be perfect agreement among people regarding any given institution. Thus we resort to seeking legitimacy at the next level:

P2: An institution is legitimate iff it is agreed upon by a majority of persons.

This is precisely the ideal imagined by modern democracy. Because a majority agreement is clearly weaker than an agreement consistently agreed upon by all, it is the case that if majority agreement is going to determine the definition of justice it needs a further limiting condition: whenever people have a common interest "x," and how to realize "x" presents several technical choices between a, b, c, and so on, then the possibility of achieving a democratic "aggregate" of preferences resulting in justice is rather significant. This is to say that when democracy is tasked with "selecting programs" rather than with "choosing between interests," then it is comparatively easy to approximate justice. Under conditions of conflict of interest, however, using democracy to shape shared choices actually becomes a mode of competition between conflicting powers. Whenever democracy isn't an art of optimally selecting programs, but rather a mode of selectively bidding among interests, then any justice that is achieved remains comparatively suspect. Democracy is indeed an efficient process for the formation of shared choices, but it is not the final arbiter of value. Democracy cannot guarantee that it will result in the most beneficial choice between the shared interests and every individual person's interest. Thus it would seem that we ought to turn to a more substantive problem inherent in the conceptual background of democracy: that is, is democracy able to attract the ardent support of the people and thus win over the people? This leads to:

P3: An institution is legitimate iff it coheres with institutions compatible with the people's shared aspirations.

Democracy is one kind of method for expressing "the people's shared aspirations" (*minxin* 民心). But can democracy sufficiently express the people's aspirations? This is a real problem. Many factors can mislead democracy into a distorted expression of the people's shared aspirations. For example, manipulation by wealthy interests, propaganda, speculation, passion, ignorance, fake news, and so on can all mislead popular opinion. Even in conditions excluding manipulation and misleading media, democracy still might not be able to accurately express the people's shared aspirations. For example, what Arrow's impossibility theorem[29] shows to be the limitations of electoral systems proves that democracy can possibly choose results that people don't truly want (it should be noted that later scholars have pointed out that Arrow's impossibility theorem has relatively little impact on actual elections). The concept of the people's shared aspirations lacks transparency. The ancient Chinese philosophers who used "the people's shared aspirations" really didn't provide a clear and distinct definition. It seems that they had a kind of unstated agreement in their understanding. At this juncture we can only draw upon classical sources and make inferences. The people's shared aspirations do not refer to the aggregate will of the people, but deals more closely with the need for benefiting each person and the interests of all.

It is not the summed up, aggregate will of the multitude then, but something closer to Jean-Jacques Rousseau's "public weal" that we are interested in here. Perhaps we could also say that the people's shared aspirations are a shared appreciation of what, through a long-term process of practical reasoning, has proven itself to be beneficial to all. This means that the mode of existence of the people's shared aspirations is a matter of *thinking* and not merely a psychological phenomenon. What the people's shared aspirations express is not a collective body of desires, but rather a conveyance of the common understanding of a set of possibly shareable experiences, traditions, and histories. This is something that has passed through a longue durée of game theoretic confirmation as "public knowledge" and isn't a result of mere special interests or some presupposed a priori masquerading as universally shared knowledge. Given the various civilizational modes of unconsciously arriving at a "universally" accepted set of legal codes and ethical principles as the "people's shared aspirations," it would seem that we are still mired in a quandary with respect to providing a clear definition of what constitutes the people's shared aspirations. Perhaps we can place the idea of the "people's shared aspirations" in a modern conceptual context to arrive at a better understanding. To do so, we might compare the "people's shared aspirations" with the modern concept of "universal values."

However, "universal values" has yet to receive an adequate definitional account, because as of yet there have been no universal standards to judge what counts as universal values. This reveals a certain irony with respect to universal values. Logically speaking, universal values should at the least mean the following: (1) some values are universal; (2) and, moreover, these values are universally good. Regarding (1), if a kind of value is useful for some situations, then it must be useful for all similar situations. In other words, if the value(s) are useful for a certain situation, then for any similar situation they are necessarily useful. This could be called the "nondiscriminatory" property of universal transitivity. This should be quite clear and uncontroversial. But regarding (2), the implications of the "universal good" are far from clear. This is because universality doesn't "analytically imply" a universal good. Universally good things necessarily imply absolutely necessary things. Thus, if we enter into "necessary values" to define universal values, then necessary values must necessarily be universally good values, otherwise they are not necessary. Here we can see, the necessity of values is the key to understanding the universality of values. Only when a certain value is simultaneously necessary and universal is it also a universally good value, and also a universal, necessary value.

The universal necessity of values must at least seek two modes of elucidation. One mode is to take the individual as a basic unit of analysis, seeking values that can be "applied to everyone." The other mode is to take relationality as the basic unit of analysis, seeking values to be "applied to every relation." The results of applying these two explanatory methods are quite different. If employing the individual as a basic unit of explanation, and wanting to prove that a certain value is universal and necessary, then one must consider the preference of every individual. Thus there exists the following type of possible situation:

1. *For "all wants"—if all want "x," then this can only prove that "x" is a universal object of desire, but not that "x" is universally right.*

2. *Universalization.* The classical Kantian principle is: "If I accept principle 'x,' then I agree that 'x' should be binding for all." This Kantian prin-

ciple is sufficient to plug the holes of "all wants" but remains unable to solve the problem of conflict among a plurality of evaluative schema. For example, if some person thinks that everyone ought to be a Christian, and another person thinks that everyone ought to use recreational drugs, it is obvious that these propositions cannot be universally accepted. Here we can see that when there exists a plurality of doctrines, universalization is ineffective.

3. *Common consent.* This is a very powerful reason. Unfortunately, it is not totally effective. Unanimity among a group can only prove that "x" has universal acceptance but cannot prove that "x" has universal benefit. For all persons to make the same mistake together or for a collective body to fall into error is certainly possible. Take, for example, the way that modern persons collectively believe that, or at least their conduct implies that, the way they consume natural resources can be projected indefinitely into the future. But such consumption patterns go beyond actual needs and undermine the very possibility of a sustainably shared life. Here we can see that, in taking the individual as a basic unit of analysis, it is very difficult to understand universal and necessary values.

If we opt instead for relationships as a basic interpretive unit of the necessity of values, then we should consider what persons would accept in their mutual relations. Thus universal values would entail:

1. *Universal benefit.* If a kind of relationship gives rise to universal benefit, then every person will agree to this. Universal benefit excludes the worst possible conditions of common consent (wherein the collective body is impoverished). Universal benefit always implies common consent, but common consent doesn't necessarily imply universal benefit. To take relationships as the basic unit of analysis has the advantage of taking objective beneficial outcomes into consideration instead of merely an aggregation of preferences. This is a more rational standard.

2. *Universal compatibility.* If a kind of relationship is sufficient to secure mutual compatibility and cooperation, then everyone will accept this. Universal compatibility in relationships doesn't intrude upon any particular way of life. Moreover, compatibility relations don't depend upon any special interest groupings or cliques. Rather, such relationships aim at the benefit of everyone involved. Thus the priority goes to relationships and not to the special interests of any individual party. Therefore universal compatibility in relations can resolve the problems of conflict between a plurality of comprehensive doctrines.

A STARTING POINT FOR POLITICAL RENEWAL

What the above analysis has attempted to prove is that through the concept of *tianxia*, together with the principle of coexistence and relational reasoning, the very concept of the political needs a conceptual renewal. The "nothing outside" and all-inclusiveness of *tianxia* opens up an expansive and truly comprehensive political discourse. Thus it can clearly determine the appropriate role of all political concepts and the scope of the problems with respect to conditionality and content. A principle of coexistence means that politics is to be conceived of as an art of shared living rather than a technique for social control and manipulation. This is the faith upon which *tianxia* politics is based. And relational reasoning is its core principle of praxis. *Tianxia* can be used to imagine a world institutional-order, and to establish new rules of the world political game, and give expression to the universal shared aspirations of the people as necessary values.

Thus a *tianxia* theory is not only a theory of world politics but at the same time involves a new conception of the political—a new starting point for political renewal and a starting point for abolishing war. In order to provide a trustworthy way of addressing the problem of the conflict between interests and values, politics must become a kind of art of determining the good and a technology for transcending the bad. More precisely stated, politics must become an art for transforming enmity into friendship rather than a technology for coping with competitive conflict. The deep political problem here is not the conflict between good and evil but rather the conflict between different goods. The conflict between good and evil is a problem without opposing positions. That good should be triumphant over evil is an incontrovertible belief of our shared humanity. But when one good, due to its difference, comes into conflict with another good and attempts to eradicate this other good, this is truly a political tragedy. Such phenomenon have led to so many tragic problems in the world with respect to existing divisions and political failures. This starting point for political renewal, as offered by a reimagined *tianxia* concept, seeks to constitute a political subject through the internalization of the world, thereby establishing a world sovereignty for everyone. This means the transforming of a world of enmity into a shared *tianxia*. And the phrase "All under Heaven is public" or the "world is common property" should be rehearsed as: "*tianxia* is a *tianxia* shared by all persons-under-heaven."[30]

PART I   The *Tianxia* Conceptual Story

1   Politics Starting with the World

There are at least two major decisive starting points by which to determine the meaning and scope of the political: the Greek *polis* constituting a concept of national politics, and China's *tianxia* constituting a concept of world politics. Before the emergence of genuine politics, humanity had a long history of various forms of rule, including many monarchies and dynasties. But mere ruling is not the same as the political. The logic of ruling is naturally a hegemonic order. Internally it is about submission to leaders and externally about submission to hegemonically realized natural orders. Within such a logic there is no way of transcending the natural order to realize a political order, and there is no basis for using the authority of rational principles to distribute benefits. Confucius defines the political as "correcting" (政者正也) and "governing through virtuosity" (为政以德).[1] This means that the political is precisely the transcendence of militaristic hegemony and the constitution of a rational order benefiting all. We should also mention another starting point of the political. This is a theocratic foundation of the political—for instance, the Jewish Kingdom of Israel. However, because ancient Israel's theocratic order goes beyond my expertise and isn't directly relevant to what we are discussing, we will not be referencing this model too much here.

The *polis* is a marvel and *tianxia* is also marvelous. To view the Greek *polis* as the starting point of European politics is not to deny that the idea of *polis* has an even earlier cultural source. Homeric epic history records the conditions of the political, the (relatively indeterminate) space of the *agora* or marketplace. The traces of the Cretan civilization also attest to an early life of the *agora*. But the Greek *polis* seems to be a more mature development of the common realm, wherein private life and a public realm are clearly demarcated in both essence and function. Similarly, the Zhou period *tianxia* system also had an early mythological form. Perhaps this is the spiritual vision and image that the early sage kings had of a yet to be realized institutional order. What is certain is that the mature institution of a *tianxia* system was a discovery of the Zhou court from over three thousand years ago. The different starting points of the political lead to very different evolutionary paths and distinctive political problems. The division between *polis* and *tianxia* as starting points for the political are, as cultural narratives, distinct "forking paths of time," to borrow language from Jorge Luis Borges.[2] Each path has its distinctive evolutionary trajectory, and it is only in modern times that the two paths give rise to conflict. The circumstances of the two narratives become entangled, and the processes of globalization take the complementary nature of these two narratives to become one possible future.

The Zhou dynasty *tianxia* system inaugurated a way of thinking that would take the problem of the world as its point of departure. It is difficult to know precisely at what time this kind of political view of the world or political ideal began to emerge. The ancient documents often trace this political view of the world back to the period of the sage-kings Yao, Shun, Yu, and Tang more than four thousand years ago. According to the tradition, during this period the "Son of Heaven" (*tianzi* 天子) led "all-under-heaven and the ten-thousand countries" (*tianxia wanguo* 天下万国)[3] as a political cooperative. This is a traditional narrative that has yet to be verified and is likely the product of a later Zhou dynasty understanding and interpretation of history based on their own political ideals. The era of the mythic sage-rulers was probably a kind of "chiefdom," where between the various chiefdoms there existed varying degrees of cooperative relationships. These sage-rulers were likely those leaders possessing awesome charisma, but we shouldn't necessarily think that they actually created any laws or established any lasting institutions.

According to the research of Wang Guowei, during the Xia and Shang periods, "there were vassal lords and the Son of Heaven, and later there were vassal lords and leaders of alliances, but there was never a role-based distinction between ruler and ministers."[4] One confirmation of this can be found in the *Exalted Documents*, where the early rulers of the Zhou dynasty still referred to the vassal lords as equals with the sobriquet "hereditary rulers from friendly states."[5] However, according to the same *Exalted Documents*, the sage-rulers seem to have already organized the various chiefdoms with their relational power dynamics to become a "harmonious alliance of the myriad states."[6] These early sages ruled over the various clans by issuing their various edicts having to do with pressing issues shared by all. For instance, the controlling of flood-waters, the institutionalization of a calendar, the standardization of measurements, the establishment of ritual and music, as well as the giving and receiving of tribute—all of these were included among the "great affairs."[7] During this time interclan cooperation became a possibility, but there still was not yet a full-blown institutionalization of any form of political cooperation. The ancients had a disposition to revere antiquity by attributing great social accomplishments to their predecessors. A reasonable inference to be drawn from this is that during this time of the sage-rulers, including the Xia and Shang periods of *tianxia* collective leadership, the mode of rulership wasn't a form of legally binding governance. This can be inferred since the political institutions under a system of law had not yet been established, and therefore rulership was likely based on the inspiring power of alliances. Even so, it is likely that during this time of the sage-rulers, as is evidenced by the narrative tradition extolling a "harmonious alliance of countries," that they already had begun to develop an ideal of *tianxia* as a political vision of world order.

The institutionalization of the *tianxia* system started in the Zhou dynasty. For an ancient society to experience an institutional revolution, it must have faced a unique assemblage of material conditions and opportunities. This is precisely the bewildering problem in need of explanation regarding the Zhou dynasty *tianxia* system: namely, why would the Zhou dynasty envisage such a world political system over three millennia ago? Such a vision is exceedingly lofty and far-sighted as a political institution. So what was happening that would give rise to such an ideal? Why would they interpret the world as a holistic political subject? What is clear is that politics always begins from world problems, but this was not a commonsensical way for political thinking to proceed. The common path historically has been to develop national politics out of tribal societies rather than starting from world politics. The Zhou dynasty *tianxia* system was not just an unusual innovation for these ancient times, but even with respect to the present world, expressive of a political problematic transcending current expectations and belonging to a new paradigm for global futures. In any event, there must have been a distinctive set of historical reasons for the institutionalizing of a *tianxia* system by the Zhou dynasty.

We might do well then to attempt to return to the historical discourse to understand the Zhou dynasty reasons for the introduction of the *tianxia* system. During the Yin-Shang dynasty, the Zhou was a small country positioned in the northwest of the "Central States" (*zhongguo* 中国) with a hybrid economy split between agriculture and seminomadic pastoralism.[8] The Yin-Shang political center was located in the Central Plain with an advanced agricultural and technological culture, and with a population possibly exceeding a million people. Precisely how large the population of the "small state of Zhou" was is hard to determine precisely, but according to some estimates, it was probably something over fifty thousand but no more than sixty thousand or seventy thousand persons.[9] The Zhou ruler was a person of virtuous reputation and began to garner a following among several smaller countries. King Wu of Zhou (周武王) raised an army to attack the Shang with the help of several allied countries.

According to Sima Qian, the Grand Historian of the Han dynasty, King Wu's forces numbered three hundred chariots, three thousand special forces, and forty-five thousand infantry. And according to the same records, King Zhou of the Shang (商纣王) sent seven hundred thousand to meet the assault, a number that is likely an exaggeration. For any of the states at this time to marshal around one hundred thousand troops and horses would be to deploy in full force. And even though the troops of King Zhou of Shang far exceeded the strength of Zhou alliance in numbers, according to the traditional historical narratives, the viciousness of

King Zhou of Shang himself was compounded by the unforeseen mutiny of some of his troops, giving King Wu of Zhou the victory. The Shang king's forces were defeated and he committed suicide. The Zhou clan then assumed the role of leading the alliance, yet the Yin-Shang regime survivors were numerous. There were also those vassal lords previously on intimate terms with the Yin-Shang leadership, and those tribes "untamed" by the Yin-Shang order founded by King Jie. There was much turmoil in the minds of the people, and there were many rebellions. On many fronts, there was a need for pacification. Thus the Zhou dynasty—this small nation that came to occupy the role as the leading political power on the Central Plain—was facing an unprecedented political problem: How to "use the small to govern the great" and how to "use the one to govern the many?"

Achieving unified governance among the many had traditionally been a matter of the biggest and strongest exercising hegemonic rule over the rest. This is to say that the one governing the many had always been based on the precondition of the powerful governing the weak. This is a natural mode of governance. In ancient societies population was not only the most important economic resource but also a most important political and military resource—it was the foundation of all power. The Zhou was a smaller country, though, whose population was limited, meaning that they couldn't possibly use the strength of numbers to govern the small. Instead, they had to be the one governing the many within the conditions of the few governing the vast. This was a wholly new situation. The reason that the Zhou were able to achieve a successful alliance among the vassal lords in overthrowing the Shang was due to the fact that they had the moral authority to rally support, and on the basis of their moral reputation, were at this critical juncture able to amass a formidable military force. But it was difficult to merely rely upon such an image of morality to maintain the sustained support and loyalty among the various tribes. This is because morality alone, in the final analysis, is unable to replace the need for power and benefits. But the actual situation of the "small governing the large" had already, as a logical possibility, negated the hegemonic model. Thus the Zhou as a political power had only one option—to invent a new kind of political institution—an institutional order with its own appeal that didn't rely solely upon military threat for governance. That is, the Zhou had to figure out how to replace mere military might with a form of institutional superiority.

From the very beginning, as a political power, the Zhou dynasty was forced to confront a complex array of problems with respect to institutional design. Because the Zhou did not have the capacity to establish a hegemonic model of governance, and because the strength of their own people was insufficient to sustain their position of exercising a collective rule of *tianxia* over the long term, they had to attempt to achieve their strategic advantage among the myriad states by other means. And the only way they could maintain their own position of power and even secure their political survival was to design an acknowledged institutional order that could secure long-term cooperation among a sufficient number of the various states. A key deciding factor in all of this was resolving the problem of "externality" among the myriad states. Zhou had to transform the external relations among the states into an internalized order of existence. This meant that the Zhou regime had to establish a world system transcending individual states in order to realize an internalization of the world. This required that a system of shared interests and shared benefits of the whole be designed that could guarantee satisfying each states' own particular interests.

Whether a world system is going to succeed depends in the first instance upon what kind of shared benefits and cooperative interests this world system can offer the various states. Such interests and benefits have to, at the very least, be more appealing to the participating states than what they could realize by the rejection of such a world political system. The interests that the multitude of tribes had in entering a world system must have been greater than the benefits they would have received by rejecting the system. And this balance of power must have been realized, otherwise no one would have accepted and supported such a system. The design of such an institutional project required a great degree of imagination. We can be sure that the unique set of challenging historical conditions that the Zhou regime faced gave rise to a profound political problem: namely, the establishing of a stable world order as a precondition for state survival. In other words, the achievement of effective world governance is a precondition for the legitimacy of any form of state governance. Thus world politics must take precedence over national politics. This dynamic is the "world internalization" problem and is synonymous with the problem of formulating a *tianxia* system.

At the time there were many different peoples that came to be referred to as the "myriad states." Even though these various states each controlled a limited territory that in sum amounted to less than half of the land area of modern China, it was this realm that the ancients considered *the world*. This realm, although much smaller than the world as we now know it, was viewed as the entire world and called "All under Heaven" (*tianxia* 天下). Land area was not all important, but what was certainly important was the positing of a world-consciousness—a kind of political consciousness that considered the entire world within its scope. *Tianxia* is a concept with a complex connotative field, but logically speaking, *tianxia* designates the entire world: that is, both a natural world and a political world. Stated precisely, *tianxia* is the combination of the natural and the political world. But because the political world and the natural world have yet to be combined, *tianxia* must be understood as a dynamic concept still in the process of becoming. Before the political world and the natural world are fully combined, *tianxia* can only remain an ideal conception of the world. And although the political world constructed three millennia ago by the Zhou dynasty was only a small part of *tianxia*, as a historically constituted concept, it can open up for us an experimental space for reimagining contemporary world politics.

The *tianxia* system introduced by the Zhou dynasty was a world political system. It defined the holistically existing political world as an "institutionally formulated *tianxia*."[10] The *tianxia* system designed during the Zhou dynasty is usually attributed to the Duke of Zhou, but it was perhaps the creation of a collective body of political thinkers led by the Duke of Zhou. The Zhou dynasty *tianxia* system was the first revolution in Chinese political history and was also, strictly speaking, the beginning of the political in Chinese history. Wang Guowei points out that "Chinese political and cultural transformations and revolutions are nothing but a drama played out after the Yin-Shang to Zhou transition" and was a "discarding of old institutions and the emergence of new institutions, and the discarding of an old culture and the rise of a new culture."[11] The many profound political problems implicated in the Zhou institutions have today taken on a clear importance. Just as with the Greek cluster of concepts such as justice, the public realm, democracy, and so on, which have for so long been a dominant and persistent political problematic, the Zhou dynasty similarly sets forth a cluster of terms such as *tianxia*, virtuosic rule (*dezhi* 德治), harmonious alliances (*xiehe* 协和), the people's shared aspirations (*minxin* 民心), and so on, as a necessary vocabulary for approaching the political. What is most important is that the *tianxia* system is primarily calling for a transformation of the natural earth into a political *tianxia*, thereby determining the basic meaning of the political for the world.

The immediate goal behind the Duke of Zhou's formulation of a *tianxia* system was to solve the unique problem of "using the small to govern the large "and "using the one to govern the many." But in addressing this problem, he produced a universally significant model of the political. The universal import of the *tianxia* system is expressed by a shared world system with the following necessary characteristics:

1. The *tianxia* system must guarantee that all states involved in the system have benefits exceeding what they would have if they otherwise remained independent and external to the system. This is the reason why every state would willingly commit to entering the *tianxia* system.

2. The *tianxia* system must also be able to constitute a system of mutual dependence and reciprocity of benefits among all of the participating states. This is in order to assure universal security for the world and an actually perpetual peace.

3. The *tianxia* system ultimately must be able to develop a set of common interests, shared benefits, and common undertakings that are universally beneficial for each state, and in so doing, guarantee the universally shared character of the *tianxia* system. In sum, a *tianxia* system must fully realize the world's internalization, making of the world an interiority without any remaining exteriority.

The formulations of the Duke of Zhou was primarily about institutionalizing the division of lands, the institutionalizing of ritual practices and musical performances, and the principles of virtuosic governance. The division of land was an institution of guardianship aimed at organizing the one body of the world for better governance. *Tianxia* was designed as a networking system that included the many different governing bodies that belonged to the main body, along with this network of the states of the vassal lords constituting the world political subject. Included within this network was the world political subject that exercised sovereignty, the *tianxia* ancestral kingdom (*zongzhuguo* 宗主国) tasked with protecting the common security and overall cultural order of the world system. This main ruling body could protect the common interests and shared benefits of the whole system. Every fiefdom was both independent and self-ruling, but also part of an entire network of the political order, thus sharing in a mutually dependent relationship with the ancestral sovereign state. These fiefdoms, in receiving protection from this centering sovereign kingdom, had simultaneously the function of protecting the ancestral sovereign state. The actual design for this institution charged with dividing territory was exceedingly complex, and a more detailed description of it will follow.

The institutionalization of ritual practices and musical performances constituted a spiritual (*jingshen* 精神) order of being. Ritual and music bestow forms of life with spiritual meaning. Suffusing all aspects of conduct and manners, the ordering of everyday affairs, and sustaining material life, ritual and music give to these things a certain solemnity and sacredness. Thus people find themselves reverentially standing in awe of heaven and earth, respecting the dignity of other persons, tending to nature with reverence, and treating the ordinary affairs of life with respect. In short, it is because ritual and music give dignity and reverence to all forms of life that we can speak of the "sacredness" (*shenjingxing* 神圣性) of ritual and music. The power that ritual and music have to sacralize the myriad aspects of life might seem to constitute a kind of religious spirit, but this is not an (ontologically) transcendental religious power, because the transformation of things into sacredness does not go beyond the spirituality latent in ordinary life. In fact, it is just the culmination of ordinary life itself.

This reverence and sacredness that is instilled into everyday life by ritual and music, and the religious transformation of ordinary experience is a distinctive feature of the Chinese cultural tradition. But due to many historical ruptures, subsumed under the rubric of "ritual destruction and musical corruption," this aspect of Chinese culture has sadly been lost to a significant degree. What remains though is a trace of the beautiful names from the ritually proper state of Zhou. However, using ritual and music to make life sacred was not the original intention of the Duke of Zhou's formulation but is a rather pleasant side-effect. This is because the Duke of Zhou was not addressing religious problems per se but rather political ones. Ritual and music are expressive of a way of life that complements the institutional divisions of territory. The aim was to create a harmonious *tianxia* at a spiritual level. Ritual propriety suffuses the myriad events and affairs with a resplendent spirituality, thus giving rise to a potentially universalizable form of shared religious experience. And ordinary events, as the qualitative embodiment of spirituality and as a basis for shareability, permits an (immanent) transcendence of things as being merely materialistic and exclusively ordered. This is the transcendence of "conflict" through "harmony." And this is what the expression attributed to Confucius means by "in the uses of ritual, it is harmony that is to be prized."[12]

It is easy to misinterpret rule by virtuosity as an ethical principle. In fact, rule by virtuosity was a principle of political economy. Before "virtue" (*de* 德) evolved into an ethical concept, it was originally a pragmatic conception of a just division of social goods. This is the origin of the expression, "virtuosity is concerned with efficacious governing, and governing is the nourishing of the people."[13] "Virtuosic rule" means an order of benefits that must be universally shared and justly distributed. A politics of virtuosity necessarily means that the benefits of all persons are optimized as distinct from a logic of maximizing benefits exclusively for some. The Duke of Zhou believed that only rule by virtuosity could guarantee political legitimacy. Mere coercive power cannot be sustained in the long-run: only virtuosity can be long lasting. Only virtuosity can suffuse the entire world, reaching all of the people and passing from one generation to the next. The enlightenment of the Duke of Zhou was a discovery of characteristics of a true conception of the political. Rule by military might is not political, it is only rule. True politics is the art of creating a universally cooperative and common lifeworld. In this sense, the Zhou dynasty's *tianxia* system was not only a kind of historical-political experiment but was also the true expression of the conception of the political.

2   The Three-Tiered World of *Tianxia*

Tianxia has a "trinitarian" conception of the world. *Tianxia* has three distinct layers of implicit meanings sedimented into this world concept. The basic layers of meaning are:

(1) Geographically, *tianxia* refers to the entire earth under the heavens as the whole world: The earliest expression comes from the *Book of Songs* (诗经): "Below the vast heavens above there is nothing that isn't the King's earth."[1] Although this *tianxia* concept references the world in its entirety, the ancients didn't know how large the world actually was. Early China's area of influence was the "Nine Realms" (九州), describing them in these terms: "To the left was the Eastern Sea, to the right sandy dunes, in the front mountain peaks, and in the rear a shady city."[2] The land area referenced here was no more than half of current China. Because of the geographical limitations of seas, high mountains, and deserts, the ancients had only a very vague knowledge of the world beyond. Before the Han expansion into the western regions there was only modes of trade with the distant world, but no political connections. The area outside of political governance was called "The Four Seas" (四海), meaning that it was vast and uncharted like the seas rather than referring to actual oceans. This

extensive domain was all part of *tianxia* but had yet to be included as realms within the *tianxia* system.

According to the perspective of the ancients, just how big was *tianxia*? The Duke Heng of Qi once asked Guan Zhong (管仲) for his instructions regarding this question. Guan Zhong's response was, "The land from east to west is 28,000 *li* and from south to north is 26,000 *li*."[3] The pre-Qin conception of *li* 里 was about 414 meters.[4] So with this estimate in mind, the *tianxia* imagined by Guan Zhong would be from east to west about 11,600 kilometers and from south to north about 10,800 kilometers. Although this doesn't cover the planet, it does account for the Asian continent. For an ancient person living more than two thousand years ago, this geographical imagination is fairly impressive. There was also forms of imagination that ranged beyond the visual realm. For instance, Zou Yan thought that *tianxia* had eighty-one separate "Nine Realms" and the area centered around the Central States was just one of these.[5] This vision obviously takes us into the realm of fantasy.

(2) In terms of social psychology, *tianxia* refers to the common deliberations of all the world's people—this is the "shared aspirations of the people" (*minxin* 民心): within the concept of *tianxia* persons are more important than land. To "get *tianxia*" (得天下) doesn't mean just to control all of the territories under heaven, but rather to receive the support of the world's multitudes. The ancients believed that if you didn't win over the hearts of the people, then even occupying land would be of no benefit, as sooner or later it would be lost. Thus Guan Zhong said, "Those who would contend for *tianxia* must first contend for the support of the people."[6] And "one cannot fail to serve the people, as this is the ultimatum of *tianxia*."[7] The *Xunzi* states: "The person who takes *tianxia* is not simply referring to someone who shoulders the weight of the territory and deals with it, but is rather the person whose way of ruling is sufficient to unite the people."[8] The aspirations of the people is the deciding factor in who really holds jurisdiction over a territory. Thus *tianxia* is not merely geographical but is even more so a psychological and sociological mode of being.

(3) In the political sense, *tianxia* refers to a world-political order: A world order defines the political whole of the world and its conception of sovereignty. In other words, a world order is what allows the world to

become a complete political being. There is a metaphysical or we might even call it a theological reason behind this claim: it is because heaven above has a perfectly harmonious order that *tianxia* as "heaven below" must also strive for a perfectly harmonious order. This is called "correlating with *tian*" (配天).[9] There is also a realist political reason: if there were no world order, *tianxia* would ultimately be a fragmented and chaotic place and perpetual peace would forever be but a hopeless proposition. This claim is what the *Mozi* references with when it states: "To reconcile what is right in *tianxia* is to govern *tianxia*."[10] In this sense it is only in bringing about a *tianxia* world order that the ultimate formation of *tianxia* can be achieved. This suggests that the ultimate achievement of *tianxia* is the full coincidence of the natural, the social-psychological, and the political worlds of value. This institutionalization of the world is what the *Guanzi* calls "institutionalizing *tianxia*."[11]

Here we can see that *tianxia* has a deeper and fuller range of meaning than the common use of the word "world." *Tianxia* is a trinitarian coordination of the natural world, the social-psychological world, and the political world. If we were to say that any problem must be placed in its "context" in order to be sufficiently understood and explained, then the limits of explaining any particular problem lies in the relative depth and breadth of this locating context. Thus, with respect to political problems, the broadest context has to be *tianxia*. This being the case, the concept of *tianxia* can serve as a viable context for interpreting and addressing all possible political problems.

3 Correlating with *Tian* (*peitian* 配天)

The order that *tianxia* depends upon is the order of *tian*. The wholeness and harmoniousness of *tianxia* as All under Heaven is secured by its continuity with the wholeness and harmoniousness of *tian* above. This faith in "correlating with *tian*" (配天) is the ideal of an (ancient Chinese) political theology. And this ideal political theology derives from a naturalistic metaphysics—that is, a metaphysics of process (*dao* 道).

Ancient Chinese culture views nature through the dual aspects of heaven and earth, and human beings are seen as existing between heaven and earth, and as serving to conjoin these two realms. The continuity and commonality among heaven—human beings—earth (天,人,地) as a trinity is the "way" (道). *Dao* means "the optimal among all possible ways of being," or in other words, *dao* is a way of being that achieves optimization in any modality. To divide being into three categories of heaven—human—earth is obviously not a scientific viewpoint, nor is it an epistemological one. Rather, this mode of categorization is the aestheticizing of a metaphysical perspective. Within human aesthetic horizons, nature is manifest as the two "prospects" of heaven and earth. The vast earth is the conveyance, supporting all actual life. It is the home of humanity and provides all the resources for human life. It is also the place where *tianxia* resides. Heaven above is the overarching canopy and encompasses all possibilities. It is the vital principle of all things and sets their boundaries. The great earth as conveyance implicitly suggests a mothering metaphor of unselfishly providing nurturing care. And heaven above, as an overarching canopy, metaphorically implies the guidance and supervision of fathering. Ancient Chinese culture did not generate any transcendent monotheistic religions and never posited the One God that is omniscient and all-powerful. Which is to say, although heaven above references the (optimal) way of existing (*dao*), this *tian* doesn't speak. How then is the way of *tian* communicated to human beings? And what kind of knowledge is conveyed?

Tian as heaven above doesn't speak, but expresses the way (天道) through the myriad transformations of nature. Just as Confucius said: "What does *tian* say? The four seasons turn and the myriad things are born. What does *tian* say?"[1] And the *Mengzi* offers a similar explanation: "*Tian* does not speak. It is only through actions and events that it gives expression."[2] The myriad changes of nature themselves indicate the rightness and wrongness of things. Since things themselves are unpredictable, thinking cannot just be focused on existing things. Since remaining focused on particular things cannot lead to comprehensive understanding, there must be an adventurous departure from existing among discrete things to the creative seeking out of the very "propensities" (*shi* 势) latent in the transformations themselves. *Propensity* means the very possibilities of one situation changing into another. And this means the condition of transcending "being as it is" and becoming "being as it is not." Propensity involves incompleteness, contingency, and openness. The most memorable literary image expressing this insight is Jorge Luis Borges's "forking paths of time." The way of *tian* is manifest as the propensities of the changes themselves among the myriad things rather than referencing an unchanging essence or the substance of things. For this reason, the metaphysics of *dao* is not concerned with defining the determinate essences of things, but instead is geared toward grasping the transformations of the myriad things conveyed in "comprehensive images" (*xiang* 象). Comprehensive images don't make any fixed categorical statements about things, but instead are always suggestive of their processual possibilities. They are the "comprehension" of an always transforming *dao*.

The metaphysics of *dao* is a "metaphysics of becoming." As such, this is a very different cogito and cogitatum from any "metaphysics of being." The metaphysics of *dao* is not astonishing or perplexing as in a metaphysics of being because existence is always an unavoidable and more or less settled fact. As such, existence does not constitute a real problem to the point of not even becoming a thematic question in the history of a *dao* metaphysics. In this classical Chinese metaphysics it is not that being or existence is being forgotten, but rather that it is never even presented as a disruption. Persons should not be disturbed by something that is necessary and absolute. It is only those things that are a matter of possible decision that should be considered as having anything to do with human destiny. Thus a metaphysics of *dao* only deals with "transformations" and doesn't get distracted by fixed "essences." We should only be absorbed with questions of "how is it becoming?" rather than being bewildered by questions such as "what finally is there?" There is what there is and this is a given in our existential condition. What is infinitely more important is the infinite possibilities latent in existence. This is precisely what the *Laozi* means in saying, "the way that can be articulated is not constant way-making; and the name that can be given fixed reference is not genuine naming (i.e., the way that can be followed just as before is not the primal way, and the concept that can be defined is not the primal concept).[3]

Nature is the ontological limit of all possible selections, and for this reason the way of *tian* is higher than the human way. Therefore human beings cannot establish natural laws. Nature won't adapt itself to human subjectivity. Human beings can only adjust themselves to accord with nature. All things are the measure of man, and not the other way around. Any human way that deviates from the way of *tian* amounts to a rejection of its own ontological conditions, and thus presents the possibility of being an unfortunate path with disastrous consequences. A metaphysics of *dao* attempts to arrive at the most efficacious way by understanding the ontology of nature. Just in terms of existence itself, the intention of existence is to continue to exist and to exist indefinitely. Existence is the unrelenting affirmation of being itself. And the self-affirmation of existence lies in the transformation of existence. To be unchanging is to be dead, since "being itself" and "essence" do not undergo change. Thus, being and essence are dead, and in fact don't exist. Only "becoming" then can "be." When the

Book of Changes says that "the greatest virtuosity of heaven and earth is called vitality"[4] and "continuity is efficacious, and completion is the native tendency of things,"[5] the text is referencing this meaning. How can we come to know that such creative vitality is the intention of existence itself? Why isn't the intention of existence to seek death? Perhaps we can understand it in this way: nonexistence is the negation of existence, and existence cannot seek its own negation. For this reason existence aims at persistence. Since the intention of existence is to persist, the meaning of existence lies in its "futurity." Efficacy is a matter of "daily renewal." The *Book of Changes* confirms that if the human way takes the heavenly way as its standard, then it can grasp its intention fully: "It is because it is similar to heaven and earth, that it does not run contrary."[6] The *Laozi* presents the same understanding: "Human beings emulate earth, earth emulates heaven, heaven emulates *dao*, and *dao* emulates spontaneity."[7]

Nature is sacred, but is not God. Since *tian* doesn't speak the information *tian* dispenses to humankind does not need to be foreknown but can be made known through the kaleidoscopic of changes within nature taken together as its meaningful gestures. The meaningful gestures of nature require human efforts to decipher, and those who can read and interpret the natural transformations of *dao* are the "sages" (*shengren* 圣人). Because concepts with fixed meanings are unable to express change, tradition has it that the sages created "comprehensive images" to metaphorically express the transformations of *dao*. According to the *Book of Changes*, there are sixty-four kinds of images, meaning that there are sixty-four unique kinds of transformational *propensities*. These images can be used to calculate the possible relationships between conduct and fortunes. The concrete quantification of fortunes cannot be ascertained and is only the speculation of mysticism. The *Zhou Book of Changes* (*Zhouyi* 周易) developed from a more ancient collection of divinatory manuals known collectively as the *Classic of Changes* (易经) and in the process of textual and philosophical evolution, these texts have progressively come to be understood as a metaphysical work. Thus the traces of the puzzling secrets of the divinatory manuals gave rise to innumerable interpretive hypotheses. Here we are not interested so much in the mystical "divinatory" aspects but instead will remain focused on the text's more subtle intimations regarding the ways of *tian*. The way of *tian* is the metaphysical basis of the way of *tianxia*, but what does the way of *tian* reveal? This is precisely the mystery that Confucius was attempting to explain.

In Confucius's compilation and interpretation of the *Book of Changes*, it is claimed that the text can be used to "penetrate the intentions of *tianxia*, to set the tasks of *tianxia*, and to resolve the doubts of *tianxia*."[8] The metaphysics of the *Book of Changes* posits an intriguing principle of political ontology: that is, ceaseless procreativity or "let all things be in their becoming" (*shengsheng* 生生). The *Book of Changes* says: "Ceaseless procreativity is called 'change' (*yi* 易)."[9] And "change" is a concept having a self-explanatory structure. The most direct meaning is "unceasingly new transformations." At the same time *yi* 易 implies a primordial explanation: "Such unceasingly new transformations are the persistently constant *dao*." Thus the meaning of this well-known phrase is "such unceasingly new transformations are what give all living things an abundance of vitality—and this is the forever constant *dao*." The "tasks of *tianxia*" implied by this ontological principle are that all life gets access to a world of compatibility and coexistence. In this world of compatibility and "coexistentiality," every existent can exist with abundant vitality. Here this ontological principle actually begins to take a turn towards the political. And since *tianxia* corresponds to the existence of heaven above, the way of heaven and the human way have a certain symmetry. Because heaven above is all-encompassing of the world, *tianxia* must become the measure of the world. And since the intention of the way of *tian* is for all existents to realize compatibility and coexistence, the intention of *tianxia* must also be that all persons realize a compatibility and coexistence. Thus the *tianxia* order must take coexistence as its principle of constitution. To formulate *tianxia* is to take a world of conflict and division and construct a *tianxia* of compatibility, and this is to effectively realize the internalization of the world. As long as the world doesn't become a *tianxia*, each person and each nation-state will only find it difficult to share in perpetual peace. This is what is meant by the expression, "If *tianxia* descends into chaos, no state can be at peace; if one country is in the throes of disorder, then no household can be at peace; if one household is in turmoil, then there is no one at peace."[10] All of this reveals that world politics are a truly holistic form of the political.

4 Institutional Layout

The core meaning of the *tianxia* system is to transform the way of heaven into the great undertaking of the human way. The institution of territorial divisions designed by the Duke of Zhou was a "one body with divided governance" system of *tianxia*. This marked a truly innovative experiment in political history. Even though the *tianxia* ideal has never been fully realized, this moment in history represents the sole actual experiment with the *tianxia* system. The successes and failures of this ancient institutional design, in terms of the future possibilities of a new *tianxia* system, is an inimitable resource for our thinking. The Zhou dynasty *tianxia* system of territorial division constructed a web-world conceived of as an "earth web of connectivity"—that is, a system structured as a web with various nested hierarchies. From a contemporary perspective, this *tianxia* network system still has relevance for today, and even a sense of futurity—although its hierarchical structure doesn't fit with the values of the current world. It is easy to view the Zhou *tianxia* system as a structure of domination. This being said, a society devoid of all hierarchy has yet to be realized because such a world is an ideal lacking the conditions to bring itself about. Not only were all ancient societies hierarchical, but today's world is in reality still thoroughly hierarchical in nature. This indicates that even though hierarchical institutions run contrary to the values of equality, hierarchy is still a necessary feature of social interaction. Axiology has its axiological standards and reality has its realistic operating principles.

Concretely speaking, the Zhou dynasty *tianxia* system as an "earth web" had an ancestral state at its center serving to oversee and protect the world. This was the special realm over which the "Son of Heaven" exercised direct jurisdiction. The second level of political units were the vassal states including the enfeoffed and tributary states. The enfeoffed states were newly established by the Zhou dynasty, while the tributary states were existing political entities that had entered into the *tianxia* system. The third level of political units were that of the various estates of the aristocracy and high officials under the auspices of the various vassal princes. These three levels together were called the "*tianxia*—state—family" (天下—国—家) model of governance and constituted a single network of divided governance. If we use standards drawn from political science, before the Zhou dynasty introduced the *tianxia* system there were no institutionalized legal frameworks of governance, there was only the *real politik* of hegemonic control.

Although there were nominally "states," what really existed was ruling clans controlling a multitude of tribes. If we rely upon historical and anthropological standards, then the effective center of large-scale governance and the ground of stable politics was the "country" (*guojia* 国家). And before the Zhou dynasty, for thousands of years there were a multitude of such "states." These two "standards" are fundamentally different and there is no real need for a detailed analysis here. In inaugurating the legally determined *tianxia* institutions, the Zhou dynasty simultaneously established the legal basis for state institutions. Using the methods of enfeoffment and tributary inclusion to set up one continuous system of political networking, the Zhou applied laws in setting up hierarchies and in demarcating distinct governing institutions. The enfeoffed states were either Zhou clan aristocrats or successful ministers with different family backgrounds. It is said that out of seventy-one enfeoffed states, fifty-three were from the Zhou clan.[1] The tributary states greatly outnumbered the enfeoffed states with, according to one account, 652 of them, and as many as 800 according to another record.[2] The vassal states existing in such numbers were in part due to a respect for the traditional configuration of political power and also in part due to a calculation of the security for the entire system. Several hundred years later, Jia Yi (贾谊 200–169 BCE) laid bare the political reasons for the *tianxia* system: "In looking for the governance and security of *tianxia*, nothing is better than setting up a multitude of vassal states and thereby reducing their power. Having little power, it is easier to get them to do what is most appropriate. And with their states being small, they will forget any rebellious ambitions."[3]

The Zhou dynasty *tianxia* system has some networking characteristics similar to the Internet:

1. Every localized realm is a structural mimesis of the whole. And every particular realm is a microcosmic model of the complete system, just like the relationship between a set and its subsets. Thus the political order is universally "transitive" while every state has independent self-governance. The ancestral ruling state is responsible for securing the institution of *tianxia*, its universal order, and the shared interests of the system, while the other largely self-ruling states settle their own internal problems. If these states were to encounter a predicament they are unable to deal with on their own, then the ancestral ruling state would intervene directly to provide support or would organize other states to be providing assistance.

2. The entire network system has an unlimited openness. In theory, this means that the *tianxia* system is equivalent to the world in its magnitude. Even though there is a significant gap between ideality and actuality, the unlimited openness means an unlimited compatibility.

3. The *tianxia* system is a voluntary, cooperative scheme, where its legitimacy comes from the acceptance and support of the multitudes of people, and the various states can freely choose to enter or exit from the arrangement.

4. Each state is potentially qualified to develop and replace the existing center as a new center, thus acknowledging the possibility of revolution (*geming* 革命). But revolution requires the confirmation of the "decree of heaven" (*tianming* 天命) (i.e., political legitimacy). If the ancestral ruling state acts unjustly, deviates from the proper way, and loses the support of the people, then it is appropriate to revolt and to replace them.

The rights and responsibilities of the ancestral ruling state and the enfeoffed vassal states according to the institutional arrangement were roughly as follows:

1. The Son of Heaven exercises complete authority over the territories within *tianxia*, and direct jurisdiction over a central realm that itself was the ancestral ruling state. Mountain ranges and large bodies of water, as indivisible and shared resources, also fall under the jurisdiction of the Son of Heaven's immediate care, while the rest of the land can be divided among the vassal states.

2. The vassal states retain rights over the territory and people of their realms, but don't have unconditional authority. Thus land and people cannot be transferred from one to another.

3. The ancestral ruling state is responsible for maintaining the shared order of the entire system. The vassal states have a high degree of self-governance over domestic matters, and at the same time have a duty to assist the ancestral ruling state in any costs associated with maintaining the shared order of the system. Therefore they had to give "tribute" and service to the ancestral ruling state, although this was not equivalent to paying taxes (in fact, it was actually much lower than taxation). Paying tribute was primarily a matter of providing the necessary resources (raw materials or special products) that the ruling ancestral state needed to carry out its responsibilities. And service is primarily a matter of providing labor (labor for governing the watersheds, creating roads, and other public projects) and military service (aimed at defense and pacifying rebellions). The vassal states also needed to attend court at intervals to give an account of themselves, and the Son of Heaven would regularly go on inspections to respond to the veracity of their accounts with rewards and punishments.

4. The ancestral ruling state would have the comparatively greater military power, while the strength of vassal states would be based on a ratio according to rank, population, and land area. The military strength of the ancestral ruling state would not overwhelm the system. In fact, the ancestral ruling state had six military units, with some sixty thousand to seventy-five thousand troops, while the large vassal states had three units, the midrange states two units, and the small states just one military unit.[4] This proportional configuration served to bring about an effective balance of power, where if the ancestral ruling state lost its legitimacy, then several vassal states could form a revolutionary coalition to overturn the corrupt central power.

Within the geographical layout of the *tianxia* system, the Zhou dynasty design was a combination of both political and theological modalities, using the clan structure as a template to develop the *tianxia* system, and developing a political system from the varying degrees of intimacy present in family-clan experience. The Son of Heaven dwells in a focal place of *tianxia* establishing a "kingly realm" as the ancestral ruling state. Since the Son of Heaven holds direct jurisdiction over "a realm of a thousand *li*," the place where the Son of Heaven resides is the "Central State" (*zhongguo* 中国), meaning the focal capital of *tianxia*. Space within this kingly realm was referred to as "inner service" and is differentiated from the numerous vassal states which were collectively referred to as "outer tribute." The numerous vassal states surrounded the kingly realm with a 500 *li* circumference on all sides. Of course, this was only an idealistic image, as the actual geographical conditions and traditional political power dynamics could not possibly have been so tidy, and at best only approximated this ideal. Together the inner and outer "service" was collectively called the "five tributes"[5] and sometimes the "nine tributes."[6] The relative intimacy of political relationships was at the same time hierarchical, with the rank of the vassal states being typically higher than those of the tributary or "service" states. These vassal states also had a much more intimate, cooperative relationship with the ruling ancestral state in terms of military, economic, and cultural matters.[7] The most distant states in the orbit had a more symbolic and titular tributary relationship.

The design that the Duke of Zhou laid out for the *tianxia* system was a combination of idealism and rationalism. The *tianxia* system attempted to incorporate all of the states within a system of coexistence, using the optimal possibilities of mutual benefit to establish different degrees of collaboration. At the same time, peaceful relations were taken as the bottom line. This was the so-called principle of "harmony of the myriad states," the basic spirit of which was to create a world with a maximization of cooperation and a minimization of conflict. The *tianxia* system designed by the Zhou dynasty lasted for about eight hundred years, the longest dynastic period in Chinese history. But the last five hundred years of Zhou history was a continual process of decline leading to an ultimate collapse. This decline had to do with an unexpected design flaw in the Zhou institutions that we will discuss later.

5 No Outside (*wuwai* 无外)

The basic character of *tianxia* is an all-inclusiveness with "no outside" (*wuwai* 无外). The literal meaning of this is that the entire world becomes interiorized, with no outside. This means to have a world of no exteriority and only interiority. Here, "no outside" means the political problem of effecting the world's interiorization. Only when all of the world's places have become interior to *tianxia*, and all persons are viewed with compatibility and coexistentiality, then and only then can the world be considered a *tianxia*.

The *Book of Rites* says, "The Son of Heaven does not speak of going outside."[1] This means that any place under heaven is part of the home of the Son of Heaven. No matter where the Son of Heaven goes, there is nowhere that is outside *tianxia*. The *Spring and Autumn Annals of Gongyang* also interpreted the demotion, expulsion, or asylum seeking of the great ministers of the Zhou dynasty as moving to the surrounding vassal states, but it would not be appropriate to describe this as "fleeing outside" because no matter where they might go, they couldn't have possibly left the interiority of *tianxia*.[2] The Son of Heaven retained all of the powers and lands of *tianxia*, and the entirety of *tianxia* was his home. Thus, it was said, "There is no outside for the King."[3] This is what the ancient poem from the *Book of Songs* was indicating: "Under the vast heavens, all is the King's land. And leading from the land to the sea, all serve as ministers to the King."[4]

According to Confucius, however, the all-inclusiveness of the King's realm, as possessing no exteriority, was still not the highest ideal of *tianxia*. This was because conceptually it had yet to reach the level of "All under Heaven as held in common."[5] This ideal meant that *tianxia* had to become the common property of all persons. Lü Buwei's explanation was most clear: "*Tianxia* is not one person's *tianxia*, it is *tianxia*'s *tianxia*."[6] The all-encompassing Kingly realm of *tianxia* was actually only the nonexteriority of the world, and was still not the realization of the world's ultimate power to realize nonexteriority. The shared properties and shared interests of *tianxia* can be seen in the conceptual gap between the practices of the historical Zhou dynasty and the ideality of the *tianxia* system. However, we cannot be transcending historical horizons to criticize the King's all-encompassing *tianxia* since the institutional structures of the Zhou dynasty had already gone as far as it possibly could in achieving the shared interests and shared governance of *tianxia* within the limiting conditions of "monarchy."

In explaining the ideal of *tianxia* nonexteriority, Lü Buwei provided an exaggerated example (probably a fabricated narrative):

> The country of Jing (荆国) had a person who lost a bow but didn't dare go to retrieve it. He said, "A Jing person lost it, and a Jing person got it, so what is there to worry about?" Confucius criticized this saying by suggesting that it would be even better by dropping the qualifier "Jing." And Laozi is said to have taken it one step further by suggesting that the qualifier "person" (人) also be dropped.[7]

The person from Jing's understanding reached a sense of compassionate equality amongst their fellow countrymen, while Confucius's understanding reached an equality among all of the world's peoples, but Laozi's understanding reached an equality among all sentient beings. Laozi's understanding actually transcends the political sphere and has more metaphysical implications. Hence it is Confucius's understanding that most closely approximates the *tianxia* ideal of nonexteriority as a governing principle. However, even if we follow Confucius's understanding, one worries that it might still be overly idealistic. This is because in actuality no institution is able to totally overcome selfishness. The practical aims of *tianxia* nonexteriority are actually quite realistic. In establishing a *tianxia* system of shared interests and shared benefits, all of the states and persons involved are willing to accept the rules of the system. In other words, the benefits that any state or person accepting the *tianxia* system can receive are greater than what they would receive by rejecting or destroying said system. In this sense, a *tianxia* system is justifiably said to have an "all-encompassing" or "no outside" (无外) political character.

Then does *tianxia* necessarily have a center and periphery ideology? For example, is there necessarily present what later gets referred to as the "Chinese and barbarian distinction?" This question must be addressed within the context of historical discourse. In early China the distinction between "civilized" (*hua* 华) and "barbarian" (*yi* 夷) was merely a way of referring to differences of natural geography, lifestyles, and cultural customs.[8] As such, this was a "descriptive" conceptual cluster without involving any racist or ethnocentric prejudices. The ancient geographical and anthropological text the *Classic of Mountains and Seas* (山海经) depicted various "strange" lifestyles of peripheral peoples. Although such depictions have a certain shock value, they were meant to be merely descriptive. If we say that the advanced Central Plain had a kind of condescending (but not discriminatory) view toward the "backward" periphery, then it must be recognized that such thinking has been a widely held view throughout human history. The ancient Central Plain was first of all a developed region. This is a historical fact. The Central Plain was the earliest to create a mature writing system and to play a leading role in rapid cultural development.[9]

Thus the Central Plain functioned as the vital core of *tianxia*, and the surrounding cultural groupings naturally tended to flow toward this heart, whether it was through imitation, study, or the plundering of resources (sometimes even usurping the Central Plain's political power). In any event the Central Plain operated as a site of shared contest among the various peoples. Whoever was victorious could occupy and continue to develop the Central Plain civilization. Mencius pointed this out quite early on—for instance, that certain sage-kings were from the "barbarian" tribes; like Shun who was from an Eastern Yi tribe.[10] What is important to note here is that the inclusive nature of *tianxia* as a concept negated a priori any oppositional exteriority, and moreover served as a kind of a priori affirmation of plurality and mutual compatibility. The Man, Yi, Rong, and Di tribes were part of the Five Auxiliaries radiating out from the central throne, and the states within the Four Seas were all considered integral parts of *tianxia*.

Although the advanced culture of the Central Plain took itself to be the standard bearer of an enlightened civilization, this did not negate the unique contributions offered by other cultures. The story of Youyu serving the state of Qin illustrates this point:

> The King of the Rong in the northwest sent Youyu on a diplomatic mission to the state of Qin. Duke Mou of Qin said, "The Central States use poetry, history, philosophy, ritual, music, and legal institutions for governing, but today there is still social chaos. Now the Rong and Yi peoples don't have such things, so how can they be governed? Isn't this a difficult problem for them?" Youyu responded, "This kind of thinking is precisely why the Central Plain is chaotic. In earliest antiquity, the sage king Huangdi [Yellow Emperor] institutionalized ritual propriety and music, promoted these institutions in his own person, and only considered governing as a minor matter. In subsequent ages, there was increasing arrogance and decadence. But the Rong and Yi people were not like this. Those above cultivated deep and illustrious virtuosity in dealing with their subordinates. And those who benefited from them felt loyalty and trustworthiness in their hearts towards the benefactors whom they served. Governing a state is like bringing proper order to one's own person. Without knowing how it came about, the true sages brought proper order to the world." Duke Mou was deeply moved and responded to the High Minister, "I have heard that neighboring states too are governed by sages."[11]

Another better-known example is the decision of King Wuling of Zhao to reform horse-riding and archery practices by allowing soldiers to wear Xiongnu clothing. Many members of the aristocracy opposed King Wuling's decision to learn from the Xiongnu culture, and argued as follows:

> The education of the sages of the Central States has all the poetry, history, ritual and music that has served as a "source of emulation for the distant realms," and a model for the barbarian tribes. But if things were reversed and "the clothes of distant lands came to change the teachings and ways of

the ancients," then I fear this could make the people perverse. King Wuling of Zhao offered the following line of rebuttal: "The ordinary people are mired in habitual customs, and the scholars are deeply invested in hearsay." Therefore, these benighted masses and the biased scholars are unable to "see broadly and discuss innovations." How then could they possibly grasp the truth that "the three dynasties (Xia, Shang, Zhou), despite having different clothes and customs, were all able to exercise sovereignty? And the five hegemons had different educational programs but all could govern? Since the past and the present have different customs, why emulate the past? The ancient sage kings didn't all dress alike, so why would we expect their ritual practices to be the same? What provides benefit to the body is called clothing, and what is pragmatic in our affairs is called education. We should establish cultural and legal norms according to the times, and establish ritual propriety according to the circumstances, in each case following what is optimally appropriate. Clothes and tools all have their own particular uses and value. Thus, in governing a particular age there is no one necessary way, and in governing states there is no need to merely copy the ancients.[12]

Moreover, the various pre-Qin rulers, noblemen, and aristocracy of the Central Plain often took the names of the Man, Yi, and Rong tribes. From this practice we can see that the use of Yi-Man naming was not considered derogatory. Wang Ke has an interesting theory as to why this practice was so pervasive. He argues the nomadic pastoralists were strong and vigorous, and so using Man-Yi names was very likely due to people desiring strong and vigorous offspring.[13]

In theory, the inclusive "no outside" of *tianxia* signified a world of shared properties and common interests. So any particular person had the right to participate in constructing a *tianxia* order, and any particular ethnic group had the possibility of becoming the leader of the *tianxia* order. Precisely because there were no predetermined cultural boundaries, the *tianxia* concept carried with it a universal attractiveness and uniquely persuasive power. Throughout history many different ethnic groups to varying degrees entered the Central Plain as the leading power—for instance, the courts of the Liao, Jin, Yuan, and Qing dynasties all used the concept of *tianxia* to explain their legitimacy in claiming the heavenly mandate.

6 Circle of Family and *Tianxia*

At the heart of the Zhou dynasty *tianxia* system was the creation of a bilateral principle of transforming the world into a family, and the family into a world. This bilateral principle established an isomorphism between family and *tianxia*. But the two different directions of transformation have different implications. Taking *tianxia* as the starting point means a political order inclusive of "*tianxia*—state—family," while taking family as the starting point means an ethical order of "family—state—*tianxia*." The two orders converge in creating a "*tianxia*—state—family—state—*tianxia*" circle. And they also form a hermeneutical circle of interpretation between the ethical and the political. This kind of hermeneutical circle is not a tautological and pointless explanation, but rather provides an ethical and political basis for a mutually entailing perspective of interpretive confirmation. From one perspective there is the ethical extension of the family into *tianxia*; and from the other perspective we have the political protection of every family through *tianxia*.

The model of extending the ethical from "family—state—*tianxia*" takes family as the root model and transforms family relationality into the *tianxia* institutional order. The Son of Heaven has a duty to maintain the shared order and interests of *tianxia*, similar to the responsibilities assumed by the heads of any household: "The Son of Heaven is a parent of the people and as such is the sovereign of *tianxia*."[1] To "receive land and receive the people" as a system of allocating territory was akin to the way that brothers might divide household property. Although this was a matter of divided governance of *tianxia*, it always preserved the relational ideal of "all within the four seas as one family."[2] The "*tianxia*—state—family" model implies that *tianxia* is viewed as shared property and that *tianxia* functions as the guarantor of the security and benefits for every state and household. If we say that the ethics of transforming family dynamics into *tianxia* is grounded in a compassionate stance that is all-inclusive with "no outside," then the political process of transforming *tianxia* into family represents a fully inclusive conception of justice. The ethics of all-encompassing and inclusive compassion is the path of humanity. This is what is meant by the expressions "respecting my elders, and extending this to the elders of others; caring for my young, and extending this to the youth of others; in doing so, governing *tianxia* is as easy as rolling a ball in the palm of your hand" and "extending concern until it suffices to protect all in the Four Seas."[3]

The political conception of all-encompassing justice is an "art of governing" and is what is meant by "without prejudice, without cliques, the kingly way is vast and broad; without cliques or prejudice, the kingly way is regular and even: without opposition and without partisanship, the kingly way is direct and just."[4] Or we might consider Confucius's saying that heaven and earth act without selfishness: "The heavens impartially cover everything, the earth impartially sustains everything, and the sun and moon impartially shine on all."[5] From this we can see clearly that the inclusive and "no outside" ethical and political orders are interpretively cyclical. On the one hand, the concept of family is being used to define the character of the world as one family within the Four Seas, thus confirming the internality of *tianxia*. And on the other hand, there is the concept of nonpartisan justice being used to define the shared interests and shared properties characteristic of *tianxia*—thus confirming the universality of *tianxia*. With the concept of family and the concept of *tianxia* thereby being coincident with each other, internality and universality too are continuous with each other.

According to the inclusive, "no outside" principle, only with the internalization of the entire world can the great governance of *tianxia* be achieved. Within an internalized world, political order is universally "transitive." Only when a political order is effectively realized among all the political levels without contradiction can it be recognized as universally effective and trustworthy. From the perspective of the Zhou dynasty's institutional design, political and ethical orders are also transitive from the bidirectionality of *tianxia*—state—family, and family—state—*tianxia*, thus constituting a comprehensive circle. Ethical and political principles are within this circle equally necessary and are therefore of equal importance. But they are still two distinct principles. There will always be situations in which one pole ends up playing either the leading or the assisting role. This problem is similar to the question of how natural order is conceptualized in the *Book of Changes* wherein *yin* 阴 and *yang* 阳 energies are both equally important factors, yet remain reciprocally complementary of one another. Although *yang* typically plays a leading role and *yin* a supportive one, in the *tianxia*—state—family structure, whether the unselfish principle of *tianxia* takes the lead or the care-extending family principle has precedence is always a potentially open question. From the late Zhou dynasty through the Spring and Autumn and Warring States periods this problem has elicited many different explanations.

According to Guan Zhong and Laozi's interpretations, the basic meaning of the *tianxia*—state—family order is its universality. *Tianxia* is the assemblage of all persons, and as such every state and family is a member of *tianxia*. This means that every basic political unit has its own uniquely personal interests and order, and that the proportionally greater political units have greater degrees of shared interests and order. Moreover, the greatest political unit with its shared interests and conception of order is *tianxia*. Thus the essential meaning of *tianxia* is conceived of akin to the unselfish protection that the heavens provides for all of the people. Guan Zhong puts it like this:

> Treating family as a village, the village cannot be managed; treating the village like a state, the state cannot be managed; treating a state like *tianxia*, *tianxia* cannot be managed. We must treat the family as family, the village as village, the state as state, and *tianxia* as *tianxia*. Without considering each other as kin, those far off will not comply; and if they don't think they are from the same village, those far off will not act on its behalf; if they don't

think they are countrymen, those far off will not conform. With the earth and the heavens, what selfishness and what family-based partiality is there? Like the moon and the sun, only exemplary persons can accord with their standard.[6]

This is to say that *tianxia* must be "like heaven and earth" in unselfishly providing standards that transcend the parochial and partisan perspectives of family, ethnicity, and nationality in order to provide *tianxia* with its universal governing order. Laozi offers an even more concise and well-known expression: "View the person as person, the family as family, the village as village, the state as state, and *tianxia* as *tianxia*."[7] Guan Zhong is earlier than Laozi, but legend has it that Laozi was an archivist of official state documents during the Zhou dynasty, and as such had likely read Guan Zhong's writings. Guan Zhong and Laozi's understanding are similar to the definition of the Kingly Way found in the *Exalted Documents* as being "without prejudice and without cliques."[8]

Guan Zhong and the Legalist thinkers all believed that the unselfish justice of the Kingly Way is given expression through "law" (*fa* 法). But the pre-Qin conception of *fa* is much broader than the modern conception of legal codes. Actually, *fa* refers to the entirety of the game rules of social life, especially the institutions concerned with "rewards and punishments." Included in these rules are the legal codes determining punishment, the distribution of social goods, and the systems of reward that together without preferential prejudice, return reward for good conduct and mete out punishment for wrongdoing. Only when a system of game rules can guarantee that good conduct receives good returns and bad conduct results in bad outcomes can it be up to the task of governing *tianxia*:

> Without regard for distinctions between familial intimates and strangers, familiarity or remoteness, wealth or poverty, beauty or ugliness, one uses appropriate measures to decide matters. Proceeding according to rule by law is to proceed like the heavens and earth in acting unselfishly.[9]

This sort of "rule by law" (*fazhi* 法制) is not the same as "rule of law" (*fazhi* 法治). The limitation of rule by law lies in the difficulty of interpreting the legitimacy of particular rules. This means there is a difficulty in ascertaining the "constitutionality" of particular rules because this is something that rule by law is incapable determining on its own. Another implicit problem here is that the implementation of an unselfish rule by law does not necessarily guarantee a good life to the extent that it in fact might even run contrary to basic tendencies of human nature.

Confucius offers another understanding of the foundational order of *tianxia*—state—family. Confucius recognized that a rational order ultimately needs to find its basis in human feelings. Any political order that transcends human feelings cannot be in accord with the shared aspirations of the people, and would necessarily result in structural conditions of hypocrisy [literally, "a discontinuity between discourse and conduct" 言行不一]. For this reason Confucius didn't endorse rule by law. Because human feelings naturally tend toward selfish desires, unless human feelings have within them another strong emotional drive tending toward unselfishness, the emotions will inevitably be an ongoing source of conflict. Human feelings must contain an alternative unselfish gene in order to produce an unselfish political order. Confucius sought for this unselfish gene in human feelings within the concept of "family intimacy" or "caring for kin." People tend to love their family members unconditionally—that is, unselfishly. Thus Confucius believed that "family intimacy" was a reliable foundation for morality. The basic social form of family intimacy is the household. So the household is the original source of love whereby human selfishness can be transcended. It is the basic conveyance of humanity's genetic capacity for love. Thus there is good reason to take family as the archetype of *tianxia*. According to Confucius, the political order of *tianxia*—state—family must ultimately be grounded in the moral order of family—state—*tianxia*. It is the ethical order of family—state—*tianxia* that secures the legitimacy of the political order of *tianxia*—state—family. Not only does *tianxia* include all states and families within a single system, but it also transforms the entire world (*tianxia*) into an unbounded family. This governing metaphor of family can also be found in the *Exalted Documents*: "It commences in family and state, and consummates in the Four Seas"[10] and "in acting as the parents of the people, the Son of Heaven becomes the ruler of *tianxia*."[11]

Confucianism understands family experience as containing within it genes for developing all human values, and thus it is akin to a sacred space for living. Family is an "irreducible" a priori source of shared meanings of individual values and social agreements. From a Confucian standpoint,

persons are constituted by their relationships. If we take somebody "a,"
it is not sufficient to just describe "a," but rather we must also show that
"the being of 'a' can exist if and only if $(a \wedge b) \wedge (a \wedge c) \wedge (a \wedge d)$ are stipulated ad infinitum." Taking this model of the household to understand life
means that we must accord with the logic of the household. This means
using a "logic of harmonious conjunction" ($\wedge$) in seeking harmoniousness,
responsibility, and contentment in all relations. By way of contrast, if we
take the discrete individual as the defining feature of persons, then we
ought to use an individualistic logic—that is, a "logic of exclusive disjunction" ($\vee$) to seek for exclusive power, self-interest, and conflict. In actual
life, household relationships can certainly give rise to conflict, but this
doesn't serve to negate the Confucian ideal as a counterexample. This is
because Confucian thinking operates at the level of possibility, and the
household can serve as that kind of ecosystem wherein individual interests
and selfish calculations are reduced to the smallest degree. The household
is the most likely place in which we form relationships of unconditional
and reciprocal caring, and serves as a matrix for forming working conceptions of mutual responsibility. In this sense, as an ideal concept, family
experience is sufficient to explain human values, and thus we have the
phrase family is "the utmost way of becoming fully human."[12] Thus family
is taken to be the optimal principle for addressing all social, political, and
world (*tianxia*) problems.

The mode of ethical extension of family—state—*tianxia* is definitely
not without its own set of difficulties. Early in the Warring States period,
Shang Yang (商鞅) raised a sharp criticism: "The way [of earliest human-
ity] advocated affection for family and loving one's own. With family-based
affection there came differential distinctions, but with loving one's own
came real risk."[13] This is to say that although the household transcends the
absolute selfishness of individuals, it still can create a "relative" selfishness
or nepotism with family as a basic unit. Every family's self-interest can
lead to conflicts similar to the conflicts engendered by individual selfishness. Thus the family-based ethics of Confucianism might be left powerless to deal with such conflicts. In the modern era, Fei Xiaotong has raised
a very important concern. In taking family as the center of radial extension like "rippling concentric circles," where each ripple is directionally
pointed outward, by the time this affective basis of moral concern gets

extended to strangers, there is not sufficient moral motivation left over to sustain the desired ethical outcome. In the process of extending the family principle, the ethical transitivity is reduced to a very weak effect. Because of this, Fei Xiaotong thought that the classical Confucian description of the *Expansive Learning* actually harbored a selfish logic: "In wanting to illuminate bright virtue in *tianxia* the ancients first governed their states; and in desiring to govern their states, they first ordered their families; and in desiring to order their families, they first cultivated their persons... with their persons cultivated they could order their families, with families ordered they could govern their states, and with their state governed they could bring peace to *tianxia*."[14] With respect to this classic passage, Fei Xiaotong writes: "(I often think that the Chinese would) sacrifice their families for their own self-interests, their party for their families' interests, their country for their party's interests, and the whole world (*tianxia*) for their country's interests."[15] Since the family model has no way of guaranteeing universal ethical concern, it is difficult to use this family model to realize a viable model for *tianxia* order.

It is certainly not the case that Confucius never considered this difficulty, but he believed that the extension of ethical caring from the family must make sufficient use of the power of moral exemplars. The problem remains though that although everyone may agree in admiring certain moral exemplars, not everyone is willing to emulate them. Seeing worthies doesn't necessarily bring about an aspiration to be like them. In many cases, instead of emulation, what is more likely to emerge is an ethical version of the "free-rider" problem. Actually quite devastatingly for the Confucian position is what Shang Yang points out:

> Persons of consummate conduct (仁者) can act caringly to others, but cannot get others to act caringly themselves. An optimally appropriate person (义者) can direct love towards others, but cannot get others to love themselves. This is sufficient to know that consummate conduct (仁) and optimal appropriateness (*yi* 义) are an inadequate basis for governing *tianxia*.[16]

This means that the consummate person can only act toward making themselves consummate persons and cannot necessarily change or influence others to become consummate persons. Here there is a problem of a discontinuity between knowing and doing. According to Confucian presuppositions, the way of becoming fully human is self-evident; every person is capable of knowing the difference between good and bad without needing external forms of proof. However, if people indeed know self-evidently what is good and bad, then they should probably also self-evidently know their reasons for violating these norms. This entails that the "self-evident" nature of morality cannot guarantee that persons will always select what is moral. This predicament faced by Confucius is precisely the opposite of the problem faced by Socrates. For Socrates believed that "no one errs knowingly"—a reason for this being that if people knew what is truly good, they certainly wouldn't foolishly choose what is bad. But actuality gives the lie to this Socratic dictum. In a *Book of Rites* chapter "Record of the Dikes" (礼记·坊记) there is depicted a portrait of a disappointed Confucius. No matter whether facing opportunity for great or small benefits, people almost always forget about what is optimally appropriate when seeing a chance for individual profit (of course not *every* person is like this).[17]

Even though the Confucian ideal regarding the power of moral exemplars cannot be totally depended upon in practice, the issue of exemplary persons that Confucius puts forward has had profound theoretical significance. It is not that exemplars are ineffective in all cases; it is just that the moral exemplars as imagined by Confucius have been ineffective. In actuality, exemplars have a power that is universal in influencing society. Emulative uptake is an important factor in understanding collective choices (the related discussion earlier in this chapter where I argued for the validity of an "imitation test" in game theory was inspired by a certain reading of Confucius). The problem though is that in most cases the truly influential exemplars are not moral exemplars, but rather exemplars who have been profitable and thus became exemplars of success. Purely moral exemplars have a difficult time exercising influence unless they are at the same time exemplars of success. This is precisely the crucial problem that Confucius overlooked. Legalist thinkers like Shang Yang and Han Fei, however, understood that only exemplars of success could possess a universal power of attraction. Thus they believed that only a legal system of "rewards and punishments" could bring about a universally effective order. Only the unselfish way of heaven, as a standard for the unselfish way of being human, could establish a *tianxia* order.

In sum, *tianxia*—state—family, and family—state—*tianxia,* as two directional perspectives on order, gave the Zhou dynasty *tianxia* system a twofold character. On the one hand, it was a "systematized coexistentiality," while on the other hand, it was a "universalized system of patronage." Together these perspectives constituted a mutually confirming hermeneutic circle. At the same time, there was an internal tension in the circle. And it was precisely this internal tension that allowed the *tianxia* system to maintain a kind of self-correcting capability as an actual institutional order. Speaking of the historical institutions of the Zhou dynasty, the two kinds of orders of *tianxia*—state—family, and family—state—*tianxia,* are theoretically equally important. And speaking from the standpoint of a logic of practice, this complex historical legacy is a most capacious resource for stimulating creative interpretations.

7 *Tianming* 天命 (Heavenly Invoked Order)

With respect to political order, political legitimacy is a matter of life and death, of existing or perishing. If there is a lack of proof for legitimacy, then any governing order will fail to receive universal acceptance and support. Such failure in turn leads to two great dangers: (1) Societal noncooperation leads to a collapse of political order. Confucius had a clear view on this matter: "If names are not correctly deployed, then language will not be used effectively; and if language is not used effectively, affairs cannot be completed successfully."[1] (2) Lacking societal cooperation and political order, it is difficult to achieve societal mobilization, and as such there is no power to resist the aggression of other political entities, so it is thus easy to be overthrown.

Political legitimacy is political power as a "heavenly invoked order" (*tianming* 天命). If *tianming* is lost, "revolution" inevitably results. A political power lacking in legitimacy can only rely upon violence in order to endure. But violence is unable to establish an effective social order, and an ineffective social order will ultimately lead to political collapse. This means that unless politics and society are harmoniously correlated, politics will ultimately result in failure. As for revolution, the important point is not the usurpation of power but rather the constitution of a new political order. In a strict sense, revolution must be an institutional revolution. If a political power is overthrown but the previous institutional setup is largely left intact, then this is really just a continuation of the status quo by another name; that is, a continuation of the established patterns of power differentials in social and political relationships—as such this cannot represent a true revolution. According to this standard, there have only been three authentic institutional revolutions in Chinese history: (1) the Zhou dynasty establishment of the *tianxia* system; (2) the Qin-Han establishment a unified system of institutional governance with its country system of territorial divisions; and (3) the still developing model of modern political institutions emerging after the collapse of the Qing empire.

The reason that China so early reflected upon the question of political legitimacy was due to the unique historical conditions of the "small conquering the great" during the Shang-Zhou transition. Before the rise of the Zhou, *tianming* 天命 (heavenly invoked order) was just a kind of religious belief. The Shang concept of *tianming* emphasized that the rulers had to receive a definitive "mandate" or "decree" from heaven. *Tianming* was thought to come from the will of heaven above which was called "the Lord on High" (*shangdi* 上帝). The concept of *shangdi* at that time, however, was not some all-seeing, compassionate, universal will. Rather, it was a protector spirit for the Yin-Shang tribal groups. It would seem that the idea of "heaven above" and ancestral spirits were imagined together as one body. Yin-Shang tribes believed that *tianming* was transmitted by ancestors. This kind of belief in ancestral lineage as being continually efficacious in human affairs had nothing to do with other tribes.[2] It was believed that as long as an unbroken line of ancestor reverence was maintained, *shangdi* could not forsake the Yin-Shang tribes. Therefore a continuous array of ritual sacrifices was created as a method to keep secure this "heavenly invoked order."

As a much smaller state than the Yin-Shang, the Zhou conquered the Shang using a human miracle to dismantle the mythology that the Yin-Shang had a monopoly on heavenly decreed political power. This demonstrated that the Yin-Shang sacrificial cult had no inherent connection with the conception of *tianming*. The proof of this was that despite the continuous grand and extraordinary sacrifices offered to *shangdi* carried out with reverence and without respite by the Yin-Shang aristocracy, the heavens above withdrew their protection for the Shang regime. Indeed, it was recorded in the *Book of Songs* that "*shangdi* transferred its care to the Western regions [Zhou]" and in seeing the virtuosity of the Zhou leaders, assisted the Zhou in overthrowing the Shang.[3] We can see from this that "heaven above" is in fact shared by everyone within *tianxia* as observed in the phrase: "the heavens unselfishly cover everything, the earth unselfishly conveys everything, and the sun and moon unselfishly shine on everything."[4] This can be understood as meaning that heaven-above, in deciding whom to protect, wasn't concerned with ritual sacrifice per se, but rather with the question of whether political practices were virtuosic in accord with the heavenly invoked order (天命). And it was because Yin-Shang had lost this virtuosity and that the virtue of Zhou had become manifest that the heavens above transferred the heavenly decreed mandate to the Zhou. The *Book of Songs* alludes to the new heavenly invoked order of the Zhou:

> King Wen is above, and shines clear and bright in the heavens. Although the Zhou is an old state, the heavenly invoked order is new. . . . As for this heavenly invoked order, it continues to exert its influence for future generations. As for future generations, the allure is immeasurable. The order of *shangdi* is upheld in the service of Zhou. Being upheld in the service of Zhou, this heavenly order is abundantly sustainable . . . in ministers performing loyalty to the King, there is no need to think of the ancestors of others. Without thinking of other's ancestors, just rightly cultivate illustrious virtuosity. Always speaking in accord with [heavenly] invoked order, even self-seeking intentions will lead to abundant blessings.[5]

With its virtuosic practices the Zhou redefined the concept of *tianming*, and in so doing, introduced a profoundly significant political revolution.

To better understand this ancient conception of heavenly decreed order as *tianming*, we must return to a very early period of this civilization. Before the emergence of the "political," the natural state was one of rule by military force. In the absence of the political, it was always a matter of the strong devouring the weak. Although early human society already had the beginnings of civilization, it still functioned largely on the continuation of this natural principle of the strong devouring the weak (a principle that persists in much of today's world). But the problem is that military force cannot occupy and dominate all space and time. There will always be some space and more time that falls outside the control of military force. It is for this reason that rule by military force alone will always be a flawed enterprise. It is likely that through experience the ancients discovered the limitations of military force and realized that a spiritual life in community was decisive in determining the ultimate meaning of the political. Spiritual life entails the enjoyable experience of being part of a shared collective body, and an orchestrating of spiritual life means to be orchestrating the spirit of the multitudes. Identifying with such a unified, shared, and consistent spirit is the true basis for political power.

The most familiar and compelling form of spiritual life is religion. Life in ancient times was dominated by forces of nature, and the ancients sought to gain the care and protection of nature. Hoping to "hear" the guiding call of heaven above gave rise to the role of shamans. Because the shamans, through the arts of communicating with heaven above, could be "listening" to the knowledge that *tian* provided, they held power over a certain type of discourse. And a most important function of religion is its discursive power. This is why the earliest shamans and tribal leaders were often the same body. From certain inscriptions on the Yin-Shang oracle bones we can confirm that the Shang kings were actually the leaders of the shamans.[6] Whether it was because shamans held discursive power and thus became leaders themselves, or that the leaders wanted to hold discursive power and thus became shamans, due to a lack of historical evidence we will never know for sure. However, a relatively reasonable hypothesis is that it is very likely that political leaders emerged out of an earlier shamanic culture. In high antiquity those who could deal most effectively with real dangers and threats were those who became leaders. And the most dangerous event at that time came from the threat of war from other tribes. Thus the early tribal leaders had to first take care of leading a military force. From this standpoint, it is reasonable to assume that military leaders could seek out and organize the support of shamanic forces. Li Zehou thinks that it was only later that an actual professional class of shamans emerged, and that originally it was the political leaders who were themselves shamanic heads seeking to control unruly spiritual forces.[7]

Apart from the shamanic arts of divination, ritual sacrifice, and prayer, the people had no other means of seeking to connect with *tian* for spiritual support. Thus the religion of the shamanic arts became the highest expression of spiritual life in high antiquity. It would seem that as a religion it could explain everything, and in dominating the spiritual life, it could establish itself as a ruling force. In order to unify and dominate the spiritual life of the people and make of them one mind, one had to exert unified control over shamanistic religion. It was necessary then for leaders to monopolize authority over the discursive power of religion, and its explanatory and procedural powers as well. In order to do this, the leaders had to bureaucratize religion and prohibit the spread of folk cults. In high antiquity the advent of the policy of "severance of communicating between heaven and earth" (*jueditongtian* 绝地通天) was revolutionary.

According to legendary accounts, at this time all of the various tribes had been at war for an extended period and their people had lost all sense of security. So individual persons were seeking out the support of the spirits, and each family was engaged in sacrificial rituals, and anyone could become a shaman. But when the shamanic arts became open to all the people like this, it lost its awe-inspiring aura and became more opportunistic and a source of deception. As a consequence, authentic spirituality disappeared and the people had little hope in their lives. Thus the sage-king Zhuanxu intervened with a religious movement. He forbade the free practice of bizarre folk religions and put an end to the shamanic practices among the people who sought to communicate directly with the heavenly spirits. This was the so-called "severance of communicating between heaven and earth" movement. This was not an abolishing of religion per se, but rather a transfer of religious authority to political leaders through a bureaucratization of religious practices. This movement was also referred to with the expression "the people and spirits shouldn't mix."

The earliest record of this movement come from the "Lü Punishments" chapter of the *Exalted Documents* (尚书·吕刑), but the discourse is not that detailed. It only says the sage-king Huang Di "commissioned (*ming* 命) Zhong (重) and Li (黎) to sever the communication between earth and heaven."[8] Later King Zhao of Chu (楚昭王) naively sought out the advice from his shaman Guan Shefu (观射父):

> If there was no severing of communication between earth and heaven "could the people climb up to heaven?" Guan Shefu carefully responded in detail

by interpreting the reason for this cultural change: "It isn't as you think. The ancients didn't let the spirits and people intermingle . . . . each accorded with its appropriate orders, and there were no chaotic relationships" and it was only later that "people and spirits intermingled, and couldn't be distinguished appropriately. Thus, the people sought out divinations and families became shamanic experts. As such, things didn't accord with actuality. The people were lacking ritual sacrifices and didn't know blessings or prosperity. The divining practices of the multitude were disorganized and the people and spirits occupied the same roles. People disregarded the organizational alliances and had no reverential awe. The spirits became inappropriately intimate with human affairs and no one had a clear idea about what to do. Auspicious life didn't emerge and nothing was in proper order. Calamity and disaster lurked in every corner and inauspicious energies were inexhaustible." Thus, the Sage Kings "led a movement to return to the old order, with no more inappropriate intermingling. This was called 'severing the communicating between earth and heaven.'"[9]

According to the analysis of K. C. Chang (Zhang Guangzhi 张光直), the popularization of shamanic practices as folk religion happened some time during the era of the Yangshao 仰韶 culture (Neolithic period, 5,000–3,000 BCE), and the "severing the communicating between earth and heaven" movement occurred roughly around the Longshan 龙山 cultural period (late Neolithic period, 3,000–1,900 BCE).[10] The "severing the communicating between earth and heaven" movement is clear evidence that the leaders of the era had already come to realize the importance of discursive power and political theology. To have a monopoly on prophetic speech was to monopolize possible futures. It is clear that if everyone had their own method of communicating with the spirits, then the authority of the political leaders would disintegrate. Yin-Shang culture had the highest kind of religiousness and it inherited a monopoly on theological power. By placing the "lord on high" (*shangdi* 上帝) into the same body of Yin-Shang ancestral spirits, they created a god whose sole duty was to protect the Yin-Shang people. In so doing, they monopolized the information coming from heaven above and became the representatives of this "heavenly invoked order." (This is more or less similar to how ancient Jewish people believed they were uniquely chosen by YHWH to be the sole receivers of his divine messages.)

The Zhou dynasty revolution was not only a political revolution but also a theological one. The theological revolution effected by the Zhou was in some ways similar to the Christian reformation of Judaism. I don't want to engage in these sorts of widely speculative comparisons, but the two historical religious transformations share at least one thing in common. Just as Christianity reinterpreted the saving power of God as universally open to all persons through God's grace, the Zhou dynasty took the original Yin-Shang monopoly on an exclusive conception of "heavenly invoked order" and reinterpreted it as a universal *tianming* 天命. The Zhou transformation reinterpreted the heavenly decreed order as belonging to a universally compassionate worldview. And the Zhou considered moral conduct as being the only criteria for interpreting the selection of *tianming*. The universality of *tianming* was a most important basis for the *tianxia* concept. Only when the heavens above had a heart of impartial universality could *tianxia* give rise to a similar universality with respect to realizing shared interests. Then and only then could *tianxia* become the people's *tianxia*, and not just a *tianxia* possessed by one or another special interest group. The vocabulary of the *tianxia* conceptual cluster probably already existed before the Zhou dynasty, but before this Zhou theological revolution *tianming* was not a universal concept. The Yin-Shang didn't use the expression *tianming* or "heavenly decreed order," but generally used instead the "thearch's command" (*diming* 帝命) or the "lord on high's command" (*shangtianzhi diming* 上天之帝命) (suggesting that the Yin-Shang idea of the lord on high was their exclusive deity).[11]

It would seem that during the Yin-Shang period the concept of *tianxia* had only geographical connotations. It only referred to the world and not to the three-tiered *tianxia* as the spatial world, the shared aspirations of the people, and the institutional order. Without a universal *tianming*, there couldn't possibly have been an all-embracing, shared, and inclusive "no outside" *tianxia*. The Zhou dynasty revolution in political theology then ushered in a series of profound changes with respect to some basic issues:

1. In using moral conduct to redefine the quality of character needed to receive the heavenly decreed order of *tianming* meant that *tianming* was subject to change. And since heaven above was not a protector deity exclusively aligned to this or that ethnic tribe, but was rather a guardian spirit for the shared interests of all the peoples under the heavens, this

meant that any criteria for receiving *tianming* couldn't be left to luck or chance. Rather, such criteria was a matter of comparing the quality of character of political leaders as expressed through moral conduct. This notion of "moral conduct" replaced the idea that heaven above would keep a protective eye upon the activities of *tianxia*. It was the power of moral conduct itself that secured and guaranteed the ongoing flourishing of the myriad people within *tianxia*, with each receiving what they needed to live up to their obligations. The basis of this theory of revolution was that to fail to live up to moral obligations was a failure in virtuosity, and such a failure was synonymous with a losing of political legitimacy.

2. Since moral conduct became the deciding factor in determining who would receive the heavenly decreed order of *tianming*, divination practices were no longer a source of authoritative information from heaven above. This signaled a revolution in envisaging the future. The future is not something that can be foretold through divination and prophecy, but is instead something that is constantly being created through human activity. It is activity that determines the outcome of things, rather than futures being revealed as a supposedly fixed and predetermined fate. The Zhou dynasty, in depending upon moral conduct for its success, directly led to the reinterpretation of the heavenly decreed order of *tianming*. *Tianming* became the bilaterally dynamic relationship between the intentionality of the heavens above with the activity of persons below. Since the heavens above could determine what kind of fortunes would be dispensed on the basis of human conduct, we should say that the future is never predetermined, but is always a result of the dynamic communicative interactions between humans and *tian*. Even so, the Zhou people didn't entirely abandon the traditions of divinatory practices, but instead understood these practices to be complementary interpretive tools for consultation and interpretive reference.

The "Expansive Plan" chapter of *Exalted Documents*[12] records an incident that can help us understand the role of divination in the early Zhou period. King Wu of Zhou sought advice from Jizi, a minister of the former the Shang regime. Jizi's counsel included reference to future activity. Whenever there is uncertainty regarding future events, the ruler should first reflect on himself before seeking counsel with the great ministers and then again with the people. And only as a secondary consideration should one consult oracle bones and divination stalks. If the ruler, the ministers, the people, the oracle bones, and the divining stalks were all in accord, then one could proceed without the slightest doubt. If two classes of people expressed dissenting opinions and two divination methods showed agreement, one could still proceed. If one divination expressed a dissenting opinion, one could proceed on the domestic front, but curtail external activity. If there was consensus on the oracle bones and divining stalks in expressing a dissenting viewpoint, then it would be best to give up on the planned course of action.[13] Since King Wu of Zhou accepted this interesting counsel of Jizi's, it is not hard to see that this way of determining future activity takes consultation with other persons as its primary modus operandi, since the dissent of oracle bones and divining stalks against a proposed course of action only made up one-quarter of the possibilities.

(3) In offering a novel reinterpretation of futurity, the Zhou conceptual revolution established a strongly historicist consciousness at its core. The importance of history replaced the importance of prophecy, and historical consciousness superseded revelation.[14] Since activity shapes the future, and at the same time creates history, historicity itself becomes the deciding factor in the flow of destiny. Moral conduct in the past will decide future fortune, and ethical lapses will decide future failures. Thus the founding sage-kings of the Zhou dynasty were insistent in rehearsing to their offspring the importance of moral conduct in securing the future. The Zhou dynasty laid the foundations for the historical consciousness of Chinese thinking (e.g., the concept that "the Six Classics are all history"). Chinese culture has become a historicist culture rather than a culture of revelation. The key reason in understanding the Chinese view of futurity is to see how a historical consciousness has quashed revelatory consciousness. In this way we might be able to explain the "Li Zehou hypothesis"—that is, the secret to understanding Chinese culture residing in the early turn from a shamanic arts consciousness to a historicist consciousness. Li Zehou thinks that such a complicated process of cultural transformation is "to this day difficult to actually understand."[15] Perhaps there is no way to recover the historical details of this transformative process, but I believe that the Zhou conception of moral conduct was the critical turning point leading to this transformation. Since moral conduct is what secures future fortunes, the historical record of such activity is the secret to unlocking future prospects.

(4) Heavenly invoked order as *tianming* (i.e., political legitimacy) is

derived from moral conduct. And moral conduct needs a credible and reliable source for confirmation. The Zhou people realized that the most direct and reliable source of confirmation for moral conduct was the shared aspirations of the people (*minxin* 民心). The expression "the feelings of the people can be seen most evidently"[16] was meant to show how the inchoate *tianming* is manifested in the feelings of the people. *Tianming* becomes a barometer of the shifting feelings of the people. There is much discussion on this issue in the Zhou dynasty documents: "The revolutions of Tang and Wu were in accord with *tian* and resonated with the people"[17]; "*tian* must yield to whatever the people desire"[18]; "*tian* sees as my people see, *tian* hears as my people hear."[19] The *Mencius* also has a passage: "Jie and Zhou (the last rulers of the Xia and Shang dynasties respectively) lost *tianxia*, because they lost the people's devotion."[20] *Tianming* is dependent upon moral conduct, and moral conduct finds its confirmation in the feelings of the people. The Zhou dynasty thinking about political legitimacy established a comprehensive interpretive framework here.

Even today this problem has not been adequately resolved. In fact, it has just begun to be addressed. If we say that moral governance finds its confirmation in the feelings of the people, what then constitutes the feelings of the people? Is it a result of a statistical analysis or a consensus based on a universal rational choice? Is this an economic concept or a political one? According to Zhou dynasty documents, the feelings of the people tracks their interests and benefits. Moral governing is to allow all of the people to benefit universally, and the feeling of the people must in turn support moral governance:

> If the King wants to win over the people of the world (*tianxia*) by first looking out for their benefit, the people will come of their own accord. It is just as with the *yang* of the winter solstice, and the *yin* of the summer solstice, without being commanded the people come of their own accord. This is what is meant by "repairing to virtuosity."[21]

Expressing this same meaning is the *Exalted Documents* passage: "The esteemed *tian* has no intimate, partial preferences, but only accords with virtuosity. The feelings of the people are not constant, but only concern themselves with what is truly beneficial."[22]

The Spring and Autumn and Warring States period documents reflect a similar understanding regarding the feelings of the people. Guan Zhong says:

> Flourishing in governance lies in according with the feelings of the people; deterioration in governance lies in going contrary to the feelings of the people. People hate anxiety and toil; I make them happy with leisure. People hate poverty; I enrich them. People hate danger; I give them security. People hate disaster and tragedy; I nurture them with life.[23]

The *Xunzi* also points out that "all of *tianxia* will repair to those who bring them the same benefits and protects them from the same harms."[24] Looking at the work the *Six Secret Strategies* (六韜) attributed to Duke Jiang, we can clearly see this line of reasoning:

> Those who would share the benefits with all of *tianxia* will gain *tianxia*; those who would arrogate the benefits of *tianxia* for themselves will lose *tianxia*. *Tian* has its seasons and earth its bounty. Those who are able to share these with others are consummate in their conduct (*ren*). And wherever consummate conduct is present, the people of *tianxia* will repair to it..... To share in the strife and the joy of others, and to share in what they like and despise is to be optimally appropriate in one's conduct (*yi*). And wherever optimal appropriateness is present, the people of *tianxia* will seek it out. People in general despise death and take joy in life, approve of moral conduct and look to benefit. What gives rise to benefit is the proper way (*dao*). And wherever the proper way is present, the people of *tianxia* will repair to it.[25]

Simply put, the feelings of the people have three significant aspects: (1) Since the people concern themselves mostly with the bare conditions of life and material benefits, the best way of winning over the people is to benefit them in this regard. And even if this is not a sufficient condition for winning them over, it is certainly a necessary condition. (2) What is supported and opposed in the feelings of the people is indicated in what they follow, and is similar to the expression "voting with one's feet." (3) What the feelings of the people either support or oppose is not only a confirmation of political legitimacy, but also can serve as proof of the legitimacy of any revolution. We can see this from the fact that the pre-Qin understanding of the feelings of the people is predominantly one of political economy. The idea of moral governance is the promotion of benefits and the avoidance of harm. In modern parlance this is to guarantee a universal provision of security and benefits. In the broadest terms good politics is a matter of planning for the well-being of all the people of *tianxia*.[26] This standard has long been accepted by the Chinese as their basic understanding of good governance.

It is clear that what ancient China understood by the expression "feelings of the people" was the people's affectivity, and not some abstract understanding of the "will of the people." The will of the people would be the result of a statistical analysis, but the people's affectivity can only represent the actually felt needs of everyone and their converging upon shared aspirations. This requires using an imaginative method of putting oneself in the place of other's and treating them accordingly in order to realize an immediate observation of "universal human feeling." This is exactly what Guan Zhong meant when he said, "Human feelings are not various, and thereby can be won over and managed."[27] However, it is very difficult to draw a clear line between subjective "wants" and objective "needs." Roughly speaking, the concept of the people's affectivity is mainly concerned with the bare needs of life, including those necessary conditions required for security and material well-being; but it also seemingly excludes ethical values and religious faith. This might have something to do with the situation that ancient society faced in terms of a perspective on basic values that had not yet progressed to the level of principled disagreement. Ancient societies had "common selections" that were more stable than any "public choice." Because of this, there was no need to appeal to statistical analysis in determining the people's affectivity. Rather, it could be understood more or less on the basis of a reasonable judgment. In this sense, moral governance in accord with the feelings of the people was an institutional arrangement wherein everyone could universally benefit.

Taking the feelings of the people as a criterion though is not without its risks. The affective dispositions of the multitudes sometimes results in wrong decisions, to the extent that on occasion there arises an incapacity to be agreeing upon shared interests and aspirations. Irrational collective decisions are harmful to the self-interests of any multitude. In a way similar to reasons Plato gave for being suspicious of democracy in the context of ancient Greek philosophy, Confucius as a pre-Qin philosopher, although highlighting the need for politics to accord with the feelings of the people, opposed following the immediate affective impulses of the multitude at any given moment. The reason for this was that the multitudes could be quite ignorant as to what was in their own genuine interest. Greek and pre-Qin philosophers alike hoped to find a universal arrangement that was beyond doubt, because then it would have the shared agreement of the (shepherded/cultivated) multitudes. The Greek philosophers sought this in knowledge that could be confirmed by universal rationality, while pre-Qin philosophers tended to seek for such confidence in morality implicated in universal human affectivity.

Universal rationality is limited by the fact that factually correct knowledge can't prevent people from making wrong choices. This is because the ultimate springs of action do not lie in truth, but rather in the seeking of benefits and the satisfying of desires. For this reason it is more plausible that universal human affect can effectively serve as a universal ground for rational choice. Confucianism makes a deep and direct observation here. No matter how perfect a rational principle might be, to the extent that it transcends human affectivity, it loses all effectiveness. To lose connection with human affects is tantamount to negating the ordinary realm of existence, and results in meaninglessness for daily life. People will always choose life over perfectly ideal concepts. But universal human affect also faces a serious predicament. Selfishness is a human emotion with the greatest degree of strength. It is not easy to find a human affect with more vigor than selfishness. Confucianism here faces a kind of paradox: Universal principles must find their ground in human affectivity, but a normative pattern (*li* 理) cannot be found in the (naturally selfishly charged) field of affects.

Any possible form of life is expressive of a certain relational dynamic between self and others. Without others there is no life, hence the external relations with others stipulates life's possibilities. It is obvious that what is rejected by others with respect to human affect cannot possibly become a universal principle. For this reason universal human affect can only emerge within webs of interpersonal relationships and cannot be inferred from some abstract conception of human nature. The optimizing of interpersonal relationships then is just the instantiation of universal principles of human affect. Confucius's breakthrough discovery was that the quality of relationships between persons is the lowest common denominator for appreciating any way of life. The principles of universal human affect must reside within interpersonal relationships. The original sense of the concept of "consummate conduct" (*ren* 仁) pertains "between two persons," which implies an "intentional agreement reached between at least two persons as to what would be a mutually optimizing relational dynamic." A relational dynamic must benefit others, or at least not harm others, in order to possibly be accepted by others. If others cannot accept a relational dynamic, then it cannot possibly be construed as "consummate conduct" (*ren*). Confucius said that *ren* is "loving others,"[28] which means to respect others (both their life and their interests). The principle here is what is meant by the *Analects* passage: "In desiring to establish oneself, establish others; in desiring to succeed oneself, help others to succeed" (the positive principle),[29] as well as by: "What you yourself don't desire, don't do to others" (the negative principle).[30] Confucius's negative principle here is the same as the negative formulation of the Christian golden rule. But the positive principle goes a long way beyond the golden rule, as it expresses clearly that what matters most in realizing what is good for self and for others is a shared imaginative process.

Universal human affect and universal reason can be complementary. Universal reason references a principle of "justice," while universal human affect refers to a principle of "reasonability." Universal reason can explain what any person *must* accept as a rule, while universal human affects can explain what any person would *enjoy* accepting as a rule. What universal reason produces as common property is law; while what universal human affect produces as common property is morality. From Confucius's perspective, what universal human affect determines to be moral is what is constant in the feelings of the people. Since the feelings of the people and morality are continuous in this way, to accord with morality is to accord with the feelings of the people. It is in this sense that Confucius believed morality to be an effective basis for political legitimacy. From this we can also understand why the Zhou dynasty believed that reverencing virtuosity resided in caring for the people and that caring for the people amounted to maintaining the heavenly invoked order of *tianming*. Wang Guowei's understanding of Zhou dynasty politics is most lucid. There is one thread that runs through the four aspects of *tian* 天 (heaven), *ming* 命 (order), *min* 民 (people), and *de* 德 (virtuosity). This is "the spirit and the great method of governing *tianxia*" of the Zhou dynasty, and "the Zhou institutions and ritual practices were all designed for the sake of morality."[31] Hou Wailu, in saying something similar, but the other way around, is even more accurate in observing that "Zhou morality emerged from Zhou institutional design."[32] These are astute observations. For the Zhou dynasty, moral principles were the core concepts of the Zhou institutional order, and the institutional order was the actual definition of moral principles.

8 Virtuosic Power and Harmony

"Governing *tianxia* with virtuosity" and "cooperation among the myriad states" were two basic political strategies of the Zhou dynasty and were closely correlated with the Zhou institutional order. Here we can reflect upon a problem: What is more important, the political strategies or the institutional order? This was not an explicit issue raised at the time, but was a problem latent in the Zhou dynasty conceptualization of the political. From a modern standpoint, if a strategy in practice achieves stable equilibrium, it is very likely to become institutionalized. According to this understanding, institutional order should be considered more important, as it is a decisive factor in any social reality. However, this theory of institutional decision-making perhaps understands society in too mechanical a manner. Moreover, with such a conception it would seem that all that is needed in wanting to design an institution is to permit societal practices to automatically give rise to institutional order. There is something dubious about this view, because people have sufficient capacities and insights to be either distorting or constructing an institution that would lead in each case to its respective demise or ongoing efficacy.

Wittgenstein's "paradox of rule-following"[1] can be understood as a way of philosophically calling into question the problem of theorizing institutional decisions. Institutional orders are a set of expansive game rules, and the ultimate meaning of any set of rules can ultimately only be understood in terms of the concrete practices that are engendered. Because rules have no means of predetermining future situations and the related details of practice, only a logic of practice itself can be expressive of the correct application of rules to concrete situations. And since concrete practical situations are never identical, even for a clearly defined rule there can be no way of determining with absolute certainty the optimally suitable application of any given rule to a logic of practice in every situation. The concrete situatedness and unrepeatability of practice is always governed by uniquely animating rules. Since practice always gives an animated, living explanation of rules, this means that there can be no way of absolutely determining in advance what would count as a correct application of a rule for any given activity in all sufficiently similar situations.

Of course, Wittgenstein's rule-following paradox is somewhat exaggerated, and does not call into question what is being stipulated as rule-governed conduct. There are exceptionally specialized and precise higher-order rules that can set limits on their flexibility within modes of practical application. But Wittgenstein's rule paradox is still pertinent to most rules encountered in life. This is because most life situations, not having the conditions of a controlled laboratory experiment, are rife with uncertainty. Wittgenstein was most definitely not a structuralist, and for the most part maintained a skeptical theoretical stance. He believes that the meaning of rules should be defined by interpretive precedents given in previous iterations of practical experience, and that rules have no way of predetermining future interpretive outcomes in a logic of practice. Simply put, rules are not sufficient to give an account of themselves, but can only be explained in terms of practice. Whatever has already been experienced in practice is what has already been understood, but drawing solely upon what has already been understood we can't infer with certainty the nature of any future practical interpretations. This problem of rule following suggests that concrete strategies are at least as important as any institutional order, and might possibly get us closer to an ideal concept of the political.

The Zhou dynasty institutional design is said to have carefully considered the successes and failures of the Xia and Shang institutions and introduced some revolutionary enhancements to these models. This suggests that the Zhou dynasty's ideal of institutional order was certainly not some unaccommodating political principle, but rather was a unique mode of expressing political principles. The Zhou dynasty's political principle defined the realm of the political and the political nature of the *tianxia* concept, and also defined good governmental strategies for moral rule and harmonious relations. We can say that the true spirit of the Zhou dynasty legacy of political order is in fact expressed in the concepts of *tianxia*, moral governance, and harmonious relations. And the institutions of feudal land division, together with ritual and music, were just at the time the most effective institutions for that particular historical time period, and not in themselves expressive of unalterable principles of political order. In actuality, in later periods of the Zhou dynasty the vassal lords began to change the institutional structures and were criticized by Confucius for bringing on a "collapse of ritual and corruption of music." And later on, the First Emperor of the Qin dynasty effected more directly and thoroughly massive "institutional change."

The Zhou dynasty's conception of the political took the strategies of moral governance and harmonious relations as basic principles for effecting political amelioration. This meant that effective institutional order could only be guaranteed by using legitimate strategies throughout the entire political process. This is to say that institutional order cannot be self-explanatory but requires an interpretation that emerges out of actual practice. Thus practical strategies are more fundamental than institutions. Only with good practical strategies can the ameliorative implementation of institutional order be guaranteed. By "institutions" (*zhidu* 制度) here is meant the various forms of official regulations and decrees, legal codes, and ritual practices that serve as the stabilizing functions of society. These can be summed up together as the "instrumentality" (*qi* 器) of politics, while the integration and "becoming one body" of strategies and practices as a set of political principles embody the "way" (*dao* 道) of the political. In the most basic terms, institutions are the result of strategies reaching a stable equilibrium and becoming formalized; and precisely because of this institutions are rule-governed bodies carrying on the structures of previous customs that have reached stable equilibrium. In this sense, institutions have their own inertia, and only those strategies that have yet to be fully stabilized are still dynamic.

According to the *Book of Changes*, what makes the metaphysical *dao* a sustainable root principle is its unchanging capacity to sustain change. Thus strategies that sustain dynamism are closer to the unalterable *dao* than institutions. The two strategies of moral governance and harmonious relations are political expressions of the principle of procreation in the *Book of Changes*: "Let all beings be in their becoming" (*sheng sheng* 生生). The respective emphasis placed upon moral governance and harmonious relations though are different. The aim of moral governance is the internalization of society, while the aim of harmonious relations is the internalization of the world. The basic spirit of these two strategies are continuous though, as they are both attempting to realize optimal cooperation while minimizing conflict—and their common spirit ultimately resides in the creating of a universal order that everyone would be willing to accept. Confucius, in defining the criterion of good political order, said "those near at hand are pleased, and those far away are attracted."[2] This meant that local people were satisfied and people from distant lands wanted to immigrate to the realm.

The concept of virtuosity (*de* 德) has been a core concept of Chinese politics and ethics from the Zhou period onward. Ancient documents and archaeology would indicate that the concept of virtuosity was likely a Zhou dynasty invention, as it seems that the Yin-Shang didn't use the concept much if at all (although this theory has yet to be confirmed). In the representative Zhou text, the *Exalted Documents* (尚书), frequent references are made to the term with extensive discussions of "moral governance." For instance, we have "virtuosity (of a sovereign) is manifest in good governance, and governing resides in nurturing the people... realizing virtuosity (in the people), deploying benefits, and maintaining a deep reverence for life is the way to promote harmony."[3] The original meaning of *de* was "uprightness and directness" that implies a principle of "public correctness" or "justice," especially in a sense of distributive justice. For example, the expression "virtuosity (*de* 德) is acquiring (*de* 得)"[4] means that to have virtuosity is to care for and help others to gain benefit. The *Guanzi* has the passage: "Caring for, generating, nurturing, completing, and benefiting the people so they get what they need and for all *tianxia* to have familial affection toward such governance is called virtuosity."[5]

Virtuosity is the political strategy of winning over the hearts and minds of the people. To love and nurture the people, to help the people receive benefits, and to refrain from greed is how to "get" (*de* 得) the hearts and minds of the people. The people get benefit and the ruler gets power. In this sense, we can say that moral governance is a political strategy of exchanging benefits for power: "The various techniques the ancient sage-kings applied in acquiring *tianxia* were aimed at expanding virtuosity, and material benefit."[6] Here we can see that the original meaning of moral governance was the guaranteeing of material benefits for all the people.

Before the overthrow of the Shang, the Zhou kings, by means of their virtuosity, won over the support of many vassal lords. It was said that the Zhou king always "cultivated virtuosity and practiced benevolence, and most of the vassal lords turned against Shang Zhou and joined Xi Bo."[7] The Duke of Zhou attempted to take the experience of "using virtuosity to win over *tianxia*" to transform it into a tradition of "bringing order to *tianxia*." The strategy of moral governance is indeed indicative of a far-sighted political awareness: (1) In the long run, moral governance is more effective than rule by military force. The *Xunzi* has a very detailed theoretical discussion on this subject that in broad outline goes as follows: there are three types of rule—rule by force, rule by wealth, and rule by virtuosity. Since rule by military force doesn't win over the hearts and minds of the people, such governance is not sustainable in the long term. Rule by wealth will attract the people, but since it is unable to satisfy insatiable greed, such governance again cannot be maintained in the long term. Since moral governance can realize distributive justice, it is the only form of political order that is sustainable.[8] (2) The strength of moral governance comes from the collective strength of winning over the hearts and minds of the people. If moral governance can be sustained, the lives of the people are properly ordered, their benefits are guaranteed, and people will naturally tend toward conservation of the current order. There is no positive reason to rebel because amply preserving good conditions is an optimal strategy for the people.

A core concept in moral governance is justice. The *Conversations of the States* (国语) says: "Reforming (*zheng* 正) is the way of virtuosity."[9] And Confucius said, "Politics is reforming [justice]."[10] Without a positive conception of justice there can be no universally effective standard, although there can be any number of reasons to deny any particular set of rules. In ancient societies, *zheng* 正 referred to a classical conception of justice. It had two principles: (1) the principle of proportionality with each according to their deserts; (2) the principle of symmetry wherein however one treats others is how others ought to be responding in treating them. The "proportionality" and "symmetry" principles that define a classical notion of justice and the "equality" and "fairness" principles that define a modern sense of justice have some very stark differences. From the viewpoint of modernity, classical justice is unacceptable because it is not based on equality. And from the ancient viewpoint, modern justice is unacceptable because in undermining relational proportionality it undermines equality, and it runs contrary to the natural principle of "simple equality is not equity."[11] This means that equity is not quantitatively equal distribution but is a matter of proportional distribution. The issue is that ancient and modern understandings of equality are importantly different.

A most important component of *tianxia* moral governance is land policy. The Zhou legal codes required that every household receive a specified amount of land, thereby guaranteeing that all farmers would have their own fields. At the same time, this legally allotted land could not be bought, sold, or transferred in any way. This guaranteed no one would lose their land. Obviously, as long as the rights of land use were stable (since all land rights ultimately returned to the Son of Heaven), the necessities of life resources could be more or less guaranteed and social order was relatively stable. The enfeoffed dukes and the chief officials of the ancestral ruling state (the various ministers of the king's territory served as prime minister, military generals and secretariat), were given varying divisions of land between 50 and 100 square *li*. The chief officials of the vassal states (the ministers of the vassal states served as prime minister, military generals and secretariat) were given varying divisions of land between 800 and 3200 square *mu*. Technology officials and expert scholar-officials (*shi* 士) were given varying divisions of land between 100 and 400 square *mu*. And commoners were given 100 *mu* divisions of lands (the same as the lowest class of scholar-officials).[12]

Whether or not this policy was in fact just would require a standard established by appeal to historical criteria. It was said that sage-kings were able to limit their own needs and let benefits be given to the people, "thin for themselves and generous for the people, limited for themselves and expansive for the world."[13] Given the historical conditions, this was the best possible way to maximize the people's benefit. If the distribution of benefits is in the interest of the people and doesn't serve to further empower the rich, it can be acknowledged to be totally moral governance. However, since the Zhou dynasty in the final analysis was a hierarchical society, it was not possible that it could've devised a distributional system of benefits that would undermine the aristocratic social hierarchy. Thus, in speaking of moral governance that would optimally benefit the people, it is probably better that we speak instead about a minimization of exploitation carried out by the ruling classes.

In addition, moral governance emphasizes that governments must create the shared conditions of a favorable livelihood for the people. This is related to the spiritual conviction regarding "procreativity" (*shengsheng* 生生). If the greatest virtuosity of heaven and earth is "procreativity" and the nurturing of life, then the greatest virtuosity of *tianxia* politics is similarly concerned with "procreativity" and the enhancement of the livelihood of the people that is in accord with the way of *tian* (*tiandao* 天道). Guanzi explains in some detail the promotion of economic and social welfare as policies of moral governance:

> Virtuosity has six modes of flourishing. These are dividing lands, improving the earthen altars, cultivating trees and milling lumber, invigorating the farmers, facilitating the sowing and harvesting, repairing the walls and houses—this is valuing life. Advancing economic potential, expanding surplus savings, fixing roads and pathways, making relations between diverse markets more convenient, caring about available housing—this is conveyance by means of wealth. Guiding the waterways, improving the sewage systems, determining the isle embankments, removing the mud and sludge, making clear the canal locks, caring for the fords and bridges—this is called improving transportation. Thinning out the army, lessening the taxation for military purposes, relaxing punitive measures, pardoning criminals, forgiving minor offenses—this is what is called lenience in policies. Caring for elders, loving the young and orphans, acting compassionately towards the widowed and bereaved, seeking knowledge about illnesses and disease, taking care of funerals for disastrous cases—this is called forestalling emergencies. Giving clothes to those who are cold, food to the hungry, assistance to the country poor, assisting the destitute, giving monetary support to those in need—this is called poverty alleviation. With regards to these six policy measures, virtuosity is key for success. In carrying out the six policy mea-

sures, with respect to what the people desire, there is nothing that cannot be had. The people must get what they desire before they will listen to their benefactors; and only in listening to their benefactors can governing be efficacious. Thus, it is said, "Virtuosity cannot but be magnificent."[14]

The *Yizhoushu* (逸周书) (*Remnants of Zhou Documents*) also describes various measures for putting moral governance into practice. Among these there are several political policies that make a lot of sense from a modern standpoint. For instance, we can see the continuity of wisdom between past and present in the following: "Establish centers for healing in the villages, and keep on hand all of the medicines needed to treat all types of illness"—this is a prescription to set up village doctors throughout the land. "Don't plant trees in the valleys for timber"—this is about proper land use in not expanding forestation at the expense of losing agricultural lands. "In the three months of spring do not log the mountains in order to the let flora and trees thrive. In the three months of summer do not fish with nets in the rivers, streams, and marshlands in order to let the fish and turtles thrive."[15] This and many other passages are all about protecting natural ecologies and securing sustainable conditions for survival.

Moral governance can also be expressed in terms of an optimally balanced distribution of power, and here too the principle of justice sets the standard. Concrete policies must give priority to and guarantee that power is in the hands of the most worthy: "Political office is only for those worthy—that is, those who are able to fulfill their obligations"[16] and even "in the remote regions there should be no forgotten worthies."[17] According to legend, the origin of a just policy for power distribution can be traced back to the era of the ancient sage-kings and their practices of "abdication," and the tradition of advancement through public acclaim. Policies aimed at selecting the worthy and capable doesn't only benefit the worthies themselves but are beneficial for the entire society. The reason for this is that while mediocre persons tend to focus only on their private interests, worthies are concerned more with common benefits and universal interests. This same phenomena has certainly been acknowledged in modern societies via various political critiques. Speaking in terms of the true function of the political, the importance of meritocratically selecting worthies based on their abilities is that it serves as a guarantee against the practical failures wrought by ineffective institutional orders. And this is a legitimate reason to uphold with respect to the shared interests of society.

In moving forward, we should consider another very important Zhou dynasty strategy—the harmonious relations or "compatibility" (*xiehe* 协和) principle. If the question of moral governance is addressing what government must do for the people, then the problem of *compatibility* is attempting to resolve how different bodies of interest can form cooperative relations. The source of all conflict lies in selfishness. Guanzi has said: "Selfish interest (*si*私) is what brings chaos to *tianxia*."[18] Selfishness is an unalterable aspect of unrefined human nature. History proves that no matter what sort of institutional arrangements are made with the aim of upholding values of equality—such as communism, the welfare state, individual rights, and so on—none of these have been up to the task of resolving conflicts that arise as a result of selfishness. Hence, within the conditions set by a presumptive selfish human nature, can a strategy for achieving optimal cooperation be realized? The strategy of compatibility offers a profoundly persuasive and meaningful response to this question. The concept of "harmony" (*he* 和) originates from the harmonious sound of an ancient musical instrument, a multihole flute, and it implies orchestrating diversity through mutual cooperation and complementarity.[19] From the *Exalted Documents* we can see that "compatibility" was a principle appealed to for guaranteeing cooperative relationships among various political bodies. This is what has been called "compatibility among the myriad states"[20] and "a sustainable harmony among the peoples of the four directions."[21]

The meaning of "harmony" (*he* 和) very clearly refers to the compatibility and complementarity of a plurality of things and events. I'm not sure why, but it seems that during a part of the Spring and Autumn period there emerged a generalized confusion regarding the difference between the concepts of "harmony" (和) and "uniformity" (同) that gave rise to the debates regarding the relative importance of harmony *he* 和 or uniformity *tong* 同. According to the *Zuo Commentary* (左传), Duke Jing of Qi thought that "harmony" was the same thing as "uniformity." And the "Yanzi" chapter goes to great length in explaining the difference between *he* 和 and *tong* 同:

The Duke said: "Are harmony and uniformity different?" Master Yan responded: "They are different. Harmony is like making a soup. You use water, fire, minced spices, salt, and plum sauce, and then set a fire under it in cooking the fish. A great chef in looking for harmony, balances the flavors, adjusts for what is missing, and mitigates any excess. The relationship between ruler and ministers should also be like this. If a ruler says a course of action is to be taken, but it actually would bring about negative consequences, then the ministers should bring attention to the negatives to present a fuller picture. If a ruler says a course of action is not to be taken but it actually would have some positive consequences, the ministers should bring attention to the positives as a way to dispel the negative aspects. The earlier sage-kings balanced the five flavors and harmonized the five sounds bringing equanimity to their own feelings and carrying out their good governance. Making music is just like the palate: there is a complementarity among the one breath, the two bodies, the three types, the four things, the five sounds, the six chords, the seven pitches, the eight airs, and the nine songs. Clear and turbid, small and large, short and long, fast and slow, sad and joyful, hard and soft, late and early, high and low, in and out, thick and thin—these are all compensatory categories. The ruler listens to proper music, bringing equanimity to his own feelings, and with such feelings, his virtuosity promotes harmony. It is like using water to flavor water; who will be able to enjoy it? It is like the various zithers having only one string; who would be able to listen to it? Relying upon uniformity is unacceptable for this very reason."[22]

There is also a passage in the *Conversations of the States* (国语), wherein Shi Bo provides a deeper analysis:

> It is actually harmony that vitalizes things. With only sameness or uniformity there can be no continuity. Using diversity to balance difference is what is called "harmony" (*he* 和). Thus, there will be an abundance of growth and things will seek it out. If sameness is added to sameness, in the end it will be abandoned.... With only one note, there is nothing to hear; with only one thing, there can be no pattern; with only one flavor, there is no dinner; and with only one subject, there can be no conversation.[23]

This set of passages explain how "harmony" (和) is the combination of diversity, while "sameness" (同) is a universal uniformity. The reason that "uniformity" is not an option is because "sameness" precludes plurality and abundance among things, causing life to lose its meaning and vitality. There is no creature that can live in isolation. Harmony, however, signifies

a vitality residing in the midst of the myriad things. It is in the complementarity and compatibility in plurality and abundance that all things
find their optimal growth. It is for this reason that harmony can serve
as a criterion for the existence and the growth of all things. Guanzi puts
this point most succinctly: "Harmony is life; without harmony there is no
life."[24]

Harmony as a concept implies a relational ontology: (1) relations determine existence. An entity has no means of existing independently. Any
entity requires the existence of related entities as a condition for its existence. Thus "coexistence" is a necessary condition for any "existence." (2)
The lowest standard for coexistence is the minimization of mutual harm.
(3) The highest standard for coexistence is realizing a maximization of
mutual benefit. In order to achieve mutual codependence and relations of
shared flourishing and minimal harm, no single perspective can be actively
seeking out the exclusively independent promotion of its individual interests. This strategy for compatibility can be expressed as follows: (1) with
regards to any two game players X and Y, there exists an equilibrium of
mutual benefit. In such ideal conditions, X would receive benefit x if and
only if Y can also receive benefit y. At the same time, X would receive harm
if and only if Y were also to receive harm; (2) X advances to receive benefit
x+ if and only if Y receives benefit y+, and vice versa. Therefore, bringing
about x+ becomes Y's optimal strategy because Y in order to get y+ must
necessarily acknowledge the advancement of x+, and vice versa; (3) within
these conditions of an equilibrium of mutual benefit, the advancing of
interests for all parties is always more optimal than individual parties
aiming to exclusively advance their own individual interests.

The strategy of compatibility is a perfect cooperative strategy because
it is able to create a stable cooperative order wherein all parties receive the
satisfaction of the advancement of their interests. The strategy of compatibility is more ideal than a Pareto improvement. Pareto improvement
can only express the progress of society as a whole, but cannot guarantee
the universal satisfaction of society. Pareto improvements can only promote the interests of some persons but has nothing to say about whether
the interests of others are being reduced, or whether the promotion of
the interests of some do not reach a level of parity with others. In such
a framework, those whose interest advancement is comparatively small

with respect to the "economic pie" might need more from the "psychological pie" as it were. If what they lose in terms of the psychological pie is greater that what they gain from the economic pie, they will likely not be satisfied. Only with the strategy of compatibility can everyone be satisfied. This is roughly equivalent to the entire social body advancing through a Pareto improvement. This strategy of compatibility expresses precisely the principle of Confucius: "I can get established iff others are getting established; I can gain improvement iff others are getting improved."[25] In order to express our reverence for Confucius, we might call this compatibility strategy a Confucian amelioration strategy. The weak point of the strategy of compatibility is that its applicability conditions are extremely limited. For obviously not every situation has the objective conditions suitable for applying this strategy of compatibility.

From the institutional practices of the Zhou dynasty we can see that this strategy of compatibility was only partially put in practice. We discover that in actual practice the concept was always weaker than its ideality. In fact, from the middle Zhou period onward, the *tianxia* system began to lose the conditions for realizing compatibility, and with continual decline it ultimately disappeared. Even though the Zhou dynasty was far from perfect, it at least presented a good institutional order. So why then would a good system collapse? Just as the creation of the Zhou dynasty *tianxia* system emerged out of a unique set of historical circumstances, the reasons for its decline are also unique. In the next chapter we will attempt to explain how a good system could collapse on account of its being too good.

9 Why Might Good Order Collapse?

We have almost come to the conclusion of this narrative history of the *tianxia* concept. In the Spring and Autumn period, the Zhou dynasty slowly entered into decline and eventually collapsed. *Tianxia* became a chaotic space with the vassal lords attacking each other in an attempt to become the dominant hegemon. With all of this, war and political intrigue became the mainstream. Speaking from a standpoint of historical conditions, the Zhou dynasty was without doubt a good society. For over two millennia it has been taken as an exemplary ruling order. But even so, the Zhou dynasty still collapsed. So from this we can infer that good political order is hard to maintain in the long run. This is a very serious problem. Chinese canonical traditions have always attributed the collapse of any dynasty to the decadence and corruption of the ruling classes in their penultimate period. However, despite there being some outlandish stories about the elites from the middle and late Zhou periods, we can say that the Zhou dynasty was overall not a corrupt political system. Hence the Zhou collapse wasn't a result of corruption. Rather, its demise was the result of a noble flaw latent in the good order—this is precisely the problem we will be addressing here.

Political order is a non-natural, humanly devised ontological order for the world. It is precisely in this sense that history is a world-creating process of humanity. Human ontology is always also a kind of cosmogony. A cosmogonic theory regarding the creation of the world is the province of God, while a cosmogonic theory concerned with the creation of history belongs to humanity. The difficult problems facing humanity all have their origins in cosmogonical predicaments that have arisen in the course of creating world-history. Even though humanity is capable of creating institutional orders, we are not capable of designing institutional orders that are totally free of contradictions. We have the capacity to create history, but not to control the future. Thus futurity has always presented a mortal problem.

As remarked upon earlier, the Zhou dynasty devised a *tianxia* system as an effective political order under the historical conditions of having to "govern the great with the small" and to "govern the many with the one." This was a unique historical situation that ensured that it was impossible for the Zhou dynasty to simply maximize their own private interests, and to date such historical conditions have not been repeated. These conditions forced the Zhou to compress their selfish interests, reducing them to a minimum. It was only in approaching governance with a just order and a reasonable distribution of interests that they could guarantee their own political authority. It was in this way that the Zhou dynasty became an exemplary political regime. Ancient societies have by and large always been authoritarian governments. But since describing the Zhou dynasty in such authoritarian terms doesn't do it justice, it might well present an exception to this historical rule. Despite the Zhou dynasty government having some authoritarian characteristics—for instance, the monarchical system and a hereditary aristocracy—the Zhou *tianxia* system was really a world system that meted out benefits and distributed power. This was a clear repudiation of a monopolization of power and interests. Moreover, the Zhou dynasty pursued the best practices of moral governance. What the ancestral state would dole out in terms of shared resources and goods was much greater than what the vassal states ever provided as tribute. Thus the costs of preserving "world peace" and "world order" came largely from the Zhou ancestral ruling state itself. The tribute from the surrounding states consisted primarily of special products from those regions (ranging from useful products such as iron tools, salt, and swords to luxury items such as precious stones, animal skins, and animals themselves such as elephants and prize horses). These were symbolic gifts expressing reverence more than any substantial form of taxation.

The economic conditions of the Zhou dynasty ancestral state, far from becoming increasingly dominant by exploiting the various regions for tribute, in fact became increasingly weak in taking on the lion's share of the burden for these shared costs. This indeed shows how the Zhou dynasty ancestral state shared political power and did not seek power for its own economic aggrandizement. Moreover, the Zhou dynasty followed the sage-king tradition of shared, deliberative governance between the "Son of Heaven" and the "scholar-officials." This so-called "shared governance" meant that the Son of Heaven couldn't monopolize control, and not only had to respect institutional limitations but also had to deliberate together with his ministers. Such shared governance is not democracy per se, but it does have a deliberative political character. In sum, given the special characteristics of Zhou dynasty politics, something like "supervisory governance" would be a more appropriate label than authoritarianism. Modern political science frequently takes authoritarianism and democracy as two mutually exclusive concepts in describing any political order, but obviously having only these two options is far too limiting to adequately cover all of the possibilities of the political.

It is precisely because the Zhou dynasty's conception of the political was effective in realizing good political order that the collapse of this good order became a problem that requires critical reflection. In the final analysis, what were the unproductive factors that led to the collapse of the Zhou order? At the end of the Western Zhou, nomadic peoples in the northwest were continuously attacking the Zhou, causing them to move the capital to the east. The period subsequent to this major transition was historically recognized as the Eastern Zhou. This dramatic change seems to indicate that the nomadic peoples increasingly wished to rebel against the Zhou dynasty system, and this insurgence might've been a direct cause leading to the Zhou decline. Again, moving the capital has frequently been viewed as a signal of the Zhou dynasty collapse. But such an explanation would seem to be putting the cart before the horse. For it should be recognized that first came the Zhou decline and its inability to maintain order, and only afterward did this lead to the revolt of surrounding peoples and states.

The Zhou dynasty *tianxia* included a vast array of diverse peoples and ethnic groups, and it had once successfully realized a "harmony among the myriad states," thereby approximating a universal peaceful order.

But the cooperation between the Zhou dynasty ancestral state and the nomadic peoples had its weak points. One of these was that, for the most part, the northern nomadic peoples and the Zhou ancestral states had only a political relationship and were lacking in any substantial forms of economic cooperation. The lifestyles of the nomadic peoples was such that since they didn't accumulate many goods and materials for their livelihood, the resources of the Central Plain always presented a temptation. As long as the Central Plain could maintain an equitable and stable trade relationship with the nomadic peoples, any enthusiasm for plundering was abated. However, as the Central Plain economies developed and their resources became abundant, they typically had little interest in what they could get from trading with the nomadic peoples and thus lacked any positive motivation for establishing a system of trade with them. Instead, for the most part there were only limited and uncertain forms of economic transaction between the more sedentary and the nomadic peoples. Moreover, the Zhou dynasty promoted an ideal of a simple and frugal life, criticizing those who valued "luxury goods" acquired from afar. For example, the *Exalted Documents* records that even though the Zhou had connections with the nine Yi and eight Man peoples, "the four Yi are all our guests without there being any near or far. Hence one ought not make a display of the goods brought from such places." Such a passage opposes the acquisition of luxury goods, complemented by expressions such as "don't put value in foreign goods" and "don't treasure goods coming from afar."[1] With such attitudes toward material goods from distant lands, positive reasons to establish economic cooperation with the nomadic peoples didn't materialize. And for this reason it was of course most difficult for the people of the Central Plain to maintain ties of political cooperation, loyalty, and trust with the nomadic groups. Even so, the revolt of the nomadic peoples was not the root cause of the collapse of the Zhou dynasty, but only an auxiliary reason.

The real cause of the decline of the Zhou dynasty was very likely a result of it being unable to live up to its own high standards of moral governance. This could be called "a catch-22 of ethical governance." Although moral governance is obviously a good thing, the Zhou institutional system had a design flaw that created difficulties in carrying out moral governance over the long haul. According to the research of Xu Zhuoyun and Ge Zhiyi, the Zhou dynasty division of land came to an end by the middle of the Western Zhou period. It wasn't that the Zhou were unwilling to continue distributing land, but that there just wasn't any more land to distribute.[2] This was an unforeseen systemic flaw of the Zhou dynasty institutional design. It wasn't simply due to the fact that the Zhou dynasty only controlled a limited amount of land, for even if they controlled the entire world, there would ultimately only be a finite amount of land in any case. Hence the end of this "divided allotment of land" system would only be a matter of time. Because later generations of the ruler's relatives and successful ministers had no opportunity to receive a division of land as their "just deserts," their motivation to be working toward the shared interest of realizing the common project of *tianxia* gradually diminished. And this quandary developed to a point where in certain cases only feelings of resentment remained.

Approaching things from another perspective, according to the Zhou dynasty institutional order vassal states were hereditary, and with the rare exception of some serious mistakes there was typically no way to withdraw or alter enfeoffed titles. Thus, for the vassal states an attractive strategy was to focus on taking care of and promoting their own enterprises while not wasting any efforts or energy toward contributing to the shared interests of *tianxia*. Merely not committing any mistakes is always easier than making significant contributions to political and economic order. The attraction of focusing attention on their own domestic economies often proved greater than the allure of contributing to the shared interests of *tianxia*. For this reason, states that had already received sufficient benefit from participating in the Zhou order eventually stopped caring about the shared interests of *tianxia*.

The institutional advantages of the Zhou dynasty *tianxia* system resided in its network of mutual interdependencies and common benefits, and in its reciprocal bonds of cooperative relationships. But the *tianxia* system proved to be too advanced for the ancient economic and technological conditions; thus the possible institutional advantages couldn't be fully realized. Even though the Zhou dynasty had established a common order of networking, in actual practice the "shareable" interests were not all that many. First, there was not sufficient economic circulation to match the shared networking order, and it was difficult to provide the common material goods necessary to serve the interests of the entire system. Because material conditions couldn't keep up with the *tianxia* concept, the political expectations of the Zhou dynasty's *tianxia* system far exceeded its economic capabilities. We can even say that the Zhou *tianxia* was only a political *tianxia* and never actually took shape as an economic *tianxia*. During the Zhou era, in terms of material production and consumption the economic order predominantly consisted of loosely aligned regional autonomy. Even though there was some trade and commerce between various states, none of the states developed a sufficiently vital order of economic interdependence. And given the significance of the symbolic political order, with core ritual practices far exceeding any forms of economic cooperation, we can understand why Confucius thought that the institutions of ritual and music were at the heart of the Zhou dynasty order.

Due to this phenomenon, the vassal states and the aristocratic scholar-officials gradually realized that *tianxia* was merely an ideal concept, and that the actual interests of the various states clearly superseded the shared interests of *tianxia*. Thus the various states committed themselves to developing their own individual power, and the increasingly powerful vassal states no longer needed to rely on the ancestral state for security or protection. Again, having taken on the lion's share of responsibility for the costs of securing the shared order and the common safety of *tianxia*, the Zhou ancestral state continued to have to pay to support the vassal states. These economic burdens and other associated costs led to the gradual exhaustion of the Zhou treasuries. And when its ability to distribute goods and power to the various regions came to an end, the ideals of moral governance devolved into a system of empty rhetoric and lost any actual influence. By the middle of the Zhou period the military prowess of the Zhou ancestral state had already lost its deterrent powers. It had gotten to the point where the regime couldn't even fend off a revolt by a renegade state, never mind exercising the power to preserve the security for all of *tianxia*. Because of its lack of power to adequately respond to the attacks of the nomadic peoples, the Zhou dynasty was forced to move its capital to the

East and thereby lost most of the land that had been directly controlled by the ancestral state. The Zhou economic strength and political authority was greatly diminished to the point where it was not even as powerful as some larger vassal states and thus was never again capable of exerting control over these states. At least nominally, the vassal rulers continued to pay respects to the Zhou king, but as soon as even their slightest individual state interests were at stake, the vassal states were unwilling to make even the smallest of concessions.

During the early Spring and Autumn period, the state of Zheng, working together with another small state, took the lead in destroying the *tianxia* order, and the Zhou king had no way of controlling the situation. At the end of the day, according to the Zhou institutional order, the vassal states had only land-use rights without total control, and any merger or transference of land was against legal codes. But the state of Zheng and Zhou came into a conflict of arms over agricultural lands, and the Zheng military wounded the Zhou King and defeated the Zhou armies. These two iconic violations of ritual propriety announced to all the realm that the rules of the game had changed. The Zhou dynasty ancestral state's right to lead *tianxia* devolved into a merely titular symbolic system. Although the Zhou continued as a nominal ruling power for several hundred more years, the Zhou's political influence decreased to a point where it was no more effective than today's United Nations. The significance of the Zhou Son of Heaven became nothing more than a plea for political correctness. The hegemonic states would claim to be representing the Son of Heaven in preserving a nominal *tianxia* order, but in actual practice they invaded or formed alliances with other states. The various states were, in name only, still part of a *tianxia* system, but in actuality the world politics of *tianxia* had already devolved into an international politics of hegemony. This historical narrative of political evolution is most unique: while the political started as a world politics (the Zhou dynasty), it then evolved into international politics (Spring and Autumn and Warring States), and finally evolved again into a national politics (from the Qin through the Qing dynasties).

The state established by the First Emperor of the Qin marks a dividing line in Chinese politics. It bade farewell to the *tianxia* system and world politics, and marked the beginning of the sovereign country as the absolute power in politics. After the ancestral state power of the Zhou dynasty had declined, the hegemonic vassals of the Spring and Autumn and Warring States were all thinking of how to bring an end to the chaos and reestablish a *tianxia* system. They all wanted to become the new leader of *tianxia*. Before having swallowed up the six most powerful states, it was not at all evident that the Qin had established a new political regime. Even though Shang Yang, Han Fei, and Li Si had all thought that politics needed a new start and opposed the "ways of the former Kings," still at the time a new politics was far from being a clear concept. And even after the absorption of the six states under one rule, the question of how to bring unified governance to such a vast realm became a pressing new problem.

Lasting for more than eight hundred years, the Zhou dynasty *tianxia* system had already become a widely respected tradition. The various countries that the First Emperor of the Qin dynasty swallowed up actually transformed a tradition even more ancient than the Zhou dynasty. With the exception of the aristocracy from the state of Qin, all the other elites upon losing their states and land would no longer be considered as aristocracy. When this ancient aristocratic tradition was severed at its roots, it ushered in a fundamental change in the structure of society. The various ethnic groupings of *tianxia* were long existing historical entities, most of whom could be traced back to prehistory. And the governing rulers of these tribal groups were all multigenerational aristocracy. The aristocratic classes had always been the basis in the organization of ancient society. The common rulers of *tianxia* could be changed, but the aristocratic class was always the legitimate representative of the various ethnic groups. After hundreds of years of the assimilations of the Spring and Autumn and Warring States periods, almost all of the aristocratic classes had ceased to exist. The First Emperor of the Qin dynasty attacked the last remnants of the Zhou aristocracy and the Qin ruling elite became the only remaining family of aristocrats. After this the aristocracy was never again part of the larger societal system. The Qin usurpation of the various states was a result of conquest by military might. Such conquest didn't need to enter into deliberation with any other groups. Instead, it could use totalizing power to construct political rule. How to continue to dominate a conquered world and how to deal with a world based in the alluring power of moral governance present two totally different sets of political problems.

Although the *tianxia* system no longer existed, the *tianxia* concept still persisted. The Qin unified rule gave rise to a vigorous debate about whether a new conception of the political was needed. Li Si strongly argued for institutional renewal and opposed any reconstruction of the *tianxia* system. For instance, the *Records of the Grand Historian* (史记) records:

> The Chancellor Wang Wan and others said, "The vassal states of Yan, Qi, and Jing (Chu) have begun to overturn the system, and are far away. They are no longer part of the King's domain. Establish a meeting with the vassal rulers and get them to accept only one ruler." The First Emperor of the Qin sent this command out to his various ministers, and they all agreed that it was a positive step. The Commandant of Justice Li Si deliberated as follows: "It was only when the Zhou sage-rulers Wen and Wu enfeoffed much territory to their sons, brothers, and other family sharing a surname that they established the distinction between near and far. But there were increasing feuds among the clans, with the vassal rulers attacking each other as enemies, and even the Zhou Son of Heaven couldn't put a stop to it. But today within the four seas there is the beneficent unified rule brought about by your highness. Everywhere is your majesty's domain, and all of the vassal rulers and accomplished ministers pay public taxes and make tribute to the extent that your rule has brought about institutional change. When *tianxia* is of one mind, it is a means for realizing peace and prosperity. But it does not serve the interests of the vassal lords." The First Emperor of Qin responded: "With these vassal 'kings,' *tianxia* has been plagued with war without respite. *Tianxia* was initially set up on the basis of ancestral temples, and again to establish various states. With them eventually raising armies again, to seek for peace and stability with such means would be most difficult. The deliberation of the Commandant of Justice is correct."[3]

Although Li Si's analysis of the weak points of the Zhou institutional order was somewhat one-sided, it is nevertheless profound. Even though the *tianxia* system of the Zhou dynasty was theoretically reasonable, in practice it lacked the means of preventing the various states from gradually drifting apart. It had no way of sustaining long-term, relational cooperation. The problem arises from the distribution of institutional power that led to the ancestral state lacking in sufficient actual power to control the chaos brought about by the competition among the vassal states.

The First Emperor of the Qin established a state system with centralized rule over many prefectures. And this spelled the end of the *tianxia* system.

10 *Tianxia* as Method

The outcome of the Zhou dynasty was certainly not a total institutional failure; for institutional design flaws can in due course be adjusted. The Zhou was an era that put forth new political ideals. Indeed, the political experiment of the Zhou *tianxia* system left us with a rich heritage of political methods and continues to offer significant resources for political theory.

The *tianxia* concept created a most capacious framework for political analysis. It introduced a political standard for thinking through world problems. Whether we are talking about global politics, international politics, or national politics, all of these conceptual domains can be interpreted within a unified framework of *tianxia*. At the same time, *tianxia* takes the world as a political subject, not merely as a physical entity. For this reason the world as such has its own political meaning. This entails that the world has an assemblage of interests that are not reduceable to national interests. Therefore world problems can only be approached through a world-encompassing viewpoint and cannot be understood from a merely (inter)national point of view. This political method can be derived from a formulation found in two classical sources—Guan Zhong's expression "take the family as family, the village as village, the state as state, and *tianxia* as *tianxia*"[1] and Laozi's "view person as person, family as family, village as village, state as state, and *tianxia* as *tianxia*"—both express this methodological point most clearly.[2]

The *tianxia* concept implies a political ontology that we might call an "ontology of coexistence." This is the ontological ground upon which political order is constructed. If we can't construct a universally shared "order of coexistence" for the world, then we can't overcome oppositional conflict and war, never mind realizing a shared lifeworld for humanity. As long as the world is oppositionally divided and conflicted, all societies will suffer the negative consequences of such exteriority. This is precisely the failure of the political. And a failure of the political will necessarily have deleterious influence on every aspect of human life. We can say that the political is not only a political problem but is simultaneously an ontological problem of life and death, of existing or perishing. Here we can feel the urgency of the "no outside" of *tianxia* as an a priori concept. The "no outside" concept a priori considers the world as a complete existence with no exteriority but only interiority. It takes a priori the world as a common resource for all persons to realize their shared interests. And it also takes a priori the negation of any noncompatible exclusionary concepts.[3] At the same time *tianxia* affirms a priori the world's plurality and relational compatibility, rejecting any one-sided, unilateral universalism and any forms of cultural imperialism. This is precisely what the *Book of Rites* means with the principle that "ritual practice shouldn't be used for indoctrination": "We've heard of ritual practice being learned from others, but not of it being imposed on others; and we've heard of studying ritual practice, but never indoctrinating others with it."[4]

To complete the interiorization of the world is an a priori mission for world governance. The cooperative nature of relational reasoning is obviously better than the competitive logic of individual rationality. Relational reasoning does not totally repudiate individual rationality, for the two are not mutually exclusive alternatives, but are rather two aspects of a common logic of practice. Relational reasoning takes precedence in reflecting on how to minimize mutual harm. It first of all excludes actions of vengeance, and then goes on to develop the optimization of mutual benefit. If the use of relational reasoning takes precedence over individual rationality, with relational reasoning serving as a limiting condition for individual rationality, it can use compatibility to limit forms of competition and can minimize conflicts by guaranteeing the optimization of cooperation. It thus can guarantee the optimization of shared interests and mutual benefits for all. The aim of relational reasoning is to create a kind of social order that allows for cooperative interests to always be transcending solely competitive interests. It attempts then to realize a Confucian amelioration—that is, a kind of ameliorating interest that necessarily takes the interests of all people into account in realizing any social improvement. A Confucian amelioration is equivalent to every person receiving a Pareto improvement at the same time, and as such can serve as a reliable and credible foundation for crafting a universally acceptable institutional order for political society.

The *tianxia* system is an "internalized world-system," and as such it is totally different from the "dominating world-system" of imperialism. Immanuel Wallerstein offered a lucid approach to understanding imperialistic world-systems: "[A world-system's] life is made up of the conflicting forces which hold it together by tension, and tear it apart as each group seeks eternally to remold it to its advantage."[5] Obviously, in imperialistic world-systems the strengthening of exclusively nationalistic interests reigns as the supreme motivation. By way of contrast, the *tianxia* system attempts to construct a world sovereignty using the political power latent in the world to realize mutual benefits that can serve the actual interests of the world. More precisely, the *tianxia* system's aim is to minimize conflict in the world and to optimize cooperation.

The *Six Secret Teachings* (六韜) provides an effective summary of the *tianxia* concept:

> King Wen ask the Duke of Zhou: "What needs to be done to establish *tianxia*? The Duke responded: "It is only when you have the capacity to cover *tianxia* that you can accommodate it; it is only when you have credibility in covering *tianxia* that you can hold it together; it is only when you arc morally consummate in covering *tianxia* that you can win it over; it is only when you cover *tianxia* with beneficence that you are able to sustain it; it is only when you can cover the exigencies of *tianxia* that you can avoid losing it. . . . Thus, *tianxia* will promote those who would benefit it and *tianxia* will shut those down who want to do it harm; *tianxia* will reward those who would bring life to it, and *tianxia* will deem thieves those who

would kill it; *tianxia* will give access to those who would enrich it and will deem enemies those who would exhaust it; *tianxia* will rely upon those who would bring peace to it and will destroy those who would endanger it. *Tianxia* does not belong to any one person, and will only give residence to those on the proper way."[6]

Although this manifesto style of expression is surely hyperbolic, it does summarize nicely what the ancient political imagination took the ideal *tianxia* to be.

PART II The Encompassing *Tianxia* of China

11 A Whirlpool Model

Providing a narrative of China is more difficult than providing a narrative account of *tianxia*.[1] Within *tianxia* there are states, and within states there are families, with each layer in the system clearly demarcated and a precise order to the overall structure. China is a nation-state, though one incorporated with a *tianxia* structure and historically deploying the idea of *tianxia* in the activities of a unified nation-state. This being the case, how can a nation-state structure and the structure of *tianxia* be integrated? And by what processes can such integration be carried out?

Before analyzing the growth of China and the dynamics of its persistence, we first need to get clear about several concepts. The Zhou *tianxia* system declined during the Spring and Autumn period and collapsed with the Qin unification. Thus the pre-Qin history was an era of *tianxia*, while the First Emperor of the Qin introduced a unified governance (*zhengyitong* 政一统) through the institution of county administrations,[2] thereby reducing *tianxia* to China as a nation-state. Henceforth the *tianxia* story was converted into the story of China. Thus here it should be said that the Qin through the Qing dynasty is what we mean by ancient China.

Even though the institutions of the Qin marked the end of the *tianxia* system, the *tianxia* concept still persisted as a political gene within

Chinese reality and enabled China to become a nation-state inclusive of *tianxia*. Despite the fact that since the Qin-Han period China never attempted to control the entire world, it has, however, tried to manage China as a condensed version of *tianxia*. These two types of systems for governance have their own distinctive aims. The ultimate goal of managing *tianxia* has been to realize an "internalization of the world" and to make the world a place without any "externalities" wherein all of the people collectively enjoy social life. Such an order includes all the political bodies in achieving a compatible orchestration of coexistence—the so-called "compatibility of the myriad states."[3] The ultimate aim in managing China is primarily to enable China to persist throughout the generations, while not worrying about the internalization of the world. Thus the exterior world became a threat and a challenge. During the Zhou dynasty, when the "distant tribute didn't arrive"[4] it was considered to have become a problem due to King Mu's ineptitude.[5] After the Qin-Han period, if the "distant submissive" tribes didn't become enemies of the imperial court of the Central Plain, there was peace and prosperity in the state. In the wake of the loss of the "nonexteriority" concept of *tianxia*, the boundary between "inner and outer" of the nation-state, became a focal problem. The main concern in managing China became focused on the establishment of an internal order sustainable in the long term. At the same time, there was an attempt to make China a state capable of facing any external challenges. The all-inclusive ideal of *tianxia* was originally intended to "make *tianxia* one family, and the Central State one person."[6] But with the eclipse of the Zhou *tianxia* system, the "no outside" ideal was reduced to just half of this ideal and became instead a principle for incorporating the interior plurality of China. And it is precisely this principle that effected the inclusion of *tianxia* as a pervasive feature of Chinese political reality.

The very character of this *tianxia* order determined that ancient China, from beginning to end, would remain imperfect in its conceptual development; this is because from start to finish, China remained ontically open-ended. This is to say that China could only exist in a process of perpetual change, with "changing" (*yi* 易) itself being its mode of existence. "Change" references the boundless changes of the sustainable *dao* 道, and the shared embodiment of an always changing changelessness. It is for this reason that China became manifest as a way of growing, with the scope of its existence constantly changing. At one time it was the Qin centralized territory; at another time it became the expansive territories of the Tang, Yuan, and Qing dynasties; and at another time manifested as the sixteen states, the Southern-Northern dynasties, the Five Dynasties and Ten Kingdoms, and also as the division of territories between the Song, Liao, Jin, and Western Xia polities. From the Qin-Han period onward, the duration of time that China was divided up into different territories was greater than the period during which it was unified. But throughout this history the ideal of a "Grand Unification" (*dayitong* 大一统) has been an article of faith for Chinese political theology. From a historical perspective, "China" has been a dynamic process of "separation" and "unification," and while the cycle of splitting up and unifying goes on unceasingly, "unification" remains the immanent *telos*. The "Grand Unification" is not just a quest for power but is also a prerequisite for living in peace. According to the ontological principle of the *Book of Changes*, "procreativity" is the basic existential aim. The "procreativity" that is beneficial to the myriad things and for the multitudes is also an enabling condition for a reasonable political state of affairs. Even though faith is an important consideration, it is ultimately necessary to have objective motivating forces serving as decisive factors. Simply believing in an ideal of "Grand Unification" does not provide enough of a compelling explanation for how China has realized its continuous and cohesive being throughout history. There must be some irreplaceable and objective dynamic for this. This is a problem that requires further analysis.

The historical narratives told by present persons typically involves anachronistic "flashbacks" drawn from contemporary experience. Even though we can be using this era's contemporaneity to be raising questions about another era's contemporaneity, still this era's contemporaneity can't be anachronistically inverted to serve another era's contemporaneity. For instance, if we take a contemporary concept to reflect back on and confirm some ancient fact, such anachronism will sever the very veins of history, making history itself into a seamless aggregation of disjointed anecdotes, and losing the coherence of its own claim to historicity. Consider how modern concepts derived from the narrative threads of Western history such as the modern nation-state, nationalism, anti-monarchy, imperialism, and so on have a natural connection with Western history. But to use these same concepts to interpret Chinese history would snap the threads of its internal historicity. Even though the narrative of post-1911 China is to a large degree a story of becoming a part of a Western-dominated global history (perhaps contemporary China, after breaking with this imperialist history can give rise to world-historical renewal and progressive growth), but if we simply take ancient China's narrative and use Western threads to give it an anachronistic reconstruction, ultimately we would lose all coherence.

The spiritual world of China was born from the techniques of shamanism and matured into a kind of historical consciousness. This is what Chen Mengjia referred to as the developmental transition "from shamans to historians."[7] According to the research of Zhang Guangzhi (K. C. Chang), at the beginnings of Chinese civilization the spiritually interpretive power of "shamans" and the political leadership of "kings" were unified in one discursive domain. This meant that spiritual power had great significance for political power. And with the emergence of writing, "history" took on a much stronger spiritual-interpretive power. Due to this dynamic, eventually the official historians and the shamans inhabited one body.[8] Li Zehou thinks that with the transformation from "shamanism" to the emergence of "history," there was ultimately the appearance of a historical consciousness that became a leading force in the spiritual tradition of China and that this historical consciousness is key to understanding Chinese civilization. Li calls this the "shamanistic-historical tradition."[9] In seeking an existential interpretive power from history, China's method of reflecting on existence took a historicist direction, and "being" got understood as "becoming." By way of contrast, Western thinking from the Greeks onward tended to take a logical-conceptual approach to reflecting on existence, wherein existence must rely upon some eternal, substantial concept for its sustenance. In contrast, China's spiritual world took history as its measure, wherein the meaning of all existents gets disclosed in their very historicity. The phrase "the Six Classics are all history" expresses this point well.[10]

The *Spring and Autumn Annals*, as interpreted by Confucius, holds this meaning as well—the idea that the historical ontology of "is" has implicated within it the axiological significance of "ought" (*dao* 道). The grand moral meanings, as found within all sorts of historical narratives, can be widely divergent and each interpretation of "orthodoxy" can be used to prop up any particular historical ideology. But what constitutes a persuasive argument for orthodoxy cannot simply be one's own personal narrative; otherwise, it would always remain an argument stemming from an ineffective relativism. Although subtle discourses can express great meanings, great meaning cannot be self-confirming. Sima Qian's thinking of "changing continuity" (*tongbian* 通变) would seem to get closer to the transformations of history itself and is a better approximation of the processual, "becoming" ontology of the way (*dao* 道). Here I don't intend to cite any specific narratives to delimit an orthodox concept of history, but instead I just want to frame the analysis as to what sorts of collective activities have shaped China. This is to say, I am not using historicist narratives and a set of dogmatic values that come with such an understanding to say what China is definitively like, but rather I am trying to understand, from a standpoint internal to the games that various historical actors have chosen to participate in, how China has become what it is. With such a method in mind, the process of China's growth can be understood as one long and continuous game. Regarding China's changes and transformations, everyone has their different evaluative standpoints, but the key to understanding the formation of China is to enter into the reasonable doings and undergoings of the historical actors. It is the doings of these actors that have defined the problems, goals, and character of the game. Along with this reasonable vision of the historical actors, there are two problems that are important to consider: (1) China has been a continuously existing entity. Hence, what are the structures and dynamics of power behind China's continuity? (2) Since the genes that tend to provide optimal benefits for life typically get reproduced, what are China's historically surviving genes?

Because historical fortunes are different, early Chinese politics started as world politics, taking the *tianxia* system as a political framework for constructing state and family order. Western politics, by contrast, started in the city-state (*polis*). The differences and similarities between these two distinct political "genes" might be mutually compensatory, but they cannot be unified as one coherent type. China, from the Qin and Han dynasties onward, became a politics of the "nation-state" (*guojia* 国家), but this cannot be equated with the Western conception of nation-state. This is because China was never a *polis*, and is not an ethno-nation-state, nor is it akin to the Western concept of empire. Although ancient China and this concept of empire have some superficial similarities (for instance, not having legally defined borders), in fact they are quite distinct in spirit. There is only a superficial likeness between "empire" and ancient China, since it didn't develop the defining characteristics of imperialism. Even though there was surely much territorial expansion, such expansions themselves were never the ideal aim of the establishment of "China" as a political entity, nor was it the motivating force behind the emergence of a unified state. Perhaps one might say that China was forced into a role of "a major leading power,"[11] but this kind of discourse fails to express the characteristics of China's national politics.

Another view might take China as fundamentally different from an ethno-nation-state and instead consider it to be a "civilization nation."[12] Such a perspective became popular in both Western and Chinese discourse. China is of course not an ethno-nation-state, but to define China as a "civilization nation" also might give rise to misunderstanding. If civilization can define China, then why can't civilization be used to define other countries? Is it the case that other civilizations lack the necessary characteristics to uniquely define their own self-identity? How are multicultural and multiethnic states like Russia, India, and the United States to be understood? Moreover, using ethnicity to define a nation-state has its clear political ramifications, but if we use civilization to define a nation-state, it becomes very difficult to achieve a similar degree of clarity with respect to political characteristics. Since a nation-state is a political being, defining a nation-state ultimately must express the characteristic nature of the political. If we only follow anthropological characteristics in attempting to understand China, then Wang Mingming's concept of "civilization body" seems more on point than "civilization nation."[13]

To differentiate China's unique characteristics from an ethno-nation-state, it is necessary to use the Chinese concept of the political as a guiding principle. This is to recognize that Chinese politics emerges from the gene of the *tianxia* concept and contains the principles of "no outside," "all-inclusiveness," and "compatibility." In this sense, China is a "microcosm" of *tianxia* because China is a "world-patterned state" that takes *tianxia* to be internal to its structure. Moreover, if we take the modern idea of an ethnostate as a juxtaposed concept, then China should be considered an "inclusive state." But such concepts are only appropriately applied to ancient China. When it comes to modern China, there now exists a dual character: traditional Chinese sensibilities with the addition of modern national characteristics. Modern China has augmented the ancient Chinese genes with characteristics of a modern nation-state, forming a contemporary sovereign state. But still China is not an ethnostate. Many debates regarding modern Chinese characteristics rest upon an overly narrow interpretation of the concept of a modern nation-state—namely, that a modern nation must be an ethnostate. Actual conditions are such that any modern sovereign state must at least belong to one of the following two basic types: (1) an ethnostate (e.g., the various states of Europe) or (2) united republics (e.g., United States, China, Russia, India). United republics all share in having legally defined borders, legally determined sovereignty, and other characteristics of modern nation-states, but they have multiethnic and multicultural differences that distinguishes them from any ethnostate. Judging from current trends, more and more ethnostates are evolving into unified republics. Many Western European countries are seeing a rapid increase of Arabic, African, Eastern European, and East Asian immigrants. Hence it is already hard to say that there are any strict ethnostates in any original sense. Thus united republics will likely become the predominant mode of constituting modern states.

Because Chinese politics have continuously included the *tianxia* gene, *tianxia* has already been condensed as part of a process of becoming China. Ancient China didn't experience the need to become an ethnostate, nor make any appeals to ethnonationalism. It was only at the end of the Qing dynasty, facing the colonialist challenges of modern Western nation-states, that China in attempting to catch up with the West began thinking about ethnostates and nationalism. Liang Qichao was perhaps the earliest to promote learning about Western ethnonationalism and corresponding ideals of an ethnostate as a way to convert China into a modern nation-state.[14] Ancient China didn't really possess a concept of sovereignty; rather, it operated with more pragmatic conceptions of "political power." In the absence of a legally defined boundary, so-called "territory" was in fact always a function of changing power dynamics. Hence ancient Chinese wars were not ethnic conflicts, but rather the results of political struggles for power. The Liao general who fought against the Song dynasty, Han De, was ethnically Han. And the Yuan general who conquered the Song dynasty, Zhang Hongfan, was also ethnically Han. If we use modern standards of ethnonationalism, these two generals would be considered traitors. But within the context of Chinese history, they were both born and raised in the northern dynasties, and the northern dynasties were also part of China, just as the Song dynasty was a part of the southern dynasties of China. It was only that Zhang Hongfan believed that the heavenly mandate had shifted to the Yuan, while Wen Tianxiang believed it should remain with the Song.

If ethnic conflict had such little relevance, what then drove the patterns of dividing and unifying ancient China? How did these dynamic historical forces take shape? China is a collection of "myriad peoples"—in modern parlance, a "multiethnic" place, and Chinese history has the power of unifying these myriad peoples, where such processes of unification are a complex and multithreaded narrative tapestry. Every kind of continuous national history has some major events or issues that will repeat over and over again. What causal reasons then might preclude a situation of disintegration from occurring again? The simplest explanation is that it all goes back to "tradition." China's unbroken existential continuity is often explained by returning to the traditions of Chinese culture, and this is again often explained by reference solely to the Confucian tradition. In this mode of explanation the Confucian tradition gets understood primarily as having displayed an illustrious morality that accounts for Chinese uniqueness. But this cultural mythology actually gives rise to some serious suspicions. First, what historical evidence is available to prove that Chinese people have a higher standard of morality than any other people? This is one glaring problem. And I'm afraid we can't overlook the gaps between actual historical practices and idealized moral education.[15] For this reason we need to recognize that in truth there is a more powerful, motivating force shaping Chinese historical practices than mere morality.

Another reason for suspicion is that Confucian political ideals only became ascendant as a governing political ideology after the Song dynasty, whereas China's general mode of being took form much earlier. This means that we must seek elsewhere for an explanation of China's distinctive political concepts. Confucianism is of course China's most important tradition, but the plurality of Chinese traditions must also be recognized as an obvious fact. A further problem remains that, even if traditions are sufficient to explain historical dynamics, traditions themselves are not ultimately *explanans*, but are themselves *explandandum* in need of explication. We must ask why traditions have become what they are? Wherein lies the attractive force in particular traditions? And what are the limits of transmission and the attendant cultural boundaries that constitute any particular tradition?

Historical events can only be narrated as stories. And behind every narrative there is always an internal plot structure and historically motivating power. What are the motive forces operating in causing particular events or situations to continuously recur throughout history? This is a question in need of explanation. Without a doubt, historical events have their unique creativity while undergoing myriad transformations, but historicity still implies a kind of overarching structure and motivating force that can explain the repetitive continuities in the ongoing myriad transformations of narrative events. This kind of immanent logic of motivating force determines what kind of game is being played in any given historical situation, and what kind of conduct can be expected to ensue wave after historical wave. Given that historicity is not only directly made manifest in mainstream historical narratives, but is always also implicitly stored in the "antinarratives" or "reversal narrativities" of dominant historical discourse, historicity always courses through history via the repetitions of difference—that is, via the repetition of unrepeatable events. It is for this reason that historicity has a metaphysical import and can contribute to explaining why something is what it is. Whenever the temporality of an existent has a self-conscious motivating structure shaping its own historicity, then and only then does such ontic temporality have a historicist ontology. There are many different ways of understanding historicity: for instance, there is transcendental theology and there is natural theology. If history is understood as having some ultimate aim, then historicity is on a kind of teleological mission. But if history is understood as an unlimited process of development, then historicity has a kind of processual existence seeking its own endurance as a mode of growth. This latter mode is precisely the Chinese historical path—that is, historicity as ceaseless procreativity and the daily renewal of meaning.

The direct motive force of existence lies in seeking out resources for survival. This is a natural condition. But whenever an existence seeks to arrive at a stable and reliable mode of surviving, or in other words, whenever an existence seeks to occupy the future, there must be a striving for political resources. It is thus that being enters a political condition. We might say that merely seeking for survival is, in the beginning, an economic problem, but when seeking for a sustainable future that has not been stolen by others it becomes a political problem. The purely economic motive of sustaining life only entails a relationship between humans and nature, and as such, belongs to a natural process that does not really give rise to history. But as soon as the question of who is benefiting from certain arrangements gives rise to the problematics of power, then we've entered into a game of human-to-human relations. It is in this sense then that history must always start with politics. Power means the establishment of social order and is concerned with taking available resources and transforming them into controlled resources. The continuation of life thereby becomes something that can be reliably anticipated. In this sense, the political is an attempt to use order to control the future. Whenever any order attempts to determine the future it necessarily follows that such order will be creating a history. From these considerations we can understand Eric Voegelin's claim that "the order of history emerges from the history of order."[16]

If a certain historical order becomes a political resource sought after by the multitudes, then this dynamic can become a game in which all participate, and from this shared participation there opens up a shared history. With respect to China, what kind of historical order was there and what kind of game emerged that could make Chinese history into a shared history of myriad peoples? Whenever a historical order, or a particular game, attracts the attention of myriad peoples, it can become a kind of "critical point"—here I am borrowing a concept from Thomas C. Schelling's game theory. A "critical point" refers to a decision made by persons without having engaged in individual deliberations or having explicitly come to some form of collective agreement.[17] Here, such a critical point can be appealed to in explaining the emergence of a shared history.

Once there was a shared common sense (it is hard to verify its original source), China was formed as the Central Plain cultures that continually expanded radially into the periphery zones. Zhang Guangzhi (K. C. Chang) maintains that the idea of the Central Plain cultures expanding outward is a misconception. In fact, the swirling interaction was a matter of all of the regional cultures having come together in various forms of mutual engagement. One reason for this misconception was that archaeological interest had focused solely on the Central Plain and thereby "tended to give an illusion of support to the hypothesis of the Central Plain nuclear status as a center of diffusion to the peripheral areas, where developmental sequences are often still incomplete and, thus, seem secondary and derivative."[18]

Reflected in new stone age civilization, there was a high degree of interaction among a plurality of different cultures. Zhang Guangzhi's observation is perhaps more accurate for this early period, but from the Xia, Shang, and Zhou periods onward the fact of the matter is that the Central Plain had become the core of China. How then to understand the nature of this core and the relationship between the center and periphery is the basic problem. In other words, how should we understand China as encompassing the Central Plain and the various surrounding regions as one holistic entity? This is the fundamental question. Within the process of China's formation there was certainly intensive cultural exchange, as well as a focal center expanding radially.

But these two phenomena are still insufficient to serve as conclusive explanation—for the mutual interaction among cultures cannot provide a definite explanation for the formation of a holistic conception of China. This is because such integration does not necessarily lead to unification, as there is always the possibility of each party taking what they want while maintaining their own independence. And the radial model of the center extending into the periphery cannot provide a definitive explanation for the formation of a holistic China either. This is because the unceasing influx of surrounding ethnic groups into the Central Plain is a historical fact that is not easy to ignore. But even more important to note is that the expansion process did not itself necessarily guarantee unity, since it might've met with resistance or even total defeat. In theory, what can guarantee the formation of a great model of governance and be sufficient to explain the basic reasons for the existence of such culture is an innate power of attraction. Confucius stated this principle as "those nearby are pleased and those from afar are attracted."[19] This is why I've chosen to refer to the model of the "focal point" to explain the basic reason for China's formation—that is, there must have been some kind of power of attraction that facilitated China becoming a shared selection.

Chinese history has itself had many focal points in need of further research. Here we want to analyze the focal point of a political game that was pervasive in ancient Chinese history—that is, the game of "stag hunting for *tianxia*" (*tianxia zhulu* 天下逐鹿) which took the Central Plain as its core. This structural dynamic was like a whirlpool with enormous centripetal and centrifugal force. Most of those involved could not resist the attractive pull of the whirlpool and one by one of their own accord entered the game as competitors. And with so many being drawn into the whirlpool game, the game gradually expanded and ultimately stabilized to form the vast realm of China.

Geographically, from the northern deserts and grasslands to south of the Yangtze River, from the vast expanse of territory between the eastern seas and the western regions—this area in total formed an undivided space for "stag hunting." The core area of this vast territory was commonly referred to as the Central Plain (*zhongyuan* 中原). This was the most developed region of early China due to its geographical and climatic conditions, and relative ease of transport. Not only was this area the economic and political center, it also became a cultural center. As the ultimate source of power that could be won from the game, the Central Plain became the contested site fought for in stag hunting for *tianxia*. "Stag hunting in the Central Plain" has become an expression that so movingly captures the game of Chinese history. It is for this reason Zhao Hui thinks that this expression effectively reflects the trajectory of China's mainstream historical development taking the Central Plain as its core.[20] If the competitors with adequate strength all had an interest in stag hunting in the Central Plain, then the additional questions we must address are: Why did the stag hunting game on the Central Plain take on a whirlpool model, even to the point of providing an explanation for the continuity of Chinese history itself? Why did stag hunting in the Central Plain become the centripetal force animating the search for a great unity as opposed to the different players remaining satisfied with a balance among a plurality of separate territories? And finally, what were the special resources of the Central Plain that were considered so invaluable as to be fought over?

Zhang Guangzhi (K. C. Chang) believes that China's "civilizational power lies in the combination of effective governance and material wealth."[21] The government's pursuit of wealth is a constant motivating factor, but there is a problem. Even though the central part of the Yellow River basin (i.e., the Central Plain) had a relatively good arrangement with respect to material civilization, it was neither an overly impressive arrangement nor was it the best in terms of technological advance. As archaeological evidence has shown, there were many relatively condensed and localized cultural sites existing in various locales in early China stretching from the belt of the northern regions of inner Mongolia and Liaoning to the southern Yangtze River basin. Each region had its own unique materials, cultural resources, and geographic strengths, with the levels of technological advance being relatively on par, and with the general quality of life being about the same. So why then would any region be dissatisfied with what it had and seek to go stag hunting in the Central Plain?

The simple fact that the Central Plain had a relative abundance of material resources is not adequate to explain why this region became the incontrovertible site that everyone sought after in the stag hunt. In particular, it is difficult to explain how the Central Plain could draw one competitor after another into the stag hunt. What then was really the decisive advantage offered on the Central Plain? This question merits further inquiry. Having abundant material resources and its serving as a pivotal site for effective transportation were certainly important assets, but it would seem that these alone couldn't have been the ultimately deciding factors. Perhaps we should seek to analyze the attraction of the Central Plain beyond its material conditions. Fundamentally different from the consumeristic values of a materialistic world, a spiritual world is always qualitatively "value added." This means that the more that a spiritual world is activated, the more it is able to augment its value and its attractiveness, and the more it can draw in the hearts and minds of people. Thus there is good reason to believe that the special position of the Central Plain must lie in the fact that its attendant spiritual world was the most replete in value and hence worth fighting over. This is because it presented a spiritual world that anyone could use to initially gain and subsequently maintain political power.

The reason that the spiritual world of the Central Plain had such evocative power and universal appeal has to do with the following determinative factors:

1. *Chinese characters*. This is the form of writing developed during the earliest history of the Central Plain. It was a knowledge system for recording and preserving wisdom and information within the China region and was able to serve as the literary conveyance of complex ideas and rich cultural narratives throughout history. For this reason spiritual China had Chinese characters as a vehicle that served as early China's most effective means of transmitting wisdom and knowledge.[22]

2. *A system of thought*. The culture of the Central Plain at the time presented a system of thought that had the most capacious explanatory force and largest capacity for critical reflection. Systemic reflection upon human conduct and the explanation of the myriad events within a coherent world-historical view can be found in texts such as the *Book of Changes*, the *Exalted Documents*, the *Zhou Rites*, the *Book of Songs*, the *Spring and Autumn Annals*, and many other early texts. This meant that the system of thinking on the Central Plain had the capacity to organize space and time as well as to facilitate a shared historical awareness and collective consciousness. It also had the capacity for large scale social organization and for creating institutions, while at the same time having its own interpretive resources for legitimizing historical, social, and institutional configurations of power. It was for this reason that the Central Plain became the most advantageous resource for realizing a Chinese spirituality.

3. *The Zhou dynasty formulation of the concept of* tianxia *was also a deciding factor*. The ideals of "all-inclusiveness" and "no outside" implicated in the *tianxia* concept signified the optimal parameters of compatibility. It did not exclude the participation of anyone and presupposed the promise that any individual persons or groups could participate in the game. And it was precisely because of this universal inclusiveness that it maintained an equal degree of attraction for everyone, and could thus serve as an equitable political resource. To complement this, the Zhou dynasty concept of *tianming* conveyed the idea that the possession of virtuosity serves as the sole legitimate reason for holding *tianxia*. This could be construed as more or less equivalent to legitimizing political revolution and hence provides an excellent reason for stag hunting. The *tianxia* concept is a good example of transforming exceptionalism into

universalism. Even though the *tianxia* concept was originally a special innovation of the Zhou court, the conceptual content of *tianxia* is replete with universal significance. It is for this reason that it received universal acceptance and has become a resource for political theology.[23]

4. *The snowball effect of political theology.* To protect their legitimate and stable use of the advantageous resources, virtually all of those victorious in the stag hunt appropriated the legacy of the narrative of "heavenly mandate" (*tianming* 天命) that had been created by the Zhou. It was by taking their own royal court as a chapter in the multivolume saga of this enduring political legacy that they could make their claim to political legitimacy. And it was in this way that a rich and unbroken historical tradition itself became a universal political theology, and of all who participated there was no one who did not want to claim this ready-made, advantageous resource.

There are perhaps even more factors, but these decisive spiritual conditions are already sufficient to support the metaphor of the whirlpool model of stag hunting in the Central Plain. Initially, as evidenced in history, the whirlpool effect took hold in its continuing centripetal pull and was the political advantage for securing the optimal resources that would draw participants into the game of stag hunting on the Central Plain. In this dynamic a whirlpool was created by drawing in a continuing increase in political advantages. As the centrifugal girth of this whirlpool continued to expand, the politically advantageous resources also continued to increase, thereby strengthening the effects of its centripetal draw. It was this continuing whirlpool effect drawing more of *tianxia* into the game of stag hunting that ultimately created China. And it was the openness of this whirlpool game—originating in the inclusive concept of *tianxia*—that ensured that China would always remain a concept open to continual growth.

12 A Condensed Version of *Tianxia*

Archaeologists typically view the New Stone Age (approximately twelve thousand years ago) as an early formative period of civilizations. When compared with the Tigris, Euphrates, and Egyptian civilizations, the formation of Chinese civilization doesn't appear all that early.[1] And on the basis of recent excavated cultural artefacts and technologies, it would seem that Chinese civilization emerged relatively independently. By the middle of the New Stone Age, the Central Plain region had already started intensive agricultural production, although it was limited to a mixed economy of farming, shepherding, fishing, and hunting. Crafting technologies were already able to produce ceramics and jade implements, and there was a primitive animal husbandry industry as well.[2] During the latter period of the New Stone Age, sericulture and bronze vessels appeared, and of particular interest here, large human settlements to the extent of walled-fortifications developed. In the southern part of today's Shanxi in the Linfen basin, the Ceramic Temple (Taosi) ruins are the remains of a large city that has an area approaching 280,000 square meters.[3] A large city of this scale has been considered to be the domain of a monarch (but this period is even earlier than the Xia dynasty, so it would perhaps be one of the legendary sage-kings), and among the excavated findings there appear to be some of the earliest writing symbols.[4]

According to the research of Zhang Guangzhi (K. C. Chang), during the late New Stone Age the Central Plain had already acquired the unique characteristics of "China" as a cultural basis. He believes that at the time there was already millet, rice, and sorghum cultivation as well as pig, dog, cow, sheep, and horse domestication. Also, there was tamped-earth architecture. And in addition to sericulture and hemp production, there were also ceramics, wood-working and bronze-based metallurgy, oracle bone divination, and ideographs. All of these features defined the unique characteristics of the core elements of early Chinese culture in the Yellow River basin.[5] In addition, excavated relics from Yangshuo, Daxi, and Hongshan have shown that from Mongolia to the Central Plain through to the Yangtze River basin, the "dragon" or *long* 龙 was used as a symbol. (Mongolia's Hongshan's jade dragon is perhaps the most archaic of the recovered *long* symbols, but according to Xu Hong's research findings, the "Green Pine Stone" dragon carving excavated at Erlitou is the most authentic and detailed expression of a "Chinese dragon").[6] This would mean that within such a wide expanse of geography there was already a great degree of cultural commonality.[7] Zhang Guangzhi infers that from around 4,000 BCE the regional cultures of northern and southern reaches had "already become interconnected as an even greater and more dynamic, interactive cultural sphere."[8]

According to legend, the period around 2000 BCE marks the beginning of Chinese monarchies or dynasties, but for a long while empirical verification for the first dynasty, the Xia, had been lacking. But in the 1960s there began to be a lot of discoveries at the remains of the Erlitou site that would seem to offer confirmation of the existence of the Xia culture (carbon-10 dating would then put the legendary Xia dynasties at around 1900 to 1500 BCE).[9] However there are also some archeologists who believe that this is just early Shang relics or materials from the Xia-Shang transition period. As of now, there is no settled consensus. And whether or not the existence of a Xia culture could confirm the existence of a Xia dynasty awaits further empirical support.[10] The Erlitou remains are located in Luoyang's Pingyuan region. From ancient times this region has been regarded as the center of *tianxia*. Including the Xia, Shang, and Zhou periods, more than half of all Chinese dynasties have been established here. Before Erlitou culture, Luoyang with its surrounding regions was the cultural center during the New Stone Age, and with the sites of both Yangshuo and Longshan cultures in this area, we can witness a continuity of culture. According to Xu Hong, the Erlitou remains should be considered the prototype of China—the earliest "China."[11] An important source of confirmation is that at the heart of the Erlitou remains is a large-scale foundation for what would seem to have been a king's palace. The surface area is about 100,000 square meters with the central palace occupying about 10,000 square meters. It is easy to see that such an architectural layout is quite similar to, although much simpler than, the concept of the Forbidden City.[12] In 1963 in Shaanxi a bronze vessel was unearthed called "Ever so Reverenced" (*hezun* 何尊). On this vessel is an official Zhou seal script inscription announcing King Cheng of Zhou's order to move the capital to the east. As part of this official edict is the phrase "I make my dwelling in these 'Central States' (*zhongguo* 中国)." This is the earliest known use of the expression "central states" that is the current term used for "China." The "central states" referenced on the *hezun* bronze vessel are indeed the Erlitou remains in the Luoyang basin.[13]

The abundance of the relics recovered from the Erlitou remains make it clear that Erlitou political power (whether this was the late Xia or early Shang government still awaits further confirmation) was already in control of a great quantity of resources and technologies. And it was making use of agriculture, animal husbandry, hunting, and fishing as a mixed economy. Jade pieces, pottery, bronze vessels, silk products, and fermented spirits were all in use as either ritual implements or objects of daily use, and they even had two-wheeled chariots. Since many sea shells were also found among the remains, it is thought that perhaps the Central Plain already had interchange with the more distant coastal peoples (since Erlitou is about 600 kilometers from the nearest ocean access).[14] But according to Xu Hong's research, the sea shells found at Erlitou are from tropical seas and are known as "shells of the immortals," more commonly referred to as "treasure shells." Thus it is not possible that these shells came from an interchange with the peoples on the Yellow Sea and East China Sea. But "if we say that the sea shells came from the southern seas of China and were transmitted northwards, why is it the case that in all the other regions of southeast China there are no archaeological traces—this doesn't make sense."[15]

It is possible that the Erlitou sea shells could have come from the distant Indian Ocean carried by northern nomadic peoples passing through the great grasslands of Eurasia and were thus regarded as a valuable treasure. The most interesting facets of Erlitou culture can also be the most controversial. Are the symbols etched into the pottery an early form of writing? The symbols discovered on Erlitou pottery resemble a writing script, but there is no way of deciphering it. The New Stone Age symbols are possibly part of the origins of later script. According to structural similarities, Xu Hong believes that Erlitou symbolic etchings and the later oracle bone writings and bronze inscriptions have an originary relationship. But whether this was sufficiently developed as a mature linguistic system must wait upon the discovery of fuller documents.[16] Zhang Guangzhi thinks that these sporadically occurring symbols fall short of a written language.[17] Later than Erlitou culture by several hundred years is the Yin-Shang culture that definitely has a mature writing system. In addition to the oracle bones serving as confirmation, there is also the ancient records of the *Exalted Documents* stating that "only with our Yin ancestors were there written archives and statutes."[18] This makes it clear that the Yin-Shang writing had already advanced to the extent that it could record institutional regulations and record historical events. Since the process of developing a writing system requires sufficient time to mature, archaeologists conjecture that "we cannot assume the Xia dynasty was not making use of writing."[19] Early on, Cheng Mengjia inferred that the origin of Chinese writing lies "at least 3,500 years ago, and at the earliest could go back more than 4,000 years" and should be included as part of the "unique culture of the Shang peoples."[20] This account seems accurate, and perhaps might require only slight revision.

It can be said that the Erlitou culture already included the basic elements or "genes" of the Central Plain culture. Even though it would be difficult to give a full account of the cultural topography of the Central Plain, we can select some genetic elements as representative. The architecture of the king's court in the Erlitou remains is an early expression of the "central axis concept" that has continued for several millennia. Xu Hong states that this was the earliest Chinese "forbidden city."[21] As a metaphorical expression with theological implications, the central axis concept is pervasive in a great many spatial designs in China—from houses, court yards, palaces, and city layouts, and even extends to an understanding of the state and *tianxia*. The symmetrical pattern of rooms laid out on a central axis is the family home which is then a microcosmic model of the state, and taken even further, is a microscopic model of *tianxia*. In addition, the Erlitou architectural structures were an early prototype for the basic style of traditional Chinese architectural forms over the millennia. According to Liang Sicheng's synopsis, China's central beam column design has a distinct outward adumbration—with the flying eaves and pointed roofs above and the many layered stairs set off from the foundation below.[22] Within such a distinctive architectural style there are adumbrated certain metaphysical characteristics: The four-cornered covered room symbolizes heaven, the thick foundation symbolizes earth, and since humans dwell between heaven and earth, the idea of "heaven-earth-human" is also conveyed as a triadic relational structure of significance. For humankind, heaven and earth are its most vast dwelling space, and a room serves as a microcosm of the same heaven and earth. For the dwelling to fully capture the meaning of heaven and earth is in part what it means for human beings "to correlate with heaven" as described in the *Zhongyong*.[23]

The Central Plain culture didn't have a transcendental religion but did express a theological understanding of nature. Nature is the ultimate criterion for the unfolding processes of the myriad things, with the way of nature serving as its own standard. This is what the *Laozi* meant by "*dao* emulating what is so-of-itself." For something to be able to take itself as its ultimate standard is the mark of an essential sacredness. Thus we can say that for China spontaneous nature is a theological concept. To become continuous with nature (the concept of "correlating with heaven") is the theological standard for taking the measure of the human world. To take heaven and earth as reduplicating the human home has the symbolic meaning of correlating with heaven and is also the point of ritual practices of reverencing heaven. From this we can speculate that the Chinese conception of "family" (*jia* 家) is not only a reference to hearth and home but is at the same time a concept of natural theology. Heaven and earth expand infinitely to encompass the myriad things and events, and the human family that takes heaven and earth as its standard reduplicates the infinite compass of heaven and earth. Heaven and earth are also reduplicated as the same structure, but on a different scale within the household garden. The household is the microcosmic model of family, while the state is a comparatively larger model of family, and *tianxia* is the family of all people. This kind of reduplication of the structure of heaven and earth is basically the same as the reduplication of the structure of the theological character of heaven and earth. Thus the bi-directional circle of "*tianxia*—state—family—state—*tianxia*" if developed further is the Chinese concept of numinosity (*shenxing* 神性) and is replete with political theological significance.

Religiosity and theological experience seem to be natural feelings for all of humanity without exception. Religiousness arises from spiritual beliefs that resolve doubts and can often be a source of cultural stability. It is difficult to imagine cultural continuity without religiousness, even though such religiousness need not amount to institutionalized or organized religion. The easiest mode of religiousness to understand is the transcendental, and for this reason most religions have posited a transcendent and superordinate being. What is so surprising is that in the continuing stability of China's indigenous culture, there has never been a transcendental religion. Scholars have offered many explanations for this mysterious fact, such as Liang Shuming's "morality does the work religion" and Cai Yuanpei's "aesthetic education does the work of religion." While morality and a culture of poesy certainly have a high place in China's cultural *dispositif*, they still do not have the status of a supreme divinity. Unlike the *dao* of spontaneous nature, morality and a culture of poesy cannot be taken as a supreme or ultimate standard. This is because they are lacking in numinosity and some uniform standard of judgment (obviously morality and aesthetic judgment are sites of disagreement and contention). Hence they cannot really do the work of religion.

For ancient China the top candidate for numinosity would be the way of nature, the next closest to nature's way would be the concept of *tianxia*, and following that would probably be the emblem of "China" numinously reduplicating the order of heaven and earth. If we can say that ancient China's moral beliefs are expressed through a kind of religious numinosity, this is because the way of humanity has always been regarded as corresponding to the way of heaven. Numinosity resides in nature, and morality is the surrogate expression of nature's numinosity. Similarly, Chinese poesy is the symbolic expression of nature. The celebrated meaning of the sun and the moon, the rivers and mountains, and the grasses and trees does not lie merely in the aesthetic results of capturing the beauty of land-scapes, but is more fully expressed in the numinosity of nature itself—that is, in the numinosity of nature as it is conveyed in ordinary life, in family and state, and throughout the ancestral lands.

The Chinese conception of numinosity, or what can be explained as the concept of China as the "middle kingdom," leads to a deeply rooted question. If the concept of China merely has the geographical sense of occupying a central place in the world, it would only be the enunciation of a subjective feeling that every place has in the world and hence would not be worthy of taking seriously. But because the concept of China also has theological significance, it should be taken seriously as a heterodox or "pagan" alternative to the monotheistic religions. Confucianism takes its moral precepts to be what makes Chinese culture different from the fundamentals of other cultures, but in fact Confucian morality should not really be regarded as a distinctive ethical theory. Matteo Ricci experienced this in China at the end of the Ming dynasty when he thought that the Confucian and Christian moral teachings were largely commensurable, and thus that China would be a great place to propagate the Christian gospel. The problems the missionaries encountered though in convert-ing the Chinese had nothing to do with differences in ethical theory, and everything to do with profound differences in worldviews. The Chinese Christian converts continued to believe in Confucianism, Buddhism, and Daoism as well as the divine agency of ancestors and even in the folk God of Wealth. And the missionaries had a hard time accepting this kind of "disingenuousness" in matters of religious belief. In actuality the basic problems of life in every place are of the same kind, and the moral dif-ferences are not all that pronounced, so it would seem that ethical theory cannot be appealed to as the ultimate explanation for China's essential uniqueness.

The process whereby the concept of China became religiously numi-nous has its own defining thread. In the imaginary of ancient China, the center of *tianxia* was China. This conceptual image probably had its ori-gins in certain geographical sensibilities. As noted above, earliest "China" was the plains of Luoyang, and somewhat later expanded to include the region stretching from Xi'an and Jin'nan to Luoyang. This is the region that came to be referred to as "the Central Plain." This territory extending in all directions served the function of locating geographical centrality. Even though the concept of China had already borrowed from the temporal and spatial arrangements of heaven and earth to imaginatively express a naturalistic conception of numinosity, during the Xia and Shang periods it probably had not yet developed to the point of being a concept of political theology. The Zhou dynasty though did establish this "worldly" *tianxia* system. The *tianxia* system, with the myriad states and China inhabiting the central position as the ancestral state, had nested layers of hierarchy all of a similar structure. When *tianxia* converged to become China, China carried on the *tianxia* gene and became a state that had a world-encompassing structure. This China carried a *tianxia* nature with the natural theology of reduplicating the orders of heaven and earth, and at the same time took on the concept of a political theology reduplicating the order of *tianxia*.

The evolution of a distinctive spatio-temporality for China was simultaneously an evolution of the concept of space-time. The original meaning of "state" (*guo* 国) was "capital city." The ideographic significance of the character is a representation of a weapon defending the surrounding city walls. The land that a "state" encompasses is not just the walled city but also the "suburbs "and the "wilds" beyond. The surrounding regions of the walled city were called the "suburbs" that included many small populations centers called "villages." Those dwelling in these places had the rights and responsibilities of "citizens." The "wilds" were the regions outside of the suburbs as large swaths of arable land, and those occupying these regions had no political rights as commoners or "unrefined" persons.[24] China as *zhongguo* was the capital of the ancestral state and was also the site of the imperial court capital. King Cheng of the Zhou dynasty proclaimed the establishment of a new capital city: "I take this *zhongguo* as my dwelling place." This *zhongguo* was Luoyang. Later the conception of *zhongguo* expanded from the ancestral state's capital to include the whole of the ancestral state—the so-called "king's domain." This realm expanded even further, probably during the Spring and Autumn period, with *zhongguo* coming to refer to the whole of the Central Plain. The Zhou dynasty system embraced within *zhongguo* a complex network of clan relations and many vassal states belonging to the music and ritual culture, including today's Yellow River basin of Henan, Shaanxi, Shanxi, Shandong, and Hebei as distinct from the Man and Yi cultural regions of the south and the northern regions respectively. This meant that in addition to a geographic reference, "China" (*zhongguo* 中国) also had cultural connotations. In the Yangtze River basin, the cultures of the Man-Yi vassal states (the Jin, Chu, Wu, and Yue kingdoms) became increasingly similar to that of the Central Plain cultures to the point of having the actual strength to contend for hegemony over the Central Plain.

Thus the concept of "China" expanded even further to include the Yangtze River basin. With more and more regions being drawn into the stag hunting game on the Central Plain, the concept of China continued to expand to the extent of including much more territory than even today's China. The greatest territorial expansion occurred during the Yuan dynasty extending to the Pamir Mountains in the west, the Sea of Japan in the east, Siberia in the north, and all the way to the South Seas in the south. The next largest expansion with a relatively stable boundary was the territory of the Qing dynasty, including the same lands but with the addition of Mongolia and a small part of Siberia. The concept of China was defined by the whirlpool effect resulting from the stag hunting for *tianxia*, which is to say that that the scale of China was determined by how many participants were drawn into the stag hunting game. And at the same time, the whirlpool effect of the stag hunting game made China a pluralistic yet unified culture.

The dynamic method by which China's culture was formed might be called "transforming" (*hua* 化). *Hua* is transformational change (变易) and is more than just one party being altered but rather always signifies mutual change. Thus *hua* needs to be distinguished from religious conversion. *Hua* is when a diversity of cultures together reconstructs existing intercultural orders. Perhaps the closest thing to *hua* could be the models of genetic mutation and replication. In this sense, perhaps, we can say that the Chinese concept of being good at "transforming" involves a sort of biological factor. Or we might borrow Nicholas Taleb's concept and say that China is "antifragile" in the sense of rejecting the conserving of a supposedly original form and instead is most adept at optimizing changing patterns within conditions of disorder.[25] The ameliorative power of China is related to faith in *tianxia*. And only a principle of *tianxia* can provide a mutually reinforcing rational and legitimate account wherein the *tianxia* gene resides in the concept of China.

In the process of the mutual transformation among diverse ethnicities and cultures, the Central Plain culture always served as a major resource for mutual transformation. Even though the many nomadic pastoralists who entered the Central Plain often preserved some of their original cultures (the Northern Wei Emperor Xiaowen, who totally embraced Hanification, is one counter example), but owing to the fact that these nomadic pastoralists were relatively lacking in quantity and quality of knowledge production in the Central Plain (by this I mean a substantial and comprehensive collection of books and documents, a holistic educational system, and the plurality of various academic disciplines), most cultures quite reasonably decided to accept the relatively advanced and developed cultural sources of the Central Plain. This process at the same time also presented a way of using and advancing the culture of the Central Plain. The meritocratic examination system has been regarded as a singularly Chinese cultural innovation, but in fact Emperor Wen of the Sui dynasty, with his northern nomadic Xianbei bloodline, was actually the creator of this system. Those nomadic pastoralist peoples who entered the Central Plain and ended up promoting Confucianism as a governing ideology did not do so as the result of Han monarchical pressures.

In fact, the kingdoms of the nomadic pastoralists gave to Confucius titles representing at least the same levels of religious reverence as any of the Han regimes. For example, the Han dynasty gave Confucius the title of "Duke" (*gongjue* 公爵) and the Tang dynasty called him "king" (*wang* 王). The Ming dynasty gave him the title of "first teacher" (*xianshi* 先师 as the spiritual leader). But the Western Xia (Tibetans) called Confucius the "Imperial Lord" (*huangdi* 皇帝, which is the highest official title). And the Yuan dynasty (Mongols) called Confucius "king" (*wang* 王), and the Qing dynasty (Manchus) also referred to him as "first teacher" (*xianshi* 先师). Another significant example is that the Yuan dynasty (Mongols) made Cheng-Zhu "neo-Confucianism" an ideological basis for the imperial examination system, while the Song Dynasty itself never gave the Cheng-Zhu philosophical system this kind of prominence.[26] The original milieu in which a culture is produced should not have sole explanatory power, since as soon as a culture is appropriated and "appreciated" by many others, it becomes a shared interpretive resource. The phenomenon of many different peoples participating in the appreciation of the Central Plain culture is similar to the way in which various European countries have drawn upon ancient Greek, Roman, and Jewish cultures.

Cultures transforming each other is an uncontested historical fact. The question of who is dominant in the mutual transformation, however, gives rise to the sensitive issue of who represents Chinese orthodoxy. The sensitive nature of this question arises from historical context. It was usually the case that participants who were continuously being drawn into the stag hunting whirlpool became Chinese. And because these participants were drawn into stag hunting on the Central Plain, the original homelands of these participants became part of China. This included the Xiongnu (Huns), Xianbei, Turks, Khitan, Jurchens, Mongolians, Manchurians, and so on. Prior to the Song dynasty, the victory of the northerners who entered the fray was relatively short-lived. But during the Song dynasty their dominance extended to a long three-hundred-year period in which their separate state was established through sheer force of arms. The Liao (Khitans) occupied northern China with their territory being more expansive than the Song. And the Western Xia (Tibetans) occupied the northwestern regions. While the Song occupied the Central Plain and the southern regions, the Jin (Jurchens) overthrew and replaced the Liao regime. The Jin expanded their realm from the Huai to the Yellow Rivers and controlled the greater part of the Central Plain. Thus the question of who actually represents Chinese orthodoxy is a really vexed problem.

In the opposition between the Liao and the Song, from the standpoint of political power, the Song was in a weaker position to the extent that in seeking peace the Song sent tribute to the Liao. For this reason the Liao ruling elite were resolute in seeing themselves as the legitimate heirs of China. But when it came to diplomatic relations, they adopted a more tolerant and harmonious stance, stating that even though "the realm is split into two states," the "affairs of the two court affairs are carried out as one family." Official documents sent from the Liao emperors Xingzong and Daozong to the Song emperors Renzong and Shenzong say as much. What is most interesting is that according to some accounts, upon conquering the Jin, the founding emperor of the Liao took possession of the jade seal passed down from the First Emperor of the Qin as a symbol of being the sole ruler of China for "ten thousand generations." Since this jade seal had so much significance regarding inheriting a political legitimacy conferred by the historical process of determining the Mandate of Heaven, whoever was in possession of it was regarded as having an exclusive symbol of legitimacy. The Liao emperor Xingzong once posed the following topic for the imperial examination system: "Possession of the State Seal as a Symbol of the Transmission of Political Legitimacy."[27]

Since the Song occupied the weaker position, they asserted a justification opposite from the Liao that emphasized the distinction between Chinese civilization and the Yi "barbarians." Wang Tongling believes that it was precisely because the Song territory was relatively small and their military prowess weaker, that in coping with the difficulties posed by the Liao, Xia, Jin, and Yuan polities, they gave in to the idea that "reverence to the King had to accommodate Yi doctrines as to what is right and proper."[28] And according to Ge Zhaoguang, what the Song was facing in terms of regnant power dynamics with the Liao, Jin, and Western Xia was an "an unprecedented anxiety regarding China."[29] Such an anxiety forced the Song political narrative to retreat from a universalist understanding of the Mandate of Heaven to a particularist understanding, and converted the notion of "the *tianxia* of all persons under the heavens" into a China of the Han people. This amounted to a betrayal of the Zhou innovation of the Mandate of Heaven tradition of universal concern by interpreting the mandate as the private property of a specific ethnic group. In some ways this might be considered similar to the Yin-Shang idea of heaven having an exclusive and particular interest in just one group of people. And although this narrative retreat might have had the effect of providing some internal solidarity, it came at the cost of giving up the capaciousness of the *tianxia* and *tianming* political narratives.

Based on this situation of divided rule, the Yuan dynasty thinker, Xie Duan, in his treatise on *Debating the Liao, Song, and Jin Legitimacy* took the Liao and Jin as the Northern dynasties, and the Southern Song as the Southern dynasty, with both having equally legitimate claims on Chinese political power.[30] This distinction between the Southern and Northern dynasties was often thought of as an ex tempore arrangement but was actually a historically baseless assertion. The Yuan and Qing dynasties were both non-Han peoples ruling over China. And though the Yuan and

Qing dynasties, to differing degrees, both appropriated the culture of the Central Plain and experienced a deep, mutually transformative relationship with this Central Plain culture, still the unique characteristics of these dynasties went beyond the limits of any traditional Confucian narratives established from the Song dynasty onward. For this reason there was no other choice but to reinterpret the concept of political legitimacy. In this process the Yuan dynasty became the hardest to justify. This is because the Yuan put into practice a system of inequality among ethnic groups. The basic policy was to promote Mongolian people and their traditions. And it was only a matter of political necessity that Central Plain cultures and institutions were appealed to. But in determining the parameters of policy, the Mongols accounted for more than half the population, and the Semu[31] and Turkish peoples outnumbered the Han.[32] The Yuan abandoned the traditional jade seal symbol of power transmitted from the First Emperor of the Qin and created a new imperial seal made from different materials.[33] This might serve to suggest that the Yuan were attempting to inaugurate an entirely novel tradition of political legitimacy.

According to Zhang Zhaosu, after Zhu Yuanzhang's establishment of the Ming dynasty, the problem of how to interpret the historical place of the Yuan was an "exceedingly difficult problem without precedent." Zhu Yuanzhang gave a two-pronged interpretation of this problem. Since the Mongolian emperors conquered all of *tianxia* to an extent that no previous rulers had, they must have received the Mandate of Heaven—otherwise they couldn't have been so successful. And since the Mongols received the Mandate of Heaven to govern all of *tianxia*, it follows that it was the intent of Heaven to let the Mongols govern China. However, because the Mongols were not suited to govern and bring proper order to China, the Mandate of Heaven had to return to the Central Plain, with it falling upon Zhu himself to be recognized as emperor.[34] With such an interpretation of history, Zhu Yuanzhang placed Khubilai Khan in the temple that symbolized the pantheon of legitimate emperors. But this new interpretation of political legitimacy was not entirely novel. What it did was to negate the distinction introduced in the Song dynasty between "Chinese" and "barbarian," and returned to the traditional Zhou interpretation of the Mandate of Heaven.

Moreover, since Zhou thinking was held in such high esteem within the Chinese tradition, with its authoritativeness far exceeding just Song dynasty Confucianism, it proved relatively easy for Zhu Yuanzhang's interpretation to prevail. Even though the Song-Ming Confucian distinction between "Chinese" and "barbarian" had some textual basis in certain pre-Qin classics with Confucius referencing in the *Spring and Autumn Annals* the principle of "resisting the barbarians" as a prime example, in fact this distinction contradicts the traditional Zhou concepts of *tianxia* and the Mandate of Heaven. Cui Shigu claims that even this reference to a purported "Chinese" and "barbarian" dichotomy rests upon a fundamental misreading: "When Confucius compiled the *Spring and Autumn Annals* and talked about resisting the barbarians, he also references the states of Wu and Chu as subjects of the Zhou who had usurped the title of King. Hence, this exclusion of the barbarians in this fashion did not happen in a historical vacuum, but occurred under very specific circumstances."[35] Cui Shigu's reading is consistent with the original sense of *tianxia*. Although the Yuan was renowned for its military power, when compared to the Song dynasty with the exception of some prominent achievements, there was a marked decline in cultural creativity. For this reason it is difficult to consider the Yuan to have been "governing through culture."[36] The Yuan opted instead for a "grand unity" model as the basis for its legitimacy. This dynamic explains the origin of the phrase "for the Kings of old, if the four seas were not one family, there could be no legitimate rule."[37] In this way the Mandate of Heaven concept was reduced to referencing territorial control—that is, a totalizing grand unity. And the concern with winning over the hearts and minds of the people gradually faded away.

However, the concept of legitimacy in its archaic sense meant "unification" and does not emphasize the idea of "orthodoxy or rectitude." Just as Rao Zongyi's research has shown, taking a statement of Li Si as a touchstone: "Previously what any discussion of legitimacy had referred to was rooted in ideas of unification."[38] But after the Song dynasty, the theory of legitimacy basically took Ouyang Xiu's interpretation as its basis. Approaching the issue from the *Gong Yang Commentary* inquiries regarding the core meaning of the *Spring and Autumn Annals*, Ouyang Xiu with presuppositions regarding "dwelling in rectitude" and "grand unity" made the following claim: "Rectifying is the way to make right all under the heavens that is wrong; unifying is the way to integrate all under the heavens that is incoherent."[39] "Interconnectedness" refers to a great unity on a spatial level, while "rectitude" means having real significance for ameliorating a public, which naturally requires the winning over of the hearts and minds of the people. This is equivalent to bringing a great unity to the hearts and minds of the people. In actual practice a complete unanimity of the hearts and minds of the people is impossible. Any system of institutional and political power can only garner a portion of the people's support, with the important difference lying in degrees of support. It is for this reason that a grand spatial unification still functions as a basic symbol expressive of the Mandate of Heaven.

The Manchurian northeast was considered to be within the jurisdiction of the Ming dynasty. After the Qing dynasty was founded, in its governance over China it continued in large degree the institutional ordering of the Ming, but with its territorial claims extending way beyond the Ming borders. The living conditions of the people flourished, and for about 150 years, from the beginning to the middle of the Qing, a "prosperous age" was reached that had few parallels in history. For this reason, with respect to the question of legitimacy, the Qing presented a very different story from the Yuan. But during the early Qing, from the perspective of the Ming dynasty Confucian refugees, the Qing still had a major legitimacy problem. Wang Fuzhi appealed to the debates regarding the cause of the Song dynasty demise as an analogy for the demise of the Ming: "The demise of the Song, was in effect the end of the cultural ways and customs of *tianxia* that had been transmitted from the Yellow Emperor, Yao, and Shun."[40] The "demise of *tianxia*" is a concept that comes from Gu Yanwu. Gu Yanwu said that "changing family names and altering official titles is to let the state perish. But when the values of consummate humanity and optimal appropriateness (*renyi* 仁义) are completely buried, to the point that beasts are being encouraged to feed on people and people to prey on each other, this is letting *tianxia* perish."[41] The way in which Wang Fuzhi appropriated this discourse seems to have departed somewhat from Gu Yanwu's original meaning. Even though Gu Yanwu was nostalgic for the Ming, his theory of "the demise of *tianxia*" was not directed at the Qing. When raising the specter of "the values of consummate humanity and optimal appropriateness" being completely buried, the example he deploys comes from the Jin dynasty, and the Jin were not a "barbarian" dynasty. Wang Fuzhi also seems to understand the idea of the "demise of *tianxia*" as signifying a rupture within the transmission of the Central Plain culture. This point, however, does not comport with historical reality. The Qing dynasty most certainly accepted and promoted the Central Plain culture—for the general worldview, understanding of history, and ethical order of the Qing continued to make direct appeal to the traditions of the Central Plain.

Part of the legitimacy question for the Yuan and Qing dynasties actually arises from the fact that emperors of both dynasties preserved their identity as Great Khans. This point has been used to argue that the Yuan and Qing dynasties were not really part of the traditional lineages of Chinese dynasties but instead were foreigner rulers subduing China. With regard to this question, we at present have no way of gaining access to the full story and can only seek after the most reasonable explanations of historical events. Using contemporary theories to deconstruct ancient realities in seeking out historical truth has a low rate of success. But to try to recover what counted as the ancients most reasonable mode of conduct, in terms of seeking to optimally realize their own interests, and to make inferences about their choices from such a principle should get us closer to historical reality. Formulating a hypothesis from this idea of "their greatest interests" (which as much as possible includes their political and economic interests together), making a choice that entailed taking on an identity of being an invading and occupying foreign power, one that totally uprooted the continuity of previous Chinese dynasties, is very likely not in accord with our principle regarding the reasonable assumptions of the Yuan and Qing rulers.

To be so identified would obviously not serve as a reasonable choice for the Yuan and Qing political actors to have made. Instead, the Yuan and Qing rulers sought to keep their dual identity because they needed to retain the continuing support of two distinct traditions and ways of life with very different means of production spanning over a vast plurality of regions. The Yuan and Qing rulers both believed that they had achieved what previous dynasties had not accomplished in terms of effecting a grand unity. And they never saw their divided territory as two separate states because the Central Plain traditions of the Mandate of Heaven and the concept of the grand unity served their greatest interest in terms of legitimating the political theologies behind Yuan and Qing governance. It was only by becoming viewed as legitimate heirs and rulers over the grand unity of China that they could realize the most effective control over resources, exercise maximal power, and achieve their greatest over-all interests. Since assuming a place in the lineage of Chinese history accorded with the optimal interests of the Yuan and Qing rulers, it is difficult to imagine that the Yuan and Qing dynasties would have imagined rejecting a political and historical resource that could prove so beneficial to themselves. Before the Ming dynasty had gone stag hunting in the Central Plain, Nurhaci[42] had written a letter to the Ming emperor Wanli that expropriated the *tianxia* concept to explain the political legitimacy of Manchurian rule over the Central Plain: "In the space between the heaven and earth, from humankind above to the insects below, all is generated and nourished by "Heaven" (*tian* 天). Do you think that it is your southern dynasty that nourishes all things? . . . This most catholic and selfless "Heaven" that nourishes all things is not something your southern kingdom can realize as a political state. . . . It is only in receiving the Mandate of Heaven that one can rule over *tianxia*."[43]

In reality, the concept of "China" has always been the outcome of mutual transformations among a plurality of cultures and the resulting shared institutional structures. But this idea of China is neither the expression of some homogenizing Hanicization, nor a result of different cultures acting externally on each other either by rejection or fragmentation. Rather, in the ongoing hybridization of Chinese culture, with the Chinese written characters conveying a profound spiritual world, the cultural genes of the Central Plain have always played a leading role. This is a fact that we don't need to rehearse here. Even when the northern ethnic groups (especially the Mongols and Manchus) entered into the Central Plain, the indigenous Central Plain culture was still a dominant resource in the process of mutual cultural transformation. As rehearsed above, it was in the optimal interests of the northern ethnic groups entering the Central Plain as potential rulers to be grafting themselves into the historical lineages of China. Hence what happened historically had a necessary logic. Whether speaking of the Yuan or the Qing dynasties, the question of their political legitimacy can be still be explained within the context of Chinese thinking, and at the very least, can be partially explained by the inherited Zhou tradition. Suffice it to say that as a state including the *tianxia* structure, the idea of China incorporating myriad peoples into one body never presented itself as an insurmountable problem.

It was only at the end of the Qing dynasty that China really encountered an identity problem for the first time where no plausible interpretation of legitimacy could be found. That is, not only was China obviously not at the center of *tianxia* in a geographical sense, but it was also no longer clearly functioning as the pivot in terms of political power and knowledge production in *tianxia*. Staying consistent with the logic implicit in the *tianxia* concept in seeking to understand world history, it follows that from the end of the Qing, "China" was no longer the "central state" in *tianxia*. Instead, China had become just one more state among many. At the same time, the internal narrative of ancient China encountered a growing skepticism with challenges coming from the outside world. And with the coming of other cultural narratives, China became implicated in alternative world logics that gave rise to a fundamental dislocation within its interpretive context and intensified problems of cross-cultural understanding.

A representative example of this is that from the Han dynasty onward (and especially during the Ming-Qing periods), the tributary institution was seen as a hierarchical structure that China forced upon the world. Fei Zhengqing calls this the "tributary system"[44] and he interprets tributary institutions as a "Chinese world order that was a totalizing system of thought and method. And for thousands of years Chinese rulers had continuously developed this system to be preserved in perpetuity."[45] However, to take the tributary institutional practices and interpret them as a tributary *system* is probably an overstatement. Even though the paying of "tribute" practiced from the Han dynasty on had nominally maintained the Zhou notion of "tributary practice," it was actually a totally different power structure and is really only nominally the same political logic. For tribute during the Zhou dynasty was a political and economic duty of the vassal lords to the *tianxia* system, and even though tribute offered was not equivalent to taxation (perhaps it was a "weak" form of taxation), it was still a basic shared financial responsibility for all the Zhou to preserve the *tianxia* system. But from the Han dynasty onward, tributary institutions functioned only as a political idea, and with the exception of a few cases of designated "vassal states" with very close relations to China (such as Joseon Korea, Vietnam, and the Ryukyu Islands), most "tributary" states didn't really acknowledge any affiliated relationship with Chinese dynasties.

Moreover, the Chinese imperial court didn't have any effective political or economic control over these tribute bearing states. So from the Han onward tributary institutions really only served an ambassadorial function and were a far cry from any totalizing "system" or "order" of control. From the Han-Tang through the Ming-Qing periods the tributary relationship was more of a policy of "thick giftings with thin returns." And for the tributary states there was enormous benefits and economic incentives for participation. A great majority of these tributary states made use of a preferential tribute policy for beneficial trade relationships. This arrangement sometimes even got to the point of various states competing over who would get to make a tributary offering. Overall, this tributary-based trade policy was a great drain for China to the extent that the Chinese imperial courts eventually had no choice but to limit the number of tributary missions and the amount of goods given and received.[46] From this we can see that the surrounding states understood the tributary order primarily in economic terms much more than its having any political implications.

We also need to recognize the phenomenon of "reverse tribute." Prior to Emperor Wu of the Han, the Western Han was beleaguered by prolonged warfare with the Xiongnu peoples. In order to seek peace, the Han court dispensed "yearly offerings" of money and goods, a clear case of what Li Yunquan called "reverse tribute" from the Han court to the Xiongnu.[47] For courts of the Central Plain to offer reverse tribute to powerful adversaries was not a rare occurrence. Both the northern and southern Song dynasties gave the Liao and Jin such reverse tribute. The phenomenon of reverse tribute shows that tributary relations was a kind of commonly used political strategy, and rather than being monopolized by the dynastic courts of the Central Plain, whoever was stronger at the moment could exact tribute.

The diplomatic policies of the dynastic courts on the Central Plain didn't stop at tribute alone. In fact, tribute for a long time was used in tandem with marriage alliances. Even though tribute was primary and marriage alliances were ancillary, we shouldn't reduce the relationship between the dynastic courts on the Central Plain and the surrounding political powers to simply tributary relations. According to the research of Yan Mingshu, the importance of marriage alliances has clearly been underestimated in modern historical research. The strategy of marriage alliances had been practiced from the Shang-Zhou periods down through the Qing dynasty and was neither a rare occurrence nor always the result of coercive tactics on the part of stronger players. Rather, forming marriage alliances served as a long-term, sustainable strategy with the dynastic courts of the Central Plain sometimes being in the passive position of enduring "negative marriage alliances" and sometimes in the active role of enjoying "positive marriage alliances."[48]

Some tributary relationships that had real political significance were investiture and the dispersal of an official calendar. To receive investiture was indicative of a relatively intimate relationship, and in times of national crisis, one could seek the aid of China. And using the official calendar meant marking time according to the Chinese emperor's reign title. So if a tributary state used the official calendar of a Chinese dynasty, this meant they acknowledged, at least to some degree, a Chinese narrative of orthodox history. According to this logic though, since now China and most of the world's countries are using a Western calendar, does this mean that we are all acknowledging a historical orthodoxy of the West?

13 Why Go Stag Hunting
   in the Central Plain?

The earliest mention of "stag hunting under the heavens" (*tianxia zhulu* 天下逐鹿) can be found in the *Records of the Grand Historian* (史记): "The state of Qin has lost their stag, and *tianxia* collectively hunts for them."[1] Herein the stag represents ultimate political power. Why use deer to represent power? This question doesn't admit of an easy answer. Power is what is being "hunted" in the political game, so using an animal to symbolize power is not hard to understand, but in ancient times there were many hunted creatures in the Central Plain, many of whom would seem comparatively stronger, bigger, and generally more imposing than deer. And the rise to prominence of the Central Plain occurred precisely during a period of intense global warming.[2] With the warmer and wetter climate, plants and trees flourished, and there was an abundance of oxen, bears, tigers, leopards, and even elephants and rhinoceros, so why then select stag as a representative of political power in the Central Plain? This question seems to elude explanation. The earliest depiction of deer in historical documents is the *Book of Songs* "Lesser Odes—Deer Cry:" "*youyou* goes the cry of the deer."[3]

The image that this song depicts is of deer representing auspiciousness and warmth, and would seem to have nothing to do with political

power. Zhang Guangzhi offers the following hypothesis: in the archaeological remains of antiquity we find deer scapula that were used for divination; thus we can reasonably infer that the ritual significance of deer
had a connection with the political symbolism of hunting stag.[4] However,
it would seem that such a conjecture is also unwarranted. For deer scapula
could certainly be ritual relics of divinatory practices, but since most of the
oracle bone remains are of oxen scapula and turtle carapaces, this would
seem to imply that oxen bones and turtle shells exceeded the ritual significance of deer bones. So we might offer another possible conjecture:
in the early history of the Central Plain, even though tigers and elephants
were more representative of power and were exceedingly fierce and violent, they weren't typically the objects of hunting, but rather could more
likely become opponents in a struggle. Only objects of a hunt would be
appropriate as symbols for competitive and/or cooperative hunting. And
the alluring beauty of a deer exceeds that of wild boars, mountain goats,
foxes, and rabbits. In addition, stag horns resemble the crown of a king
and hence would be suitable for symbolizing political power. And here
is another piece of collateral confirmation for this hypothesis: the *Book
of Changes* states that "when stag have no fear they go deep into the forest, and it is better for the lord to let them go."[5] What this meant is that
without receiving counsel from officials overseeing the hunting parks, and
with deer hiding in the forest, the ruler would be wise not to pursue them.
This implies that at the time, stag hunting had already become recognized
as a competitive game overseen by professional officials and prepared for
by the aristocracy. Perhaps this is the real reason that deer became a symbol of political power.

The key to the stag hunting game lies in an alluringness that is difficult
to resist. Stag hunting meant to vie for political power in the expansive
realm that had the Central Plain at its center, with most political competition depending upon who had control over the greatest resources. Some
contests were actively entered into, while some were due to a series of
relational events that drew one in as an unwilling participant. As has been
rehearsed above, a unique characteristic of the stag hunting game is its
whirlpool dynamic. Being drawn into the gyrating fray, it is exceedingly
difficult to wholly extricate oneself unless one is ready to retire completely
by surrendering all interests and territorial claims (as was the case with

some Xiongnu and Turkish peoples who decided to flee to distant reaches). Rather than simply being the outcome of a historically settled configuration of power, victory or defeat in the stag hunting game depended on the circumstances prevailing in any given moment. Here we have, in broad brushstrokes, considered the logical inferences behind the reasons why the Central Plain came to be the focal point of political power. In what follows, we need to go further in understanding this historical context and how it was that the Central Plain became a focal point.

Why does stag hunting take place in the Central Plain? Xu Hong offers two points that are helpful in answering this question. One is Robert Carneiro's "circumscription theory of the role of warfare in the formation of states"[6] that takes as a set of preconditions (for focal state formation): (1) being a place in which circumstances are optimal for gathering together of resources; (2) having a continuous flow of peoples that leads to exponential population increases; (3) involving a situation in which the inhabitants of the central region respond to being surrounded by others. Under such circumstances there is no choice but to increase power and expand the scale of a base of operations to facilitate self-preservation and the defeat of competitors. The result is that in such a geographical focal point there is an intensification of operations due to fierce conflict. Xu Hong believes it is possible that in the ancient Central Plain, precisely this kind of situation occurred. An alternative explanation can be found in Zhao Hui's "centrality theory." On this model the Central Plain region is located at the center of an expansive territory and thus became the focal point of transportation and communication, trade, and information networks. For this reason the Central Plain accumulated the most political experience and emerged as a relatively mature power, while the peripheral regions, with a relative lack of opportunities to be learning, were put at a relative disadvantage in the competition for power. Zhao Hui infers then that the success of the Central Plain had more to do with favorable transportation modalities and effective communication conditions than with economic forces playing a decisive role.[7]

These two theories would both seem up to the task of explaining, at least in part, the historical conditions behind the emergence of the Central Plain as a focal point, but there still some remaining questions. The natural resources and population density of the Yangtze River basin was by no means significantly less than that of the Yellow River basin. Moreover, the emergence of this civilizational center occurred not later (or only slightly later) than the Central Plain, and the material technologies and transportation conditions were not significantly inferior. So why then didn't the Yangtze River basin come to be the central region, and instead was considered through the Spring and Autumn period as a region of uncouth barbarians? Moreover, if communication and trade were decisive factors, why didn't the highly developed western regions become the center? Given the vaster territories to traverse, the western regions stretched out in all directions as a nexus of trade and information sharing. To the east of this region was the Central Plain, and to the west they were connected with Central Asia and the Middle East. With such conditions they had all the advantages of trade and technologies coming from both east and west. Indeed there was a great deal of trade and technology that passed through these western regions on its way to the Central Plain to the extent that these western reaches became the major hub of the Silk Road. Why then was the (cultural-political) status of the western regions considered to be inferior to that of the Central Plain?

Mancur Olson's theory of state formation proposes an alternative explanation.[8] For Olson, the success of a state must necessarily entail a strengthening of its capacity for collective action. However, Olson's theory shows that small groups can relatively easily realize collective action, whereas for large groups there is always a serious free-rider problem that can lead to the abortion of such action. Hence states that are successful in large scale collective action must at least satisfy the following basic conditions that can transcend the free-rider problem: (1) they must be able to form universal shared interests that are similar to the Confucian ideal of "an ethical state"; and (2) they must have institutionalized selective incentives similar to the Legalist promotion of a clear institutional distinction between rewards and punishments. According to the historical narratives, the royal courts that emerged on the Central Plain had both of these with the tradition of the sage-kings and their styles of ethical governance and requisite institutions for distributing rewards and punishments. This would seemingly satisfy Olson's basic conditions. But even if Olson's theory can account for the basic conditions that could lead to victory in the stag hunting game, it still cannot fully account for the necessary and continuous role that the Central Plain occupied as the only place for stag hunting. Why did the Central Plain become this irrevocable site for engaging in the stag hunt? The question we are trying to resolve here is, "What in the end were the special resources that the Central Plain possessed that inspired such contention?" Certainly the social development of the Central Plain in terms of transportation, economics, and politics taken together were sufficient to make it the site on which various forces, one after another, joined in this game of contestation. But this is the later story of the Central Plain; what we are concerned with here is the original narrative.

Of course, the Central Plain becoming a focal center had something to do with resources. But we can't overlook another possible reason for the emergence of this pivotal region. In comparison with other similar regions rich in resources, the Central Plain was comparatively easy to occupy, thereby making the costs of war relatively low. Hearing this rather mundane reason might cause some to despair, but perhaps it was a positive factor. While economic conditions, transportation logistics, and the cost of warfare as decisive factors can account for contingent reasons that the stag hunting occurred in the Central Plain, such reasons remain insufficient for explaining the paramount central *necessity* this region possessed for stag hunting. What we need to come to understand here is not why stag hunting on the Central Plain was an occasional occurrence, but rather why the stag hunting game had such a focal point and was carried out as a continuous thread throughout Chinese political history. More precisely, we need to explain why the stag hunting game took on a whirlpool dynamic. What in the final analysis were the reasons for this game to take shape as a whirlpool model? What were the factors that sustained the Central Plain as a centripetal force in this whirlpool? Perhaps it is precisely because stag hunting took on a whirlpool model that, far from expressing contingent behavior, became a necessary site of contest for achieving political power in the Central Plain.

Before humanity developed all sorts of technologies aimed at conquering nature, the world was an indomitable and largely unfathomable place. For this reason humanity tended to approach the riddles of existence via paths of sorcery and magic. Divination was a very early type of magic, but with the subsequent emergence of literary culture and books, writing became the greatest magic outshining all else. Writing subsumed all things and events, preserving them in a form that human beings could readily possess in perpetuity. Not only could writing preserve the past, but it could also attempt to predict the future. Writing took natural temporality and transformed it into human historicity. Hence writing created a world of ideality. And this idealist world could employ a summoning of deceased souls as a method for narrating the objective nature of the materialist world. This is the greatest magic. With the help of writing, humans came to wield profound spiritual power. It is said that when the legendary scribe of the Yellow Emperor, Cang Jie, created the written script, the ghosts and spirits wailed all night. Before humanity had the means of objectively representing the world via materialism, they used a kind of idealism to possess it. They created a fictional spiritual world capable of giving a complete explanation for all things and events. Thus they could raise up life in order to transcend the constraints of simply located time and place, living ideally within dimensions that included the entire world and all of time. Numinosity is power, and therefore early peoples had to contest over it. The ancient Central Plain movement of "severing the communicating between earth and heaven" was actually a struggle over who could possess this numinous discourse. When the sage-kings revoked the shamanistic powers of the common people and made it a state prerogative, this meant that only the central court could be ruling the world. Different from shamanistic techniques, though, writing as the greatest magic naturally had a universal character that could be shared, and hence could not become the sole possession of any particular power. For this reason a spiritual world opened up within the historical contestation and an invitation to share in the magic of writing culture became a universalizing activity of life.

It was in the Central Plain that a written script was first developed, and moreover this development entailed the emergence of a spiritual world that was conveyed through written characters. And in deploying what the spiritual world of these forerunners had to offer was not only the power to interpret the world but also the power to possess the very historicity of this thing called "China"—and from this dynamic emerged a reliable spiritual path. To share in this spiritual world was equivalent to sharing a history, and the sharing of this history by ever more peoples meant an expanding scale of political order. This entailed a sharing of a world for optimizing possibilities. In this sense, then, among all the resources of the Central Plain, the most uniquely valuable was its written characters and the conveyance of a distinctive spiritual world. This intangible cultural resource was much more important than mere geographic centrality or abundant material resources. Of course, there was a complex combination of many causal factors that brought about the emergent dynamic of the whirlpool model of the stag hunting game on the Central Plain; but in the midst of all this, the most decisive factor was the competition over the right to contribute to the formation of this spiritual world, which was in fact a competition to be authorizing history and creating knowledge.

Of course, this is all only a hypothesis based upon a rational interpretation of historically political factors. If we accept this hypothesis, though, the following narrative will by and large make good sense. In the history of the struggle to control the spiritual world of the Central Plain, the most successful exemplar ought clearly to be the Duke of Zhou who emerged as a leader of the original Western Zhou political faction. The Zhou dwelled in the northwest near the western Rong tribes. And after the Zhou conquest of the Shang on the Central Plain, the Duke of Zhou bloc used the concept of "virtuosity" (*de* 德) to redefine the "Mandate of Heaven" (*tianming* 天命) as a basis for political legitimacy. In thus reforming the Shang tradition that claimed its ancestors had sole possession of a Mandate derived from a mono-theoarchical Heaven, the Zhou transformed the concept of the Mandate of Heaven into an impartial and universalizing way of Heaven that could be a "benefactor of virtuosity alone." For any action to be authenticated as "virtuosity," it must manifest as action constituting historical meaning. From this dynamic we can infer that it was the Zhou dynasty that first established the historicity of the spiritual world of the Central Plain. And this reformist spiritual turn successfully installed a new concept of the political with the Zhou continuing Xia and Shang dynastic traditions. This conceptual turn legitimized authorizing power with a spiritual world and a political history focused by the Central Plain.

Additionally, the Zhou institutionalization of the *tianxia* concept expanded the spiritual world of the Central Plain beyond its previously recognized territorial boundaries. We can say that the Duke of Zhou's thinking was, in both temporal and spatial dimensions, a revolution in political theology; with natural temporality becoming historicity, and spatial worlding becoming *tianxia*. Through this conceptual transformation, China's mode of being encompassed a more profound historicity and a more expansive understanding of the world. With the inexhaustible heavens above as a counterpart, there could be unbroken historicity; and with the vast expansiveness of earth as a counterpart, there could be nonexteriority in understanding of the world. The capaciousness made possible by this spiritual world approached the ultimate in scale. Here we can go a long way toward explaining the early maturation of Chinese culture, and the persistent reasons provided for its continuity in succeeding generations.

With the demise of the Zhou dynasty the various great powers had another opportunity for stag hunting. The centuries of the Spring and Autumn and Warring States periods further laid the foundations for the ongoing whirlpool model of stag hunting in the Central Plain, which brought about an increase in the stability and strength of its centripetal and centrifugal attraction. Subsequently, every dynastic period continued to strengthen this whirlpool effect. It should be noted that the whirlpool wasn't always fixed in the Central Plain, but no matter how far the center of the whirlpool drifted away from its original heart, the stag hunting game never deviated from the spiritual world opened up by the Central Plain. As the northern desert and grassland peoples incrementally became the strongest competitors in the stag hunt to the point of establishing parity with the indigenous powers of the Central Plain and even exceeding them in political authority, the whirlpool center of the stag hunting game moved from its original Central Plain location to the Youyan belt (stretching from present-day Hebei north to Liaoning), and with this shift the Chinese dynastic capital moved from Xi'an and Luoyang to Beijing. According to the analysis of Zhou Chenhe, the reason behind the Jin and Yuan dynasties establishing their capital cities already revealed their reinterpretation of the focal center of *tianxia*. The Jin dynasty established Beijing as its capital and called it the "Central Capital" (中都), and an early expression of the reason for this move was, "Yanjing is at the center of heaven and earth."[9] Yuan dynasty reasons for making Beijing their capital offer a similar set of explanations: "The Son of Heaven must live at the center," and "if not Yan, nowhere else will do."[10] From the Song dynasty on,

China's economic center moved south of the Yangtze River, which shows that the political center of the whirlpool game need not necessarily be isomorphic with its economic centers.

Growth and diminution in this stag hunting game bore an obvious relationship with the respective economic considerations of both aggressors and defenders. Within the strictures of economic and military might, each contestant would weigh up the differential risks and benefits and decide on whether to embark on any particular military adventure—and with such a logic in mind, strategies of attacking or defending can all in the end be understood simply as a matter of attempting to control access to optimal resources. This logic can also account for why the various dynastic courts on the Central Plain, while holding a clear power advantage over the nomadic pastoral peoples of the northern steppes, typically did not attempt to conquer the grasslands, but instead were content to keep the northern steppes in check with various strategies of deterrence. Conversely, this stag hunting logic can account for the historical fact that when the northern steppes peoples did achieve a clear power advantage they always moved south to establish themselves as sovereigns in the Central Plain. This is because the optimal resources were in the Central Plain. In the *Salt and Iron Discourses* (盐铁论) it is recorded that during the Han dynasty, when deciding on whether to use military force to conquer the Xiongnu, the main faction pointed out an unstated assumption that it is not proper for the sovereign of the Central Plain to use military force to conquer the pastoral nomads: "The Xiongnu lands are vast, and the barbarian horses are fleet of foot, and the power differential is easily upset. To do too little is to fail to deter them; but to do too much is to impose an untenable military burden on the people. If military conscription is vexing, strength is lost; and if used in excess, resources are exhausted."[11]

And even in dispatching the armies, they could never catch up to the Xiongnu: "The lands that the Xiongnu ride herd over are inexhaustible, extending in all four directions, and even with light chariots and fleet horses, you can't possibly defeat them."[12] Thus in dealing militarily with the pastoral nomads, it was considered better to stick to self-defense: "There is no benefit to be had in occupying barren lands, since it comes at such a high cost to the people."[13] Conversely, the people of the northern steppes had relatively little to lose in invading and governing the

Central Plain and had only huge advantages to gain. Once in control, not only could they gain a full measure of economic security, but moreover they could acquire the greatest apportionment of spiritual and political resources. Li Hongbin's research here shows that the intercourse between the northeastern tribes and the peoples of the Central Plain was relatively intimate such that they had a high degree of mutual understanding. These tribes in particular had the greatest interest in stag hunting in the Central Plain because they possessed the optimal conditions for successful entry into the game.[14] Indeed, such was the case to the extent that, with the exception of the Mongols, every tribe that successfully entered the Central Plain to eventually rule over it were peoples from the northeast (Xianbei, Khitans, Jurchens, and the Manchus).

The rise and decline of various powers in the stag hunting game gave rise to a distinctively Chinese mode of dynastic orders punctuated by various interregnum. In European history there was also of course periods of division and unification, with imperialism being one major reason for unification, and ethnic conflict and religious sectarianism being major reasons for division. In many historical cases European interests in division would seem to have trumped any motivations for unification. One reason for this was that the centripetal allure of ethnic and religious factionalism typically remained stronger than that of imperialism. By contrast, because ancient China didn't develop a monotheistic religion, the various faiths didn't have any overarching desire for totalizing power but could instead coexist with a relative appreciation for diversity. Similarly, in Chinese history there wasn't any ethnonationalism or racism as such. And cultural differences leading to divisiveness were, at a spiritual level at least, typically weaker than the faith in *tianxia* as one family. Thus it was relatively easy to embrace coexistence.

However, such spiritual reasons are only necessary conditions for unification but not a sufficient condition. Ultimately what was needed to make unification operational in actual practice was the centripetal force of the stag hunting whirlpool. When the centripetal force of the stag hunting game reached a certain pitch to the extent that becoming engulfed in the gyre was irrevocable, China itself was transformed into a whirlpool and functioned as a necessary precondition for unification. For each vying participant it could be said that their greatest interest wasn't division; and settling for disunity was only a viable strategy for self-preservation. In other words, unification served as a propensity of the whirlpool dynamic itself, while division was an expedient tactic only when competitors became bogged down in an impasse and had to resist the whirlpool effect.

From the Qin dynasty onward, whether in the configuration of the many players of the northern and southern dynasties or during the periods of grand unification, the amount of time that China was ruled by northern tribes (including the Xiongnu, Xianbei, Turfan, Khitan, Jurchen, Mongolian, and Manchus) amounts to more than half of Chinese history. And for the period wherein northern tribes were ruling what we recognize today as China's political body, the time spans more than three hundred years (i.e., the Yuan dynasty together with the Qing). Of course, there is also the case of long durations of separation for peoples in the southwest. But in any case, within the whirlpool model it always remained difficult for the losing competitors to fully extricate themselves or entirely withdraw from the centripetal dynamic. And for those losers who rejected unification by fleeing, they typically forfeited everything to the extent of losing their family estates. This historical Chinese whirlpool model, with all different peoples continuously entering the fray, could not but pro- duce a domain in which ethnically and culturally diverse peoples coex- isted. The question "How to sustain the coexistence of a diverse ethno- cultural domain?" or put differently, "How to maintain *distinction* within *unity*?" became a problem that each succeeding dynasty had to find ways of resolving. And the reality of the myriad peoples coexisting led to China's continuously implementing hybrid institutions such as the "one country, two systems" or "one country many systems" ideals.

Who was it then that invented this "one country, many systems" model? Was it invented in the Zhou dynasty? Even though the Zhou *tianxia* system was all-inclusive with each region having its own local customs, the *tianxia* system was not meant to be a single state order but rather a world order. Hence it cannot be a "one country many systems" state, but instead was a kind of multicultural system. It was only with the institu- tional reforms of the Qin dynasty that China became a single state. But the *tianxia* gene of inclusiveness has allowed China through the ages to always strive to approximate the Zhou dynasty ideal of "not seeking to alter local customs"[15] as a political legacy. In fact, though, it was never a case of totally refraining from altering local customs since the coexistence of all participating ethnic groups entailed a continual process of mutual transformation.

With the Han dynasty and the Xiongnu entering the whirlpool game together and the western regions becoming increasingly open to exchange, the problem of how to coexist together with many different peoples came fully into relief. The Han had largely inherited the institutions of the Qin, and institutionalized an order of "unification" to replace the Zhou dynasty's ideal of "mutual compatibility." Moreover, the institutionalization of unification only solved the problem of how to bring homogeneity to divided territories and was unable to address the problem of harmonizing diverse ethnic groups. With respect to actual military prowess, since the Han court had only the same or slightly superior strength, it was exceedingly difficult for them to pacify the Xiongnu. The Han thus deployed a strategy of marriage alliances as a way of bringing the Xiongnu into a tributary relationship with the Han court. However, because the Xiongnu were competitive rivals of the Han and not collaborative allies, the practice of having a tributary relationship was only nominal, and did not actually work all that well. But the Han court acquired the new political experience of making inroads into the western regions that had many diverse tribes, many existing on a smaller scale than the Xiongnu and living without any political sense of unity among them. There were many conflicts among these diverse tribes and also between them and the Xiongnu. And because these tribes were living along the Silk Road, and enjoyed together with the Han dynasty the trade benefits of these routes, they were motivated to cooperate with the Han court and to seek out its active protection: "The western regions reflect on the awesome virtue of the Han, and share in the joy of belonging to its realm."[16]

As Han governance expanded into the western regions, it met with the problem of cultural alterity. Because the county system and direct governance were not suitable models for the western region peoples who had joined the Han alliance, the Han court invented an institution that extended this order called "capital protection" (*duhu* 都护) which was a kind of guardianship.[17] When the Han set up the capital protection infrastructure, it functioned in a similar fashion to a county seat but was not actually considered a county. For example, the capital protection administrative centers didn't have a governor (an executive administrator) but only military commanders. This meant that the capital protection offices served the role of military protection and didn't function as social administrative units. The capital protection offices served primarily a military function, with garrisons and granaries all having the purpose of "protecting" the western regions. Under the Han policy of "protection" of the western regions, there were at the most fifty small states involved.[18] Because the capital protection offices did not carry out governing and administrative functions, this meant that they didn't get involved in the autonomous rule of the various peoples of the western regions and only sought to maintain conditions for a cooperative relationship to persist between the western regions and the central court. These capital protection offices were something like China's earliest version of a "one country many systems" policy, and the tactics of ruling by "halter and bridle" (*jimi* 羈縻)[19] laid the foundation for its institutionalization during the Sui and Tang.

During the period of the Sixteen Kingdoms, the northern nomadic peoples entered the Central Plain and established many separate political regimes. During this time, due to the majority of subjugated peoples being Han, the practice of "governing through separating the non-Han *hu* peoples from the Han" was instituted.[20] The Xiongnu founder of the Han-Zhao kingdom (304–329 CE), Liu Yuan, was the first to establish the divided governance of the *hu* and Han peoples. Under this system the emperor would be the common ruler of both the *hu* and Han peoples, and a lower level of officials would be divided into two domains of power dealing with the *hu* and Han peoples, respectively. The basic structure was that the *hu* peoples would deal primarily with military affairs and the Han would deal primarily with agriculture, with *hu* officials in command of the military forces and Han officials having responsibility for administering economic and social affairs. Thus the *hu*-Han division of governance was at the same time a division between military and civilian domains.[21]

This way of dividing the country into a military and civilian society as two separate domains with two distinct sets of institutions was not the governmental model of "one country two systems," but it functioned more like a social distinction. It was only with the onset of the Tang dynasty rule by "halter and bridle" system that such policies, for the first time, took on a truly political character. The territory of the Tang was vast and its peoples were diverse. The setting up of the "halter and bridle" prefectures served to carry out the political administration of the regions outside of the Central Plain. The institutions in each separate area were tailored to fit the local cultural customs of each region. And for the most part the regions exercised a high degree of autonomous rule. Each prefecture had a different degree of autonomy though, with some exercising a high degree of self-governance maintaining intact the traditional institutions of its people, and administrators at every level of government being commissioned from the local population. The next level of autonomy was for the central powers to appoint an official to oversee local governance, and the weakest degree of autonomy was for the central powers to appoint garrison officers who would share administrative responsibilities with the locally appointed officials.[22]

The later system of appointing hereditary tribal heads among minority peoples (*tusi* 土司) is best understood as an extension of this "halter and bridle" model. The Liao dynasty also implemented a government that divided the non-Han and Han peoples, with the northern Council of Advisors using established Khitan policies to administer the Khitan people, while the southern Council of Advisors used Han law to manage the Han people.[23] This division of Han and non-Han in governance didn't operate with a logic of racial segregation and was not based on a divided administration of foreigners and Han people. Rather, it was based on a reliance upon local custom to best realize social and political order. In the Liao court many Han persons served as high officials, even gaining titles of prime minister, chancellor of military affairs, grand tutor, official historian, minister of rites, general, and so on. Han De, for example, who was already serving as a high official, gave up his positions of prime minister and concomitantly the chancellor of the southern and northern militaries, to be enfeoffed as the king of Jin.[24]

The Yuan dynasty's institutional dynamics were even more complex. For the most part, they respected the Mongolian order of things while at the same time augmenting it with Han law and a diversity of other institutions. For instance, the legal codes were an amalgam of Mongol, Han, and Hui Muslim law.[25] The Yuan territories were vast beyond compare, with most of the regional dynamics representing a totally new experience for the Yuan court. Indeed, in many locales the Yuan had still not yet implemented mature and stable political institutions by the time of its demise. Broadly speaking, the Yuan court under its military governance, acted somewhat like a military regime, and maintained only the traditional customs of the different regions.

The Ming dynasty basically appropriated the Tang dynasty model of "one country many systems," with each population in the border regions preserving their traditional institutions. And during the Ming the system of appointing hereditary tribal heads among minority peoples for self-governance (*tusi*), a system that was introduced for the peoples of the southwest by the Yuan dynasty, reached a certain institutional maturity. The Qing dynasty continued with the developed institutions of the Ming and underwent a high degree of "Hanification" in governance on the Central Plain, while opting for continual progress in the administration of the border regions through a hybridic combination of local autonomy and centralized guardianship. In broad outline, China has continuously maintained a political order inclusive of many diverse institutions. In the pre-Qin *tianxia* era it was a multicultural system, while in the post-Han eras it maintained a "one country many systems" structure.

The China that has been formed through the stag hunting whirlpool model is a hybridic, multicultural, and multiethnic entity—with one important aspect being the mutual transformation occurring among many cultures, and another being the intermingling of many different ethnicities. Even though there has been mutual assimilation and fusion, a persistence of what is called "Han people" and "Han culture" has in the end been a mainstay, and for this reason the complex processes adumbrated above have often been taken to actually be a kind of "Hanification." This is a relatively messy problem. For the concept of "Han" (汉) is not only quite complex in and of itself but is regularly haphazardly lumped together with the concept of "China." The Han ethnicity is a modern concept that has been retroactively defined, with the real problem being that China has never been an ethnostate. Instead, China has undergone continuous, virtually parthenogenetic growth, with its elastic expansion and development always being determined by the dynamic of the stag hunting game. The various regions and peoples who have joined in the whirlpool game then are all creators of China. The Yellow Emperor and the Yan Emperor were from the Western Rong and Eastern Yi peoples. The Shang dynasty originated with the Eastern Yi, while the Zhou had its origins in a fusion of Western Rong and Xia peoples. The Sui-Tang imperial blood line was predominantly Xianbei, and the Yuan and Qing histories are well-known. The ancient Central Plain ethnicities (Xia, Shang, Zhou) intermingling with the peoples on the Zhou hinterlands as they continuously entered the Central Plain (the Xiongnu, Tujue, Xianbei, Qiang, Tibetan, Khitan, Jurchen, Mongols, Manchus, Man, Miao, and so on) together became a "new" Central Plain peoples, and it is only as the outcome of this multiethnic hybridity that we have what is designated by the modern name, Han peoples (*hanzu* 汉族).

Stated more precisely, early China did not deploy a distinction between Han and non-Han peoples. Already during the Xia-Shang-Zhou eras, some northern and northwestern peoples had already deeply inhabited the Central Plain. According to the research of Wang Tongling, through the Spring and Autumn period there were still many northern and northwestern peoples enfeoffed as vassal states in the Central Plain that were distributed over what is currently the areas of Shaanxi, Shanxi, Ningxia, Hebei, Shandong, and Henan. It was only after losing in the stag hunting game that some of these peoples retreated north of the Gobi desert (Outer Mongolia). The last powerful northern Di state called Zhongshan (in the middle of today's Hebei) existed up until the middle of the Warring States period when it was finally conquered by the state of Zhao.[26] Beginning with the Han dynasty, the prowess of the northern desert peoples steadily increased, and one after another they entered the stag hunting game. Entering the game comparatively late were the Tufan Tibetan peoples, while the Tibetans (Zangzu) living in Qinghai and Gansu entered much earlier and, on several occasions, partitioned vast amounts of the Central Plain territories. Most remarkably, in 763 BCE the Kingdom of Tibet carried out a surprise attack on the capital of the Central Plain at Chang'an.

From this stag hunting whirlpool dynamic we can see that "China" is a much broader category than the concept of "Han." Putting any kind of valorized historical narrative together with the concept of China will obviously carry certain biases. Hence it is only by following the dynamic structure of the stag hunting whirlpool and the history of its growth that we can hope to adequately understand China. The idea of "historical reality" found in history books tends to be constructed from historical narratives.

We can take perhaps the most complicated Yuan dynasty as an example. The Ming histories, the Yuan official narrative, the traditional narratives of the Mongols, and the narratives of the western regions regarding the Yuan each offer a fundamentally different understanding about the true character of the Yuan dynasty, but all of them are value laden narratives. Here we are striving to appeal only to a minimalist use of "the commensurable facts," just as we determined above that it is only in using the interpretive principle of "the reasonable greatest interest" as our standard in using political and economic considerations to adequately contextualize historical events. From this principle we can reasonably infer that even though the Yuan dynasty had a profound reverence for Mongolia proper, its greatest interest was actually in the Central Plain. Thus Khubilai Khan's decision to become the emperor of China was a reasonable choice. This can also explain the decision of Emperor Shun of the Yuan to keep the title of a Yuan emperor even after being defeated and having to retreat to the northern desert regions—what history knows as the Northern Yuan. And it was only when counterattacking became entirely hopeless that this dynasty ultimately fell apart.

Wang Tongling's *A History of Chinese Ethnicities* describes the process of how China's diverse ethnic groups mutually transformed each other in exquisite detail. According to his carefully documented research, from the time that the Qin empire became China, a diverse array of ethnicities had established relatively stable dynastic orders. The Jin and Qing were created by the Manchus; the early and later Zhao, the Xia, the Northern Liang, and the Yuan were all founded by the Mongolians; the early and later Yan, the Western and Southern Yan, the Western Qin, the Southern Liang, the Northern Wei, the Northern Zhou, the Northern Qi, and the Liao were established by peoples of Manchu-Mongolian mixed ancestry (i.e., the Xianbei and Khitan peoples); the later Tang, the later Jin, and the later Han were formed by the Hui Muslims; the early Qin, the later Qin, the later Liang, and the Western Xia were founded by the Tibetans. And among the states of the so-called Han, the state of Qi was actually a blend of Han and Eastern Yi peoples; the state of Qin was a mix of Han and Western Rong peoples; the states of Jin and Yan were a blending of Han and Northern Di peoples; and the Dali Kingdom was the result of Han and Miao blending. Similarly, the dynasties of great unity of the so-called Han peoples—the Qin, Han, Jin, Sui, Tang, Song, and Ming—were all also mixed ethnicities.[27]

Whether the various peoples of ancient China possessed a natural sense of ethnic self-consciousness is an open question, but what is important to note is that in any case other ethnicities were never viewed with a sense of necessary disapprobation or as inherently degenerate, and there seem to be, historically speaking, few interethnic boundaries that couldn't be easily traversed. For any regime, acquiring and maintaining political power was the most important advantage to obtain. Whether a dynasty excluded other ethnicities sharing in political power would be a great test of its relative degree of ethnic self-consciousness. It is Wang Tongling's discovery that no matter who held political rulership in China, in general, political power and being a member of the ruling class was open to all ethnicities. He provides many concrete and detailed examples to illustrate this fact that in every dynasty, the ruling elites came from all ethnic backgrounds. For example, during the dynasties wherein Han people were in charge, we can find in historical records examples of many non-Han officials. During the Sui dynasty, there were 51 Xiongnu, Xianbei, and other central Asian peoples serving as government officials. During the Tang dynasty there were all together 122 Xianbei, Turkic, Korean, Tibetan, Khitan, Uighur, Japanese, Indian, and other non-Han peoples serving in elite positions (among them many notable generals and ministers—such as Yuchi Jingde who was Xianbei, Ge Shuhan who was Turkic, Gao Xianzhi who was Korean, Yuan Zhen who was Xianbei, and Li Ke who was Uighur). During the Song dynasty there were 34 officials of Xianbei, Xiongnu, Turkic, Dangxian, and Arab ethnicity (including the famous general Hu Yanzan who was Xiongnu).

During the Ming dynasty there were around 174 Mongolian, Jurchen, and Uighurs serving in high positions. And to reverse the order, according to official historical records, during non-Han ruled dynasties we see a similar phenomenon. During the Khitan Liao dynasty there were 68 Han officials (including the very important ministers Han Derang and Zhao Yanshou). During the Jurchen Jin dynasty there were over 277 Han officials. During the Mongol Yuan, as part of the meritocratic system of giving Mongolian names to Han officials, there were 37 Han persons serving in high positions (including the notable generals Shi Tianze, Zhang Rou, and

Zhang Hongfan).[28] During the Manchu Qing dynasty the innumerable Han officials far exceeded the number of their Manchu counterparts, and the number of famous generals and scholar-officials is difficult to tabulate.

Another important measure for evaluating this phenomenon of mutual ethnic accommodation was intermarriage. Historically it was simply matter-of-fact and never proscribed for ethnic groups in China to practice intermarriage (including between the royal families and persons outside of their own ethnic group). Only during the Song and Yuan dynasties did some restrictions exist, with the Song dynasty being the most extreme, since the royal family never intermarried with other ethnic groups. And the imperial clan of the Yuan court seldom intermarried with Han peoples. Only nine Han women entered the Yuan royal court, and no one from the royal family ever married a Han person.[29]

And with respect to what is called "Han culture," this is also a product of diverse cultural hybridity. If we have to give a description of the most characteristic features of Han culture, perhaps we would say that it is the spiritual world conveyed by and made accessible through written Chinese characters. This spiritual world is in a process of continuous growth, and historically has already absorbed much substance from diverse cultures. In the process of mutual transformation among diverse cultures, institutions, costumes, arts, music, cuisine, technologies, language, and customs have all undergone many changes. Only the spiritual world conveyed by Chinese characters could sustain such hyperstability, with the Han culture conveyed in the Chinese script serving as its most basic genes.

The hyperstability provided by Chinese characters and the pictographic-ideographic nature of the Chinese script itself are related. On the one hand, Chinese writing as a medium expresses the external world and constructs an objective world; while on the other hand, Chinese writing as largely ideo-pictographic, constructs a imagistic world replete with meanings. This kind of unique ideo-pictographic character of the Chinese script allows it to transcend its function as a mere symbolic "signifier" by possessing its own independent sense. The phonetic meaning of language lies in the "signified" or in the "referent," which is to say that the meaning of any phonetic symbols are purely a matter of "reference." This means that symbols themselves don't have any independent meanings. If the fixed relationship between referent and reference is severed, then symbolic meaning is empty. But the pictographic-ideographic nature of the Chinese script always has a double structure of meaning: the signified meaning and the apparent meaning. It is quite possible that Gongsun Long's famous paradox that "all things have their significance, but signification itself does not signify"[30] is pointing to this unique feature of Chinese script. Things can all be objects of linguistic reference, but the meaning of a written character itself does not reduce to reference. A Chinese character as a "signifier" of course has its referential function as a symbol, but Chinese characters as signifiers are always also themselves an image, and thus they can constitute a spiritual world independent of any world of supposedly objective reference—that is, as "something that the world otherwise does not have."[31]

What this imagistic nature of Chinese writing constructs is not only a spiritual world, but at the same time a spiritual subject that itself serves a constitutive function, having the capacity to be simultaneously both a "cogitatum" and a "cogito." Of course, this is a sort of anonymous subject—that is, a purely cultural subject. Because of this, a thinking Chinese person always possesses a double subjectivity: that is, an individuated psychological subjectivity and a common Chinese character subjectivity. And in acting with these two subjectivities simultaneously, a distinctive Chinese consciousness is directed on the world. While an individual psyche is viewing the world, the Chinese character subjectivity is also "seeing" the world. A paradigmatic instance of this phenomenon of double seeing can be found in classical poetry. On the one hand, what is expressed in classical Chinese poetry is simply a poet's view of the external world; while on the other hand, what is also always expressed is the poet's self-construction via Chinese characters within a self-sufficient, imagistic world. This allows for classical Chinese poetry to have overlapping visible effects of expressing both a naturalistic and an imagistic world. The images of Chinese characters are the formal receptacle of spiritual embodiment and a place wherein the metaphysical and empirical converge.[32] It is for this reason that individual uniqueness can also have universal features, and that the past can always be present such that history has contemporaneity. Without a doubt this deep significance of Chinese characters has its unique spiritual allure.

Any "Hanification" of China then should be conceived of as having an intricate connection with the spiritual attraction of Han culture, and the reasons that Han culture became a focal selection point by the many of those who displayed stag hunting prowess had to do with their own rational choices as they engaged in the game. What is called "rational choice" here is first of all a seeking out of optimal security, and is secondarily a seeking to optimize resourcefulness. The hybridically constituted "Han peoples" make up a majority of the Chinese population, and it is for this reason that other ethnic groups who entered into the Central Plain (either partially or entirely) tended to appropriate Han culture as a kind of "dominating strategy." Not only does such a strategy prove useful in guaranteeing political stability and economic interests in the long term, but moreover it takes advantage of the interpretive spiritual capacities and knowledge producing power of the Han culture to secure an optimal mode of political sustainability. Since the spiritual world conveyed through Chinese characters had the greatest capacity for storing knowledge and for producing wisdom—in other words, the greatest capacity for epistemic flows (both input and output)—it was a must-have resource in the construction of a political theology and historical narrative used in establishing institutions and organizing society focused in the Central Plain. Before the Western spiritual world entered East Asia, the spiritual world conveyed through Chinese characters was an unparalleled spiritual resource for this vast region, and it was because of this that Han culture became a common resource that could be appropriated by all.

With China as the contested site of stag hunting by many different ethnic groups, deciding winners and losers always remained an uncertain proposition. Vitally important was the fact that the greater the expanse of the whirlpool dynamic of the stag hunting game became, the greater the expanse of China became. All regions that entered into the stag hunting game tended to become an integral part of China, and those regions that did not join the stag hunting game tended to remain more exterior to China. As to what is internal and external to China, this is a concept that is all too easily misunderstood. In the pre-Qin *tianxia* era, according to the principle that there can be no exterior to *tianxia*, *tianxia* was considered unbounded. Nevertheless various regions were cleaved off by local political powers and did maintain precise territorial boundaries vis-à-vis the Central States. For this reason, relative to the territorial divisions made by these political powers, there was a distinction between inner and outer. With respect to the "kingly domain" of the ancestral state of the Zhou dynasty, all of the vassal states were considered "exterior" (*wai* 外) regions. Among the vassal states themselves, they considered each other as exterior. As for those enfeoffed states that had family relations with the Zhou lineage (the so-called Xia vassals), the Eastern Yi, Northern Di, Western Rong, and Southern Man in the four directions, who were all allied with the vassal states, were all considered exterior. For all of the vassal states viewed internal to the *tianxia* system, for all the regions of the four quarters and four seas that had yet to enter into the *tianxia* system, they were left to be considered as exterior.

With the eclipse of the *tianxia* system, the entire Central Plain became territory directly administered by the Qin court (somewhat similar to the way the kingly domain region was the territory administered directly by the Zhou kings). The regions outside of the Central Plain were considered an exterior realm that was yet to be governed, but this was still different from being considered as foreign countries. After the Qin-Han period, *tianxia* was never again implemented as a political institution, but it still functioned as a kind of ideal conceptual horizon. For this reason the interior and exterior distinction did not refer to the interior and exterior of China, but rather pointed to a difference between governed and ungoverned regions. It was a concept of inner and outer with respect to political power, and not a concept of inner and outer relative to the boundaries imposed by a discrete sovereign state.

At this point we should also not avoid discussing the far too often misunderstood Great Wall. Earlier than the Great Wall of the Qin dynasty, China had already constructed several great walls, and the ruins of many of these still exist. During the Spring and Autumn and Warring States periods, with vassal states contending for regional hegemony, wars of incursion were frequent, and each state, in service to its own self-preservation, began to construct walls. These military fortifications constructed accorded with the topographical constraints present at the forward position of each state. The state of Qi was the first to construct a great wall, erecting a long wall along its southern border that extended for over a thousand *li*. The southwest portion protected Qi from incursions by the state of Jin, while directly south and to the southeast it protected it from

Chu and Yue.[33] Even though the state of Qi didn't share an immediate border with the states of Chu and Yue, as many smaller states existed between them, the great states of Chu and Yue frequently launched military campaigns that transgressed the borders of other states. The vassal states of Chu, Lu, Wei, Qin, Yan, Zhao, and Zhongshan all followed suit by building their own great walls. Most of these great walls were used to secure borders or to carry out attacks against other states in the Central Plain, and only a small portion of them were used to protect against the nomadic peoples of the northern desert regions. For instance, the whole of the great wall of Qi was used to defend against other vassal states in the Central Plain. While both Yan and Zhao had northern and southern walls, with the northern walls being used to protect against incursions from northern nomads and the southern walls protecting them against invasions from other vassal states in the central region. The state of Zhongshan (composed of the "white *di*" nomads) had a wall to the west of its capital to protect against the state of Chu.[34] The state of Chu's great wall was in the north for both defensive and offensive purposes in the Central Plain.

It is clear that the location of the great walls of each state was largely determined by the orientation of its competitor states. The Qin dynasty's great wall was constructed for the sole purpose of defending against nomadic peoples because, after Qin had unified the Central Plain, the only remaining competing powers were the peoples north of the desert, since the western regions hadn't yet entered into the stag hunting game. After the Qin dynasty the many walls constructed in different periods show clearly that the decisive factor in the significance of the wall depended upon who was the leading competitor. For instance, the Northern Wei court built a great wall in the region today called Inner Mongolia in order to defend against Rouran, who were also nomadic peoples.[35] The Goryeo (Korean) kingdom built a great wall to defend against invasions from the Tang dynasty.[36] The Liao kingdom in today's Heilongjiang built a very long great wall from Liaoning to Inner Mongolia, and what is worth noting is that the lands beyond its great wall were not foreign countries but territories the Liao already claimed (e.g., part of contemporary Russia, the entire northeast of China, and portions of eastern and western Siberia). This meant that the Liao wall was built entirely in Liao territory and had nothing to do with demarcating territorial boundaries between states.

Rather, it was built to defend against possible internal rebellions by the Jurchens, the Shiwei Mongols, and others.[37]

The fact that most of the great walls were coincident with or near the walls built by the Qin and Ming dynasties, and usually not far from the division between north and south, was because these walls served to divide the two great economic zones of ancient China—that is, the dividing line between the predominantly nomadic economies (fishing and hunting) and the predominantly agriculture economies. These walls were also at the time a division between the eastern regions of China that had a monsoon climate and the more arid western reaches. This division is marked by a line demarcating China's wet climate with at least 400 millimeters of annual precipitation: that is a division between a typically wet and dry climate. This division also roughly corresponds to the so-called "Hu Huanyong Line" reflecting differentials in population distribution[38] that was drawn from the Black River to the mountains of Tengchong in southwest Yunnan. This "jagged dog tooth" line is not uniformly straight but winds and curves with the lay of the land: a continuous line with jigsaw-like deviations. Hu Huanyong was the first scholar to use statistical analyses to confirm that the several maps of China—geographical, precipitation, and population maps—exhibited a more or less isomorphic pattern. These overlapping lines have a multilayered and intersectional set of implications. To a significant degree, these lines exerted a profound influence on the configuration of the stag hunting game, probably splitting ancient China between the power differentials of nomadic and agricultural regions, and serving as functional dividing lines in the "one country two systems" or "one country many systems" modalities. But, of course, this is only an approximation, since beyond the Great Wall there were also many agricultural lands.

Taking a long historical view, the military power of these two regions was relatively balanced, each experiencing cycles of relative dominance and decline. But in terms of their economic modes of production and differences in ways of life, the Great Wall line was the easiest way to differentiate between two great, evenly matched powers in the stag hunting game. When the two great powers in the game found reasons to cease fighting or enter into peace talks, the cessation of hostilities would usually occur along the lines of the Great Wall. Of course, each separate occasion on which there was achieved a relative balance of power was unique. For example, there was the Hetao region that, even though belonging to the dry lands, had substantial irrigation that allowed for both farming and animal husbandry, and that from the Warring States period onward frequently changed hands.[39] In broad strokes we can say that after the China game had moved from an east-west to a north-south oriented competition, unless one party with overwhelming force was able to establish unity, the line constituted by the Great Wall became representative of a balance of power in the game.[40] Of course, this Great Wall was not the only decisive factor in establishing a line dividing a balance of powers in the game. In the history of the south-north conflicts, the northern regions defeated the southern regions with relative frequency. Apart from the great walls in the balancing power game, there were also the belts between the Huai River and Qin Peaks, and again there was the Yangtze River. In summary, the Great Wall was not only a functional border, but was also a focal region for the stag hunting game and served as a balancing-dividing line between the north and south of China. This can also explain why the heartland of China, following the changes introduced by the whirlpool game, moved from the Central Plain to Beijing. In the dynamic of the stag hunting game, the location of Beijing was right in the middle of this relative balance and proved the most effective place to be simultaneously controlling the north and south of China. It was for this reason that those Chinese dynasties able to simultaneously rule over north and south China took Beijing as their capital.

14 Existing through Change

Taken together, all the indeterminate flows coupled with the relatively settled factors of ancient China was to be sure a complicated and highly mutable process, but for all of the changes it never wavered far from its ancestral patterns. Zhang Guangzhi has called Chinese civilization a "continuity pattern."[1] The reason for China's continuous existence lies in the fact that China itself is a method of growth. The metaphysics of the *Book of Changes* is the root of Chinese modes of thinking. Herein the aim of existence itself is persistence. What is persistence? It lies in changing, in ceaseless procreativity, and in daily renewal. This means that the metaphysics of the *Book of Changes* is not an "ontology of substance" but is rather an "ontology of process." The ontology of the *Book of Changes* became a method for China's existence: everything is in a state of perpetual change, with the variables in any process of change being uncertain.

The "way" of existence, then, is a continuity in change, which is from start to finish, the sustaining of a kind of harmonious coordination within processes of transformation. Continuity in change, or repetition with a difference, is more than simply continuing to exist, but is a matter of making *this* existence increasingly accommodating in order to better cope with all of the changes. It is only in being able to cope with the myriad changes that effective perpetuity can be realized. In the *Daodejing*, Laozi uses "water" as a metaphor for depicting this adaptive mode of thinking. A way of being with optimal results is to be like water in taking shape only according to circumstances and in moving forward according to what opportunities arise. This "water methodology" can perhaps go some way toward explaining how China has been so good at changing and persisting. With its method of growth and existence being a limitless "existing through change," China has been enabled to exist as a "world." And with this "worlding" capacity in full effect, China can always grow by way of "being what it is not" [i.e., becoming pure potentiality]. The *Mencius* says: "That which is passing is transforming, and that which persists is numinous."[2] This passage might serve as a most appreciative footnote explaining China's mode of a sustainable historicity.

There is also the Greek story of the Ship of Theseus that tells of a wooden ship that in the course of its journey has all of its old planks replaced with new ones. But at the end of the journey, the wooden ship still looks just like the vessel that had set off on its original journey...

PART III   The Future of *Tianxia* Order

15 A World History Yet to Begin

World history is a dubious concept, for humanity has yet to accomplish "taking the world as a world" (an allusion to Guanzi's "taking *tianxia* as *tianxia*"). Therefore "the world *qua* (political) world" has yet to exist. Under these conditions the idea of world history is nothing more than a kind of misleading fiction. The "world" in which we are living is still only a world in a physical sense, that is as the planet Earth. But we have yet to imagine a world defined by world interests and a world to be shared by all. For this reason the world we are living in, apart from its material substance, has no political identity or political order of being. So until now, when we say "world" it actually only refers to a "nonworld."

In this "nonworld" world that we inhabit, there has hitherto been no universal, shared history. Prior to the modern era, each region had its own version of history. With the movements of modern colonialism, the opening up of foreign markets, and the effects of imperialism, it would seem that the various regions of the world have become more interconnected. And the multiple histories of the various regions have been organized under the banner of a European history conceived of as a "complex history of histories." However, this is definitely not a true world history, but only an expansion of European history through colonial domination.

The various local histories of the world have been recast in the narratives of European hegemony as playing only passive or auxiliary roles. This is European expansionist history masquerading as world history and has until now served as the mainstream for the basic model of what gets called world history. The modern development of this extreme form of globalization has had the effect of drawing all persons into an all-pervasive and inextricable game, but up until now the world has yet to produce a universally acceptable set of rules. The world has given rise to a game from which no one can extricate themselves, but it has yet to become a shared world, and as such represents nothing but a "failed world." Modern globalization would seem to be producing its own grave diggers. At the very least it has resulted in the modern political game falling into a self-induced state of chaos and the loss of any progressive road forward. This is especially true when globalization is coupled with the plethora of negative consequences brought about by strategies deployed within modern imperialisms seeking to dominate the world. In such a global predicament world order is lost. Although this is surely tragic, it does present opportunities to be creating new game rules.

With the end of the Cold War, the notion of an "end of history" (cf. Francis Fukuyama) has appeared as a thesis that announces an overly romantic and naive ideal. Applying a Hegelian narrative structure, such a view illegitimately takes up a kind of theological account of history. But even assuming that someday a messiah might finally arrive, God never promised that such an event would immediately follow the Cold War. Moreover, God never claimed democracy to be messianic, and according to the existing prophetic proclamations concerning God, it would seem that he wouldn't be all that inclined to be a supporter of democratic institutions—for God's divine fiat hardly requires democratic consensus. I don't mean here to stand for or against any specific religious narrative, but just want to say that prophetic stories always depend upon prophecy, just as democratic stories depend upon an ideal of democracy; and that these two types of stories shouldn't be conceived of as overlapping in identical narrative logics. Democratic stories belong to a modern logic of progress, wherein progress like evolution, isn't to be construed as having a terminal point (unless humanity were to go extinct). And if we marry progress with a narrative logic of Christianity, then it clearly becomes a kind of modern superstitious story. The result of blending these two logics is neither scientific nor theological, but instead represents a kind of superstitious ideology.

A genuine world history, then, must take world order as a starting point in crafting its narrative of a shared life of humanity. World order should not be conceived of as some hegemonic superpower or an alliance of dominating states ruling the world, but should rather be a kind of sovereign world order wherein communal interests are the guiding standard of governance. Rather than one state, or faction, establishing the rules of the game for the world, the world should be establishing game rules for all of the states. The Zhou *tianxia* system represented just such a "world" political order that covered a relatively limited terrain. So the Zhou was a conceptual experiment in world politics and the heralding of a coming world history. But the world has yet to become a *tianxia*, and a genuine world history has yet to begin.

The reason the world has yet to become a *tianxia* is that until now the world has persisted in conditions of anarchy, even frequently lapsing into a Hobbesian-like state of nature.[1] This is because until now there hasn't been a world institution capable of receiving universal acceptance, or even a universally acceptable worldview. Thus it has hitherto not been possible to constitute the world as a political subject. For human beings the world has only had geographical significance, and with respect to the political, only nation-states are deemed significant. It is for this reason that the world has only been exploited as a "common" resource and treated as a domain to be fought over and abused. The real problem of world politics does not lie in so-called "failed states"[2] but rather in a "failed world." If the world continues for much longer as a failed world, then all nation-states, including large and powerful states, will have a very difficult time overcoming the negative aspects of this world exteriority. It is exceedingly difficult for a world lacking coordination and cooperation to be ensuring security and peaceful development.

The real absurdity lies in the fact that even though every nation-state knows all too well that world security and cooperation are necessary conditions for their continued existence and development, there has never been a sufficiently robust effort made to attend to the problems of world politics. One reason for this is that the shared interests of the world are not felt to be as pressing as the given objectives of discrete nation-states. Moreover, the more hegemonic nation-states are always trying to maintain an exploitative international system. We have good reason to believe then that as the world's various crises intensify, we have to be approaching the concept of world politics with the same degree of seriousness that we currently approach problems of national interests, individual rights, and governmental taxation.

As rehearsed above, except for the special case of the Zhou *tianxia* system, the natural development of the political would seem to have been determined only by national politics. And if we use national politics to engender international politics, there is no way to progress into world politics. National politics are domestically directed politics, with the core problems being concerned with power and interests, and the distribution of rights and responsibilities within given nation-states. International politics are externally directed politics insofar as they are focused on political relations between nation-states. For international politics the core problems remain the interest games between nation-states—be it based in logics of cooperation, competition, conflict, or warfare. Even though the kind of issues international politics has to deal with are the world's political problems, it has yet to be world politics as such. This is because international politics are not carried out for the sake of world interests, but only for national interests on a world scale. World peace and cooperation are not sought-after goals (even though international peace and cooperation are popular slogans within current paradigms of international politics). What is sought after, though, is a total domination over opponents and the maximization of exclusionary, selfish interests. We can even say that international politics seldom has been able to justly adjudicate conflicts of interest between nation-states. In fact, it would seem to be exactly the opposite, as international politics often only serves to intensify international contradictions, causing interstate conflicts of interest to increase. If international politics were somehow to fairly resolve international conflicts, it would have to be because a real balance of power was occurring between two parties or because of the presence of some necessary and sufficient reason for the two parties to engage in cooperation.

With respect to the core of national politics, the aim is to be establishing the most just set of institutions with game rules that don't from the outset exclude the possibility of discrete, irrational governments (and nonstate actors) to be seeking only the maximization of their own exclusive self-interests. International politics on the other hand does not have effective institutional frameworks and is not even seeking to work out agreement upon what would count as just rules of the game; instead, international politics has only so many "strategies" for harming others for selfish benefit. One type of strategy is the systematic organization of domestic affairs for a nation-state, and another is a system for competing against foreign powers. The two together form one body politic. This means that international politics is not on a separate order from national politics, but rather belongs to the same set of strategies of national politics, but is just directed against foreign powers. This is sufficient to explain why the world has never emerged from its anarchic condition to realize a genuinely political arrangement. International politics have actually been nothing more than a false packaging of international hostilities (including warfare), with the result being that the world has become an anarchic commons. In other words, the world has become the largest tragedy of the commons. This is especially the case within ideologies of hegemonic nation-states, where other nation-states and even the high seas are conceived of as just so much territory to be dominated. Although such truths are typically never so baldly stated, international politics essentially has such a character.

The *Peace of Westphalia* was an epoch-making response to the problem of the world as a tragedy of the commons.[3] On the foundation of this treaty model, a system of sovereign states was incrementally introduced wherein a mutual acknowledgment of the world commons was divided along the lines of national sovereignty, with each nation having its own clearly demarcated set of property rights. There can be no doubt that this clear demarcation of discrete national property rights was an effective solution to the tragedy of the commons, but it also gave rise to a new set of problems. This system of national sovereignty legitimized the fragmentation of the world; or put in another way, the very idea of national sovereignty negated the concept of world sovereignty and of world interests. This revolutionary modern system of sovereign nation-states was a great advance for the development of nation-states, but not all states benefited equally. Technological and economic advances led to a small group of powerful countries conspiring to dominate the world. During this phase of early modernity, from the perspective of the stronger players, although the various powerful nation-states generally recognized each other's sovereignty, the vast majority of the rest of the world's nations and nonstate regions were not granted their share of the global commons. In such a world order these areas could be freely invaded, conquered, and occupied as colonial subjects. It was only after two world wars that revolutionary worldwide liberation movements brought about a situation in which all nation-states could hope to be recognized as sovereign. This system of sovereign nation-states thus became pervasive for the entire world as its basic mode of division, and since then there has never again been a world commons.

But the pervasiveness of this system of sovereign nation-states is not a world system that serves the aspirations of world cooperation and common interests. Rather, it belongs to an imperialistic system of hegemonic nation-states. The field of mainstream economics tends to maintain that this clear demarcation of property rights will produce rational cooperation, or at least provide a basis for rational negotiation in the resolution of problems based in conflicts of interest. And this basic principle is partially valid. To be precise, such a principle is only effective under conditions wherein the rules of the game are already just. But within an imperialistic system it does not work. Even though the universal recognition of national sovereignty has in great measure held in check both the consolidation and the parsing up of territories (although not in any absolute sense), with the model of territorial consolidation giving way to a model of competition, still the modern rules of competition do not allow for the world to benefit universally. Rather, first it was Europe and then the United States that have set up the rules of the game to serve their own interests as imperialistic rules aimed at world domination in economics, politics, and culture.

"Domination" is an intriguing concept as it doesn't denote direct aggression, but rather refers to more subtle and invisible modes of oppression, exploitation, and control. Karl Marx was the first to discover the problematic of capitalism exploiting the world. Influenced by Marx, many modern radical thinkers have continued to go deeper by further exposing the exploitative nature of capitalism. This problem has already become common knowledge, and there is no need for further elaboration here. Even so, the critique of capitalism leveled by radical thinkers has never really gone beyond the concept of "class." In seeking to find a concept of class applicable around the world, many thinkers actually obscure the ways that international exploitation can be even more insidious than national exploitation. And, furthermore, how European and now the American nation-state has been exploiting the rest of the world. In fact, the "exploited" peoples within Europe and America are at the same time relatively speaking, acting as "beneficiaries" of the European and American systems for exploiting the rest of the world.

For this reason the real interests of the common peoples of Europe and America and the interests of the people in the rest of the world cannot be entirely coincident. Even though all may be "workers" in some abstract sense, they basically do not belong to the same class concept. And when the people of the world's "other places" carry out political liberation as envisioned and promoted by Europe and America, they cannot actually be realizing economic liberation because they will always remain in a different class structure from European and American peoples. Therefore a concept of class that does not seriously reflect upon international exploitation is very suspicious. Until the problem of international exploitation is resolved, or more accurately, until the rules of imperialistic domination are eliminated, the diverse peoples of the world cannot belong to the same class concept.

Recently there has been a renewed interest in Marxist ideals of the unification of the world's proletariat classes—including the ideas of recent radical thinkers such as Thomas Piketty's notion of a progressive global tax on wealth concentration,[4] and Michael Hardt and Antonio Negri's conceptual imaginary of the "multitude"—that is a gathering of peoples to resist capitalism, and a practical movement taking shape to promote a self-governing, pluralistic and democratic organization of "the commons."[5] Even though there are some new ideas in their theories, none of these thinkers are able to adequately respond to Mao Zedong's Three Worlds theory, which directly addressed the problem of global inequality. Equality and democracy can alter the distribution of wealth within nation-states, but are ineffective in changing the situation of weaker countries within an exploitative international system. These are two equally important issues and cannot be confused. It is an open question within developed nation-states as to whether or not implementing Piketty's tactics for achieving equality, or Hardt and Negri's tactics for initiating social equality and collective self-governance might be beneficial. Such theories always pose a real conundrum on a global scale where it is most difficult to predict the outcome. There are many possible results, one of which would be to cause developing nations to further lose their competitive edge and fall into the trap of a declining economy before ever achieving prosperity. Thus the vision of "globalism" advocated by the Euro-American radical leftists might help in improving the interests of their own citizens, but whether such visions would be helpful in diminishing the system of international exploitation and oppression, or whether it could bring about real changes in the inequitable rules of the international game, are questions that are most certainly awaiting considerably more evidence to even be initially decided upon.

The contemporary system of international exploitation is perhaps an apotheosis of imperialism (e.g., V. I. Lenin once thought that imperialism was the apex phase of capitalism). Because it entails very highly developed methods of domination, and as the efficacy of military incursion diminishes, control over every aspect of the vital lifelines of states and peoples is clearly advancing. Increasing control over global systems of financial capitalism and new developments in advanced technology that function to exert control over basic resources (such as energy production and agriculture) are becoming more and more pronounced. And this increasing control over vital lifelines functions as a further step toward guaranteeing a deepening domination of the world by imperialism, with its totalizing power to set game rules and to exercise interpretive power over what can even count as knowledge. This monopoly over the setting of game rules and over knowledge production itself clearly amounts to a totalizing capitalism.

Even though the logics of domination and world control exercised by modern imperialism are most powerful, they also have their fatal weaknesses. We have already analyzed the problems of imitation in tactical deployments and counterstrategizing. Both of these problems deal with forms of resistance open to weaker parties within structures of domination, and in such dynamics we find that the weaker party's counterstrategies can always have a certain destructive effect on imperialist orders, even if they cannot be fully overturning modes of imperialist domination. It is precisely the problem of tactical imitation though that presents imperialism with a problem most difficult to address. This is because imitative tactics can lead to the effective obsolescence of imperialist strategies— that is, to be hoist by one's own petard, as it were. As "imitation tests" show, within any adversarial situation, one cannot afford to be accepting the consequences of imitative revenge by an inimical party, because that would necessarily bring about the unfortunate impasse of a prisoner's dilemma—that is, a situation that could possibly result in mutual annihilation. It is only within strategies of shared flourishing that tests of universal imitation can endure. Thus only game rules that are aimed at guaranteeing peace and cooperation—that is, rules based on shared interests—can stand the tests of imitation. This would seem to be a self-evident truth. Is it not most perplexing then as to why global justice remains such an unrealizable possibility? The reason might not be particularly mysterious or profound, though, as it is based solely on the fact that hegemonic nation-states still possess a pronounced strategic advantage, and hence they remain intent on making use of every possible means to preserve their advantage based in structural inequality. Another difficult problem that might lead to feelings of despair, is that within the current global order, it is only the regnantly powerful that really have any means to be establishing institutions that are universally beneficial to the world order. However, the powerful always remain set on stubbornly seeking to maximize their own exclusive self-interests.

Transcendent Truth cannot solve any actual problems. To really be resolving problems, one must be looking for critical junctures within history. We should be looking back over the unique historical reasons that enabled the Zhou dynasty to have established the *tianxia* system. The fortunate victory of the Zhou gave them a leading position in an alliance among many states. And since the Zhou was a relatively smaller state, it had to attempt to solve the political problem of "the one governing the many" and "the small governing the large." For these reasons, establishing a world institution of universal flourishing seemed to be the only rational choice. But this kind of opportune historical moment cannot be repeated. In fact, such opportunities are never repeated, and the future would seem to bode little promise. However, it is possible that current forces of globalization and certain advances in scientific technologies might be creating another critical point in history that brings about either great fortune or misfortune. On the one hand, highly developed future technologies might usher in an era wherein small groups, and even individuals, might be able to exercise the power of destroying any existing national order. And this would mean that minority communities—those that are currently being oppressed or small groups with unbridled ambitions—could, in possessing advanced technologies, become extremely dangerous by presenting a fatal challenge to imperialistic systems. On the other hand, advanced developments in technological systems might indicate that societies and nation-states are becoming unprecedently powerful while at the same time becoming extremely fragile.

Nassim Nicholas Taleb has interestingly analyzed how fragility has become extremely difficult for modern societies to deal with in its various forms.[6] And along with this increasing fragility, there might be profound difficulties in enduring the destruction wrought by various irrational modes of resistance to fragility. In a certain sense, then, the possibility of such totally destructive challenges looming on a future horizon represent a kind of "apocalyptic question." Put more precisely, the destructive capabilities inherent in advanced technologies are not only a threat to hegemonic powers but also to the entire world. Such technological advances might catapult any conflict of interest or those between spiritual (worldview) disagreements into extremely dangerous situations. This kind of danger is not just an apocalyptic problem for hegemonic powers, but even more so for humanity at large. The real danger of these apocalyptic predicaments lies not in some final decision or last decisive battle but rather in the fact that humanity cannot possibly endure the destructive forces unleashed by advanced technology, which is far more likely to lead to the end of the world. Facing this problem, the only possible deliverance is to be establishing world institutions that can secure the flourishing of all persons and all states. And this would require the creation of new rules of the game that alter a logic of competition in order to bring about a world system based in universal compatibility and peaceful coexistence.

Herein resides the contemporary relevance of the *tianxia* system—or perhaps we might say its very futurity.

16 Kantian Questions
and Huntington's Problem

In response to the fatal threat that warfare posed for humanity, Immanuel Kant posited his ideal of "perpetual peace." For his time, Kant's raising of this issue was very progressive. In fact, at this historical juncture Europe had fallen into an intense competition over who could carve up the world, and the temptations to go to war outweighed any motivations for peace. Indeed, it wasn't until after World War II that in the European context the allure of peace again finally exceeded the temptations to go to war. Actually, it is difficult to determine whether this desire for peace overcoming the appetites for war was a result of hard lessons learned from two world wars, or merely due to the new the threat of nuclear annihilation.

Kant's theory of peace is simultaneously an idealistic fantasy and a realistic anticipation. The idealistic fantasy comes from his positing of a "world republic" constituted by "world citizens." Such a conception takes the world to be just a larger scaling of the model of a nation-state. Kant himself rejected this unrealistic fantasy for the reason that it would be impossible for a world republic to result from the convergence of the ideal aspirations coming from each individual nation-state, since each state would have to be agreeing upon ultimately being subsumed within one great state. Moreover, if the world really were to become a single state, then it would likely develop into an authoritarian regime. For these reasons Kant recommended a rational plan for insuring peace—namely, a peaceful alliance composed of "free nations."[1] At the time, for Kant "free nations" referred to nations distinct from authoritarian, republican states. The key reason that an alliance of free nations could be considered capable of realizing peace was that free states had similar, nonauthoritarian institutions, a common political culture, and a shared set of values. Kant's theory has come to fruition in actual practice as the European Union.

Kant posited a wonderful theory, but it falls short in being unable to address the problem of achieving peace on a global scale. In the first place, Kant's criteria for realizing peace requires that the institutions and prescribed values for each state be the same. But this condition cannot possibly be satisfied on a world scale. The various nations of the world have different cultures, values, and political institutions, so it is difficult to imagine that all nations could converge as one. And it is even harder to imagine a unity in cultural and religious terms. For these reasons the largest scope to which Kant's proposal would be applicable is a region that shares a relatively similar culture—Europe, for example. But, of course, such historical cultural achievements of relative similarity cannot solve the problem of world peace. Moreover, political and cultural homogeneity between nation-states doesn't necessarily entail an absence of conflict. Kant's proposal for peace is merely an international agreement among nations, and is not a system wherein shared interests are actually conceived of as transcending national interests. It is thus that Kant's proposal cannot guarantee serious conflict or mutual injury will not eventually arise between various states. Kant believed that between free states a potential always exists for resolving disagreements via rational means. This rational faith could be redefined in the present age as a story about the absence of war between democratic countries. While such a story is certainly not without its reasons for misgivings, this is not important. For the problem lies in the fact that even if certain states do not resort to open military conflict, they might still be carrying out warfare by other means such as financial warfare or other pernicious strategies that can be seriously harmful to the interests of other states. National interests and pressures for national survival are intimately connected, and one cannot expect that these motives will cease to exist just because of a supposed similarity in political culture.

Kant's proposal might be able to promote regional cooperation, but it is much more difficult to rely on it to resolve international disputes, especially the new conflicts resulting from increasing trends of globalization. In particular, Kant's proposals fail to address Samuel Huntington's thesis regarding civilizational clash: for example, the Israeli-Palestinian conflict, the opposition between the West and Russia, grievances between the Middle East and the West, the ongoing contradictions between China and America, and the list goes on and on. There is much to be suspicious of in Huntington's thesis of civilizational clash such as his reductively dividing of the world up into major civilizational groups with corresponding descriptions of unique civilizational essences. But still within the general problematic that he raises there is a profound insight—namely, that similarity in cultural and political institutions alone is not sufficient to prevent civilizational conflict. This means that dissensus in political ideology is not as deeply problematic as civilizational conflict. The end of the Cold War could not have possibly signaled the "end of history" (cf. Fukuyama), but rather only marked a new phase in world history. On this particular point Huntington is indeed visionary. The transformations in the nature of world conflicts have already confirmed that "the end of history" was an alarmist and empty declaration. Even so, whether civilizational clash is really the deepest source of conflict is still a debatable question. In the wake of several events that seemed to confirm Huntington's thesis of civilizational clash, a kind of covert cold war has been reinstigated. But this time around the rhetoric is different. It is no longer just a cold war between communism and liberalism, but now seems to be a cold war between authoritarian and democratic nations. Still, this can't simply mean a return to Cold War models of engagement.

Rather, what is more likely happening is the realization that the various modes of contradiction which have beset the modern world have never disappeared. And it doesn't matter if such contradictions are expressed as a conflict of political ideologies or as civilizational clash, a conflict between national interests or as class conflict. And especially, it doesn't matter if this is conceived of as a result of a conflict between rights and interests. It is simply that all these various contradictions, important as they are in different epochs, are always returning in different guises. Perhaps what we need to consider more carefully is that, just as the sameness of political institutions is insufficient to preclude the possibility of contradictions and conflict, civilizational similarity cannot possibly guarantee the absence of contradictions and conflict. In fact, it is more likely that concessions being made between countries with similar civilizations happen on the basis of deliberations regarding rights and interests rather than appeals to civilizational similarity. This point doesn't negate the seriousness of the problem of civilizational clash, but it does suggest that civilizational clash is not necessarily the most entrenched root of conflict. Since any type of conflict, occurring under different circumstances, can in turn emerge as a dominant contradiction, the truly important question isn't what kind of contradiction is most fundamental, but rather what kind of order is capable of guaranteeing that no matter what type of contradiction arises, things won't progress to the fatal conflict of warfare.

Many moderns have hoped that through rational dialogue we can resolve disagreements and have thus developed various dialogical theories of ethics and politics. According to these ideals, dialogue is the least costly game to be engaging in and can actually replace the openly violent contests that deploy real weapons with more deliberative counteroffers. In theory, if rational dialogue is capable of resolving conflict, then Kantian peace could be realized. If not on a world scale, then at least on a local level, we could achieve "perpetual peace." However, the effectiveness of replacing war games with language games remains always at best a fervent hope. What this actually shows is that disputes in language cannot replace disputes in action, and that rational dialogue is ultimately capable of resolving rather insignificant disagreements.

Perhaps the limitations of rational dialogue are a consequence of the fact that most dialogues are not entirely rational. If dialogues were entirely rational and were actually engaged in with good intentions by all parties, could they then be effective in resolving problems of conflict? Here we can turn to Jürgen Habermas's concept of dialogue carried out within ideal speech conditions—that is, modes of dialogue that are fully rational and entered into under conditions of full equality, sincerity, and honesty. Habermas's ideal dialogue situation approximates a utopia to the point of being naïve and of little practical use. For example, Habermas requires that ideal dialogue be "truthful," but not only is true speech not always necessarily sufficient in resolving conflicts, but in some cases, truth can actually lead to disastrous outcomes. It is the utopian nature of Habermasian discourse ethics that is the root of the problem. The limitations of Habermasian ideal dialogue theory lies in its ignoring a basic fact. With respect to those things that involve our most fundamental interests, it doesn't matter how rational the dialogues that we engage in because none of them can lead to effective conflict resolution. In those things that have immediate impact on the meaning of life such as religion, spirituality, and values, it is well-nigh impossible to achieve mutual agreement through rational dialogue alone.

The theoretical limit of a dialogue that is fully rational and carried out with good intentions is that it can at most achieve a degree of mutual understanding and mutual sympathy. But it can never be the case that participants in an ideal dialogue, just because of their mutual understanding and sympathy, will necessarily make interest-effacing concessions regarding issues relating to their personal life narratives and deeply held values. This limitation can be summed up in the phrase "mutual understanding cannot guarantee mutual agreement."[2] The difficulty lies in the fact that from a mutual understanding of "minds" we cannot infer a mutual agreement of "hearts." Nor should we be inferring that even where interests for individual "bodies" converge, there might not also be changes happening at the level of mutual understanding and mutual agreement.

John Rawls is generally recognized as carrying on and developing this tradition of Kantian thinking. Rawls's new version of a "law of peoples"[3] certainly gets into even larger-scale political questions previously unthought of in Kantian theorizing on cosmopolitan peace. But because Rawls's hypotheses in many places run counter to Kant's principle of a universally good moral will, it is hard to imagine that Kant would agree with these Rawlsian developments. And with respect to international politics, Rawls's theory is hardly that compelling. Still, it is a big departure from the domestic political theory he articulated in *A Theory of Justice*. The reason I want to discuss Rawls's theory of international relations here is the huge difference between his theory of international and domestic conceptions of justice. This difference reveals, in a rather paradigmatic way, the limitations of international political theory. According to Rawls, the principles of justice to be applied to domestic societies are not appropriate for international societies. This is especially true regarding the "difference principle" as a condition of preferential consideration for the most vulnerable in deciding matters of distributive justice. Rawls thinks that this principle ought not, nor can be used at an international level. This is because the difference principle gives preferential consideration to the interests of the weakest in ideally distributing economic goods as a necessary investment that must be made in order to sustain social order. Otherwise, the possibility of the oppressed becoming the destroyers of the social order becomes an increasingly realistic predicament.

The difference principle is a precondition for guaranteeing that a society will not devolve into a state of the strong devouring the weak. And when Rawls negates the application of the difference principle for international societies, this is basically equivalent to negating any sense of international justice. In a world where the strong devour the weak, the oppressed obviously have no duty to be upholding the conditions of their own oppression and exploitation by the oppressors. Under such conditions it is likely that exceptional means of resistance will be employed, leading to a world in crisis. In thinking of how to resolve this problem, Rawls came up with the method of interventionism. According to Rawls, under certain conditions it is necessary to use "condemnation and coercive intervention " against uncooperative nations. The reason for this is that under the Law of Peoples, liberal and decent peoples have a right to be intolerant of "outlaw states."[4] There is nothing at all new in this proposal as it is nothing more than a form of modern neoimperialism. It is definitely not something Kant could recognize as an international principle. Actually, Kant had already, in advance as it were, rejected Rawls's international theory by announcing that in conflict between states that neither party can be declared an unjust enemy since this would already presuppose a judgment of right.[5] Obviously, no single party can or should possess the power to be unilaterally determining standards of justice.

In the ongoing efforts to resolve international conflicts and to uphold world peace, the United Nations represents a great achievement. Stephen Angle has pointed out that in my previous book, *Tianxia System*, with an "overly narrow reading" of the United Nations, I offered a rather inadequate assessment.[6] However, the United Nations is in the final analysis only an international consultatory organization that belongs to a system dominated by certain nation-states, and as such cannot be a mechanism for world management, and even less, a universally acceptable world political institution. The UN is still limited by a political culture of "internationalism" and hence does not reach the realm of a true political "worlding." Thus all of the rules of the UN are not suited to world institutions but are fit only for international regulations. For each nation-state the UN can serve as a kind of space for public consultations in which to carry on its (exclusively domestic and self-centered) forms of negotiation and brokering. The UN is an institutional attempt to replace violence with communication and is a hybridic product that fuses ideals of peace with concepts of rational discourse.

However, when multiple parties, using the institutional frameworks set by the UN, are able to arrive at a consensus, it is always the case that the disputes being addressed are never too serious. But when encountering issues directly impacting questions of vital national interest, there is always substantial difficulties faced in terms of what the UN is capable of achieving in arriving at any effective consensus, resolutions, or substantive agreements. A still deeper problem is that typically no parties are ever fully satisfied with the supposedly just decisions reached through UN procedures. And with each sovereign state seeking to maximize its own exclusive interests, it is difficult for them to see matters of international justice as actually being "just." Moreover, it is also exceedingly difficult to satisfy UN determined conditions of justice. In reconciling international disagreements, the UN has already done all that it can, but its institutional power is ultimately limited. Without a doubt, dialogue and mediation can to some degree help to diminish warfare, but these methods alone have never been able to decrease the contradictions that give rise to reasons for conflict in the first place. Even when multiple parties realize a kind of effective balance, it is usually only a result of noncooperative games reaching a sort of Nash equilibrium, and very seldom signals the fantasy of a "win-win" outcome being achieved via rational dialogue.

We have no reason to be criticizing the UN here, though, because the UN is ultimately an organization lacking in effective power on a global scale. In essence, the UN is merely a mechanism for international negotiations rather than an effective means for exercising world political power. This becomes especially true when we consider that as an entity, the UN has less political power than any sovereign nation, and thereby is naturally incapable of forestalling the behavior of any cohort of imperialistic powers and their quest for world domination. It is for this reason that the UN remains a long way from being an exemplary model for world governance and has no real power to be transcending the international system set by sovereign nation-states. When all is said and done, the United Nations ideal doesn't offer a "world concept" that is any higher than the concept of national sovereignty.

Stephen Angle has a constructive idea here. He believes that changing the character of the UN and developing it into more of a *tianxia* system might be a relatively economical road to take: "It may be a easier to move from existing international institutions toward a more genuinely global institution, than to reject the existing institutions and try to start from scratch."[7] However, because the character of the UN is essentially governed by the political logics of a system of modern state sovereignty, it is extremely difficult for it to be wholly remolded into a world institution that belongs to the world. I believe that if a *tianxia* system is to become a possibility in the future, then its foundation will most likely be based on those structures and organizations that have real power such as systems of global finance, global technologies, and the internet. Or perhaps we should say that remaking global financial systems, global technological systems, and the internet into a world system that more readily allows for common flourishing, collective ownership, and shared governance is a necessary condition for the realization of any new *tianxia* system.

Of course, the most important question for a future world lies in how to change the regnant logics of political action and modes of political thinking. And without a spiritual revolution, any merely material revolutions might just bring the world to an even more apocalyptic place.

17 Two Types of Exteriority:
Naturalist and Constructivist

Political logics are determined by political orders and their underlying modes of thinking. And political orders and their modes of thinking are ultimately determined by the influence of basic political units. From the early days of modernity to the present, political logic has largely been determined by the basic political units of discrete "individuals" and sovereign "nation-states." Because the political unit of *tianxia* has been absent, the largest and most effective category of political logic has been limited to the nation-state, and the very ideal of world order has been forsaken. As we have rehearsed above, international politics belongs to an extension of national politics, and as such can only serve nations, not the world. Because of this, modern politics has been destined to be unable to resist its own internal logic that precludes developing a truly world-based politics. In a strict sense the reasons we might have for hoping for a future world politics do not arise from seeking after ideals of "a best possible world," since we can't state with certainty that a world politics would necessarily entail a better politics (for the question of whether or not a kind of politics is better than another form is, in the absence of some universal standard, always determined by unique interpretive contexts). Instead, our hope derives from the fact that human life has come to a point wherein we need most urgently a world politics. Without such a politics it becomes nigh impossible to secure the universal human need for peace, safety, coexistence, and cooperation. This is to say that world politics fulfills certain objective needs, and as such is more than simply a matter of appealing to relative and subjective values. Herein we will be discussing the effectiveness of a world political logic.

From a most basic standpoint the political is simply a means of resolving human life issues relating to security and cooperation, and is a way of resolving problems that arise from negative "exteriority." It is for this reason that politics aims to construct an order capable of pacifying conflicts emerging through exteriority—that is, an order that can resolve the negative aspects of exteriority via positive forms of cooperation. As a natural phenomenon, in order to transcend every individual standpoint, and to transcend every "we" grouping, there must exist a naturally exterior "otherness" that reciprocally limits all freedom of action. This is an objective fact recognized by Xunzi, Hobbes, and many other original position theorists. Recognizing such naturally exterior alterity, though, leads to problems of conflict, and just as Hobbes described, such conflict is necessarily a nasty and brutish competition. However, despite competition for mere existence within conditions that are nasty and brutish, it is not the case that such natural conflicts must go unresolved. This is an important feature of natural exteriority. Speaking both theoretically and practically, despite having experienced numerous examples of destructive zero-sum games, it is always possible to hope that conflict for existence will come to an end via some kind of a rational equilibrium reached in the course of competition. Whether in cooperative or a noncooperative balance, both parties can explicitly or implicitly acknowledge a shared division of interests. And this suggests that struggles for existence don't have to end in a life-or-death battle, but can precipitate a search for an acceptable distribution of benefits.

According to the natural logic of an original position, there are at least two kinds of possibilities for political evolution: (1) *Xunzi's model* which uses the benefits of cooperation to entice outsiders to become internal participants, and in so doing, establishes a stable cooperative order. This is a logic of interiorization. (2) *Hobbes's model* which expects the strong to set up a powerful government to induce outsiders to submit to its hegemonic order. This is a logic of a subjugating exteriority. In fact, these two kinds of political logics always exist simultaneously in the midst of any regional political dynamics. From the course of history we can see that a logic of interiorization is more akin to a Chinese style of political thinking, while a logic of subjugation is more akin to European styles of political thinking. This is simply an empirical fact, not a necessary principle. If we take a long view of history, though, and especially if we consider the future as well, we can see that there exists a phenomenon and tendency toward "institutional convergence."

In the wake of the political experience and institutional formation of various regions and nation-states, there is gradually emerging a constitutive and mutually illuminating common understanding. The governments of each region undergo a process of learning from the strong points of others to offset their own weaknesses, and gradually produce a more hybridic set of institutions that have assimilated much knowledge. Already the political institutions of many states of the world today are clearly composed of many hybridic factors, to the point that it is difficult to simply refer to a country as capitalist, socialist, or any other term of ideological significance. For example, the institutions of Europe, China, and the United States all have both socialist and capitalist elements, although their proportional emphasis and ways of approaching these political-economic concepts remain quite different. The deep reasons for institutional convergence are that even though the distribution of benefits do not entirely put an end to the conditions of a natural struggle, it is never necessary for a zero-sum game or a battle-to-the death to ensue. For this reason societies gradually make the adjustments necessary for realizing a reasonable mode of distribution, and all reasonable institutions always end up being at least partially similar. What this means is that in facing the most serious problems of life, the choices people make are likely to be rational, and thus there is hope to establish cooperative relationships and to achieve reconciliation. By contrast, when it comes to issues that don't directly impinge upon life and death issues, it seems that human beings are more likely to reject cooperation and to go their own idiosyncratic ways.

The hardest conflicts, then, in which we might even find reconciliation to be impossible, are usually a result of cultural contradictions that have little or nothing to do with struggles for existence. This fact might call to mind something similar to Huntington's thesis, for the cultural or civilizational exteriority of others is not in itself a fatal threat to one's own existence. Cultural difference simply means a different spiritual world, and differences in spiritual worlds do not necessarily lead to zero-sum games. We could imagine a more or less total indifference obtaining between two spiritual worlds to the extent of "each appreciating the beauty of its own culture" (cf. Fei Xiaotong)[1] and having little or no concern with the lives of each other. Obviously, the intolerance of the cultural exteriority of others is a human artifice. In other words, cultural alterity has no correlate in a naturally given negative exteriority but can only come to be viewed as such via an artificially constructed order of values. In early history, given the geographical separations of certain cultures, there were no significant intercultural interactions. But as soon as the opportunity arose, mutually beneficial interactions between cultures was a natural occurrence, resulting in either mutual transformation or hybridic fusion. It can hence be said that for early cultures there were no clearly demarcated borders, but rather only a fluid boundaries and mutual forms of evolution. Why, then, is it that intercultural relations have become so marked by opposition and enmity? This is a question that requires explanation.

Every kind of culture represents a spiritual world, and such a spiritual world can provide an explanatory framework for all things and events occurring within a culture. Different spiritual worlds give rise to different explanatory frameworks. And such differences aren't simply a matter of right and wrong but rather reflect different perspectives. Divergences in perspectives don't necessarily lead to envy or jealousy because each culture "in appreciating its own beauty" can remain satisfied with itself, while not feeling a need to look upon cultural alterity with enmity. Even in situations of mutual mistrust between cultures, this doesn't necessarily entail that things must escalate into open hostilities or wars caused by cultural differences. This is because viewing the cultures of others as an enemy requires at least the following two exclusionary factors: (1) *Dogmatism*—that is, the belief that one's own culture, as a spiritual world, is the only truth, and all other spiritual worlds are false. This is an "epistemological fallacy" as it mistakenly applies the concept of empirical truth to the realm of values. (2) *The right of an exclusive orthodoxy*—that is, thinking that one's own culture as a spiritual world is the only correct one, and thereby necessarily being in possession of the right to make absolute value judgments about other cultures; and moreover exercising the right of usurping the interpretive authority of other spiritual worlds. Involved here is a mission to be converting adherents to other spiritual worlds to one's own. These two factors together are necessary in the production of cultural insularity.

Among the various kinds of cultures, it is only monotheism that can possibly give rise to this twin need for dogmatism and a right of exclusive orthodoxy. However, it is not the case that all monotheistic religions necessarily embrace both of these factors. For instance, even though Judaism is a monotheism, it is typically a "particularist" monotheism that is limited only to "God's chosen people" and isn't meant to apply in the same way to everyone else. Thus certain forms of Judaism might only have dogmatic beliefs without making claims to an orthodoxy that is universal and exclusive. The real turning point in history came with the appearance of Christianity. Christianity took the particularist monotheism of Judaism and turned it into a universalistic monotheism, resulting finally in the copresence of both dogmatism and an exclusive orthodoxy functioning as its equally important determining characteristics. Passing through the "four great discoveries" of Christian politics, a "spiritual politics" was created with its four great discoveries being propaganda, psychological control, massification, and the creation of spiritual enemies.[2] With all of this, other cultures came to be regarded as unacceptably heretical and as intolerable spiritual enemies that had to be either rejected or converted. Despite being a self-avowed basis for "universal civilization" in the West, Christianity remains the true source of intercultural hostility. It is in this sense, then, that it can be said that the advent of Christianity was a world-impacting event that actually sought to "sever communication between earth and heaven" as it attempted to abrogate the religious rights of other cultures, wipe out their unique sense of sacredness, and assert a monopoly over the religious rights of the entire world.

The great enterprise of Christianity, attempting to create a single unified spiritual world, did not really succeed, leading to a series of worldwide spiritual wars. This is what Huntington meant by "clashes of civilization" and is also what Carl Schmitt conceptualized as the "friend-enemy distinction" model of the political. From the time that Christianity conquered

Greek civilization, a logic of a struggle against heresy has taken shape in the West; with this, the West has come to see the world as being mired in conflictual opposition and warfare. With this Western hegemonic mission of subjugating the world via its dissolution of the a priori integrity of the "world" as a concept, the world itself has become disenchanted. Instead of being viewed as a sacred space, the world has become a mere stage for the universal realization of "Christianity."[3] In other words, the world itself has ceased to have any potential for subjective agency and has now become a mere object. Because of this, all the myriad things and events of the world and all its diverse peoples have lost their unique histories. Any history and culture existing prior to becoming part of this totalizing "Christian" civilization is viewed as forsaken and having hitherto existed only in a meaningless, existential absurdity.

This political-theological logic of Christianity has henceforth been expanded and applied in many different secular versions. For example, before being modernized by the "universal civilization" of the European Enlightenment, all other cultures were deemed as persisting in a state of benighted ignorance. And similarly, before their liberation through Communism, all nonliberated local cultures were viewed as hopelessly occulted; and prior to realizing democracy, illiberal societies wallowed in their misery, and so on and so forth. If the world can only have one kind of spirituality, then this signifies a loss of "the worldness of the world." For the nature of a world is not simply a matter of its spatial scope but is also most importantly a matter of its radical abundance and diverse plenitude. If a vast space is lacking in diversity and plurality, then it's not actually a world, but at most, just a "thing." The philosophical debates about "sameness" (*tong* 同) and "harmony" (*he* 和) occurring during the Spring and Autumn period already addressed this dynamic principle. If the myriad things are ultimately all the same, then the myriad things are really only one thing as just so many copies of "it." Only when there is a plurality of things can there actually be a "harmony," and only with a harmonizing of plurality do we have a world. For a world to be unified with one religion, one set of values, one spiritual world, then even if such a world was a vast expanse in its spatiality, in terms of spirit it would actually be nothing more than just one thing—and as such cannot count as a world.

Using the theological logic of monotheism as a political logic to con-

struct cultural exteriority in turn leads to intolerance and hostility in relations with other cultures. Such a politics can only remain in an immature
state, for it is only on the basis of a "harmonizing compatibility" that politics can come to be genuinely political. Politics established on the basis
of a "homogenizing universality" are merely a matter of exercising control, and control is not political. The concept of the political has a deeper
meaning than hegemonic control and dominating power. If a politics cannot realize orders that are "correlated with Heaven" (*peitian* 配天)—that
is, orders that advance a procreative growth of things in "letting all beings
be in their becoming," or said another way, orders that advance an abundant "richest plurality of beings"—then it is not really a political order.
Even though the political realm necessarily employs power, its goal cannot
be power for power's sake, but rather must lie in the institutionalization
of a compatible order of being that allows all things to achieve optimal
growth. The political then should be "correlated with *tian*," rather than
with any monotheistic conception of God.

The spiritual worlds of every culture has their own conception of the
sacred. And what sacred things in each culture provide explanation for
is not just the goods required for sustaining life, but to serve as a means
of explaining the very meaning of life itself. Every spiritual world has its
sacred mountains and rivers, lands, flora and fauna, along with its historical narratives and peoples. And together these sacred figures constitute
an indestructible realm existing beyond mundane time and space. It is in
these sacred mountains and rivers and their common histories that gives
a people their shared souls and cultural common sense that can mobilize
a feeling of collective agency. The sacredness inherent in every spiritual
world gives rise to its own indomitable transcendence, but different spiritual worlds, constructing as it were each other's exteriority, don't necessarily have to give rise to antagonistic relationships. It is only in the universalism of monotheism that, in the attempt to dominate the world, an
intractable enmity among spiritual worlds is engendered. As an alternative to this monotheistic spirit of world domination, the worldview proposed by the *tianxia* concept is able to accommodate a plurality of diverse
spiritual worlds, providing each and every spiritual world with its unique
sense of peace and contentment, and its freedom to live free from mutual
harm. In this sense, *tianxia* represents "an inclusive world of all possible

worlds." As such, *tianxia* is not part of a worldview that appeals to one homogenous spirit but is rather one that appeals to an achieved sense of existential continuity.

It is the West's use of a theological logic of monotheism as a political logic that has given rise to the modern challenge of a conflict of civilizations. Just as Huntington has allowed, the challenge that the West presents to other cultures is one-dimensional. And moreover, as even Huntington admits, the "West won the world not by the superiority of its ideas or values or religion (to which few members of other civilizations were converted) but rather by its superiority in applying organized violence."[4] As a result of such organized violence, by 1914 Westerners controlled about 84 percent of the world's territory. Yet, as the *tianxia* theory demonstrates, one might succeed in conquering and occupying a material world, but the truth remains that a spiritual world cannot be usurped. This guarantees that logics of domination will always eventually encounter a point of reversal. Throughout history the rise and fall of many great empires would seem to indicate that there is an unavoidable fate involved in the rise and decline of empires. But this is a historical claim without verification—a kind of superstitious mythology. So herein when we refer to "a point of reversal," it is not meant to be part of any mythology. Rather it is the conceptualization of a balance achieved via resistance, or in other words the "production of counterstrategies" from parties of alterity. In this achieved balance, a key condition is that modern game theory, new technologies, globalizing modes of organization, and antihegemonic social movements have steadily become more and more part of a shared repository of "common knowledge," which means that the deployment of effective counter measures to the logics of domination have become a real possibility.

In other words, the oppressed now have unprecedented access to operative means of retaliation and resistance, and this access effectively diminishes or dissolves any of the advantages that might have been accruing to imperialism. For the political logic of imperialism to be dismantled there must have emerged several points of reversal. First, after World War II, there was a proliferation of postcolonial sovereign states. Next, there was the balance of power that emerged during the Cold War with the proliferation of nuclear weapons—the situation of so-called MAD (mutually assured destruction). Implicated in this balance is of course an extreme danger. And again, there was the emergence of various forms of terrorism coming from nonstate actors that have prophesized global destruction. But perhaps the most important turning point has been the processes of globalization itself of which the internet might be a fair symbol. This is a largely positive transformation and even provides some reasons for optimism. These several turning points together suggest that imperialism as a kind of political logic is now unsustainable.

18 Borders and No Outside

A characteristic marker of modern politics are "borders." In other words, a foundational principle of modern politics is to clearly and distinctly define everything via processes of clear and distinct "demarcations." The result of this has been the production of all kinds of legally determined borders. Exerting the most influence among these borders has been the designations of individual rights and of national sovereignty, wherein individual rights define the boundaries of individuals and sovereignty defines national borders. Of course, the demarcation of things is not a modern invention, and even less a proprietary cultural product of Europe, since every civilization has, to varying degrees, drawn webs of demarcation within their traditions. But it is only with these particularly modern methods of demarcation that modern politics has affected a profound transformation on our ways of living in the world.

The demarcating boundaries of modern politics have at least the following life-altering characteristics:

1. *Clarity.* Traditional demarcations were frequently found to be insufficiently clear and distinct. Usually traditional demarcations resulted from implicitly acknowledged customs, leaving plenty of room for contestation. The different kinds of modern borders, on the other hand,

have been demarcated via legal methods and can be clearly defined. Hence they bring clarity to the rights, responsibilities, powers, and limits of everything.

2. *Closure.* Since the demarcations of traditional societies tended to be uncertain, it was seldom the case that a totally closed border was formed. This is to say that traditional demarcations were sufficient to pick out the unique features of things but faced difficulties in drawing clear dividing lines between one thing and another. In terms of logic, traditional demarcations imply propositions such as "the necessary properties or conditions for a thing X are a, b, c, and so on," but this description doesn't rule out whether there might be other features of X that are discontinuous with a, b, c, and so on. Modern demarcation implies something like "this thing X has the following necessary and sufficient features as enabling conditions: a, b, c, d," and moreover, the demarcating logics of modernity can rule out all other inconsistent features.

3. *Sovereignty.* Being able to clearly define closed borders also establishes a totalizing, internal power within such borders, and this is the concept of sovereignty. In the political logic of (Western) modernity the smallest political unit of sovereignty is the individual, and the largest political unit is the nation-state. The philosophical foundation of sovereignty is subjectivity, as both individual rights and national sovereignty require the possession of subjectivity. However, not all things that have subjectivity are by virtue of this feature recognized as sovereign. Take, for instance, the fact that modern politics has not clearly defined cultural sovereignty—a condition that has become a very complex issue.

Borders are constructed with the aim of setting off a clearly bounded, independent existence from other things. As has been stated earlier in this chapter, the basic units of politics determine political thinking and political order. And since the basic units of modern politics (namely, individuals and nation-states) maintain an independent existence by drawing clear boundaries in the face of any alterity, this mode of thinking is destined to give priority to seeking the maximization of exclusive interests. In other words, exclusive interests are necessarily prioritized over shared interests. According to this logic, except for those who are collaborating, all other "others" are in varying degrees a "negative exteriority." Because of this, conflicts between the independent basic units of politics cannot be avoided. Moreover, the maximization of exclusive interest are an interminable process, and because of this conflict also remains practically interminable. The problem of exteriority among individuals has already been resolved by nation-states. Societies, as defined by the legal frameworks established by nation-states, have transformed the exteriority existing among individuals into problems of interiority. However, for so-called "international societies"—although this concept is not really accurate as hitherto there hasn't been any truly world community within international space—the situation is totally different.

While international "society" on the surface has international law and various other international agreements and organizations to appeal to, in actuality it remains always potentially mired in a Hobbesian state of nature. With respect to the notion of international society, borders present a paradox. On the one hand, borders make clear distinctions regarding inviolable sovereignty and imply a kind of mutual recognition and a division of interests; on the other hand, it is only by transgressing or destroying the boundaries of others that individual nation-states can achieve an increase in their exclusive interests. For this reason, all regions outside of one's own borders are tacitly recognized as a potential commons to be plundered. In the current system of sovereign nation-states, if a sovereign nation becomes sufficiently powerful according to the logic of maximizing exclusive interest, such a state will develop into an imperialist hegemon. This is the basic story of modernity. But let us please be patient as this modern narrative is currently playing itself out. Despite our modest reasons for maintaining hope, there is at present an even more terrifying postmodern culture that is conniving to carry out further crimes against humanity.

Let's first continue with the modern narrative. It is the basic character of imperialism to view the entire world as so much territory that can be arbitrarily plundered. Put concretely, any region outside of Europe and North America as "the *rest* of the world"—including Asia, South America, and Africa—are all tacitly assumed to be common lands that can be exploited. This mode of imperialism, with the British Empire as a paradigmatic example, continued until the end of World War II. In this sense, we can take World War II as a point of reversal for the logic of imperialism. As colonial, semicolonial, and other traditionally oppressed states became sovereign nations, they modeled themselves on European institutions, technologies, and policies. As such, since previously oppressed states could now exercise a degree of resistance or even revenge, and at the very least always had the capacity for noncooperation, the earlier imperialistic strategies were no longer the most effective way for the Western imperialist powers to occupy the world commons. And because the world had already become full of sovereign nation-states, there was no longer an external "commons" to be exploited. It is for this reason that American imperialism, continuing in the role of world hegemon, carried out some institutional renovations within imperialism, turning modern imperialism into a globalizing imperialism.

American imperialism continued and intensified a portion of the strategies of modern imperialism that were still effective. The colonial system of modern imperialism was no longer possible, but maintaining an unequal system of international trade was found to be effective. This was a legacy of the British Empire. In addition, the hegemony of knowledge and the unequal systems of communication, as they had been conveyed in the English language, were also found to still be effective—this was another important inheritance of the British Empire. This system of hegemony of knowledge, facilitated by methods of communication and maintaining a monopoly over the production of discursive rules, has exerted a broad influence over the theological narratives of all things—be it in interpreting society, history, ways of living, and values. Cutting the lifelines of the knowledges and histories of other cultures, such an interpretive imperialist monopoly has reduced other spiritual worlds into meaningless shards. It has caused these spiritual worlds to lose their sacredness and integrity and has used a faith in progress (a kind of secular version of monotheism) to negate the historicity of all forms of cultural alterity. It has divided the world into a center and periphery, and further dichotomizes the world as either "having history and progress" or being "ahistorical and stagnate."

The ultimate result of these unequal narratives has been the effective devolution of other kinds of knowledge and spiritualities, even to the point of bringing about a mass extinction of certain cultural traditions. American imperialism is a clear intensification of the political despotism, economic domination, and epistemic hegemony of modern imperialism, and has conspired to create a kind of global "dependence" on the American framework.[1] According to an expression enjoyed in America, this is simply "American leadership." This kind of "American leadership" has been candidly explained by Joseph S. Nye as leading either by "hard" or "soft" power, in the ongoing manipulation of global political power dynamics, global capital markets, and global language systems.[2]

American imperialism has initiated two other "world structures" that permit a system transcending national sovereignty. One is financial hegemony, and the other is a strategy of using individual human rights to trump national sovereignty. According to analysis by Qiao Liang (a leading People's Liberation Army military strategist and geopolitical theorist), America has used the hegemony of the US dollar to set up the world's first "financial empire." This is an entirely novel and ingenious innovation. In 1971 the value of the US currency was decoupled from the gold standard. This event signaled the collapse of the global financial order agreed upon at the Bretton Woods Conference:

> The United States has propagated the development of a perfect storm in the world—namely, globalization. Using US currency as a foundation, America has established a historically unprecedented financial empire. This empire's tentacles reach into every corner of the globe, as every region mechanically and homogenously develops in an imitative manner. The US dollar flows ubiquitously into the world, and wealth flows towards America.[3]

The hegemony of US currency is not only a means of controlling world trade and a method for manipulating global financial markets, but at the same time in serving to secure American capital interests and its position of dominance, it is also a direct form of profiteering. In this process there is a miraculous turn that allows for wealth to be accumulated *creatio ex nihilo*. The unmatched military might of the United States is converted into a kind of "credit" system then for the US dollar, which in turn secures the exporting of the US dollar. And the exporting of the US dollar returns as unlimited wealth. The hegemony of the US dollar has become a pure and totalizing method of capitalist exploitation by using fictitious "capital" to in effect be exploiting the entire globe. And whenever there is a challenge to this system, the United States uses its currency's capital advantage to instigate financial warfare. This ensemble of strategies inflicts severe damage on other national currencies and regional economies, and sometimes even results in direct military aggression. According to Qiao

Liang's speculations, the various wars instigated by the United States over the past two or three decades have all been wars to protect the hegemony of American currency.

Another invention of American imperialism is the hegemony of human rights discourse, with its characteristic slogan being "human rights trump sovereignty." This means that under the banner of human rights it becomes possible to "legitimately" invade, contain, and manipulate other nations, and can even serve as a pretext for initiating wars. In theory, human rights as a universal principle, represents a real breakthrough for the previous ethno-nation-state system, but in practice it has largely been used to protect American special interests. The hegemonic art of "transforming universality into particularity" is a result of the power of interpretation wielded by America in determining the scope and application of universal values. This clever art of "transforming universality into particularity" can be contrasted with the early Christian art of "transforming particularity into universality." Saint Paul interpreted the unique Christian faith in the story of the suffering and resurrection of Jesus as a narrative about the universal salvation of the world, thereby giving Christianity its universal character. Today the United States relies upon economic and military pressures to ensure that the power of interpretation over universal human rights resides solely with America, thereby privatizing the right to interpret a universal concept. This in effect is to back up the use of "soft power" with a guarantee of "hard power." And is similar to the always incomplete Christian fantasy of a grand unity under God's sovereignty. There is a double conversion here moving from "transforming particularity into universality" to "transforming universality into particularity." This is a ravenous strategy that allows one nation to control the world, and in its shrewdness it is truly a marvel to behold.

In this game of globalized imperialism, America not only wins through its exertion of supreme power but also has effectively become the sole decider of what kind of game it will be by maintaining a monopoly over the creation and interpretation of the geopolitical game rules. In this fashion, America has successfully become the only extra-legal subject in the world game, in its exceptionalism taking on three roles in one. That is, the United States acts as an *arbiter* of who can play the game, a *legislator* of the rules of the game, and a *decider* of what kind of game it will be.

Because of this, America becomes the only truly exceptional nation-state in the world, transcending the system of national sovereignty by maintaining such "double-edged borders." What having "double borders" means is simultaneously maintaining internationally recognized borders existing between sovereign nations *and* possessing unilaterally determined, invisible borders always suited to exclusive American interests. This is the international system that covers most places in the world, including those places that are actually controlled or dominated by the United States. This is especially obvious when we consider financial systems, media production, the internet, and the general nature of globalized discourse. And of course, this set up involves a globalized military power.

These invisible US borders span most parts of the world. And with American hegemony being so successful, and seeming to possess the conditions necessary to create a world system approximating that of a *tianxia* system, why then is it the case that "pax Americana" even in all its splendor, is finding it increasingly hard to endure any longer, even to the point that it now seems to have entered a slow but steady phase of decline in global authority? Though there are many theories regarding the possible demise of the American empire, virtually all of them belong to traditional theories about the rise and fall of empires. Most of these involve either an analysis of the mistaken use of specific strategies *or* speculations about an external challenge of some sort. What all of these traditional theories fail to recognize, though, is that the real cause for decline resides in the limitations of the logic of imperialism itself.

Even though imperialism has an ambition to govern the entire world, it lacks a worldview that can take the world's interests as a standard. Imperialism is only capable of taking on a nation-state perspective. And since it can only take the nation-state as its ultimate subject in seeing the world as a mere object to be dominated, for this reason, regardless of what degree is reached in the extending of its imperial powers of domination, its interests and its values are always curtailed to the measures of the nation-state. This then is the true limitation of the logic of imperialism. It can be said that insofar as it is lacking the worldview of imagining "nothing exterior to *tianxia*," it has no hope of establishing a truly universal order. And it is just because imperialism lacks a "nothing exterior to *tianxia*" worldview that from its very conceptual root, it will always be operating with only an inverted understanding of the enabling conditions for universal order. Its fatal error lies in thinking that "universality" comes from "universalization." Whether in logic or in practice, universality has to be a precondition for universalization—not the other way around. This is but to say that only with universality can there be universalization, and that in no way can universality be inferred from universalization. Herein lies a basis for the distinction between a unilateral universalism and a compatible or inclusive universalism. This is also the root of the basic difference between an imperialistic world system and a harmonizing of myriad states in a *tianxia* system.

The root significance of the *tianxia* concept is that it can explain clearly the idea of a world with "no outside." This is a world with only interiority and no exteriority, and is a necessary condition for the establishing of universal order. This means that if a world order is to become truly universal, as a precondition it must realize the interiorization of the world. Interiorization is an ontological condition for universality. And only by realizing the interiorization of the world is it possible to establish a universal order; for then and only then is it possible to advance the universalization of a universal order. To put it the other way around, as long as political exteriority exists, the world cannot become a true world, and the universal order of the world cannot exist. Under conditions that lack an interiorized world, trying to unilaterally promote one's own exclusive order as a universal order is certain to encounter external resistance. It is for this reason that the construction of a world order must first of all recognize "the nonexteriority of *tianxia*" as an a priori concept. Only then, with the political logic of interiorizing the world, can we hope for the establishment of a universal world order.

Any political logic that rejects a principle of "nonexteriority" is bound to seek the maximization of its exclusive self-interest, and because of this, it ensures that the world will be divided into the exploiters and the exploited, the rulers and the ruled. This then is the logic of exteriority and is precisely the opposite of a "nonexterior" interiorizing logic. The reason why the political logic of imperialism cannot ultimately succeed lies in the inevitability of encountering problems that it cannot possibly resolve of itself. These problems are always paradoxical. The following paradoxes are possible variations of this basic contradiction at the heart of imperialist logics:

1. *The Xunzi Paradox* which could also be called the "cooperation paradox." Cooperation can produce an increase in the overall amount of
   possible benefit, and hence people need to cooperate. However, if people
   must seek the maximization of their exclusive self-interests (the working
   hypothesis of "homo economicus"), then this necessarily would bring
   about the problem of conflict over private interests and lead to hostility
   and the dissolution of the very possibility of cooperation. This problem
   can only be resolved in political units that have been interiorized.
   Modern theory and historical experience have both proven that only
   with the interiorizing of a basic political unit, whether it be a nation-
   state or some other collective body politic—even the mafia—can there
   be an overcoming of this problem of conflict between private interests
   by establishing effective legal mechanisms for securing fair economic
   distribution and for recognizing property rights. The problem remains
   though that until the world itself becomes an interiorized unit of politics, it is impossible to realize a universally acceptable institutionalized
   distribution of interests on a global scale. It is for this reason then that
   unless there is a resort to coercive violence or the deploying of certain
   technological advantages used to exert dominance, any imposed hegemonic game rules imposed will inevitably be met with continuous resistance, open revolution, and the dissolution of cooperative possibilities.
   But strategies of violence and domination are bound to meet up with
   even greater problems down the road.

2. *The Imitator's Paradox.* According to our previous strategic "imitation
   test," any game scenario wherein knowledge and technology can't be
   monopolized, all competitive game strategies will in the long run
   become common knowledge. Since every game will ultimately reach a
   state wherein all participants imitate the most competitive strategies,
   the inevitable result is a realization of game-theoretic balance as seen,
   for instance, in iterations of the Prisoner's Dilemma and scenarios of
   assured mutual destruction. The key to note here is that strategies seeking a maximizing of exclusive self-interests, or the resorting to violent
   tactics, will inevitably result in calculations that are intolerable from a
   standpoint of universal imitation; of course, including the most intolerable conduct of seeking revenge. It is for this reason that it is impossible
   to establish a universally recognized or universally effective set of institutionalized game rules under such conditions. This means that using
   hegemonic logics to construct a universal order is necessarily paradoxical. For with such operative logics as soon as one is seeking to establish
   a universal and peaceful order, one is simultaneously undermining that
   very order.

3. *The paradox of preserving the right to exclusive interpretation.* Controlling the media through which spiritual modalities can be expressed would seem to lead to an exclusive right to be interpreting spirituality, values, and truth; but it is difficult to secure public trust with such an exclusive monopoly over interpretations. The problem with the strategy of monopolizing exclusive interpretations is that in order to affirm the legitimacy of hegemony, the concept of "justice" has to be used to describe and interpret various hegemonic actions. For example, there is the appeal to the values of "peace," "human rights," and "liberation" used to initiate wars. And then there is the nominal uses of "freedom" and "democracy" used to destroy freedom and democracy, and the use of "human rights" to negate the human rights of others, and the appeals to political correctness to negate traditional values, and so on. Such rhetoric has all sorts of evil intentions and consequences implicated in the working concept of "justice." And this contradiction gives rise to a fundamental paradox in monopolizing the power of interpretation. If the concept of "good" implies all legitimate actions, then the concept of good itself is actually self-refuting because "bad" is also implicated in the "good." For as we know, as a matter of logic, "from any false proposition (that is, a contradiction) any proposition (including true propositions) can be derived." In deductive logic this is a valid axiom; but for a similar logical construction to be used in political interpretations, the results are always disastrous. For if a (paradoxical) concept of justice has implicated within it all actions, then this proves that this concept of justice is a false concept. From a different angle, if we claim as a logical principle that "a true proposition has implicated within it every proposition (including false propositions)," then this principle will self-destruct. If from true propositions we can derive false propositions, then the true propositions are not credible. In a similar fashion, if the concept of justice has implicated within it legitimating reasons for any course of action (even evil ones), then the concept of justice has implicated within it all kinds of wrong. This being the case, such a concept of justice would similarly self-destruct.

To use the individual, ethnicity, the nation-state, or religion as the basic units of politics is to define political logic in such a way as to make it extremely difficult to develop a universally shareable world order. And this makes it extremely difficult to resolve problems on a world scale. This is because all these basic political units as boundary concepts have not developed with the world in mind. Thus, as formulated concepts, they are not up to this world-political task. Given the current conditions of globalization, what the world urgently needs is a kind of universal order that can guarantee a common sharing of interests. Otherwise the world will remain unable to cope with this postimperialist era of chaos. As the old orders of imperialism decline to a point where they exist in name only, the world is increasingly beset by all kinds of unthinkable plights such as large-scale terrorist activities, fundamentalist mass religious movements, and other such irrational dangers. This is why the future world really needs a new *tianxia* system. In other words, the world needs to become a *tianxia* to vouchsafe world peace. It is only when the logic of "nothing outside of *tianxia*" can be appealed to in producing an integrated world that is internalized without any exteriority, that there can be hope for establishing a universally shared world order.

19 Materializing Conditions for a New *Tianxia*

What is coming to an end is a certain form of modernity, not history itself. Perhaps at some unforeseen time, history will come to an end, or perhaps it will continue on indefinitely. This is not something we can know. Francis Fukuyama's thesis regarding the end of history has already proven to be an overly hasty conclusion in light of Huntington's clash of civilizations notion. But civilizational clash is just a rather remarkable longstanding problem that has yet to be resolved. A genuinely new history belongs to the new game rules that are being created by globalization. Despite there being no indications of an end of history as such, this concept still harbors a serious question.

This question has its origins in a Christian imagination, although the end of history as imagined by Christianity is only one possible version. If at some point in the future, history actually were to come to an end, I fear it is unlikely that it would be due to some final battle between good and evil, or because of God's final judgment regarding our ultimate salvation. What is much more realistic as a possible apocalyptic scenario is the end of humanity itself, a kind of suicidal end wherein humanity's final judgment is that there is ultimately no salvation. Logically speaking, this worst-case scenario is in fact the most likely. For the suicidal activities of humanity began in modernity with the aims of making the human the measure of all things, an attempt to become God, and this resulted in a radical recasting of human greed now seen as a legitimate right.

First, modernity recognizes the legitimacy of selfishness. In defining rational conduct with the consistent logic of seeking to maximize self-interest, this modern principle necessarily entails all bad things. Selfishness already entails the *possibility* of all bad things, but the legitimation of selfishness as a principle implies the *necessity* of all bad things. Another foundational pursuit of modernity is seeking to conquer nature through limitless development. This aspect of progressivist thinking greatly increases the risks brought on by human conduct.[1] This modern political logic not only increases our capacities for self-inflicted harm and destruction (e.g., nuclear weapons, biological weapons, digital weapons, genetic weapons, and so on), but also increases the chances of human extinction due to overstepping natural boundaries (e.g., genetic engineering, artificial intelligence, machine learning, robots, and so on). While prophecies concerning technology and various science fiction scenarios may not necessarily come true, these narrative fictions can reveal the real operative logics of current humanity—that is, the fantastic fictions humans come up with expose what they are actually thinking. With the advent of the requisite technological capacities, humans are now very likely to act out many of these dangerous fantasies. Science fiction then isn't just mere fantasy, but indicative of the heartfelt confessions of deep human longings.

As a new game, globalization is currently in the process of deconstructing the orders of modernity: not just its political order but also the social order and various cultural traditions as well. The accelerated rate of technological development brought about by globalization has brought with it an unprecedented danger for human societies in the form of a critical imbalance: that is, our technological capabilities far exceed our capacities for exercising self-control in the current order. And this critical imbalance is becoming increasingly dramatic. The rate of separation between our technological capabilities and our capacities to realize effective order are rapidly increasing; on the one hand, technological innovations are accelerating daily, and on the other, our capacity to be effecting order is in rapid decline. As soon as technological capabilities reach a critical point, this capability could be transformed directly into power. And when human capabilities close in on a God-like power, this might be the critical point of human extinction—an apocalypse. Progressivist theorists tend to optimistically reject such dire warnings as alarmist. But such optimism is based entirely on a faith that has no guarantees. Why can't human beings become God? While there is no definitive proof as to what will occur in the future, there is always a logic of concern. In contrast with God, humans are not omniscient nor omnipotent and do not have a God's control over an infinity of possible worlds. Moreover, there is no "backup" world for humans; all we have are our best attempts to realize the limitless in a limited world. And this indeed is an impossibility. Cantor's world only exists in mathematics.[2]

In the real world such a concept can only bring about the destruction of the world. Infinity implies a plurality of limitless possibilities. And this in turn implies that for humanity, with limited power, there will always exist unexpected and uncontrollable factors. Unless humans become like God, and were to possess an infinite range of capabilities to be facing an infinite range of possibilities, there can be no way of realizing this fantasy of limitlessness in a limited world; and any attempts to do so will only bring about the collapse of this actually limited world. This coming apocalypse is a kind of trial of humanity itself. It is likely that humanity, having created an uncontrollable power, will bring about its own extinction—either as a consequence of self-inflicted destruction or through the vengeance of nature.

As rehearsed above, the games of modernity based in zero-sum competition and antagonistic contest truly thrive in times of growth and prosperity. The secret to such success is the asymmetrical advantage won by a small group of nation-states as a result of relying on technologies that allow them to carve up and exploit the world. But as globalization increasingly becomes the universal process of modernization, and especially as informational networks are rapidly universalized, monopolizing and colonizing knowledges are more and more becoming common knowledge. The asymmetrical advantages of the exploiting nation-states will gradually disappear, and all the hitherto ordered zero-sum competitive political games will become increasingly pointless.

We have already joined the game of globalization, but new institutions have yet to take shape, and hence we are stuck using the old game rules of modernity. This lack of coordination has already begun to bring about frequent failures in both thinking and action. As reality confirms, using modernity's methods of thinking and acting to deal with new games and new problems not only frequently results in failure, but can even bring about the most untoward of consequences. For example, the various crises we already face such as the global financial crisis, climate change, terrorist movements, territorial conflicts, and so on, have brought us to our wit's end. A characteristic condition of activity during this era is a pervasive feeling that things never turn out quite as they should. And for this reason the issue of world governance has already become an urgent problem. Before the era of rapid globalization, to speak of the "common future of a global human community" would've just been rhetorical, but this ideal is now in fact a most pressing problem.

At present, because the game of globalization lacks a suitable set of rules, it has again returned to a kind of "original situation." This is indeed the world we now see with crisis lurking in every direction brought about by a general lack of stability. Under these conditions lacking a world order, humans tend to engage in extremely risky projects with outcomes that are difficult to foresee. This is especially the case with the implications of the quantum leap enhancement of capacities brought about by the integrated technological revolutions that are occurring in the fields of biology, artificial intelligence, and the internet. This revolution in technologies is likely to totally transform the human experience in all aspects. According to the predictions offered by some scientists, a seismic revolution in our technologies is not far off. What is especially dangerous here is that technological progress is often considered to be an indubitable indicator of humanity's progress. But could an uncontrollable advance in technology lead to a huge disaster or even the extinction of humanity itself? In theory at least, technology is perhaps blameless, but technology can give rise to irresistible temptations leading to conditions that humanity itself might not be able to foresee. And the self-confidence of humanity is the least credible thing there is.

Even if it is difficult for us to fully judge of all the inherent risks of technology, the fact that the development of technology might give rise to political problems is an obvious possibility. For instance, might technological progress in the future bring about a form of intractable neodespotism?

This is entirely possible given current trends and would seem to be simply a question of will power. For instance, humanity covets technologies that could provide every individual with comprehensive services. There is thus a generalized acceptance of technological systems that require mass surveillance and manipulation over every bit of human data, to the point that no matter where one now goes, there is possibly surveillance equipment immediately recording the entirety of the biometric data points of any individual, ostensibly for the purpose of providing individuals with their "useful" information sets and offering them the "best" delivery of services.

However, precisely because of this technological facility, individuals might become totally dependent upon the comprehensive services offered by the new technologies in ways similar to a drug addiction (at present the use of the worldwide web and cell phones are actually already highly addictive). Comprehensive services would seem to provide a vast array of free choices and a more robust equality, but at the same time, these services can exercise a manipulative control over every aspect of an individual's lifestyle and thinking. This heralds a totally new form of authoritarian control. In providing liberty and equality, there could be a realization of total control. This would seem to be a paradox, as every individual might appear to be free and equal, but in reality all of their "free choices" are entirely defined and predetermined by the technologically controlled, comprehensive services. Because of this technological control the exercise of political freedom would lose any kind of creative agency. This indeed would be an extremely comfortable form of neodespotism, as it would be providing what everyone wants via optimal services that they just can't live without. It is not difficult to imagine that future neoauthoritarianisms will be made successful by their constant appeals to upholding "freedom" and "democracy."

Perhaps some can refuse this or that service, but it seems nearly impossible that anyone could truly exercise their right to be choosing freely because, if they were to actually do so, they would have to be forfeiting many of the services they require for daily life. When services are systematically provided to cover all of life's necessities, such a provision becomes a supreme power that no one can resist. Again, this is not a directly coercive power, but a manipulating one. Everyone is "willingly" controlled, because they need these life services provided by the comprehensive technological systems. And speaking to present conditions—systems such as banks, the internet, communication media, market systems, and so on, have all already begun the process of fully implementing a totalizing convergence of comprehensive services and manipulative power. We can easily imagine that future technological regimes, in developing comprehensive systems of service, will exercise a totalizing authoritarian control. Previously it has been assumed that insofar as economic and technological progress is being made, the basic problems of survival will someday be solved, and all that will remain will be to live a life of pure "freedom" and "democracy." This is of course an illusion of modernity, an illusion shared by both liberalism and communism. In fact, high-level advances in technology might just actually plant every individual's basic life conditions deep within complex systems of technology, and then the problems of life could become even more difficult to deal with than ever before, way more difficult than the age old problem of mere survival. Life problems will no longer involve a simple equation that can only be addressed by physical labor. Instead, life will require persons to be continually inserting themselves into high-tech and manipulative systems to survive, ultimately a tedious and mechanical process that provides little sense of accomplishment or room for personal creativity.

In the future, power might indeed be decided by service, fulfilling the maxim: "service is power."[3] In the era of globalization, global services that are more convenient, more systematic, more comprehensive, and more capacious will become the basis of a new kind of political power. Mao Zedong once pointed out that power must "serve the people." At one point this might have just been an ideal political aspiration, but viewed from the present day, this slogan seems to reveal a kind of implicit and unintentionally suppressed premise: namely, those who are able to serve the greatest number of people can garner the greatest amount of power, and hence the greatest delivery of services can be converted into the greatest political power. What we have to remember here, though, is that the goal of power is not service; rather, it is through service that some can come to acquire autocratic power. Future humanity might have no choice but to give allegiance to various comprehensive systems of service, and under its hypnotic spell they might be "willingly" institutionalized. Neoauthoritarianism is not a problem that modern freedom and democracy can solve, because a neoauthoritarianism that negates freedom and democracy is at the same time always appropriating nominal "freedom" and "democracy" in order to succeed. Neoauthoritarianism is a paradoxical product of freedom and democracy. The markets and democracies that modern people have developed have overturned traditional forms of despotism, but these same thoroughly progressive markets and democracies have again produced a new form of despotism.

This seemingly incoherent turn of events actually has a necessary logic. Democracies and markets have an isomorphic structure. Both are expressive of the choices of people, and both are effective means of avoiding power monopolizations. But the problem remains that power is always inevitably more cunning than any specific democracies or markets. Power will not miss any opportunity to aggrandize itself, and new power always employs new tactics. The first step is to cater to the preferences of the masses, and then to manufacture their choices, and finally control what the masses need in terms of service. Hence we ultimately arrive at a neoauthoritarian power that has been realized through liberal democracy and market economies. The great advantage of this new despotism lies in the fact that it functions with no way of extirpation, since it grows parasitically in and through free markets and liberal democracies. This might call to mind Plato's prophecy that the fate of governments are cyclical, with autocracy causing people to seek democracy, and democracy ultimately metamorphosing into authoritarianism. At present this problem is irresolvable.

A danger inherent in the "systematized power" of neoauthoritarianism is its implicit "systematized violence." As all-pervasive, systematized modes of living, there is latent a kind of irremediable and inexcusable violence. Responsibility for this violence cannot easily be assigned to the conduct of any single subject, since the oppressed too are utterly dependent on the system for their very livelihood (if I'm not mistaken, Slavoj Žižek has somewhere denounced a similar sort of violence). Systemic violence not only arises from technological and economic systems, but also from media and discursive systems, and any other modality that brings a certain organizational system to persons and affairs. This kind of systemic violence doesn't typically harm people directly, but rather erodes their freedom through the implementation of rules, institutions, and procedures. And it is through the limiting all kinds of possibilities that such systems actually exercise their control. It is difficult to define the boundaries of blame for such controlling mechanisms, especially since the control of hearts and minds is apparently achieved "legitimately" as it were, through generally accepted game rules. By comparison, despotic governments wherein the people dare not express their frustrations are low-level forms of authoritarian control. Systemic violence on the other hand represents high-level form of authoritarian control since it employs methods of determining even what is available in the conceptual repository in order to ensure that people lose their capacities for critical reflection, so that even when people do think, they are limited to a politically correct vocabulary that has been approved by the system. Systemic authoritarianism of this sort gives rise to a false consciousness in persons, which is akin to living a robotic existence—that is, just mindlessly carrying out commands.

Such false consciousness takes the form of producing chaotic thinking through a vocabulary that has been so thoroughly addled that when thoughts are expressed, the language can only be selected from an extremely limited and politically correct vocabulary. Even when expressing something wrong or "sinful" one must always be using a correct vocabulary. For example, in using the language of human rights as a pretext for instigating a war, the reasons given for forgiving those implicated in the killing of others is human rights. Continuing this logic, to right the wrong for those who have been injured and to punish those implicated in the killing of others actually becomes a violation of human rights. This is a commonly observed phenomenon in the media and even in academic discourse, and is a very dangerous point because it seems that only such a ridiculous discourse is capable of being universalized. There is good reason to believe that the discourse of the mainstream media has already become a sort of modern political theology. And it is just such an enslavement of consciousness that is itself indicative of the most profound violence.

Democracy has already been hijacked. And it is hard to liberate democracy because democracy itself has certain weaknesses that everyone knows makes it difficult to avoid being hijacked. For instance, the "aggregation of preferences" is a very imperfect mode of collective decision making because an "aggregation of individual rational choices" inevitably results in "collective irrational choices." It is difficult for democracy to prevent the collective interests from being dominated by propaganda and rigged elections, for these manipulative tactics are considered more or less legitimate procedures. We must also consider a relatively hidden problem: namely, constitutions would seem to be final arbiters in democracy, but how is the legitimacy of a constitution itself to be determined? This question has never been sufficiently addressed. Democracy has been tacitly recognized as a confirmation of the legitimacy of a constitution, but there are so many points in such confirmation processes that are questionable. Logically speaking, since constitutions effectively provide governance for the collective body of all citizens, then constitutions should be unanimously agreed upon by every individual citizen as a kind of universal contract. How to actually confirm what a collective body of citizens would unanimously agree upon is a most difficult problem. Clearly a plurality of viewpoints cannot be equivalent to a unanimously agreed upon consensus. For this reason, in theory it is only a "universal reason" that could possibly confirm what a universal consensus should be, but the problem remains that universal reason cannot possibly be definitively determined within the actual activities of any democracy.

As people are still defending and enjoying modern democracy, new powers have been covertly altering democracy. Democracy is metamorphosing into a "publicracy."[4] I use the term "publicracy" to explain the political transformation involved in democracy that was originally grounded in individual choices, but is now being grounded more through "public opinion." Public opinion shapes and dominates the preferences of individual persons and is expressed as the mainstream ideas and viewpoints found in popular media. And such public opinion is itself created by a certain systematization of power. In this process there is a shift from organization through persuading of hearts and minds to a state of willingly being controlled. It is worth noting that "publicracy" is not necessarily antithetical to democracy. In fact, a publicracy can result from what is always implicit in democracy. Power will never pass up an opportunity to dominate others. And since democracy creates a public sphere, power has an opportunity to be surreptitiously dominating the public sphere using a "publicracy" that passes for a democracy. Thus democracy becomes a mere hollow shell for authoritarianism, and the truly operative powers are the systems that determine the rules of the game and issue the rewards of the game (i.e., life benefits). Speaking from a standpoint of logical possibility, publicracy is not necessarily authoritarianism. For it is possible that public opinion might not be formed behind a veil of power, but really results from a universal deliberative reason. In such a scenario there might even be good governance. Aristotle's anticipation that a method of rational dialectic might replace attempts in the marketplace to win over the public with so much nonsense, was a notable historical instance of seeking such an edifying publicracy.

The new powers currently being produced by globalization are not necessarily working within the same methods of determining borders previously found in modern political forms of subjectivity. Rather, new powers are making use of new forms of subjectivity in selecting for a globalized network existence. This signals a kind of fundamental transformation in politics. As previously outlined, the subjective units of politics—namely, the basic units of calculating interests—always determines the specific game rules and the available ways of thinking. The individual and the ethno-nation-state, as the basic units of subjectivity in modernity, both seek to maximize exclusive, self-interests as a subjective body. It is for this reason that the political games of modernity are necessarily competitive and antagonistic. What, then, in the games of globalization are the basic units for calculating interests? Because the globalization game still has much space that has yet to be opened up, I would not dare to claim here an absolutely certain understanding regarding the rules of this global game. Though, from what can be gathered from present circumstances, it would seem that we can say with some degree of certainty that within current global game dynamics the operative basic unit for calculating interests is a kind of "network existence." This entails that the appearance of a new model of political subjectivity that goes beyond the concept of a sovereign nation. For the first time in history there is a new subjectivity appearing currently as a bundle of economic interests, but in terms of the political potential of this model, it is very likely in the future to become a basis for a new form of political subjectivity as well—a form of subjectivity that might develop alongside sovereign nation-states or that might even use sovereign nation-states in a manipulative way.

Following the deepening patterns of globalization, we can see that the greatest beneficiaries of globalization are not any single nation-states.

Rather, it is the network existences themselves that benefit the most as a basic unit of new global power. So far it has been the world financial capitalist systems, new media systems (like the internet and cellular services), and other advanced technological systems that are at present the greatest beneficiaries within this global game. And these beneficiaries have the most reasons to be hoping to become the world's dominant power. Even if financial systems, media systems, and other technological systems might still be partially controlled by nation-states, both in terms of current practice and in future trajectories, all networking models of power systems are expanding their networking capacities. Over the entire world, this networking is like a vast spider's web expanding everywhere, always forming new connections. Without a stone remaining unturned, this web ineluctably comes to control all practical activities and discursive spaces, and step by step will come to manipulate and exploit each nation (currently this has already been partially realized), even to the point of making every national government a mere puppet of the global capitalist and technological systems. Media determines what opinions will be welcomed, and financial capital determines what actions will be rewarded, while advanced technology determines all future possibilities. The global financial system, new media systems, and high-tech systems are beginning to coalesce to form a new authoritarian power. This power uses methods totally different from the sovereign nation-state in attempting to control the world. Even if at present this is just an early stage in such global control, and is mainly limited only by economic factors, in the future it is likely to evolve into a truly world political power.

Power always finds the most suitable path and space in which to grow, and power always uses new methods to adapt to new games. Under the conditions of globalization, network existence has the optimally advantageous conditions for a growth of power. For this reason any system that is able to grow like a network model will become a member in the most powerful group within the global game. Such new powers don't have to establish a world government, nor do they need armies or a police force. Rather, such powers will continue to provide universal and necessary "optimal services" to create a dependent and docile populace. Moreover, in using systems that people are totally dependent upon, these powers can take the next step in dominating nation-states and governments. It is precisely in this sense, then, that service is power. Put more accurately, the combination of capital, technology, and services form a trinitarian body of power. Capital will never miss an opportunity to use new technologies to increase its power. And in the future this new power will have a clearly transgovernmental and transnational capacity for control, and as such will become a new political subjectivity. Compared to the modern "boundary powers" of sovereign nation-states, it could perhaps be called a "systematical power" orientation of the political.

The global game set by systematical powers alters the "ontological conditions" of the political. Systems are constituted by "relations," so the currently actual basic-units, the nation-state and the individual, are receding into an auxiliary position. Under the conditions of ongoing global systematization, the character of relations determines the nature of any actual subjectivity, and might even completely redefine the nature of subjectivity. At the same time, the character of relationality determines what counts as effective conduct and what the rules of any new game will be. "Existence" then no longer has a complete and independent character, but rather becomes a kind of functional placeholder for "coexistence." This seems to confirm an implicit metaphysical premise of the *tianxia* concept: "existence presupposes coexistence." Forming an increasingly powerful mutual codependence between a multiplicity of existing entities represents the greatest opportunity for survival, and the most successful mode of preservation can no longer be the modern strategies of pursuing the maximization of exclusive self-interest. Rather the optimal strategy becomes an internalizing of the world in order to seek the optimizing of shared interests. Under such conditions of mutual interdependence, seeking the maximization of exclusive self-interest is bound to be self-defeating. Why has imperialist hegemony become increasingly ineffective? The reason is that the conditions of the global game have changed. When shared interests transcend exclusive interests, strategies of resistance are of no use because they bring no ultimate payoffs. It is only with the systematization of network power that through an orchestrating of common interests there can be an optimization of shared benefits.

In a possibly imagined future, all of the various global systems will bring the world ever closer together. Global systematization is a necessary material precondition for the possible emergence of a new *tianxia system* world order. But the mere systematization of the material world won't automatically evolve into a *tianxia* world. This is because in a world of globalization that does not possess a *tianxia* spirituality, the selfish systematization of power cannot possibly establish world institutions of shared interests. A political world held in common by all persons must develop according to a world-ideal. And a world-ideal here is what the Guanzi meant by "taking *tianxia* as *tianxia*" and what the Laozi meant by "viewing *tianxia* as *tianxia*." This world-ideal is obviously not aimed at systematizing a new authoritarian power operating with the trinitarian logic of global capitalism, technology, and comprehensive services. Even though such power is of a different order from the previous forms of political subjectivity like the sovereign nation-state, it still can only seek the maximization of self-interests and exclusively held power. In attempting to become the ruler of a neoauthoritarian world, these systematic powers cannot become the protector of the world's shared interests. Speaking in terms of their potential capacity for violence and destruction, such neoauthoritarianisms are even more dangerous than forms of modern imperialism.

We cannot know what the future will bring, but we can consider future possibilities. If the newly emerging power of world systematization maintains the trinitarian "capital—technology—service" model without alteration, and simply moves from economic power to further develop itself as political power, then the following are all possibilities:

1. The interest in global exploitation exceeds the interests leading to war, and there might then be a total avoidance of open conflict. This would count as progress, but it wouldn't totally rule out that under certain circumstances, the manipulation of sovereign nation-states might threaten war or operate with a pretext of military invasion in order to eradicate various stubborn obstacles.

2. As soon as there is a power able to exercise total control over the world, interest in political power will transcend economic interests. The ideal of these new systematized powers could very possibly then become a "technological utopianism" in attempting to use new high-tech methods of continuously altering and constantly redefining human lives. On the one hand, such an ideal needs to continue to provide optimal services, but on the other hand, it would have to maintain its authoritarian domination.

3. The unlimited development of technology becomes the highest interest, at least on par with interest in political power. The new systematized powers might then possibly transform scientific technology into the only "religion" of the future. And getting rid of all cultural restrictions without any scruples, it could challenge utterly the traditions of nature, God, and morality. Because of this, these systematized powers could possibly develop extremely dangerous technological advances, especially revolutionary accomplishments in the fields of biology, artificial intelligence and new forms of energy resources. With respect to the possible alarming consequences of such technological attainments, scientists have all sorts of conjectures. It is impossible to be certain which future scenarios are more likely to come true, but we can be sure of one thing: it is possible that future technologies will provide humanity with great power, but they cannot themselves provide humanity with a noble morality relevant for the wise application of this power (for morality is a cultural rather than a technological product). It is for this reason that it is far more likely that the unrestricted development of technology will bring about apocalyptic results, rather than resulting in any significant benefits for human life.

4. It is possible that technological revolutions could give rise to dominating rulers and even to a near absolute power of a superhuman ruling class. In the weakest sense, this group of superhuman rulers would become a new governing class. But in an even stronger sense, these superhumans could become a very powerful, new posthuman species. Disparities in capacities could rule out any possibility of revolution, and the absolutely powerful superhumans would then dominate totally with any idea of class struggle existing only as an antiquated narrative. It might go so far as to produce a new "speciesism" that could make modern racism look quaint by comparison, and all the so-called civilizational clashes would be a thing of the past.

In any event, coming revolutions in technology will lead to a future in which a great majority of our current political problems no longer exist. Just as Ludwig Wittgenstein pointed out, some problems are resolved not by finding definitive answers, but by getting over the thought paradigms that produced them. We might be able to get over old problems, but a world apocalypse is becoming a serious issue, and no longer just part of our literary imagination. A problem we are now frequently facing goes as follows: if a world institutional framework for recognizing common interests isn't created that is capable of altering the political logic of seeking to maximize exclusive self-interests, then the marriage of unlimited technological developments and unlimited selfishness will very likely lead to an apocalyptic end of human civilization. As humans attempt to conquer nature with their technologies, as long as they still preserve their original selfishness, this will necessarily lead to an imbalance in living and the probable extinction of humanity. At the same time, it is not possible to change the naturally selfish natures of human beings. For if a living thing abandons its naturally selfish nature, it would directly lose its mechanism for protecting life itself, and would have no way to continue to exist. Being a part of nature, humans must follow their nature. So in attempting to transcend nature, human beings are likely to lose control and self-destruct. The natural order is an ontological boundary that scientific technologies should not transgress. Hence it can be said that the unregulated development of technology is the greatest existential threat humanity is currently facing.

At present, the technological authoritarianism being brought about by the new systematized powers still belongs to the future. A more pressing crisis at the moment is that those hegemonic powers of imperialism still around have a similarly profound interest in these terribly risky technological developments, with the aim of preserving their hegemony. Developing technologies without countenancing the risks involved is a highly irrational behavior, and yet this very irrational behavior is coming from the most powerful forces currently vying for world domination. Thus we cannot hope for the existing international organizations to arrest the irrational conduct of national and systematized powers. It will only be by establishing a kind of supranational body as a universal world order that we could possibly hope to restrict imperialist hegemony and the new authoritarianism of systematized powers. Only then can we hope to avoid the malaise of technological authoritarianism and the concomitant madness of world extinction. This is precisely wherein lies the vital significance of imagining a new *tianxia* system.

20 New *Tianxia*: A Vocabulary

We have been rehearsing a historical narrative of an ancient *tianxia* system as an exemplary political innovation that emerged from a very unique set of historical circumstances. Today's geopolitical configuration marked as it is by globalization represents another instance of very special historical circumstances. Even though the problems currently being encountered are entirely different from those faced three thousand years ago, there is a similar urgent need for political innovation on a global scale. To enable the world to avoid domination by hegemonic systems, and to allow it to avoid possible futures of high-tech warfare and totalizing control by technological systems, what we need is the establishment of a new *tianxia* system. Such a system would be a world order belonging to all the people of the world, and would transcend the regnant hegemonic logics that have been in play since the advent of modernity. In this sense the ancient *tianxia* system has contemporary significance for today's world and future relevance for tomorrow's world.

The problems that a new *tianxia* system needs to resolve are those of the contemporary world, and thus it cannot simply be a replica of the ancient *tianxia* system. A new *tianxia* system cannot be some myth that promises humanity universal happiness, but rather should offer concrete plans for seeking universal security and the shared well-being for humanity as a whole as part of a global institutional framework. Also, it certainly can't simply be a new kind of system for world domination, but instead should be offering us an "inclusive" guardianship system. This guardianship system would attempt to use methods of "coexistence" as a basis for continued existence; and, as such, would reject all forms of "exclusivity" that have been inherited from modernity. This is our only hope to avoid the complete failure of human destiny.

We have no way of predicting whether or not a future *tianxia* system could be actualized. And we have no way of forecasting the concrete institutional arrangements of a future *tianxia* system. This is because there are no means of acquiring perfect foreknowledge regarding future social conditions. But if a future *tianxia* system is going to be a possibility, then a working "lexicon" for a new *tianxia* system will definitely include some key terms continuous with the ancient *tianxia* concepts. We could reference John Rawls's idea of a "lexical order" as a means of explanation.[1] However, the understanding of "lexical order" here will be slightly different from Rawls, since Rawlsian order is aimed at establishing "priority," wherein the former conception is more important than what comes later in a lexical order. Rawls does this in order to avoid the difficulties of selecting between things viewed as equally important. In contrast, the sense of "order" I am using here is meant to assert that the former terms have a logical priority over the latter, but that the former terms are always implicated in the latter terms, and vice versa. Hence, here there is not meant to be a comparison of relative importance, since we cannot do without the former or latter terms, and all the related concepts are equally important.

1. THE HEAVENLY WAY (*TIANDAO* 天道). The way of *tian* or "Heaven" is the way of nature, and is a concept of natural theology or natural metaphysics. *Tiandao* does not require confirmation because it is already wholly manifest in the modes of existence of the myriad things and events. When Confucius said that Heaven doesn't speak but still makes its intentions manifest, he was referring to this. Alluding to a similar saying of Wittgenstein's, we might say that the way of Heaven is "ineffable." The way of *tian* is the ontological limit for humankind, as humans cannot possibly transcend this limit in order to confirm the nature of *tiandao*. In other words, *tiandao* is a priori and any conduct that contravenes the

operations of *tiandao* is necessarily self-destructive. *Tiandao* as "the way of nature" is not a scientific object, nor is it simply the "laws of nature" as they might be stipulated by modern science. Rather, *tiandao* is a way of changing in nature that maintains natural harmony (i.e., a way of auto-harmonizing). This is the way that nature has of self-harmonizing that can be acknowledged by human persons as so many evaluative standards that they can consult and emulate:

1.1 CORRELATING WITH *TIAN* (*PEITIAN* 配天).　Since *tiandao* or "the way of nature" is a standard for the coexistence of all things, the "way of humanity" being derived from *tiandao* must accord with such standards. This is what is meant by correlating with *tian* (*peitian*). Correlating with *tian* implies that nature limits freedom, and that the myriad things are the measure of humanity, but that this limiting-measuring process is expressive of the very intentionality of *tian*. To act contrary to these limits is to offend against *tian*. This is to say that whenever nature gets understood as a mere object to be conquered by human freedom, or whenever exclusively human intentions are taken to be the measure of all things, is to offend against *tian*. If human beings oppose the intentionality of *tian*, they are acting against the "*telos* of being," and when humans create an imbalance with nature, they are self-destructing. Thus *tiandao* is the ultimate limit of human being. Human beings can only practice freedom and creativity within the bounds of *tiandao* (e.g., the inventions of the wheel, of languages, and of antibiotics were all done in accordance with the way of nature; while developing nuclear weapons, using genetic engineering trying to create superhuman immortals, and inventing new chimeric species of cyborgs are examples of creations that offend against nature). *Tiandao*, being the limit of human freedom, basically entails that insofar as any free creation has implicated within it certain risky possibilities that humans lack the capacity to effectively manage, then such a creation is an offense against *tian*. A most fundamental responsibility of a new *tianxia* system then will be using institutional powers to constrain modes of human conduct that, insofar as they are not being held accountable for their consequences offend against *tian*, and inevitably lead to consequences entailing technological and political risks over which humans cannot possibly exercise any control. Such global institutional constraints are necessary for the sake of human survival and basic security.

1.2 PROCREATIVE GROWTH (*SHENGSHENG* 生生). Since nature produces the myriad things, the basic intentionality of nature is to let all beings persist in their becoming, and to let all life flourish and proliferate. In order for all beings to be able to persist, the most important condition is coexistence. In other words, if things are not able to coexist, then no single existence is possible. Since this is the intention of *tian*, it must also be included within the goals of a *tianxia* system. An institutional order that promotes universal flourishing must be appealed to in order to preserve a plurality of things in the world. And a principle of coexistence must be used to construct a mutually sustaining relational ontology, thereby creating a diverse world in which the shared interests of coexistence are more attractive than pursuing exclusively conceived selfish-interests.

1.3 NONEXTERIORITY (*WUWAI* 无外). A necessary condition for humanity's coexistence, and a key condition for universal security and perpetual peace, is the "no outside" ideal of *tianxia*. The interiorization of the world means a world that has only interiority and no exteriority. A *tianxia* system becomes an institution for guardianship with no outside, a system that could maintain a universal world order. Since a *tianxia* system has to belong to the world and not to any specific nation-state, as an institution it must be anti-imperialistic and anti-hegemonic. This is what the Guanzi meant by "taking *tianxia* as *tianxia*" and what the *Book of Rites* means by "*tianxia* for all." The ideal of a world with no outside means a world aiming at making all the peoples within the four seas one family, and a world wherein *tianxia* is the shared home of everyone. This ideal version of a world with no outside is not necessarily realizable, and we can only be *hoping* then for a basic version of it to come about through ongoing processes of world interiorization.

2. RELATIONAL REASONING AS A BASIC PRINCIPLE FOR THE HUMAN WAY. The human way takes "the way of Heaven" or *tiandao* as its standard, and thereby must take as a first consideration the universal security and well-being of all people. It is for this reason that the rational principles governing the human way emerge from relational reasoning. Relational reasoning gives first considerations to mutual security, rejects war as a matter of principle, and attempts to limit competition within a framework of minimizing harm. The institutional rationality of the *tianxia* system takes relational reasoning as its principle because *tianxia*

is not an "other-excluding" basic unit, but instead presupposes as its largest scale a basic unit of coexistence. Thus we have:

2.1 THE MINIMIZATION OF MUTUAL HARM. This is a direct application of the principle of procreative growth. The minimization of mutual harm is a necessary precondition for relational coexistence. This satisfies the rational choice of avoiding maximizing risk and, as such, is a robustly rational principle. Since the minimization of mutual harm means a minimization of danger, in terms of rational choice theory it is clearly a better option than seeking to maximize one's exclusively defined self-interest.

2.2 THE MAXIMIZATION OF MUTUAL BENEFITS. This expresses the tandem strategies of virtuosity (*de* 德) and harmony (*he* 和). If we admit that the minimization of mutually inflicted harm is a negative rational principle, then the maximization of mutual benefits is a correspondingly positive rational principle. However, whether the maximization of mutual interests is more rational than seeking to maximize self-interest cannot be a matter of direct comparison but needs to be decided within specific, concrete conditions. Since *tianxia* presupposes the interdependent conditions of globalization, given the higher degree of interdependence among people, the maximization of mutual interests in comparison with maximizing private interests are better able to advance personal and national interests. For this reason it appears to be a more rational choice. And, in this sense, the maximization of mutual interests takes priority over the maximization of exclusive self-interests. This is concretely realized as:

2.2.1 CONFUCIAN AMELIORATION (孔子改善). A fundamental implication of the maximization of mutual benefit comes from a Confucian ideal of "in desiring to establish oneself, establish others; and in desiring to succeed, help others to succeed."[2] This Confucian ideal is a broadly universal principle, and has many implications in the areas of politics, economics, and ethics. In ethics it is clear that the Confucian principle, negatively expressed, is markedly different from the positively expressed golden rule from the Bible (even though the Confucian principle's negative expression as "what you don't desire, don't put upon others"[3] and the positively expressed biblical golden rule are entirely compatible). Here we understand the Confucian principle in its political and economic sense as "Confucian improvement." The basic implication of this is that any institution is legitimately universal if and only if said institution is capable of securing a collective Pareto improvement of benefit distribution for all. In other words, only if everyone's interests without exception are included in a scheme of Pareto optimization, then and only then can it be said that a Confucian amelioration has been achieved. And this is the same as claiming that a Pareto optimization of the interests of social collectivities must not only avoid harming any individual's legitimate interests but should always also involve an overall improvement of every individual's life conditions.

2.2.2 THE WAY OF BENEFITING FROM SIMPLIFICATION. There is a principle for regulating the natural balance derived from the *Laozi*: "the way of *tian* resides in reducing excess and supplementing insufficiencies."[4] Laozi believed that if any thing or event were to develop too far in any one direction, or if the wealth of some were to reach an excessive degree or accumulation, then it would necessarily lead to imbalance, and such imbalances necessarily lead to disaster. For this reason we must provide limiting conditions preventing such imbalances. Laozi's principle and Rawls's economic "difference principle" share some commonalties, but their respective modes of reasoning are quite different. Rawlsian principles take equality as a reason, while Laozian principles have nothing to do with equality but are instead derived from equilibrium as a reason. Since all things can only exist by persisting amid relational equilibriums, a loss of equilibrium for anything leads to the loss of its vitality. And for things that achieve a maximization of benefits to an excessive degree, they will for that very reason begin to decline. This is what the *Laozi* meant by "things have their cycle between diminution and gain." It is for this reason that reducing the benefit of the powerful is a strategy for preserving the existence of the powerful, otherwise they will meet the fate of "powerful oppressors never getting a good death."[5] Here we can see that the Laozian principle is not biased toward achieving equality for the weak, but is rather aimed at securing equilibrium in order to promote the vital well-being of everyone through mutual benefit. This kind of equilibrium principle probably comes from the concept of yin-yang balance found in the *Book of Changes*. This yin-yang conceptual pairing takes shape as a functional metaphor for achieving dynamic equilibrium, meaning that the vitality of everything is ultimately derived from a dynamic equilibrium.

2.2.3 MUTUAL SALVATION. This is the most positive goal within the principle of maximizing mutual interests. Even though this is an idealist principle, it is not without a certain practicality. The ideal of mutual salvation is all about actualizing "moral power" (*de* 德): "helping people to avoid death and resolving their difficulties, saving the people from bad predicaments, and providing emergency relief, this then is 'moral power.' And wherever there is such virtuosic governance, the world will repair to it."[6] This means that when robust moral power is realized by going to the rescue of others or providing relief for nations in the grips of disasters without attaching conditions or expecting trade benefits, the world would then approach a *tianxia* concept of becoming one family within the four seas.

3. COMPATIBILIST UNIVERSALISM. This is another important legacy of the ancient *tianxia* system that has contemporary significance. That the world has so many divergent and even conflicting cultural values is a given fact. The way of political thinking associated with monotheism tends to view one's parochial values as normative for the entire world considering them universal values, while viewing other values as so much cultural "diversity" to be tolerated. This kind of "tolerance" is not a way of truly respecting other cultures, but rather merely represents a means of placing other cultures into a fringe or periphery position vis-à-vis the self-avowed dominant culture. Implicit in this concept of tolerance is a radical inequality. A *tianxia* system, however, would recognize cultural "pluralism" that is different from this derogatory sense of "diversity." There has been an implicit fallacy with regard to the understanding of universal values. Typically, universal values get interpreted as values that have application to every individual. But this sort of understanding is illogical, because every culture believes itself to be in possession of the values to be applied to every individual. This leads to an inevitable contradiction. Since any culture can consider its values to be applicable to every individual, then *every* culture can take its values as universally applicable to all individuals. The result of this logic can only be a kind of particularism, not a universalism. By contrast, compatibilist universalism understands universal values as being "applied to every relation." But this is just to say that universal values can only be determined in "relationships" and not with respect to "discrete individual units." The universal values defined by compatibilist universalism avoid this contradiction. Thus:

3.1 VALUES DETERMINED IN RELATIONS WITH OTHERS ARE TRULY UNIVERSAL VALUES. Golden rules in every culture, such as the Confucian principle and the biblical golden rule, are all expressed as universal values defined in terms of relations with others. This is a confirmation of relations with others as a source of universal values. The universal values defined within relationality can necessarily be recognized as universal. This is a logical confirmation of the relational nature of universal values.

3.2 VALUES THAT CANNOT BE DEFINED IN RELATIONS WITH OTHERS ARE PARTICULARIST VALUES. Particularist values mean that because of the collective bias of a given culture, such values can only be applied within a given culture, and have no application to external relations and, as such, should not be imposed on others.

Because the future cannot be foreknown, this working lexicon of the *tianxia* system must preserve a certain openness. The vocabulary of the *tianxia* system discussed here is in varying degrees a continuation of the "genes" transmitted from the ancient *tianxia* system. But these genes of ancient thinking are all to be reimagined and newly contextualized in light of contemporary problems. This means that if there is to be a new *tianxia*, it cannot be the same as the ancient *tianxia*. Many foreign scholars have raised skeptical questions about the possibility of a new *tianxia*. For example, if the future world really becomes a *tianxia* system, then whose *tianxia* will it be? Whose order will govern it? Will this lead to a Chinese hegemony? In other words, even though in theory the *tianxia* system is supposed to consider the interests of the world, doesn't it also secretly harbor a plan for China to rule the world? William Callahan is a representative example of these kinds of skeptical worries wherein the *tianxia* system possibly signals the ambitions for a new "pax Sinica." Callahan worries that although "Zhao Tingyang criticizes the West for universalizing its particular worldview at the considerable expense of other ones, is he doing anything different? Is he not trying to universalize the very particular Chinese concept of Tianxia in order to apply it to the world?"[7] And again, "Zhao's argument that Tianxia is all-inclusive seems to miss the point that not everyone wants to be included."[8]

These are indeed interesting questions. But I want to say that even if the concept of *tianxia* comes from China, its relevance belongs to the world, just as we might say that even though the idea of human rights originates with Europe, it now belongs to the world. And regarding the problem of those not "willing to be included in the *tianxia* system," Callahan has I'm afraid conflated the *tianxia* system with current Chinese political realities. He rightly believes that in today's world many peoples and nations are not willing to be ruled by China. This is an obvious truth, but it has nothing to do with the argument for *tianxia* as a world system of governance. Today's China is a sovereign nation-state and is not a *tianxia*. So critiques directed at modern China should not be used to criticize the viability or desirability of a global *tianxia* system. In this argument for a new *tianxia* system I have attempted to show that (1) a *tianxia* system belongs to the world, and not any particular nation-state; (2) a *tianxia* system is an open system and is a universal invitation for all peoples; (3) and most important, a *tianxia* system attempts to create a relational order of universally shared mutual benefits, making the world's shared interests and mutually enjoyed benefits greater than any exclusive interests. Of course, even if a future *tianxia* system could be realized according with these ideals, it is not necessary that every nation-state be willing to join in. To each their own.

And the question of whose *tianxia* it would be in the future is an unanswerable question because no one can predict the future. The most I can offer here is a kind of Borgesian response. The future is a forking path of time, and possibilities abound. But such a response is obviously unsatisfying, because it doesn't really answer the question. What this question is really asking is, whose *tianxia* should we hope the world to be? However, even in this sense I don't hope for *tianxia* to "belong" to anyone in particular. This is a problem of misunderstanding caused, to a greater or lesser degree, by certain modes of modern thinking. According to the political logic of modernity, it would seem that out of a world of conflict there must at some point emerge a most powerful nation-state or a certain ethnic group that in the competition for possessing the world would achieve a final victory and could thereby establish a dominant world order. This modern political imagination has, within present world conditions, already become an illusion and will hopefully continue to become ever more illusionary heading into the future. As has been rehearsed above, the nation-state as a basic unit of power, is in the process of losing its actual allure, and in its place is emerging a new model of power—that is, the new systematized power, a power that is at present dominating global systematization processes and controlling the power of many nation-states.

This systematized power is likely to hold the real power in future world politics, and nation-states will likely just serve as representatives for this power. It would seem that the future world cannot remain a system of hegemonic nation-states, and this will spell the end of the international system of national hegemonies. For this reason, and at this point all of this is only speculation, a new *tianxia* system is likely to be established across the multiple global systems as a unifying supervisory power. This is especially relevant for global financial systems, the internet and high-tech sectors. The ancient *tianxia* system (the Zhou dynasty) used ancestral ruling states to guard and supervise the myriad states within a networking system. And according to this institutional gene and following a logic of evolution from within current conditions of globalization, a new *tianxia* system might just emerge from within shared world structures in a supervisory role. We can then imagine that this new *tianxia* system could not possibly belong to any single nation-state but would be a world power shared by all nations (and all systemic powers). This could prove to be the most rational political outcome.

Last, I want to briefly discuss another difficult theoretical problem. Can the institutionalized orders of ritual and music from the ancient *tianxia* systems still serve as a "gene" for a new *tianxia*? Not only did the lead designer of the ancient *tianxia* system, the Duke of Zhou, introduce an institution for land divisions (a world political institution allowing for divided governance over one body), but he also established an institutional order of ritual and music (*liyue zhidu* 礼乐制度). We have only briefly discussed the order of ritual and music above without offering much explanation. This is because the institutions of ritual and music belong to the particular culture of ancient China and, as such, don't pertain to the problem of universalizing world institutions. The ancients already realized that the *tianxia* system was universal, while the institutional orders of ritual and music were particularistic. And for this reason they rejected the possibility of expanding the ritual-musical order as universal on the principle that "ritual shouldn't be exported through education."[9] It is said that the Duke of Zhou consulted the successes and failures of the Xia and Shang cultures in creating the institutions of ritual and music that came to be representative of the elegant lifestyles of the ancient Central Plain cultures. Such refined culture became a model for emulation by the myriad states of *tianxia*. In sum, the Duke of Zhou set up the ritual and music as a model culture for other states of their own accord to come and study without it being imposed on others or their being coerced to conform. Herein we can see that the Duke of Zhou had a clear grasp of the conceptual distinction between universal political principles and particularistic cultural institutions.

I am willing to raise a sort of meta-question here, though, about the problem of ritual and music. Even though ritual and music might not belong to a world institutional order, they are certainly still relevant to world spirituality. "Ritual" (*li* 礼) means that every unique situation, person, or event requires a distinctive ritual response or adaptation. This means that different ways are required to respect different beings. Xunzi accurately defined ritual as a "dividing up" (*fen* 分). The way of ritual adaptation requires responding to different beings (persons, situations, and events) differently and had a complex cultural character with so much ethical, social, and aesthetic significance. As such, *li* 礼 was a holistic transmission of social values and created the possibility for sharing in practices of mutual respect. But if ritual practice was lacking in sufficient personal commitment and was just a matter of superficial showing off, then it did not measure up to sincere reverence. This is what Confucius meant by: "If people are not consummate, what is the point of ritual? If people are not consummate, what is the use of music?"[10] And when it comes to the concept of "music" (*yue* 乐), it was not limited to musical sounds alone, but rather refers to the possibilities honeycombing any experience that could be shared via modes of aesthetic expression and appreciation. The significance of *yue* 乐 lies in using shared aesthetic modes to express experience, thereby reverencing any affective experience for its possible refinement, and at the same time, showing reverence to those who are sharing in the experience.

The Duke of Zhou introduced the institutions of ritual and music with their profound significance lying in reverence for the particularities of ordinary life and in their unique ways of making life sacred, thereby making all things and the entire world sacred. The sacredness of all things didn't come from God but from a profound reverence for life. On this point ritual and music are consistent with the relational thinking of the *Book of Changes*. Through the myriad orders of nature, and through its changes and transformations, a divine message is relayed to human beings. It is for this reason that everything is worthy of reverence. And to reverence the myriad things is to reverence heaven and earth. This then is the continuity of the ways of humanity and the ways of *tian*, and is how human lives come to have their sacredness. It is only when the affairs and responsibilities of life are full of sacredness that life can have real meaning. If the flow of life itself cannot generate sacredness in its invisible processes, and if sacredness is regarded as the sole property of an absolute, eternal, and perfect God, then ordinary life indeed has no meaning. It was because ritual and music were indeed the confirmation of the sacredness of life that Confucius saw the collapse of the ritual and musical order to be the greatest of all evils. For as soon as ritual collapses and music is corrupted, human beings are no longer able to reverence all things, and are no longer able to respect the myriad things as their appropriate measures. Instead, using human freedom as the measure of all things inevitably leads to the collapse of any evaluative standards, and all experiences, feelings, and aesthetic responses become decadent. In such a condition our wayward and willful intentions appear and disappear in the blink of an eye, and there is not a scrap of any meaning left over.

Political institutions can only guarantee a good world—that is, a secure, peaceful, and cooperative world. But a good world does not necessarily guarantee a good life—that is, a life in which the process of life itself has meaning. A good world is a necessary condition for a good life, but it is not itself a sufficient condition. In this book I have limited myself to a discussion of the reasons for how a *tianxia* system might possibly create a good world, but have not touched upon the problem of how the world would have to be in order to lead a good life. In today's world, wherein many senses of spirituality have been lost, what sorts of ritual and music might possibly save us? Regarding this question, even in his own time, Confucius was at his wit's end. Apparently the *Classic of Music* (乐经), one of the Six Classics, had already been lost for some time during Confucius's life, and so even for Confucius it was difficult to fully understand the Zhou rituals and music in their entirety. Archaeologists have subsequently found many texts within the ancient tombs, but they have yet to discover the *Classic of Music*. This missing *Classic of Music* might perhaps serve us well as a leading metaphor going forward.

Jizi's Lost Democracy

My reimagining of the concept of *tianxia* (All under Heaven) suggests a system of world order for and by all the world's peoples. This political ideal is not some unrealizable utopia but rather an accessible *contopia*. The concept of *tianxia* was a political starting point of China. In contrast to the Greek *polis* as the political starting point of Europe, *tianxia* as a concept indicates that Chinese political thinking had begun with an all-encompassing "world" rather than an exclusionary and discrete conception of sovereign "states." At the beginning of the political story of *tianxia*, the ancient concept perhaps proved to have emerged too early for the world, being untimely in the sense of being ahead of its time. But now it just might prove to be an optimal juncture to be using *tianxia* to reimagine a reasonable mode of restarting a process of realizing future world governance within the trends of globalization and new technological conditions.

Being so much more than a solution to the challenge of Huntington's thesis regarding the inevitable clashes of civilizations, *tianxia* is also an effective response to the failure of international politics with its regnant paradigm of zero-sum competitive logics obtaining among states and its woefully ineffective game rules that use only hostile strategies which are incapable of solving any world political problems. *Tianxia* then comes on the scene offering an alternative concept of the political. Contrary to the popular yet misleading thinking regarding the concept of the political, if such a conception is actually going to help to resolve problems, it should not be taken to mean merely the *designation of friend and enemy*. Furthermore, war should no longer be defined as the *continuation of politics* by other means.

As a matter of fact, hostility and war reveal nothing other than the total failure of the political. Therefore the political should be redefined as the art of transforming hostility into hospitality. Otherwise, the political remains nothing more than the abuse of power and a totally useless enterprise. A shocking spectacle of the world as it currently exists is that the anarchy of the whole world is completely inconsistent with the relatively more well-organized states existing in the world. This means that we have a failed world lacking in both political and metaphysical world-ness. The *tianxia* system is intended to aid us in remaking a world so that we might better manage the world-scale problems of the present global era, including the challenges brought about from the rise of new advances in technologies, globalizing economic forces, climate change, and conflicting civilizational values. We need to realize that the modern theories established from the seventeenth through the nineteenth centuries lag behind the times and have been thoroughly exhausted. Such theories of the political can no longer be relied upon to deal with the new challenges of the present and the future.

Throughout this book I have argued that a future *tianxia* system ought to be established upon a new ontology of coexistence, with three *constitutional* concepts:

1. *An internalization of the world*, inclusive of all nations in a shared system that constitutes a political world with no more negative externalities.

2. *A relational rationality*, with priority given to the minimization of mutual hostilities over the maximization of exclusive self-interest. This conception of rationality stands in stark relief from an individual rationality that only pursues the maximization of its own shallowly conceived self-interest.

3. *A Confucian amelioration*, which requires that *one is improved if and only if all others are improved*. A Confucian improvement signals the

nonexclusive improvement for all and is thus more acceptable than a Pareto improvement in thinking about the operative game rules of world politics. In other words, a Confucian improvement is equivalent to a coinstantaneous Pareto improvement for everyone insofar as their relational potentials are being politically ameliorated.

The story of *tianxia* has not yet come to an end. After the development of a philosophical theory, the next movement requires the articulation and implementation of legitimate institutional arrangements. As I see it, a future *tianxia* order needs a practical "smart democracy," if we can so call it, as a functional alternative to currently practiced democracies. This concept of a smart democracy is based upon the voting project proposed by a great politician, Jizi (箕子) who offered it to the Zhou dynasty *tianxia* (around 1123–1120 BCE), but it was never carried out because it was not needed nor desired by the monarchical system of early China.

It is a story that came up in the early days of Zhou dynasty, recorded in "The Expansive Plan" (洪范), a chapter in the Chinese earliest political history named the *Exalted Documents* (尚书). About three thousand years ago, after defeating the huge army of the Shang dynasty, the king of Zhou assumed the power to rule over the vast land that was *conceptually* supposed to be coextensive with the world (*tianxia* 天下) and was later recognized as China. The king of Zhou decided to establish a universal *tianxia* system harmonizing with the whole world as he saw it. Upon considering that world governance was a completely new thing, obviously more complicated than anything that he had previously experienced, the king attempted to gather all the inspiring and illuminating advice from various sources of wise counsel in the realm. Jizi, one of the most respected politicians at that time and a former minister of the Shang dynasty, was invited by the king of Zhou to share his political ideas and to become a high minister of the Zhou. Jizi declined the official offer, since he did not want to betray his own dynasty, but agreed to share his political insights for the sake of all the people of *tianxia*, a cosmopolitan community greater than any single nation.

Jizi's ideas have been recorded and summarized as the famous "nine constitutional counsels" which broadly cover his insights into world governance in the enumeration of laws and political economy. It seemed that the king was highly appreciative of the fifth constitutional proposal that suggested political impartiality should be maintained with respect to all nations and all cultures, so that the king could administer the *tianxia* system with universal consent. Actually, the king accepted eight ideas of the "nine constitutional counsels"—all except the seventh idea that implied a "smart democracy" as I am calling it here. In this proposal we can find a formula for democracy that is an alternative to the ancient Greek and to most modern formulations. I suppose that, depending on one's perspective, it is surprising that China does not boast about the practice of democracy and yet in ancient Chinese wisdom we can find a very novel theory of *smart democracy*: a theory written on paper so old, yet so very new and profoundly resonant for the geopolitical situation today.

Let us briefly delve into the details of Jizi's smart democracy. The original subject was to seek a solution to the uncertainty of making large-scale political decisions. This is an issue integral to any democracy, and yet Jizi did not invent the word *democracy* (*minzhu* 民主) and there was no such word in ancient Chinese. Jizi's proposal was concerned with the *consent of human votes and heavenly votes*. It presupposed a voting system of five representative votes wherein three votes were to be cast by human beings (including one vote by the king, one by the majority of the ministers, and one by the majority of the people) while two additional votes were cast "by heaven" using two modalities of divination techniques. At the time, the practice of divination was carried out with professional skills, astrological calculations, and geographical measurements. It should be noted that, in the early days of civilization, divination had been regarded as a reliable form of acquiring knowledge, just as we trust the sciences today. Hence there shouldn't be any doubt that in this style of smart democracy for our present age, divination votes would in the contemporary context be replaced by scientific votes. We will discuss this later. The key point to recognize, though, is that smart democracy essentially means a *knowledge weighted democracy*.

The inspiring rules of Jizi's method for voting can be outlined as follows:

R1: If the king, ministers, peoples, and both divination techniques all consent with a proposal, then this result suggests an optimal public choice;

R2: If a proposal receives only one human vote, whether by the king, the ministers, or the people, but is supported by both divinations, then the proposal is to be considered conditionally reasonable;

R3: If one of the divination techniques does not support a proposal, even if it is supported by all of the human votes, then such a proposal might be worth a try for a manageable domestic situation but considered inappropriate for any risky actions abroad;

R4: If neither of the divination techniques supports a proposal, then no action should be taken, even if receiving unanimous consent from the human votes.

From these rules it is obvious that the knowledge-weighted votes are given a higher priority than the human votes. This proposal for weighing votes indicates that a knowledge-weighted democracy aims at allowing knowledge to lead democracy, so that the political body can be making more intelligent decisions.

A knowledge-weighted democracy must be revised or improved upon for a new *tianxia* system. Within the contemporary situation, it would entail rejecting authoritarianism and monarchy in all forms. The five votes could be reduced to three: one by the majority of the people, similar to the ideal espoused by modern democratic theory (e.g., "one person, one vote"), and the two remaining votes given to two scientific committees—one in the natural sciences and the other based in the humanities. These two committees would consist of meritocratic representatives selected from a pool of respected experts from the natural sciences and humanities scholars. These two committees would be able to cast votes representing reliable knowledge that can remain independent of special interests, partisan politics, and ideological governments. It would require two steps in the voting process: (1) people vote for what they want among an array of policy preferences; and (2) the two knowledge-weighing votes approve or disapprove of the initial popular vote. Thus, such a voting system would define a separation of political powers: the people have the independent power to decide the *desirable*, and the scientific committees have an independent power to decide the *feasible*.

I will offer here one more effort to improve the "intelligence" of democracy by suggesting a modification of the voting system drawing upon this ancient counsel. To let it better represent the true will of voters and to respect the concepts of *minimizing harm* and *maximizing compatibility* in democratic politics, my recommendation would be a *two-way voting* system—that is, a "one person, two votes" model as an alternative to the popular system of "one person, one vote."

Let a case be that a proposal A will benefit all, and that each will get a payoff N, whereas proposal B will benefit 51 percent of people with a payoff N+1, while decreasing the payoff for 49 percent of people by N-1. The partial proposal B would most likely defeat the impartial A in the usual voting system due to an underlying selfish human nature. In the interest of reducing the harm of this naturalized "tyranny of the majority" to minorities, a system of two-way votes might help a little. Suppose that a person has two votes instead of only one vote—that is, each voter could vote with one pro vote and one con vote at the same time, expressing simultaneously their approval and disapproval within their rational and affective disposition. The briefest argument for this arrangement could be that everyone has their assents and dissents, their positive and negative preferences for things. Hence with these two votes allowing for an unambiguous expression of both for and against, there is to be found the full and fair representation of preferences in both directions. It should be noted that the undesirable matters more than the desirable in many cases. The undesirable relates more directly to one's personal security and liberties, whereas the desirable gets closer to the maximization of self-interests that tends to produce interpersonal conflict more than cooperation. Obviously, the vote of disapproval is essential in protecting the irreducible needs of life and should therefore not be totally neglected.

I would suggest that the basic rules for a "one person, two-votes" system function as follows: (1) *the net pros rule*—that is, net pros = pros minus cons. Suppose that proposal A gets 51 percent pros and 31 percent cons, then 51 percent minus 31 percent = 20 percent net pros; and suppose proposal B gets 41 percent pros and 11 percent cons, so 41 percent minus 11 percent = 30 percent net pros. Hence, B should be considered the winner; and (2) *the conditional majority rule*—namely, if A and B coincide in their net pros, then the one with more initial pros wins.

In some cases, the two-way voting system might lead to different results than a "one person, one vote" system and would hence better represent what people truly want and do not want. This could partially restrain certain abuses of democracy and reduce the harm done by the majority winners to the minority losers, and hence it might fortify the legal protection of the oppressed and disadvantaged persons within societies. Moreover, such a two-way voting system could remind the candidates and policymakers to be more mindful and attentive to more reasonable, inclusive, and impartial goals rather than focusing on more factional agendas. And such a voting system could certainly be more conducive to representing the general interests of people which would in turn avert a larger number of cons.

If so designed, I believe democracy could become more *institutionally intelligent*. Being smart in itself and by itself, democratic politics could strive to remain free from all irrational choices. Here I've offered two concrete policy proposals drawing inspiration from the classical ideal of Jizi's *tianxia* politics. But the future story of the *tianxia* system will always remain open to the best efforts of all of our political imaginations.

Notes

FOREWORD TO THE CHINESE EDITION

1. Translator's note: The term "theology" (*shenxue* 神学) here should probably be understood to mean more a mythic-historical narrative and accompanying culturally embodied moral imagination used to legitimate certain ethical values and political projects rather than being understood as a strictly rationalist discourse regarding the existence of purportedly transcendent spiritual beings or divine entities. The oft encountered problem of translation and "creative misreading" in a postmodern context is surely encountered here as well. Perhaps some productive cross-cultural philosophical resonance can be discovered in a shared working interest in "things unseen" evoking hope and ameliorative energies within *Tianxia* thinking and traditional Abrahamic theological horizons shaping the rather nascent field of political theology.

2. Translator's note: The "stranger problem" is the author's way of succinctly stating one of Fei Xiaotong's key reservations regarding the Confucian tradition. See Fei Xiaotong's *From the Soil: The Foundations of Chinese Society: A Translation of Fei Xiaotong's Xiangtu Zhongguo*, translated by Gary Hamilton and Wang Zheng (Berkeley: University of California Press, 1992).

3. Zhao Tingyang's *Tianxia System* (天下体系) (Nanjing: Jiangsu Education Press, 2005).

NEW FOREWORD

1. For good discussions, from different angles, of the uses of the *Tianxia* concept, see Wang Mingming, "All Under Heaven (Tianxia): Cosmological Perspectives and Political Ontologies in Pre-Modern China," *HAU: Journal of Ethnographic Theory* 2, no. 1 (2012): 337–83; Ban Wang, Mei-yu Hsieh, and Mark Edward Lewis, eds., "Tianxia and the Invention of Empire in East Asia," in *Chinese Visions of World Order: Tianxia, Culture, and World Politics* (Durham, NC: Duke University Press, 2017), 25–48; and, for its later uses, Timothy Brook, Michael van Walt van Praag, and Miek Boltjes, eds., *Sacred Mandates: Asian International Relations since Chinggis Khan* (Chicago: University of Chicago Press, 2018).

2. *Analects*, part 17, here from http://classics.mit.edu/Confucius/analects.4.4 .html.

3. All quotes from Zhao are from this book, unless otherwise noted; emphasis added.

4. See Yaqing Qin, *A Relational Theory of World Politics* (New York: Cambridge University Press, 2018), and Xuetong Yan, *Leadership and the Rise of Great Powers* (Princeton, NJ: Princeton University Press, 2019). See also Yan Xuetong, Daniel A. Bell, and Sun Zhe, eds., *Ancient Chinese Thought, Modern Chinese Power*, trans. Edmund Ryden (Princeton, NJ: Princeton University Press, 2013).

5. Quoting the *Book of Documents* (书经). The best English edition is still James Legge, *The Chinese Classics*, vol. 3, *The Shoo King or The Book of Historical Documents* (London: Trubner, 1865).

6. Interestingly, both for the old Mao (of the 1970s) and Zhao, this emphasis on "oppressed states" comes to the exclusion of Marx's class struggle; "the Marxian ideal of 'internationalism' based on a theory of class is also untenable," Zhao says.

INTRODUCTION

1. Translator's note: This expression gets translated as "universal problems of the world" here, but I wanted to begin to highlight how the *Tianxia* system being offered by Zhao requires a radical rethinking of historically regnant Western notions of transcendence and universality. Since this cultural paradigm shift in thinking about "universal" problems is largely still yet to come, I've also opted for "shared" and "common" in many places to translate Zhao's creative uses of *pubian* 普遍.

2. Translator's note: *zhuti* 主体 is usually rendered "subject" in the sense of subject-matter and a "leading body" in a discursive field. Here I want to highlight the anti-individualistic stance of taking the world as political subject and allude to the dynamic activity. Hence "agency" for *zhuti*.

3. (管子·牧民): "以家为乡, 乡不可为也; 以乡为国, 国不可为也; 以国为天下, 天下不可为也. 以家为家, 以乡为乡, 以国为国, 以天下为天下." *Guanzi* "Shepherding People": "A village cannot be managed in the same way as a household. A state cannot be managed the same way as a village. A political realm (*tianxia*) cannot be managed the same way as a state. Manage instead the household as household, the village as village, the state as state, and this is taking *tianxia* as *tianxia*." Cf. W. Allyn Rickett, *Guanzi: Political, Economic, and Philosophical Essays from Early China—A Study and Translation* (Princeton, NJ: Princeton University Press, 1985), vol. 1, 56.

4. 老子(道德经·第五十四章): "修之于身, 其德乃真; 修之于家, 其德乃余; 修之于乡, 其德乃长; 修之于邦, 其德乃丰; 修之于天下, 其德乃普. 故以身观身, 以家观家, 以乡观乡, 以邦观邦, 以天下观天下. 吾何以知天下然哉? 以此." *Laozi Daodejing* Ch. 54: "Cultivated in your person, the virtuosity is real; cultivated in your family, the virtuosity will be replete. Cultivated in the village, the virtuosity will be extended. Cultivated in the state, the virtuosity will be abundant. Cultivated in *tianxia*, the virtuosity is encompassing. Thus, use one's own person to view persons, one's own family to view families, one's own state to view states and all of this is to use *tianxia* to view *tianxia*. How do I know that *tianxia* is like this? From this." Cf. James Legge, *The Sacred Books of China: The Texts of Taoism* (Oxford: Oxford University Press, 1891), part 1, 98.

5. (公羊传·隐公元年 1.1.6): "王者无外, 言奔则有外之辞也" (周的天下是无所不包的世界, 其中不存在外国, 如果周的官员到诸侯国去谋职或避难, 就不能说是出奔, 不是出国, 因为所有地方都属于天下). *Gongyang Zhuan* "Duke Yin Year 1 1.1.6": "There is nothing outside of the ruler—so to say that [the Earl of Zhai] 'fled' to Lu would imply that there is an outside." (The *tianxia* of Zhou is a world that is all encompassing, with no state lying outside of it. If the Zhou officials go to the enfeoffed kingdoms in order to seek employment or refuge, they are not absconding or going into exile because all realms are part of *tianxia*.) Cf. Harry Miller, trans., *The Gongyang Commentary on The Spring and Autumn Annals* (New York: Palgrave MacMillan, 2015), 10.

6. (礼记·孔子闲居第二十九): "天无私覆, 地无私载, 日月无私照." 几乎一样的语句也见于(吕氏春秋·孟春记·去私): "天无私覆也, 地无私载也, 日月无私烛也, 四时无私行也." *Liji* "Kongzi's Relaxed Dwelling (ch. 29)": "*Tian* provides no private canopy, earth provides no private conveyance. The sun and moon provide no private illumination." What seems to be the same phrase appears in the *Lushi Spring and Autumn Annals* "Meng Chun Record—Expelling Selfishness": "*Tian* provides no private canopy, earth provides no private conveyance, the sun and moon provide no private radiance, the four seasons provide no private rotations." Cf. James Legge, trans., *Li Chi Book of Rites: An Encyclopedia of Ancient Ceremonial Usages, Religious Creeds, and Social Institutions*, edited by Ch'u Chai and Winberg Chai (New York: University Books, 1967), vol. 2, 281.

7. Schmitt points out that the meaning of the political is "distinguishing

between enemies and friends." See Carl Schmitt, *The Concept of the Political* (Chicago: University of Chicago Press, 1996).

8. An early formulation of the original position was Hobbes's state of nature. But contemporary references frequently cite John Rawls's original position. Rawls's position has more potential than Hobbes's as it allows for a purely imaginative theoretical construction and isn't limited by an idea of "nature". [Translator's note: For more on this comparison, see Zhao Tingyang's *The Fulcrum of First Philosophy* (第一哲学的支点) (Beijing: Sanlian Press, 2013), 151–72. Here Zhao elaborates upon this problem by distinguishing between the "original position" and the "evolutionary position."]

9. Even if we limit ourselves to contractual theory, Rawlsian presuppositions are unable to necessarily result in Rawlsian conclusions. This is due to at least the following two logical vulnerabilities: (1) within the conditions set by the veil of ignorance, according to the principle of "risk-aversion" people are more likely to choose the equal distribution of wealth set by a Communist society rather than the free competition and welfare for the poor of a neoliberal society; and (2) once the veil of ignorance is removed, according to the principle of persons seeking to maximize their individual self-interest, at least a portion of society will be more willing to alter or destroy the original contract and not continue to accept the conditions established under the original veil of ignorance.

10. Translator's note: Throughout the text Zhao frequently uses the term "gene" (*jiyin* 基因) as a political concept. It should be noted that the Chinese transliteration of this biological metaphor also has ideographic significance, as the term implies some sort of latent, but also grounding, transformative potential.

11. See *Xunzi* "Kingly System" (荀子·王制): "人生不能無群"; cf. Eric Hutton, trans., *Xunzi: The Complete Text* (Princeton, NJ: Princeton University Press, 2014), 76.

12. *Xunzi* "Discourse on Ritual Practice": "人生而有欲, 欲而不得, 则不能无求. 求而无度量分界, 则不能不争; 争则乱, 乱则穷. 先王恶其乱也, 故制礼义以分之." (荀子·礼论). Cf. Hutton (2014), 201.

13. *Book of Rites* "Ritual Conveyance": "Thus human feelings are the field of Sage Kings. By refining ritual, they cultivate them; by promoting propriety, they plant them; by teaching and learning, they tend the fields." (礼记·礼运): " 故人情者, 圣王之田也, 修礼以耕之, 陈义以种之, 讲学以耨之." Cf. Legge (1967), vol. 1, 383.

14. *Book of Rites* "Ritual Conveyance": "Thus when the Sages established normative patterns, they had to take heaven and earth as roots, *yin* and *yang* as sprouts, the four seasons as handles, the sun and stars as record, the moon as measure, ghosts and spirits as companions, five phases as material, ritual propriety as vessel, human affect as field, and the four luminosities as nurturance." This discourse is traditionally attributed to Confucius, but perhaps generations of students after Confucius brought more into play within the original discourse.

(礼记·礼运): "故圣人作则, 必以天地为本, 以阴阳为端, 以四时为柄, 以日星为记. 月以为量, 鬼神以为徒, 五行以为质, 礼义以为器, 人情以为田, 四灵以为畜." 这是传说的孔子言论, 可能是孔子后辈学生加工发挥的. Cf. Legge (1967), vol. 1, 383.

15. Translator's note: Here as elsewhere the term "safety" or "security" (*anquan* 安全) as used by Zhao is ideographically alluding to a comprehensive or all-inclusive (*quan* 全) peace and general sense of well-being (*an* 安) as an immanent teleology or limit-horizonal concept within his *tianxia*-rooted political theorizing.

16. *Book of Rites*, "Ritual Rhythm" (礼记·礼运): "大道之行也, 天下为公 (the world as common property), 选贤与能[这一点接近柏拉图的想象), 讲信修睦[与霍布斯丛林相反的安全状态) . 故人不独亲其亲, 不独子其子, 使老有所终, 壮有所用, 幼有所长, 矜寡孤独廢疾者皆有所养, 男有分, 女有归.货恶其弃于地也, 不必藏于己; 力恶其不出于身也, 不必为己. 是故谋闭而不兴[这一点最重要, 如果有一种存在秩序能够导致所有竞争谋略失效, 就必定是和平世界), 盗窃乱贼而不作, 故外户而不闭, 是谓大同." Cf. Legge (1967), vol. 1, 364–66, where he renders the expression as "a public and common spirit ruled all under the sky." [Translator's note: The parenthetical commentary is of course Zhao's own.]

17. (礼记·中庸): 辟如天地之无不持载, 无不覆帱……万物并育而不相害, 道并行而不相悖. Cf. Legge (1967), vol. 2, 326.

18. For more on this, see Zhao Tingyang's "The Forking Paths of Time—Contemporaneity as an Ontological Problem" (时间的分叉—作为存在论问题的当代性), *Philosophical Researches* (哲学研究) 6 (2014).

19. Since the May 4th movement, the oft-leveled criticism that Chinese culture opposes individual freedom and rights is not accurate given the historical discourse. Actually, because the individual was never a political unit in itself, problems of individual liberties and rights just didn't exist (and hence it also isn't the case that such discourse was always consistently opposed).

20. Translator's note: "Optimum" (with its noun-bias) is used here in conscious distinction from "optimal" (with its adjectival preference) to signify a zero-sum competition, and mutually exclusive conception of the "best possible world" from the standpoint of a foundational individual or sovereign nation-state, rather than a relationally realized flourishing as a best possible world.

21. Ethical dilemmas occur when distinct ethical goods cannot both be realized; for example, in deciding whether to sacrifice one person's life in order to save another's.

22. Translator's note: I have decided to translate *zhengzhi youxi* 政治游戏 as "political language game" in an inclusively Wittgensteinian manner. The idea of a language game captures nicely the scope of the discursive field implied by Zhao's theoretical and practical vision of a world political subject.

23. *Exalted Documents* "Yao's Canon": "In seeking into antiquity we find that when Yao was made ruler he was styled as Fang-xun. He was reverent, intelligent, cultivated, thoughtful, and effortlessly and peacefully comported. He was

abundantly polite and most effectively deferential. His luminous influence was expressed throughout the four realms and was on par with the heavens above and earth below. His intelligence was most effective and his virtuosity most distinguished. He cared for the nine clans and the nine clans became harmonious. He also ordered and refined the hundred surnames, and the hundred surnames became ever so illustrious. He achieved a *compatibility between the countries*. And with these timely changes, all of the multitudes found their flourishing."

(尚书·尧典): "曰若稽古帝尧, 曰放勋, 钦明文思安安, 允恭克让, 光被四表, 格于上下. 克明俊德, 以亲九族, 九族既睦. 平章百姓, 百姓昭明. 协和万邦, 黎民于变时雍." Cf. James Legge, *The Chinese Classics: With a Translation, Critical and Exegetical Notes, Prolegomena, and Copious Indexes* (Hong Kong: James Legge; London: Trubner and Co., 1865); vol. 3, pt. 1, 14–15.

24. See Fei Xiaotong's *From the Soil: The Foundations of Chinese Society— A Translation of Fei Xiatong's Xiangtu Zhongguo*, translated by Gary Hamilton and Wang Zheng (Berkeley: University of California Press, 1992), 62–70; Fei Xiaotong 费孝通, *From the Soil* (乡土中国) (Beijing: SDX Joint Publishing Company, 1985), 21–33.

25. *Daodejing* ch. 54. (道德经·第五十四章): 以身观身, 以家观家, 以乡观乡, 以邦观邦, 以天下观天下. 吾何以知天下然哉? 以此. Cf. Legge (1891), pt. 1, 98.

26. Translator's note: Legalism (*fajia* 法家) is the school of philosophy associated with figures like Han Feizi and Li Si (both traditionally thought to be students of Xunzi), who argued for a mechanistic view of state power grounded in law and the "two handles" of punishments and rewards. Latitudinalism refers to a strain of European political philosophy emerging from the new physical sciences that offered entirely mechanical explanations of physical phenomenon but reserved the right of a sovereign God to intervene in psychological and social explanations of human phenomena.

27. Confucius's original statement of this ideal is: "In desiring to establish themselves, consummate persons establish others; and in desiring to make creative advance, they help others make creative advance" (论语·雍也). Cf. James Legge, *The Chinese Classics* (Oxford: Clarendon Press, 1893), vol. 1, 194.

28. Translator's note: "Political justice" *gongzheng* 公正 conceptually implies a public order and social rightness. As such, it would seem to go beyond the more familiar "procedural" and "substantive" notions of justice as *a priori* givens. Instead, the concept entails a shared working out of the political in public or the always ongoing, gerundive "correcting" of an emergent public sphere.

29. Translator's note: Kenneth Arrow was a social theorist who in *Social Choice and Individual Values* (New Haven, CT: Yale University Press, 1951) claimed to have proved that given certain parameters, it is impossible to derive collective decisions from an aggregate of individual choices.

30. See *Lüshi Spring and Autumn Annals* "Revering the Public": "*Tianxia* is not one person's *tianxia*. *Tianxia* belongs to *tianxia*." And "Martial Strat-

egies: Opening Instructions" section of the *Six Secret Teachings*: "*Tianxia* is not one person's *tianxia*, hence it is *tianxia*'s *tianxia*." 参见 (吕氏春秋·贵公): "天下非一人之天下, 天下之天下也"; 另见 (六韬·武韬·发启): "天下者非一人之天下, 乃天下之天下也."Cf. John Knoblock and Jeffrey Riegel, trans., *The Annals of Lü Buwei* (Stanford, CA: Stanford University Press, 2000), "Honoring Impartiality" I/4.2, 71; and Ralph and Mei-Chun Sawyer, trans., *The Seven Military Classics of Ancient China* (Boulder, CO: Westview Press, 1993), 54.

CHAPTER 1

1. *Analects (Lunyu)* 12.17 and 2.1; cf. Legge (1893), vol. 1, 258 and 145.

2. Translator's note: This expression is from Borges's novel *El jardín de senderos que se bifurcan* (Buenos Aires: Editorial Sur, 1941).

3. *The Exalted Documents* "The Yi and Ji" [Shun's Forester and Minister of Agriculture] chapter has: "Under the bright heaven and throughout the corners of the seas and amongst the myriad lifeforms, the ten-thousand countries have superlative harmony." "光天之下, 至于海隅苍生, 万邦黎献." (尚书·益稷). Cf. James Legge, *The Sacred Books of China: The Texts of Confucianism*, part 1 (Oxford: Clarendon Press, 1879), 58. And the *Records of the Warring States*' "Qi Records" has, "During the time of the Great Yu there was heaven encompassed the myriad states." "古大禹之时, 天下万国." (战国策·齐策). Cf. J. I. Crump, trans. and annotated, *Chan-kuo Ts'e*, revised edition (Ann Arbor: Center for Chinese Studies, University of Michigan, 1996), 173.

4. Wang Guowei 王国维, *Collected Writings—Discourse on Shang-Zhou Institutions* (观堂集林·殷周制度论) (Shijiazhuang: Hebei Educational Press, 2001), 296.

5. (尚书·牧誓), (尚书·大诰); cf. Legge (1879), "The Speech at Mu," 131, and "The Great Declaration," 125.

6. (尚书·尧典); cf. Legge (1879), "The Canon of Yao," 32.

7. (尚书·尧典)(尚书·舜典); cf. Legge (1879), "The Canon of Yao," 32, and "The Canon of Shun," 38.

8. According to Sima Qian's 司马迁 *Historical Records "Zhou Annals"* (史记·周本纪) the Zhou tribe started as predominantly agricultural and later became nomadic pastoralists, only to later return to farming. Cf. William H. Nienhauser et al., trans., *The Grand Scribe's Records*, vol. 1, *The Basic Annals of Pre-Han China* (Bloomington: Indiana University Press, 1994), 55–60.

9. Xu Zhuoyun 许倬云, *History of the Western Zhou* (西周史), (Beijing: SDX Joint Publishing Company, 2001), 77–78.

10. (管子·霸言). Cf. *Guanzi* "Conversations of the Hegemon." Rickett (1985), 356.

11. Wang Guowei (2001), 287–88.

12. "礼之用, 和为贵"(论语·学而). Cf. Legge (1893), vol. 1, 143.

13. "德惟善政, 政在养民"(尚书·大禹谟). Cf. Legge (1879), vol. 3, 46.

CHAPTER 2

1. "溥天之下, 莫非王土."(诗经·小雅·北山). Cf. James Legge, (1876), vol. 3, 273.

2. "左东海, 右流沙, 前交趾, 后幽都."(淮南子·泰族训). Cf. John Major et al., trans., *The Huainanzi* (New York: Columbia University Press, 2010), 224.

3. (管子·地数). Cf. Ricketts (1985), 45.

4. Cui Guangzhu 翟光珠, *The Standardization of Ancient China* (中国古代标准化) (Taiyuan: Shanxi People's Press, 1996), 80.

5. Sima Qian 司马迁, *Records of the Grand Historian*, ch. 74 (史记·卷七十四), (Beijing: Zhonghua shuju, 1982), 2344. Cf. Nienhauser et al. (1994), vol. 7, 180–81.

6. "夫争天下者, 必先争人." (管子·霸言). Cf. Rickett (1985), 357.

7. "人不可不务也, 此天下之极也." (管子·五辅). Cf. Rickett (1985), 194.

8. "取天下者, 非负其土地而从之之谓也, 道足以壹人而已矣." (荀子·王霸). Cf. Hutton (2014) [where he takes "shouldering the land" literally as "carrying soil"], 106–107.

9. (礼记·中庸). Cf. Legge (1967), vol. 2, 327. Translator's note: The expression *peitian* 配天 from the *Zhongyong* challenges any simple translation as arguably there is no readily available correlative conception of creativity in English that would allow for human sages to be "equal with Heaven" (Legge) without presupposing a theological arrogance or human hubris—something Legge himself rather dramatically alludes to in a footnote of his commentary. Roger Ames and David Hall have rendered this expression as "complementing *tian*" and implied in this is a co-equal or co-creative sense of ethical-political artistry. See their *Focusing the Familiar: A Translation and Philosophical Interpretation of the Zhongyong* (Honolulu: University of Hawai'i Press, 2001), 113.

10. "一同天下之义, 是以天下治也" (墨子·尚同上). Cf. Ian Johnston's *The Mozi: A Complete Translation*, "Exalting Unity I," (New York: Columbia University Press, 2010), 95. Translator's note: Here "reconciling what is right in tianxia" as a profoundly communicative and deliberative process seems to be more in line with the *Mozi* than "making uniform the principles of the world" and moreover fits much better with Zhao's creative refashioning of this ideal.

11. "创制天下"(管子·霸言). Cf. Rickett (1985), 356.

CHAPTER 3

1. "天何言哉? 四时行焉, 百物生焉, 天何言哉? " (论语·阳货). Cf. Legge (1893), vol. 1, 326.

2. "天不言, 以行与事示之而已矣" (孟子·万章上). Cf. James Legge, *The Chinese Classics* (London: Trubner and Co., 1875), vol. 2, 281.

NOTES TO CHAPTER 4

3. "道可道非常道, 名可名非常名" (可因循之道便不是根本之道, 可定义之概念便不是根本概念) , 老子: (道德经·第一章).Some translations interpret this passage as "the *dao* that can be *spoken* is not the universal *dao*. And the name that can determinately fix a concept is not a universal concept." Although such interpretations are not completely off the mark, they do depart from the *Laozi*'s original intention. Whenever the received *Daodejing* is discoursing on what is *dao*, it is very clearly saying that only the transforming *dao* is the changeless *dao*. Cf. Legge (1891), part 1, 47.

4. "天地之大德曰生" (周易·系辞下传·第一章). Cf. James Legge, *The Sacred Books of China: The Texts of Confucianism* (Oxford: Oxford University Press, 1882), part 2, 381.

5. "继之者善也, 成之者性也" (周易·系辞上传·第五章). Cf. Legge (1882), 356.

6. "与天地相似, 故不违" (周易·系辞上传·第四章). Cf. Legge (1882), 353.

7. "人法地, 地法天, 天法道, 道法自然" 老子: (道德经·第二十五章). Cf. Legge (1891), 68.

8. "以通天下之志, 以定天下之业, 以断天下之疑" (周易·系辞上传·第十一章). Cf. Legge (1882), 371.

9. "生生之谓易" (周易·系辞上传·第五章). Cf. Legge (1882), 356.

10. "天下大乱, 无有安国, 一国尽乱, 无有安家, 一家皆乱, 无有安身"(吕氏春秋·卷十三·谕大). Cf. Knoblock and Riegel (2000), "Illustrating the Great," 299.

CHAPTER 4

1. According to the *Zuozhuan*, "In the past King Wu of Zhou in conquering the Shang and emerging as the sole ruler of *tianxia*, gave enfeoffed titles to 15 of his own brothers and 40 others from the Ji (Zhou) family line." "昔武王克商, 光有天下, 其兄弟之国者十有五人, 姬姓之国者四十人." (左传·昭公二十八年). Cf. Stephen Durrant, Wai-yee Lee, and David Schaberg, trans., *The Zuo Tradition* (Seattle: University of Washington Press, 2017), 1689. And the *Xunzi* states: The Duke of Zhou 周公 "in institutionally bringing together *tianxia* set up 71 countries with the Ji family clan occupying 53 of these." "兼制天下, 立七十一国, 姬姓独居五十三人." (荀子·儒效). Cf. Hutton (2014), 52.

2. *Remnants of the Zhou Documents*—"Prisoners of this Age" (逸周书·世俘), *Spring and Autumn of Master Lü*—"Observing the Age" (吕氏春秋·观世). Cf. Knoblock and Riegel (2000), 378.

3. "欲天下之治安, 莫若众建诸侯而少其力, 力少则易使以义, 国小则亡 邪心" (汉书·贾谊传). Cf. Burton Watson's *Courtier and Commoner in Ancient China: Selections from the History of the Former Han by Pan Ku* (New York: Columbia University Press, 1974).

4. (周礼·夏官司马), (左传·襄公十四年). Cf. Durrant, Li, and Schaberg (2017), 14.5, 1023.

5. The *Guoyu* states, "The order of previous kings was that inside the state

there was an internal realm of order, and outside there was an external service. The protecting principalities served as an auxiliary service. The Yi and Man peoples served as a stable service. And the Rong and Di people were a kind of uncouth source of service." (国语·周语上)曰: "夫先王之制, 邦内甸服, 邦外侯服, 侯卫宾服, 夷蛮要服, 戎狄荒服."

6. The *Rites of Zhou* "Summer Offices—Grand Cavalry" chapter has: "For a span of a thousand *li* is called the state realm. Outside of this for a span of 500 *li* is called the Marquis's realm; and after that for another 500 *li* is the cultivated fields; and after that for 500 *li* is the realm of the barons; and 500 *li* beyond that is the realm for gathering; and 500 *li* beyond this is the realm for guarding; and for 500 *li* beyond that is the *man* 蛮 realm; and then beyond that for 500 *li* is the realm of the *yi* 夷; and beyond that for a span of 500 *li* is the realm of market-places; and then beyond that for 500 *li* is where wild animals track." (周礼·夏官·大司马)曰: "方千里曰国畿, 其外方五百里曰侯畿, 又其外方五百里曰甸畿, 又其外方五百里曰男畿, 又其外方五百里曰采畿, 又其外方五百里曰卫畿, 又其外方五百里曰蛮畿, 又其外方五百里曰夷畿, 又其外方五百里曰镇畿, 又其外方五百里曰番畿."

7. The *Exalted Documents* "Yu's Tribute" chapter has: "Five hundred *li* is the vassal realm of the sovereign. From the first hundred *li* tribute was brought as grain fresh on the stalk; from the second hundred *li* it was brought with a portion of the plant; from the third hundred *li* it was brought as hemp to make clothing; from the fourth hundred *li* it was brought as grain still in the husk; and from the fifth, tribute was brought as cleaned grain. Five hundred *li* beyond constituted the realm of the Vassal Lords. The first hundred *li* was occupied by the cities and lands of the sovereign's ministers and officials; the second, by the jurisdiction of the barons; and then the other three hundred *li* was the domain of various princes. Five hundred *li* beyond was the peace-securing domain. In the first three hundred, they cultivated learning; in the other two they engaged in military exercises and defensive tactics. Five hundred *li* remoter still was the beltway. The first three hundred *li* was the land of the *Yi* people; and the other two hundred were for the *Cai* sacrifices. And the most remote five hundred *li* was a wild region. The first three hundred were the land of the *Man* peoples and the other two hundred were a space of flowing transitions." (尚书·禹贡): "五百里甸服: 百里斌纳总, 二百里纳铚, 三百里纳秸服, 四百里粟, 五百里米。五百里侯服: 百里采, 二百里男邦, 三百里诸侯.五百里绥服: 三百里揆文教, 二百里奋武卫. 五百里要服: 三百里夷, 二百里蔡.五百里荒服: 三百里蛮, 二百里流." Cf. Legge (1879), 75–76.

CHAPTER 5

1. "天子不言出." (礼记·曲礼下). Cf. Legge (1967), vol. 1, 113.

2. (春秋公羊传·隐公·1-1-6). Cf. Miller (2015), 10.

3. (春秋公羊传·隐公·1-1-6). Cf. Miller (2015), 10, and Sima Guang's 司马光

Comprehensive Mirror to Aid in Government "Vol. 27: Record of the Han, ch. 19" (资治通鉴·卷二十七·汉纪十九): "春秋之义, 王者无外, 欲一于天下也."

4. "溥天之下, 莫非王土, 率土之滨, 莫非王臣." (诗经·小雅·北山). Cf. Legge (1876), vol. 3, 374.

5. (礼记·礼运). Cf. Legge (1967), vol. 1, 364.

6. "天下非一人之天下也, 天下 (人) 之天下也." (吕氏春秋·卷一·贵公). Cf. Knoblock and Riegel (2000), 70.

7. (吕氏春秋·卷一·贵公). Cf. Knoblock and Riegel (2000), 71: [Translator's note: It is suggested that Jing荆is likely a textual variant of the state of Chu楚国].

8. *Book of Ritual* "Kingly Institutions": "When it comes to the people's dwellings, it must be planned in accordance with the patterns of heaven and earth, cold and hot, dry and moist. In the vast valleys and expansive rivers there are a plurality of institutions, and amongst the people there are many different customs. Having a firm or compliant character, a light-hearted or serious temperament, being slow or quick witted—these are regulated by different customs. The five flavors have their own distinctive ways of harmonizing, tools and machines must be regulated differently, and different clothes and vestments have their unique benefits. Refine the people through education, don't change their customs. Bring proper order through governing, don't change their benefits (i.e., what they find culturally suitable). The people of the middle states, the Rong, and the Yi, the people of the Five Directions all have their characteristic natures (*xing* 性) and this can't be altered. The Yi of the east wear their hair unbound and tattoo their bodies, and they sometimes eat raw meat. The Man of the south tattooed their foreheads and walked on their tiptoes, and some ate raw meat. The Rong of the west wore their hair unbound and wore animal skins, and don't eat grains. The Di from the north wear animal skins and feathers and dwell in caves, and also don't eat grains. The people of the middle states, Yi, Man, Rong, and Di all have their comfortable mode of dwelling, harmonizing flavors, stylizing suitable clothing, making beneficial use of things, and preparing implements. Generally speaking, the people of the Five Directions all have their distinctive languages and their preferences and desires are not the same." Cf. Legge (1967), vol. 1, 228–89.

(礼记·王制): "凡居民材, 必因天地寒煖燥湿.广谷大川异制, 民生其间者异俗.刚柔轻重迟速异齐, 五味异和, 器械异制, 衣服异宜.修其教, 不易其俗; 齐其政, 不易其宜.中国戎夷, 五方之民, 皆有性也, 不可推移.东方曰夷, 被发文身, 有不火食者矣.南方曰蛮, 雕题交趾, 有不火食者矣.西方曰戎, 被发衣皮, 有不粒食者矣.北方曰狄, 衣羽毛穴居, 有不粒食者矣.中国、夷、蛮、戎、狄, 皆有安居、和味、宜服、利用、备器, 五方之民, 言语不通, 嗜欲不同."

9. According to ancient legend, the writing system of the Central Plain was developed earlier than the era of the Yellow Emperor (Neolithic Period), but according to Chen Mingjia's research, and verified by archaeological finds, a Central Plain writing system capable of expressing a complete and distinctive

style of thinking is not that old. Rather, Chen thinks we should date it to the early Shang or perhaps slightly early, around thirty-five hundred to four thousand years ago. See Chen Mengjia 陈梦家, *Studies in Chinese Writing* (Beijing: Zhonghua shuju. 2011), 11–15, and *A Comprehensive Overview of Shang Divination Discourse* (殷墟卜辞综述), (Beijing: Zhonghua shuju, 1956), 644.

10. (孟子·离娄下). Cf. Legge (1875), vol. 2, 253.

11. (史记·秦本纪). Cf. Burton Watson, *Records of the Grand Historian: Qin Dynasty* (New York: Columbia University Press, 1993), 16.

12. (战国策·赵策·武灵王昼间居). Cf. Crump (1996), 292.

13. Wang Ke王柯, *Peoples and Countries: A Comprehensive Overview of Thinking Chinese Multi-Ethnic National Unity* (民族与国家: 中国多民族统一国家思想系谱) (Beijing: Chinese Academy of Social Sciences Press, 2001), 32–33.

CHAPTER 6

1. (尚书·洪范): "天子作民父母以为天下王." Cf. Legge (1879), part 1, 144.

2. (荀子·议兵). Cf. Hutton (2014), 154.

3. (孟子·梁惠王上): "老吾老, 以及人之老; 幼吾幼, 以及人之幼.天下可运于掌," 故"推恩足以保四海." Cf. Legge (1875), vol. 2, 135-35.

4. (尚书·洪范): "无偏无党, 王道荡荡; 无党无偏, 王道平平; 无反无侧, 王道正直." Cf. Legge (1879), part 1, 143-44.

5. (礼记·孔子闲居): "天无私覆, 地无私载, 日月无私照." Cf. Legge (1967), vol. 2, 281.

6. (管子·牧民): "以家为乡, 乡不可为也; 以乡为国, 国不可为也; 以国为天下, 天下不可为也.以家为家, 以乡为乡, 以国为国, 以天下为天下.毋曰不同生, 远者不听; 毋曰不同国, 远者不行; 毋曰不同国, 远者不从.如地如天, 何私何亲? 如月如日, 唯君之节." Cf. Rickett (1985), 56.

7. 老子: (道德经·第五十四章): "以身观身, 以家观家, 以乡观乡, 以邦观邦, 以天下观天下." Cf. Legge (1891), part 1, 98.

8. (尚书·洪范第十二下): "无偏无党, 王道荡荡.无党无偏, 王道平平.无反无侧, 王道正直." Cf. Legge (1879), part 1, 143-44.

9. (管子·任法): "不知亲疏,远近,贵贱,美恶, 以度量断之. 以法制行之, 如天地之无私也."

10. (尚书·伊训): "始于家邦, 终于四海" cf. Legge (1879), part 1, 93.

11. (尚书·洪范): "天子作民父母以为天下王" cf. Legge (1879), part 1, 144.

12. (礼记·大传). Cf. Legge (1967), vol. 2, 61.

13. (商君书·开塞): "其道亲亲而爱私, 亲亲则别, 爱私则险." Cf. Yuri Pines, ed. and trans., *The Book of Lord Shang* (New York: Columbia University Press, 2017), ch. 7, "Opening the Blocked," 167.

14. (礼记·大学): "古之欲明明德于天下者, 先治其国, 欲治其国者, 先齐其家, 欲齐其家者, 先修其身……身修而后家齐, 家齐而后国治, 国治而后天下平." Cf. Legge (1967), vol. 2, 411-12.

15. Fei Xiaotong 费孝通 (1985), 27: "一个人为了自己可以牺牲家，为了家可以牺牲党，为了党可以牺牲国，为了国可以牺牲天下." [Translation slightly modified from Gary Hamilton and Wang Zheng's *From the Soil* (1992), 69.]

16. (商君书·画策): "仁者能仁于人，而不能使人仁；义者能爱于人，而不能使人爱.是以知仁爱之不足以治天下也." Cf. Pines (2017), "Charting the Policies," 220.

17. Translator's note: Zhao is here referring to a chapter of the *Rites* wherein Confucius discusses the "canaling" (*fang* 坊) effects of ritual on natural human desires and social conduct. Despite the best efforts of the sages in constructing a good ritual order, though, common people will still on occasion tend toward forms of conduct favoring selfish competition over mutual benefits, thereby "forgetting" optimal appropriateness (*min you wangyi er zheng li* 民猶忘義而爭利). Cf. Legge (1967), vol. 2, 292.

CHAPTER 7

1. (论语·子路): "名不正，则言不顺；言不顺，则事不成." Cf. Legge (1893), vol. 1, 264.

2. K. C. Chang 张光直, *The Bronze Age of China* (中国青铜时代) (Beijing: SDX Joint Publishing Company, 1999a), 414–15; Xu Zhuoyun (2001), 101–103.

3. (诗经·大雅·皇矣) cf. Legge (1876), vol. 3, 347.

4. (礼记·孔子闲居) cf. Legge (1967), vol. 2, 281.

5. (诗经·大雅·文王): "文王在上，于昭于天.周虽旧邦，其命维新……假哉天命，有商孙子.商之孙子，其丽不亿.上帝既命，侯于周服.侯服于周，天命靡常……王之荩臣.无念尔祖.无念尔祖，聿修厥德.永言配命，自求多福." Cf. Legge (1876), vol. 3, 331–34.

6. K. C. Chang, *Art, Myth and Ritual: The Path to Political Authority in Ancient China* (Cambridge: Harvard University Press, 1983), 44–55; Chinese translation: Zhang Guangzhi 张光直 (美术、神话与祭祀), (Beijing: SDX Joint Publishing Company, 2013), 37.

7. Li Zehou, *The Origins of Chinese Thought: From Shamanism to Ritual Regulations and Humaneness*, trans. Robert Carleo III (Leiden: Brill, 2018), 14–15; original Chinese version: Li Zehou 李泽厚. (由巫到礼，释礼归仁) (Beijing: SDX Joint Publishing Company, 2015), 6–7.

8. (尚书·吕刑): "乃命重、黎，绝地天通" cf. Legge (1865), 257. Translator's note: Here Legge notes that Zhong and Li are obscure figures in the context of the *Exalted Documents* (*Shujing*), but based on a parallel narrative in the *Conversations of the States* (*Guoyu* 国语),there is a possibility that these figures were the Minister of the South and Minister of Fire respectively, but became tasked with carrying out a social-religious reform movement to bring about a more centralized order to the Shamanic-religious bureaucracy by limiting the rituals carried about by the common people (*pingmin* 平民), while also eradicating the Miao people, and their practices of ancestor worship, because they had become too

dependent upon harsh punishments in oppressing people during the early emergence of King Shun's compassionate reforms. According to the Minister Guan Yifu in the *Conversations of the States*, the "Great Lord" (*Huangdi*) was none other than Shun (舜) and he gave Zhong and Guan the additional titles of Minister of Religion and Minister of Education to carry out these "severing" reforms in society.

9. (国语·楚语下): 假如没有绝地天通, "民将能登天乎"? 观射父详细解了这个事件的前因后果: "非此之谓也.古者民神不杂……各司其序, 不相乱也," 而后来" 民神杂糅, 不可方物.夫人作享, 家为巫史, 无有要质.民匮于祀, 而不知其福.烝享无度, 民神同位.民渎齐盟, 无有严威.神狎民则, 不蠲其为.嘉生不降, 无物以享.祸灾存臻, 莫尽其气", 于是颛顼" 使复旧常, 无相侵渎, 是谓绝地天通."

10. K. C. Chang 张光直, 中国考古学论文集 (*Collected Essays on Chinese Archaeology*) (Beijing: SDX Joint Publishing Company, 1999b), 393.

11. Chen Mengjia 陈梦家 points out that the heavenly mandate during the Yin-Shang period referenced "The Lord's commandment" (*diming*帝命) and that *tianming* was a distinctively Zhou expression. See his *Explanation of the Exalted Documents* (尚书通论) (Beijing: Zhonghua shuju, 2005), 207.

12. (尚书·洪范) cf. Legge (1865), 139–47.

13. (尚书·洪范) cf. Legge (1865), 145–47.

14. Translator's note: Zhao's use of "revelation" here, given the previous discussion of the nonexclusive Zhou sense of *tianming*, contrasts a unilateral transmission of meanings and values derived from a transcendent, single-source deity with a hermeneutic of historical consciousness understood as an ongoing, active conversation with past and living cultural contributors deliberately rendering *tianming* in process and in any context as being morally prophetic without presupposing any ontologically fixed or transcendent revelations.

15. Li Zehou 李泽厚 (2015), 13–20. Cf. Li Zehou (2018), 22.

16. (尚书·康诰第十五): "敬哉! 天畏棐忱, 民情大可见" *Exalted Documents* "Records of Kang Chapter 15": "Be reverent! *Tian* has an awe-inspiring capacity to empower sincerity. This is most evident in the affects of the people." Cf. Legge (1865), 167.

17. (周易·革·象): "汤武革命, 顺乎天而应乎人" cf. Legge (1882), 254. Translator's note: Tang 汤 and Wu 武 were the military leaders of political revolutions that respectively overthrew the Xia and Shang regimes.

18. (尚书·泰誓): "民之所欲, 天必从之" cf. Legge (1865), 127.

19. (尚书·泰誓): "天视自我民视, 天听自我民听" cf. Legge (1865), 128.

20. (孟子·离娄上章): "桀纣之失天下也, 失其民也; 失其民也, 失其心也" cf. Legge (1875), vol. 2, 241.

21. *Remnants of the Zhou Documents* "Interpreting the Great Assembly"; (逸周书·大聚解): "王若欲求天下民, 先设其利, 而民自至, 譬之若冬日之阳, 夏日之阴, 不召而民自来.此谓归德"

22. (尚书·蔡仲之命): "皇天无亲, 惟德是辅.民心无常, 惟惠之怀." Cf. Legge (1865), 212.

23. (管子·牧民): "政之所兴, 在顺民心; 政之所废, 在逆民心.民恶忧劳, 我佚乐之; 民恶贫贱, 我富贵之; 民恶危坠, 我存安之; 民恶灭绝, 我生育之." Cf. Rickett (1985), 54.

24. (荀子·正论): "兴天下之同利, 除天下之同害, 而天下归之也." Cf. Hutton (2014), 185.

25. (六稻·文稻·文师): "同天下之利者则得天下, 擅天下之利者则失天下.天有时, 地有财, 能与人共之者仁也.仁之所在, 天下归......与人同忧同乐, 同好同恶者, 义也.义之所在, 天下赴之.凡人恶死而乐生, 好德而归利, 能生利者道也, 道之所在, 天下归之." Cf. Sawyer and Sawyer (1993), "Civil Secret Teaching," 41.

26. Translator's note: I have had some difficulty here in translating this seemingly direct phrase in Zhao's Chinese because the expression *tianxiaren mouxingfu* 天下人谋幸福 can mean either "planning for the happiness of all the people in *tianxia*" (understood as an aspirational achievement of extending political cooperation to the entire world) or as "planning for the happiness of the people of tianxia" (understood as an ethical-political category of ideal designation for those people with the appropriate affective dispositions to support an ideal political regime of tianxia). In any event, as often is the case in Zhao's writings, the multifaceted historical, linguistic, and conceptual resonances are powerful resources for thinking through new possibilities for political theory.

27. (管子·权修): "人情不二, 故民情可得而御也." Cf. Rickett (1985), 95 (Where he takes *qing* 情 as a variant of *xing* 性 and renders it "human nature/is all the same").

28. (论语·颜渊). Cf. Legge (1893), vol. 1, 260.

29. (论语·雍也): "己欲立而立人, 己欲达而达人" cf. Legge (1893), vol. 1, 194.

30. (论语·颜渊): "己所不欲, 勿施于人" cf. Legge (1893), vol. 1, 251.

31. Wang Guowei (2001), 301–302.

32. Hou Wailu侯外庐, *Theorizing Ancient China's Social History* (中国古代社会史论) (Shijiazhuang: Hebei Education Press, 2003), 206: "周之道德, 实皆因其制度而生."

CHAPTER 8

1. Ludwig Wittgenstein, *Philosophical Investigations* (New York: Macmillan Company, 1964), 201.

2. (论语·子路): "近者悦, 远者来" cf. Legge (1893), vol. 1, 269.

3. (尚书·大禹谟): "德惟善政, 政在养民....正德、利用、厚生、惟和" cf. Legge (1865), 47.

4. (礼记·乐记): "德者得也" cf. Legge (1967), vol. 2, 95.

5. (管子·正): "爱之, 生之, 养之, 成之, 利民不德 (自得) , 天下亲之, 曰德." Cf. Rickett (1998), 137.

6. (管子·霸言): "夫先王取天下, 术术乎大德哉, 物利之谓也" cf. Rickett (1985), 358.

7. (史记·周本纪): "修德行善, 诸侯多叛紂而往归西伯" cf. Nienhauser et al. (1994), vol. 1, 58.

8. *Xunzi* "Debating Military Affairs": "In terms of bringing cohesion to the people there are three methods: virtuosity, force, and wealth. Because one wants to get others to respect one's name and reputation, to refine one's virtuosic conduct, and to desire to act on behalf of the multitudes, therefore they should expel crudeness and invite my teachings in. Grounded in the people, and elegantly disposed [in ritual attire and decorum] the masses will be at ease. In establishing laws and issuing edicts, nothing will be opposed. This is how to secure the realm and solidify power, unify the people and strengthen the military. This is to use virtuosity to bring cohesion to the people. Without having one's name and reputation revered or refining one's virtuosic conduct, but just having others approach one with awe due to a firm grip on the propensity of things, even if the people are inclined to resistance, they won't dare revolt because of the differentials in military might. There must be expansive spending for the military force and the control of the realm through their discretionary power (*quan* 权) will be weakened; so to use military force to bring cohesion to the people is a lesser option. Without having one's name and reputation revered or refining one's virtuosic conduct, but using poverty to seek wealth, hunger to promote fullness and empty stomachs to get to get people to open their mouths, is to get the people to depend on the nurturance of the sovereign. As such, one needs to have control over every little grain of food, over the wealth of the economy, and efficaciously distribute [food and wealth]. If this is done for three years, the people will have a kind of trust. And then one could control the realm but discretionary power will be weak. Social cohesion can be achieved but the state will be weakened; this is called using wealth to bring cohesion to the people. In terms of realizing social cohesion, to deploy virtuosity is kingly, to use force is weak, and to use wealth is impoverishing. This is the same in all times." (荀子·议兵): "凡兼人者有三术: 有以德兼人者, 有以力兼人者, 有以富兼人者.彼贵我名声, 美我德行, 欲为我民, 故辟门除涂, 以迎吾入.因其民, 袭其处, 而百姓皆安.立法施令, 莫不顺比.是故得地而权弥重, 兼人而兵俞强: 是以德兼人者也.非贵我名声也, 非美我德行也, 彼畏我威, 劫我势, 故民虽有离心, 不敢有畔虑, 若是则戎甲俞众, 奉养必费.是故得地而权弥轻, 兼人而兵俞弱: 是以力兼人者也.非贵我名声也, 非美我德行也, 用贫求富, 用饥求饱, 虚腹张口, 来归我食.若是, 则必发夫掌窌之粟以食之, 委之财货以富之, 立良有司以接之, 已期三年, 然后民可信也.是故得地而权弥轻, 兼人而国俞贫: 是以富兼人者也.故曰: 以德兼人者王, 以力兼人者弱, 以富兼人者贫, 古今一也." Cf. Hutton (2014), 161–62 [using "capturing the people" for *jianren* 兼人].

9. (国语·周语下): "夫正, 德之道也."

10. (论语·颜渊): "政者正也." Cf. Legge (1893), vol. 1, 258.

11. (尚书·吕刑), (荀子·王制): "维齐非齐" cf. Legge (1865), 263 [who has "to secure uniformity in this (seeming) irregularity"], and Hutton (2014), 70 [who has "total equality is not order" for this expression].

12. Cui Tongzu 瞿同祖, *China's Feudal Society* (中国封建社会) (Shanghai: Shanghai Century Press Group, 2003), 87–200.Translator's note: A *mu* 亩 is a traditional Chinese land measurement and is equivalent to about 1/6 acres.

13. (晏子春秋·内篇问上·第十一): "薄于身而厚于民, 约于身而广于世" cf. Olivia Milbourne trans., *The Spring and Autumn Annals of Master Yan* (Leiden: Brill, 2018), 254.

14. (管子·五辅): "德有六兴.曰: 辟田畴, 利坛宅.修树蓺, 劝士民, 勉稼穑, 修墙屋, 此谓厚其生.发伏利, 输㳛积, 修道途, 便关市, 慎将宿, 此谓输之以财.导水潦, 利陂沟, 决潘渚, 溃泥滞, 通郁闭, 慎津梁, 此谓遗之以利.薄征敛, 轻征赋, 弛刑罚, 赦罪戾, 宥小过, 此谓宽其政.养长老, 慈幼孤, 恤鳏寡, 问疾病, 吊祸丧, 此谓匡其急.衣冻寒, 食饥渴, 匡贫窭, 振罢露, 资乏绝, 此谓振其穷.凡此六者, 德之兴也.六者既布, 则民之所欲, 无不得矣.夫民必得其所欲, 然后听上; 听上, 然后政可善政也.故曰, 德不可不兴也." Cf. Rickett (1985), 196.

15. (逸周书·大聚解): "乡立巫医, 具百药以备疾灾"; "不可树谷者树之材木"; "春三月山林不登斧, 以成草木之长; 夏三月川泽不入网罟, 以成鱼鳖之长."

16. (尚书·武成): "建官惟贤, 位事惟能" cf. Legge (1865), 137.

17. (尚书·大禹谟): "野无遗贤" cf. Legge (1865), 46.

18. (管子·心术下): "私者, 乱天下者也" cf. Rickett (1998), 59.

19. Translator's note: Here is the Zhou dynasty seal script variant of the character *he* 和 that Zhao is alluding to as referencing a wind instrument: 龢.

20. (尚书·尧典): "协和万邦" cf. Legge (1865), 32.

21. (尚书·洛诰): "和恒四方民" cf. Legge (1865), 189.

22. (左传·昭公二十年), 也见于(晏子春秋·外篇·第五): "公曰: 和与同异乎? 对曰: 异.和如羹焉, 水火醯醢盐梅以烹鱼肉, 燀之以薪.宰夫和之, 齐之以味, 济其不及, 以泄其过.君臣亦然.君所谓可而有否焉, 臣献其否以成其可.君所谓否而有可焉, 臣献其可以去其否"; "先王之济五味, 和五声也, 以平其心, 成其政也.声亦如味, 一气, 二体, 三类, 四物, 五声, 六律, 七音, 八风, 九歌, 以相成也.清浊, 小大, 短长, 疾徐, 哀乐, 刚柔, 迟速, 高下, 出入, 周疏, 以相济也.君子听之, 以平其心, 心平德和"; "若以水济水, 谁能食之? 若琴瑟之专一, 谁能听之? 同之不可也如是." Cf. Durrant, Lee, and Schaberg (2016), 1587.

23. (国语·郑语): "夫和实生物, 同则不继.以他平他谓之和, 故能丰长而物归之; 若以同裨同, 尽乃弃矣"; "声一无听, 物一无文, 味一无果, 物一不讲."

24. (管子·内业): "和乃生, 不和不生" cf. Rickett (1998), 52.

25. (论语·雍也) cf. Legge (1893), vol. 1, 194. Translator's note: This is Zhao's unique philosophical translation of the well-known *Analects* passage into more logical-analytic terms.

CHAPTER 9

1. (尚书·旅獒): "四夷咸宾, 无有远迩, 毕献方物," "不贵异物" "不宝远物." Cf. Legge (1865), "The Hounds of Lu," 151.

2. Xu Zhuoyun (2001), 311; Ge Zhiyi 葛志毅, *Studies in Zhou Institutions of Land Distribution* (周代分封制度研究) (Harbin: Heilongjiang People's Press, 2005), 229.

3. (史记·秦始皇本纪): "丞相绾等言: 诸侯初破, 燕,齐,荆地远, 不为置王毋以填之.请立诸子, 唯上幸许.始皇下其议于群臣, 群臣皆以为便.廷尉李斯议曰: 周文武所封子弟同姓甚众, 然后属疏远, 相攻击如仇雠, 诸侯更相诛伐, 周天子弗能禁止.今海内赖陛下神灵一统, 皆为郡县, 诸子功臣以公赋税重赏赐之, 甚足易制.天下无异意, 则安宁之术也.置诸侯不便.始皇曰: 天下共苦战斗不休, 以有侯王.赖宗庙, 天下初定, 又复立国, 是树兵也, 而求其宁息, 岂不难哉! 廷尉议是." Cf. Watson (1993b), 44.

CHAPTER 10

1. (管子·牧民): "以家为家, 以乡为乡, 以国为国, 以天下为天下" cf. Rickett (1985), 56.

2. 老子: (道德经·第五十四章): "以身观身, 以家观家, 以乡观乡, 以邦观邦, 以天下观天下" cf. Legge (1891), vol. 1, 98.

3. Translator's note: "exclusionary concept" here refers to concepts that are (ethically and politically) incompatible with the *tianxia* ideal of all-encompassing nonexteriority. As such it does not rule out dissident politics—as long as dissent would be operating to promote the political ideals of common interests for all the people of *tianxia* as a future world-political subject.

4. (礼记·曲礼上): "礼, 闻取于人, 不闻取人; 礼, 闻来学, 不闻往教." Cf. Legge (1967), vol. 1, 63.

5. Immanuel Wallerstein, *The Modern World-System*, vol. 1, *Capitalist Agriculture and the Origins of the European World-Economy in the Sixteenth Century* (Berkeley: University of California Press, 2011), 347: Chinese translation: 华勒斯坦, (现代世界体系·卷 1) (Beijing: Higher Education Press, 1998), 460. Translator's note: Immanuel Wallerstein (1930–2018) was an influential political sociologist who theorized the historical emergence of the "world-economy" (the disconcatenating hyphen here is most important) in the long sixteenth century wherein various European powers functioned as a "center" with the "periphery" of the Americas and Asia functioning more or less as an "external arena" serving to prove that the only two hitherto possible world-systems have been either *world-empire*, which is no longer possible under conditions of global modernity, or a *world-economy* that has so far only been capitalist-imperialist in orientation.

6. (六稻·武稻·顺启): "文王问太公曰: 何如而可为天下? 太公曰: 大盖天下, 然后能容天下; 信盖天下, 然后能约天下; 仁盖天下, 然后能怀天下; 恩盖天下, 然后能保天下; 权盖天下, 然后能不失天下……故利天下者, 天下启之; 害天下者, 天下闭之; 生天下者, 天下德之; 杀天下者, 天下贼之; 彻天下者, 天下通之; 穷天下者, 天下仇之; 安天下者, 天下恃之; 危天下者, 天下灾之, 天下者非一人之天下, 唯有道者处之." This is apocryphally attributed to the Grand Duke Jiang (姜太公); it is likely a writing from the Warring States. Cf. Sawyer and Sawyer (1993), 53–54.

CHAPTER 11

1. Translator's note: To forestall confusion, it should be noted here that throughout the term "China" is being used to translate *zhongguo* 中国, literally "the Focal State(s)." Occasionally, Zhao is playing upon the conceptual ambiguity of this term in its historical transition from a pre-Qin designation of political authority to the modern notion of a sovereign nation-state.

2. In the past many historians appropriated Western historical concepts and took the Qin through Qing dynasties to be "feudal " in their governance. This is a category mistake. The Zhou dynasty was truly "feudal" [literally "division of territorial establishment"] (封建), while everything after the Qin was a county administration (郡县) system. Currently most scholars avoid employing these erroneous concepts and have instead taken to using the categories of Western political science to refer to the Qin-Qing institutions as "centralized power" or "authoritarian politics" and so forth. These concepts in degree approximate the reality but are not really accurate. Even though from the Qin onward, the monarchical system took the emperor as the highest power, it still partially preserved the ancient tradition of "shared governance." With the exception of those violent dictators who ignored the institutions, an emperor under normal conditions could not be an autocrat. The Qin-Han period established a multilayered system of "deliberative governance" wherein the internal, court-appointed officials regularly carried out public deliberations that would determine state policy and affairs. If there was a particularly important or difficult situation that required decision, there would be a convening of a centralized body of hundreds of officials to deliberate in congress. The ultimate conclusion awaited confirmation from the emperor. Each historical period had unique systemic differences, but basically the principle was the same. According to the research of Yu Yingshi, the system of governance during the Song dynasty was the apex. Thus it is wrong to simply describe the history of imperial China as an "authoritarian" system. But a "shared governance" designation is probably too much of an exaggeration also, since the emperor ultimately held final decision-making power. Because modern political science is lacking in the conceptual terminology to accurately describe a Chinese monarchical system, herein we will be referring to the Chinese monarchical system as a "unified system of administration." This is just an expedient name, though, as it awaits further consideration. The main reason for this is that the most important political condition in the Chinese monarchical

system was the division between the official class and the common people. The emperor was the unifying linchpin in this relationship between the body of officials and the common people. Thus we can call it a "unified administration."

3. The *tianxia* system hopes to achieve a compatibility in political order. The so-called "compatibility of the myriad states" as an expression comes from the most ancient collection of political writings, the *Exalted Documents*. "Compatibility" references the ability to transform enmity into friendship and to use inclusivity to guarantee a peaceful political order.

4. Because the King Mu of Zhou was fond of war, he had attacked the Quan and Rong people for not paying tribute on time. Although this particular military campaign was hugely victorious, it destroyed the tradition of Zhou compatibility in governing. The result was a great loss of distant tributes and of the willing participation of various regions. These various distant regions never again paid tribute to the Zhou.

5. Attributed to Zuo Qiuming 左丘明, *Conversations of the States* "Discourses of the Zhou"; (国语·周语上).

6. (礼记·礼运): 以天下为一家, 以中国为一人. Cf. Legge (1967), vol. 1, 379.

7. Chen Mengjia 陳梦家, "Myth and Shamanism in the Shang Dynasty" (商代的神话与巫术), *Yanjing Xuebao* (燕京学报) 20 (1936).

8. K. C. Chang, *Art, Myth and Ritual: The Path to Political Authority in Ancient China* (Cambridge, MA: Harvard University Press, 1988), 91. Chinese translation: 张光直 (美术、神话与祭祀) (Beijing: SDX Joint Publishing Company, 2013b), 85.

9. Li Zehou (2018), 13. Cf. 李泽厚: (由巫到礼·释礼归仁), (Beijing: SDX Joint Publishing Company, 2015), 13–21.

10. Translator's note: This reference "that the Six Classics are all histories" (六经皆为中国古代史书的一种主张) is not easily sourced to a particular text but was a common idea in debating the philosophical import (*yili* 义理) of the core Confucian classics: *Book of Changes* (易), *Exalted Documents* (书), *Book of Songs* (诗), *Book of Rites* (礼), *Classic of Music* (乐), and *Spring and Autumn Annals* (春秋).

11. In previous essays I've used the term "great power." Lu Xiang has suggested using "leading power" because "great power" in contemporary political discourse already has a rather negative connotation as a kind of euphemism for hegemonic power. I've made the correction here.

12. Joseph R. Levenson, Lucian Pye, and other Western sinologists consider China to be a civilization nation. An earlier analysis of this dynamic comes from Marcel Granet. Granet didn't directly use the language of "civilization nation," but his *La civilisation chinoise* (Paris: La Renaissance du livre, 1929) analyzed Chinese society as a distinctive kind of civilization. Modern Confucians have a similar understanding. Qian Mu believes that Chinese "people and nation are both cultural existences" (*A Guide to Chinese Cultural History* [中国文化史导论] Beijing: Commercial Press, 1994, 23—first edition from 1948). And Liang Shum-

ing says, "China proceeds as a society instead of as a nation-state" (*China's Modern Academic Classic—Liang Shuming Edition* [中国现代学术经典·梁漱溟卷] Shijiazhuang: Hebei Education Press, 1994, 23—first edition published in 1949). Liang Shuming refers to a letter from a friend regarding Bertrand Russell's 1920 visit to China. During this visit at a Shanghai lecture he reportedly said: "China is in fact a cultural body and not a nation-state" (Liang Shuming [1949], 255). From this we might infer that the earliest positing of China as a civilization nation could have been Russell.

13. Wang Mingming 王铭铭, "China: Ethno-body or Civilization-body?" (中国: 民族体还是文明体?) *Beijing Cultural Review* 文化纵横12 (2008).

14. In 1901 Liang Qichao 梁启超 promoted ethnonationalism ("National Thinking of Transformation and Change: A Theory of Difference and Similarity" [国家思想变迁异同论], in *Ice Drinker's Studio: Collected Writings*, vol. 1, collection 6 [飲冰室合集 Shanghai: Zhonghua shuju, 1936]; and in 1902 he promoted the ethnostate ("Treatise on the Great Power of Ethnic Conflicts" [论民族竞争之大势], in *Ice Drinker's Studio: Collected Writings*, vol. 2, collection 10). But later he turned to nationalism.

15. Folk sayings are more accurate than official doctrines when it comes to reflecting true social conditions. Li Qingshan 李庆善, in *A New Theory of Chinese People: Viewing the People's Heart from Folk Sayings* (中国人新论: 从民谚看民心) (Beijing: China Academy of Social Sciences Press, 1996), observes that the many contradictions in traditional folk sayings reveal two aspects behind behavior. One aspect is they are promoting honest, unselfish conduct, and the other is recommending the crafty pursuit of personal benefit.

16. Eric Voegelin, *Order and History*, vol. 1, *Israel and Revelation* (Baton Rouge: Louisiana State University Press, 1956), ix. Chinese translation: 埃里克·沃格林、霍伟岸、叶赢译: (秩序与历史·卷一·以色列与启示) (Nanjing: Yilin Press, 2010), 19.

17. Thomas C. Schelling, *The Strategy of Conflict* (Cambridge, MA: Harvard University Press, 1980), 42. Chinese translation: 托马斯·谢林, 赵华等译: (冲突的战略) (Beijing: Huaxia Press, 2011), 48–51. Translator's note: Thomas Schelling thinks through game theory, for games of strategy rather than chance or skill, wherein a decisional rationality is always being adjusted in response to the constantly changing strategies of others to optimize the interests of individual agents and all concerned parties. This particular quote is in the context of an "essay on bargaining" ranging from gangsters to international agreements between states involving threats of open conflict aiming at deterrence. And it is especially in these cases wherein a shared moral or ceremonial vocabulary (e.g., "cross-my-heart" promises as communicating trustworthiness) are largely or entirely absent, that situations arise in which rational collective decisions cannot be reliably foreseen: "When the act to be deterred is inherently a sequence of steps whose cumulative effect is what matters, a threat geared to the increments

may be more credible than one that must be carried out either all at once or not at all when some particular point has been reached. It may even be impossible to define a 'critical point' with sufficient clarity to be persuasive."

18. K. C. Chang, *The Archaeology of Ancient China*, 4th edition (New Haven, CT: Yale University Press, 1986), 369. Chinese translation: 张光直: (古代中国考古学), (Beijing: SDX Joint Publishing Company, 2013c), 434 .

19. "近者悦，远者来" (论语·子路). Cf. Legge (1893), vol. 1, 269.

20. Zhao Hui赵辉, "The Formation of the Historical Trend of the Central Plain as Core," (以中原为中心的历史趋势的形成). *Wenwu* 文物 (*Cultural Relics*) 1 (2000).

21. "文明动力是政治与财富的结合" K. C. Chang 张光直, 考古学专题六讲 (*Six Lectures on Archaeology*), (Beijing: SDX Joint Publishing Company, 2013a), 156.

22. According to yet-to-be confirmed sources, in early China, in addition to Chinese characters as *hanzi* 汉字 there was also ancient "Yi Script" (*yiwen* 彝文). But the research is inconclusive. It is thought that the Yi script could have been the ancient writings of peoples from the southwest and would then have a certain affinity with the Yi writings of today's Yi (*nuoso burma* writing or the language used by the Nuosu Yi people of the Liangshan Yi Autonomous Prefecture). Most of the Yi writings preserved today date from the Ming and Qing periods and the content is primarily shamanistic and divinatory. It would seem that it has an earlier source. But in terms of how early ancient Yi script was used, and what kinds of complex abstractions it was capable of, these are part of a set of questions that need further expert research.

23. Christianity is another successful example of the exceptional becoming universal. Jesus's crucifixion and resurrection are exceptional narratives but became expressed as a universal belief system open to all.

CHAPTER 12

1. In Europe and America it is popular to think that the Sumerian civilization is earlier than Chinese and Indian civilizations, but there is definitely room to be skeptical of such views. Over the past decade there have been many archaeological discoveries such as early agricultural tools and earthenware that would indicate Chinese civilization has traces at least as early as Sumerian civilization. But it would seem that Sumerian civilization was more advanced, and pending more archaeological finds, I herein follow the mainstream opinion.

2. See Chinese Academy of Social Sciences Archeological Research Center 中国社会科学院考古研究所, "Chinese Archaeology: The New Stone Age Volume" (中国考古学·新石器时代卷), (Beijing: Chinese Academy of Social Sciences Press, 2010), 198–202.

3. Chinese Academy of Social Sciences Archeological Research Center (2010), 568.

4. Chinese Academy of Social Sciences Archeological Research Center (2010), 768–95.

5. Chang (1999), 54–55.

6. Xu Hong 许宏, *Earliest China* (最早的中国), (Beijing: Science Publishing, 2009), 152.

7. Chang (1999), 36.

8. Chang (1999), 158–59.

9. Chinese Academy of Social Sciences Archeological Research Center 中国社会科学院考古研究所, "Chinese Archaeology: The Xia-Shang Volume" (中国考古学·夏商卷), (Beijing: Chinese Academy of Social Sciences Press, 2011), 81.

10. Zhang Guangzhi believes that the Erlitou culture's origins coincide with the Xia culture, but ultimately the reason we cannot conclude that it is Xia or Shang is because "so far we haven't discovered any Erlitou written sources." (张光直: *Archaeology in Ancient China* (古代中国考古学), Beijing: SDX Joint Publishing Company, 2013c, 376–77). The problem though is that, according to current sources, the Erlitou period hadn't yet developed a written script, so it is feared that we will never find any "written sources."

11. See Xu Hong's 许宏 *What Is China?* (何以中国), (Beijing: SDX Joint Publishing Company, 2014), 145–48.With respect to "the earliest China," archaeologists commonly agree that the formation of China was a long-term process. But when it comes to selecting out concrete, representative emblems of the earliest Chinese characteristics, there is no agreement at all. For example, Su Qiqi is inclined to believe that the Taosi culture "formed the basis of Hua and Xia ethnic groupings." Su Qiqi 苏秉奇, *A New Exploration into the Origins of Chinese Civilization* (中国文明起源新探), (Beijing: People's Press, 2013). This age would seem to correspond to what the ancients have said about the era of Yao and Shun. And then there is Han Jianye, who believes that Miaodigou culture is the earliest China. Han Jianye 韩建业, *Early China: The Formation and Development of a Sino-Sphere Culture* (早期中国: 中国文化圈的形成和发展), (Shanghai: Shanghai Classics Publishing House, 2015), 268. This age would seem to correspond to what the ancients have said about the Yellow Emperor era. Although these theories are all reasonable, herein I make use of Xu Hong's preference, using the Erlitou culture as the earliest China that would correspond to somewhere between the end of the Xia and the early Shang. The Yellow Emperor, and Yao and Shun, were certainly key figures and periods in the formation of China, but the archaeological materials are limited, and moreover what we do have is insufficient to prove at what time the great region of China formed a definitive center. Perhaps we might think that the psychological import the Yellow Emperor, Yao, and Shun have had upon Chinese culture are more important than such proof. Even though the legends about such exemplary figures are quite possibly a record of actual history, the civilizational levels achieved do not necessarily reach a core strength. And the legends are likely derived from later eras as core civilizations

on the Central Plain projected backward. However, in comparison, the civilizational level of the Erlitou remains is impressive enough to be persuasive as an expression of the symbolic structure of the Chinese cultural "gene." Thus I've opted to align with Xu Hong's reading of prehistory.

12. Xu Hong (2014), 117–19.

13. Liu Qingzhu ed. 刘庆柱主编, *Chinese Archaeological Discoveries and Research, 1949–2009* (中国考古发现与研究 1949–2009), (Beijing: People's Press, 2010), 196.

14. Chinese Academy of Social Sciences Archaeological Research Center (2011), 107–23.

15. Xu Hong (2009), 205–207.

16. Xu Hong (2009), 146–47.

17. Zhang Guangzhi 张光直 (2013c), 346. Cf. Chang (1986), 295.

18. (尚书·多士). Cf. Legge (1865), 198.

19. Chinese Academy of Social Sciences Archaeological Research Center (2011), 125.

20. Chen Mengjia 陈梦家, *Studies in Chinese Writing* (中国文字学), (Beijing: Zhonghua shuju, 2011), 11.

21. Xu Hong maintains that although the surface area of the Erlitou palace is about one-seventh of the size of the Forbidden City, in terms of its structural elements it can serve as the prototype for all subsequent Chinese palatial court architecture. See Xu Hong (2009), 80–84.

22. Liang Sicheng 梁思成, *Chinese Architectural History* (中国建筑史) (Tianjin: Baihuawenyi Publishing, 1998), 15.

23. This phrase "correlate with heaven" (*peitian* 配天) is earliest seen in the *Exalted Documents* "Lord Shi" chapter (尚书·君奭): "While the ritual refinement of Yin lasted they could correlate with heaven" (殷礼陟配天) [cf. Legge (1865), 207]. For an early interpretation of the concept of "correlating with the heavens," see the *Book of Rites* "Focusing the Familiar" chapter (礼记·中庸): "Only those of optimal sagacity in the world have the brilliant intelligence and luminous wisdom capable of overseeing the realm. And only these exemplary figures can also have the broad appreciation of diversity and flexible adaptability to exercise empathic understanding. And only these exemplary persons can display the strenuous energy and moral fortitude to keep a firm grasp on their qualities of leadership. And only these exemplary persons can exercise the equipoise and awesomeness to command respect in all situations. Their cultural refinement and accordance with reason is enough to maintain proper deference. So broad, so expansive, and most deep, but timely springing forth like the heavenly encompassing of all things—what a profound chasm. Manifesting as such, the multitudes express reverence, speaking as such the multitudes are trusting, acting as such and the multitudes are pleased. It is for this reason that their good

name spreads throughout the Central States and exceeds even to the Man and Mo barbarians in the south and the north. Wherever boats and carriages ply and human strength penetrates, wherever heaven's canopy extends and earth holds us up, everywhere that is illumined by the sun and moon, wherever frost and dew condense, and wherever can be found breath and blood there is sure to be reverence and love. This is called "correlating with the heavens" (*peitian* 配天). "唯天下至圣, 为能聪明睿知, 足以有临也; 宽裕温柔, 足以有容也; 发强刚毅, 足以有执也; 齐庄中正, 足以有敬也; 文理密察, 足以有别也. 溥博渊泉, 而时出之. 溥博如天, 渊泉如渊. 见而民莫不敬; 言而民莫不信; 行而民莫不说. 是以声名洋溢乎中国, 施及蛮貊. 舟车所至, 人力所通, 天之所覆, 地之所载, 日月所照, 霜露所队: 凡有血气者莫不尊亲, 故曰配天." Cf. Ames and Hall (2001), 113. And also: "Vast and sturdy it [utmost creativity, *zhicheng* 至诚] is a companion of the earth; exalted and brilliant, it is a companion to the heavens; farsighted and enduring, [such creativity] is unlimited." 博厚配地, 高明配天, 悠久无疆. Cf. Ames and Hall (2001), 107.

24. Yang Kuan 杨宽, *An Institutional History of Ancient Chinese Cities* (中国古代都城制度史), (Shanghai: Shanghai People's Press, 2006), 25–36.

25. Nassim Nicholas Taleb, *Antifragile: Things That Gain from Disorder* (New York: Random House, 2012), 3.

26. Yao Dali 姚大力, *Mongolian Yuan Institutions and Political Culture* (蒙元制度与政治文化), (Beijing: Peking University Press, 2011), 270.

27. Regarding all the Liao Dynasty materials, see Wang Ke's 王柯 *Ethnicities and States: A Comprehensive Overview of Thinking Chinese Multi-Ethnic National Unity* (民族与国家: 中国多民族统一国家思想系谱), (Beijing: Chinese Academy of Social Sciences Press, 2001), 119–28.

28. Wang Tongling 王桐龄, *A History of Chinese Ethnicities* (中国民族史), (Changchun: Jilin Publishing Group, 2010), 376.

29. For "all these perspectives regarding China," see Ge Zhaoguang 葛兆光 *Here in "China" I Dwell* (宅兹中国), (Beijing: Zhonghua shuju, 2011), 41–42, trans. Jesse Field and Qin Fang (Leiden: Brill, 2017).

30. Rao Zongyi 饶宗颐, *A Theory of Political Legitimacy in Chinese History* (中国史学上之正统论), (Beijing: Zhonghua shuju, 2015), 157–61.

31. Translator's note: The Semu 色目人 (literally "colored-eyed people") was a name used to refer to a wide array of central Eurasian ethnic groups as part of the fourfold hierarchy proposed during the Yuan reign.

32. Chen Gaohua 陈高华 and Shi Weimin 史卫民, *A Comprehensive History of Chinese Political Institutions*, vol. 8 (中国政治制度通史·第八卷), edited by Bai Gang (白刚主编), (Beijing: People's Press, 1996), 60.

33. Chen Gaohua and Shi Weimin (1996), 37–38.

34. Zhang Zhaosu 张兆裕, *The Chinese-Barbarian Distinction in the Ming Dynasty* (明代华夷之辨) in *Ancient Historical Documents: Ming and Qing*

dynasties (古史文存·明清卷上), edited by Chinese Academy of Social Sciences History Research Center (Beijing: Social Sciences Literature Press, 2004), 265-77.

35. Cui Shigu 瞿式谷, *Notes on Unofficial Matters* (职方外记小言). See Xie Fang谢方, *Commentary on Notes on Unoffical Matters* (职方外记校释), (Beijing, Zhonghua shuju, 2000), 9.

36. Translator's note: *wenzhi* 文治 can be read either as a verbal compound, that is "using 'literary culture' (*wen* 文) to achieve order" or as an adverbial phrase indicating a "governing culture."

37. "自古帝王非四海一家不为正统." Song Lian 宋濂, *Yuan History*, chapter 161—Biography No. 48 (元史·卷一百六十一·列传第四十八) (Beijing: Zhonghua shuju, 1976).

38. Rao Zongyi (2015), 6.

39. "正者, 所以正天下之不正也; 统者, 所以合天下之不一也" Ou Yangxiu 欧阳修, *A Theory of Political Legitimacy* (正统论上) in Rao Zongyi 饶宗颐 (2015), 114.

40. Wang Fuzhi 王夫之, *On the Song Dynasty*, chapter 15, "Ancestral Order" (宋论·卷十五·度宗). *Complete Works of Wang Fuzhi* (船山全书), (Changxia: Yuelu Publishing House, 2011).

41. "易姓改号, 谓之亡国. 仁义充塞, 而至于率兽食人, 人将相食, 谓之亡天下." Gu Yanwu 顾炎武, *Record of Daily Realizations*, chapter 13, "Origin of Order" (日知录·卷十三·正始). *Sikuquanshu* 四库全书, (Chinese Text Project digital library, 1773).

42. Translator's note: Nurhaci (1559–1626) was a Jurchen chieftain who united various tribes in northeast Asia, later all identified as "Manchu" and carried out many military attacks on the Ming dynasty and Joseon Korea. He is recognized as the founder of the Qing Dynasty.

43. "天地之养, 上自人类下至昆虫, 天生天养之也, 是你南朝之养之乎?......普养万物之天至公无私, 不以南朝为大国容情. ......天命归之, 遂有天下." "Nurhaci's Letter," in *Historical Materials from Before the Qing Invasions* (清入关前史料选辑 1) (Beijing: People's University of China Press, 1984), 289–96.

44. Fei Zhengqing, ed. 费正清主编, *Chinese World Order: Traditional China's Ambassadorial Relations* (中国的世界秩序: 传统中国的对外关系) (Beijing: Chinese Academy of Social Sciences Press, 2010), 283.

45. Fei Zhengqing (2010), 1.

46. Zheng Youguo 郑有国, *Researching Traditional China's Institutes of Foreign Trade* (中国市舶制度研究), (Fuzhou: Fujian Education Press, 2004), 214–20.

47. Li Yunquan; 李云泉, *The Myriad States Come to Court: A History of Tributary Institutions* (万邦来朝: 朝贡制度史论), (Beijing: Xinhua Press, 2014), 13.

48. Yan Mingshu 阎明恕, *A History of Marriage Alliances in Ancient China* (中国古代和亲史), (Guiyang: Guizhouminzu Press, 2003), 157.

CHAPTER 13

1. "秦失其鹿, 天下共逐之." Sima Qian 司马迁, *The Record of the Grand Historian*, "Biography of the Marquis of Huaiyin" (史记·淮阴侯列传), (Beijing: Zhonghua shuju, 1982). Cf. Watson (1993a), 183.

2. Man Zhimin 满志敏, *Climate Change Research in the History of China* (中国历史时期气候变化研究), (Jinan: Shandong Education Press, 2009), 92–118.

3. (诗经·小雅·鹿鸣), "呦呦鹿鸣. . ." Cf. Legge (1876), vol. 3, 182.

4. Zhang Guangzhi 张光直, *Collected Writings on Chinese Archaeology* (中国考古学考古文集) (Beijing: SDX Joint Publishing Company, 1999b), 53.

5. (周易·上经·屯卦三) cf. Legge (1882), 62.

6. Translator's note: Robert L. Carneiro offered a theory of the origin of major political powers (viz., large-scale cities and states) based in a circumscription model using three factors: (1) environmental limitations, (2) population pressures, and (3) warfare. See R. L. Carneiro, "A Theory of the Origin of the State," *Science* 169 (1970): 733–38.

7. Xu Hong (2014), 96–99.

8. See Mancur Olson, *Power and Prosperity: Outgrowing Communist and Capitalist Dictatorships* (New York: Basic Books, 2000); *The Rise and Decline of Nations: Economic Growth, Stagflation, and Social Rigidities* (New Haven, CT: Yale University Press, 1982); and *The Logic of Collective Action: Public Goods and the Theory of Groups* (Cambridge, MA: Harvard University Press, 1965).

9. "唯燕京乃天地之中" Translator's note: *Yanjing* (literally "Swallow City") is a literary name for Beijing and is a reference to the region being conquered by the state of Yan during the Warring States period. The name was restored to the city during the reign of the Khitan's in the tenth through the twelfth centuries during the Liao dynasty.

10. "天子必居中," 于是 "非燕不可." Zhou Chenhe 周振鹤, *Sixteen Lectures on Chinese History and Political Geography* (中国历史政治地理十六讲), (Beijing: Zhonghua shuju, 2013), 256.

11. "匈奴之地广大, 而戎马之足轻利, 其势易骚动也. 少发则不足以更适, 多发则民不堪其役. 役烦则力罢, 用多则财乏." Huan Kun 桓宽, *Salt and Iron Discourses*, chapter 38, "Containing the Barbarians" (盐铁论·备胡第三十八).

12. "匈奴牧于无穷之泽, 东西南北, 不可穷极, 虽轻车利马, 不能得也." Huan Kun 桓宽, *Salt and Iron Discourses*, chapter 46, "Western Regions" (盐铁论·西域第四十六).

13. "非贪壤土之利, 救民之患也." Huan Kun 桓宽, *Salt and Iron Discourses*, chapter 45, "Attacking Methods" (盐铁论·伐功第四十五).

14. Li Hongbing 李鸿宾, "Stag Hunting on the Central Plain: The Secret Behind the Expansion of the Northern Peoples into the South" (逐鹿中原: 东北诸族南向拓展的秘密) in *Social Sciences Weekly* (中国社会科学报) January 29, 2015.

15. "不求变俗" (礼记·曲礼). Cf. Legge (1967), vol. 1, 102.

16. "西域思汉威德, 咸乐内属" Ban Gu 班固, *Han History*, chapter 96, "Biographies of the Western Region" (汉书·卷九十六下·西域传).

17. Ban Gu 班固, *Han History*, chapter 70, "Biography of Zheng Ji" (汉书·卷七十·郑吉传).

18. Meng Xiangcai 孟祥才, *Comprehensive History of Chinese Political Institutions*, vol. 3, (中国政治制度通史·第三卷), edited by Bai Gang (白刚主编), (Beijing: People's Press, 1996), 257–58.

19. Translator's note: The "halter and bridle" model (or *jimi* 羁縻) refers to strategies of incentivizing participation in the leading central state power configuration while also controlling mechanisms to deter actions detrimental to the whirlpool balance of power.

20. Translator's note: The term *hu* 胡 was an appellation for any nomadic and seminomadic tribes north of the Central Plain.

21. Huang Huixian 黄惠贤, *Comprehensive History of Chinese Political Institutions*, vol. 4 (中国政治制度通史·第四卷), edited by Bai Gang (白刚主编), (Beijing: People's Press, 1996), 72–80.

22. Yu Lunian 俞鹿年, *Comprehensive History of Chinese Political Institutions*, vol. 5 (中国政治制度通史·第五卷), edited by Bai Gang (白刚主编), (Beijing: People's Press, 1996), 256–60.

23. Li Xihou 李锡厚 and Bai Bing 白滨, *Comprehensive History of Chinese Political Institutions*, vol. 7 (中国政治制度通史·第七卷), edited by Bai Gang (白刚主编), (Beijing: People's Press, 1996), 74–87.

24. Wang Tongling (2010), 394–98.

25. Yao Dali (2011), 280.

26. Wang Tongling (2010), 18–28.

27. Wang Tongling (2010), preface.

28. Wang Tongling (2010), 335–525.

29. Wang Tongling (2010), 440–41.

30. "物莫非指, 而指非指" (公孙龙子·指物论). Cf. Kirill O. Thompson, "When a 'White Horse' Is Not a 'Horse,'" *Philosophy East and West* 45, no. 4 (1995): 490–91.

31. "天下之所无" (公孙龙子·指物论). Cf. Thompson (1995).

32. Translator's note: The phrases *xing er shang* 形而上 and *xing er xia* 形而下, literally "above/before form" and "below/after form" with "form" (*xing* 形), simply understood to mean gestalts that are made manifest in experience are taken from the *Appended Words* 系辞 commentary to the *Book of Changes* (易经). In the modern project of translating Western philosophical concepts into Chinese characters, the former term got employed to translate "metaphysics" (形而上学) and hence I've made a distinction between what is structuring experience (i.e., "metaphysics") and what is manifest in experience (i.e., empirically verifiable reality).

33. Duan Qingbo 段清波 and Xu Weimin 徐卫民, *China's Great Wall through*

History: Discoveries and Research (中国历代长城: 发现与研究), (Beijing: Science Press, 2014), 1–17.

34. Duan Qingbo and Xu Weimin (2014), 114–56.

35. Duan Qingbo and Xu Weimin (2014), 247–48.

36. Duan Qingbo and Xu Weimin (2014), 284–85.

37. Duan Qingbo and Xu Weimin (2014), 304.

38. Hu Huanyong 胡焕庸, "China's Population Line: Attaching Statistical Tables and Density Maps" (中国人口之分布: 附统计表与密度图) in *Acta Geographica Sinica* (地理学报), 1935, 2.

39. Zhou Chenhe (2013), 75–77.

40. Fu Sinian 傅斯年, *Ethnicity and Ancient Chinese History* (民族与古代中国史), (Shijiazhuang: Hebei Education Press, 2002), 3.

CHAPTER 14

1. K. C. Chang, Chinese translation of *Art, Myth and Ritual: The Path to Political Authority in Ancient China* (2013b), 130.

2. "所过者化, 所存者神." (孟子·尽心上). Cf. Legge (1875), vol. 2, 349.

CHAPTER 15

1. Translator's note: "Anarchy" here doesn't refer to the various traditions of political theory and praxis that leveled critiques against imperialist capitalist orders and settler-colonial states from the nineteenth century on, but merely to the chaotic arrangement of powers resulting in the blind exercise of state-sanctioned violence and ruthless, self-interested, and unenlightened competition.

2. The notion of "failed state" is frequently used in an (imperialistic) American perspective. It mainly refers to a nation-state whose functions have basically become ineffective, leading to social chaos.

3. The *Peace of Westphalia* refers to the agreement reached on October 24, 1648, in the divided Holy Roman Empire in the Westphalian cities of Osnabrück and Münster. It was a culmination of a series of treaties that put an end to the Thirty Years War. The treaty included the parties of the Holy Roman emperor Ferdinand the Third, the king of Spain, the king of France, the king of Sweden, the Dutch Republic, various dukes of the Holy Roman Empire, and Free Cities from the Empire.

4. See Thomas Piketty, *Le capital au XXI de siècle* (Paris: Edition du Seuil, 2013); *Capital in the 21st Century* (Cambridge, MA: Harvard University Press, 2014).

5. See Michael Hardt and Antonio Negri, *Empire* (Cambridge, MA: Harvard University Press, 2001); *Multitude* (New York: Penguin Books, 2004); *Commonwealth* (Cambridge, MA: Belknap Press of Harvard University Press, 2009).

6. See Taleb (2012).

CHAPTER 16

1. See Kant's *Idea for a Universal History with a Cosmopolitan Intent* (1784) and *Perpetual Peace: A Philosophical Sketch* (1795), translated in *Critique of Historical Reason—Collected Writings* (历史理性批判文集), (Beijing: Commercial Press, 1997).

2. See Zhao Tingyang, "Understanding and Acceptance," in *Les Assises de la Connaissance Reciproque*, ed. Alain Le Pichon, (Paris: Le Robert, 2003). Here I develop a critique of Habermasian discourse ethics.

3. John Rawls, *The Law of Peoples* (Cambridge, MA: Harvard University Press, 1999).

4. Rawls (1999), 37ff and 48. [Translator's note: I had significant difficulty here locating the original phrase cited from Rawls from the translated Chinese text (Zhang Xiaohui et al. trans. 2001). I think part of the difficulty had to do with an understandable interpretive gloss by the translators of Rawls here to be highlighting the contrast between so-called "Well-Ordered societies" (viz., either liberal or decent hierarchical peoples) with unliberal and outlaw states that, according to Rawls, might require military intervention going beyond any mere justification of "self-defense" grounded in supposedly reasonable conceptions of a "Law of Peoples." However, since I couldn't actually find a sufficiently correlate sentence in the source text wherein Rawls stated so baldly an acceptance of intolerance allowing for military intervention and coercive sanctions (i.e., imperialist warfare by other hybrid, economic means), I slightly modified the original quote by turning it to a paraphrase. And for further context I cited two places wherein more or less the same point is being made. In any event, without getting too bogged down in the niceties of a Rawlsian analytic vocabulary, I think Zhao's critique of liberal triumphalism here, and all the associated abuses of human rights rhetoric used to be justifying imperialist economic sanctions or worse, stands clearly on its own strengths.]

5. Immanuel Kant, *Perpetual Peace: A Philosophical Sketch* (1795), in *Perpetual Peace and Other Essays*, trans. Ted Humphrey (Indianapolis, IN: Hackett Publishing Company, 1983).

6. Stephen C. Angle, *Contemporary Confucian Political Philosophy* (Bristol, UK: Polity Press, 2012), 79.

7. Angle (2012), 79.

CHAPTER 17

1. Translator's note: This phrase comes from a lecture Fei Xiaotong gave on the occasion of his eightieth birthday celebration. The entire sixteen-character slogan highlights the importance of cultural pluralism and world harmony: "Each appreciating their own beauty, and thus appreciating the beauty of others, sharing in this shared cultural aesthetic, the world becomes a great harmony!" (各美其美, 美人之美, 美美与共, 天下大同).

2. For a more detailed analysis, see Zhao Tingyang, *Bad World Investigations* (坏世界研究), (Beijing: People's University of China Press, 2009), 200–10.

3. Translator's note: Although not in the original, I've placed "Christianity" here in scare quotes because it is clear from the context that Zhao is referring not to an umbrella term capturing the various forms of religiosity around the world related, however loosely, to the figure of Jesus of Nazareth but more directly to a Western imperialist political logic derived from a certain religious milieu that can now operate just as much in a secular framework as it did in more traditional religious modalities.

4. Samuel P. Huntington, *The Clash of Civilizations and the Remaking of World Order* (New York: Touchstone Books, 1996), 51.

CHAPTER 18

1. So-called "dependence" refers to the fact that "some national economies receive limits from the growth and development of the national economies that they are dependent upon . . . the dependency condition leads to the dependent nations falling into a backward and exploited status vis-à-vis the hegemonic nations." See Theotônio dos Santos, *Dependency and Social Change* [*Dependencia y cambio social*] (Santiago: Centro de Estudios Socio Económicos, Universidad de Chile, 1972); Chinese translation: 特奥托尼奥·多斯桑托斯: (帝国主义与依附) (Beijing: Social Sciences Literature Press, 1999), 301.

2. Joseph S. Nye calls for America to strengthen its soft power to supplement its hard power. And although America is already "the greatest power since the Roman Empire," to rely just upon its hard power is not sufficient to "act in the world as it desires." See Nye, *The Paradox of American Power: Why the World's Only Superpower Can't Go It Alone* (London: Oxford University Press, 2002).

3. Concerning the theory of the hegemony of US currency, see Qiao Liang 乔良, "Why Americans Go to War" (美国人为何而战), *China Youth Daily* (中国青年报), February 25, 2011; and "Finance and War: Hegemony of American Currency and Sino-American Chess Games" (金融与战争: 美元霸权与中美棋局), *National Defense Reference* (2015), no. 11–12.

CHAPTER 19

1. Translator's note: By "progressivist" (*jinbulun* 进步论) here Zhao seems to be critiquing an idea of political modernity marked by a post-Hegelian triumphalist logic of endless progress and a linear, teleological model of historical understanding. This is obviously not a critique of "progressive" politics or any form of melioristic political theorizing per se.

2. "Cantor's world" is a mathematical concept. It is derived from Georg Cantor's set theory and the supposed reality of transfinite sets/worlds.

3. See Zhao Tingyang and Jules Régis Debray, *Words from Two Sides: A Correspondence Concerning the Problem of Revolution* (两面之词: 关于革命问题的通信), translated by Jean-Paul Tchang 张万申, (Beijing: CITIC Press, 2014), 179–83.

4. "Publicracy" is an English term the author created using a structural etymological method. See Zhao Tingyang and Debray (2014) for more on how this term can be used.

CHAPTER 20

1. John Rawls, *A Theory of Justice* (Cambridge, MA: Harvard University Press, 1971), 42–43.

2. *Analects* 6.30, "己欲立而立人, 己欲达而达人" (论语·雍也) cf. Legge (1893), vol. 1, 194.

3. *Analects* 15.24, "己所不欲勿施于人" (论语·卫灵公) cf. Legge (1893), vol. 1, 301.

4. *Daodejing* chapter 77, "天之道, 损有余而补不足"老子: (道德经·第七十七章) cf. Legge (1891), 119.

5. *Daodejing* chapter 42 (道德经·第四十二章) cf. Legge (1891), 85.

6. "免人之死, 解人之难, 救人之患, 济人之急者, 德也, 德之所在, 天下归之." (六韬·卷一·文韬). Cf. Sawyer and Sawyer (1993), 41.

7. William A. Callahan, "Tianxia, Empire and the World: Chinese Visions of World Order for the Twenty-First Century," in *China Orders the World*, ed. William Callahan and Elena Barabantseva (Baltimore, MD: Johns Hopkins University Press, 2011), 105.

8. Callahan, "Tianxia, Empire and the World," in Callahan and Barabantseva (2011), 104.

9. Translator's note: The expression *li bu wang jiao* (礼不往教) comes from an adaptation of a verse in the Quli chapter of the *Book of Rites*. In its original context it seems to be referring to the idea that ritual learning should be naturally occurring as a result of spontaneous desire rather than used to coercively inculcate values in impressionable heartminds. Cf. Legge (1967), vol. 1, 63.

10. *Analects* 3.3, "人而不仁, 如礼何? 人而不仁, 如乐何?" (论语·八佾) cf. Legge (1893), vol. 1, 155.

Bibliography of Works Cited

Ames, Roger T., and David Hall. 2001. *Focusing the Familiar: A Translation and a Philosophical Interpretation of the Zhongyong*. Honolulu: University of Hawai'i Press.

Angle, Stephen C. 2012. *Contemporary Confucian Political Philosophy*. Bristol, UK: Polity Press.

Arrow, Kenneth. 1951. *Social Choice and Individual Values*. New Haven, CT: Yale University Press.

Borges, Jose Louis. 1941. *El jardín de senderos que se bifurcan*. Buenos Aires: Editorial Sur.

Brook, Timothy, Michael van Walt van Praag, and Miek Boltjes, eds. 2018. *Sacred Mandates: Asian International Relations since Chinggis Khan*. Chicago: University of Chicago Press.

Callahan, William, and Elena Barabantseva, eds. 2011. *China Orders the World*. Baltimore, MD: Johns Hopkins University Press.

Carneiro, R. L. 1970. "A Theory of the Origin of the State." *Science* 169: 733–38.

Chang, K. C. 张光直. 2013a. *Six Lectures on Archaeology* (考古学专题六讲). Beijing: SDX Joint Publishing Company.

———. 2013b. 美术、神话与祭祀. Chinese translation of *Art, Myth, and Ritual*. Beijing: SDX Joint Publishing Company.

———. 2013c. 张光直 (古代中国考古学). Beijing: SDX Joint Publishing Company. Chinese translation of *The Archaeology of Ancient China*, 4th edition.

——. 1999a. *The Bronze Age of China* (中国青铜时代). Beijing: SDX Joint Publishing Company.

——. 1999b. *Collected Essays on Chinese Archaeology* (中国考古学论文集). Beijing: SDX Joint Publishing Company.

——. 1986. *The Archaeology of Ancient China*, 4th edition. New Haven, CT: Yale University Press.

——. 1983. *Art, Myth and Ritual: The Path to Political Authority in Ancient China*. Cambridge, MA: Harvard University Press.

Chen Gaohua 陈高华 and Shi Weimin 史卫民. 1996. *A Comprehensive History of Chinese Political Institutions*. Vol. 8 (中国政治制度通史·第八卷). Edited by Bai Gang（白刚主编）. Beijing: People's Press.

Chen Mengjia 陈梦家. 2011. *Studies in Chinese Writing* (中国文字学). Beijing: Zhonghua shuju.

——. 2005. *Explanation of the Exalted Documents* (尚书通论). Beijing: Zhonghua shuju.

——. 1956. *A Comprehensive Overview of Shang Divination Discourse* (殷墟卜辞综述). Beijing: Zhonghua shuju.

——. 1936. "Myth and Shamanism in the Shang Dynasty" (商代的神话与巫术) in *Yanjing Xuebao* (燕京学报) Vol. 20.

Chinese Academy of Social Sciences Archeological Research Center 中国社会科学院考古研究所. 2010. *Chinese Archaeology: The New Stone Age Volume* (中国考古学·新石器时代卷). Beijing: Chinese Academy of Social Sciences Press.

——. 2011. *Chinese Archaeology: The Xia-Shang Volume* (中国考古学·夏商卷).

Crump, J. I. (trans. and annotated). 1996. *Chan-kuo Ts'e*. Revised edition. Ann Arbor: Center for Chinese Studies, University of Michigan.

Cui Guangzhu 瞿光珠. 1996. *The Standardization of Ancient China* (中国古代标准化). Taiyuan: Shanxi People's Press.

Cui Shigu 瞿式谷. 2000. *Notes on Unofficial Matters* (职方外记小言). See Xie Fang 谢方, *Commentary on Notes on Unofficial Matters* (职方外记校释). Beijing, Zhonghua shuju.

Cui Tongzu 瞿同祖. 2003. *China's Feudal Society* (中国封建社会). Shanghai: Shanghai Century Press Group.

Duan Qingbo 段清波 and Xu Weimin 徐卫民. 2014. *China's Great Wall through History: Discoveries and Research* (中国历代长城：发现与研究). Beijing: Science Press.

Durrant, Stephen, Wai-Yee Lee, and David Schaberg, trans. 2017. *The Zuo Tradition*. Seattle: University of Washington Press.

Fei Xiaotong 费孝通. 1992. *From the Soil: The Foundations of Chinese Society—A Translation of Fei Xiaotong's Xiangtu Zhongguo*. Translated by Gary Hamilton and Wang Zheng. Berkeley: University of California Press.

——. *From the Soil* (乡土中国). Beijing: SDX Joint Publishing Company, 1985.

Fei Zhengqing, ed. 费正清主编. 2010. *Chinese World Order: Traditional China's*

Ambassadorial Relations (中国的世界秩序：传统中国的对外关系). Beijing: Chinese Academy of Social Sciences Press.

Fu Sinian 傅斯年. 2002. *Ethnicity and Ancient Chinese History* (民族与古代中国史). Shijiazhuang: Hebei Education Press.

Ge Zhaoguang 葛兆光. 2011. *Here in "China" I Dwell* (宅兹中国). Beijing: Zhonghua shuju. Translated by Jesse Field and Qin Fang. Leiden: Brill, 2017.

Ge Zhiyi 葛志毅. 2005. *Studies in Zhou Institutions of Land Distribution* (周代分封制度研究). Harbin: Heilongjiang People's Press.

Granet, Marcel. 1929. *La civilisation chinoise*. Paris: La Renaissance du livre.

Gu Yanwu 顾炎武. 1773. *Record of Daily Realizations* (日知录). *Sikuquanshu* 四库全书. Chinese Text Project digital library.

Han Jianye 韩建业. 2015. *Early China: The Formation and Development of a Sino-Sphere Culture* (早期中国：中国文化圈的形成和发展). Shanghai: Shanghai Classics Publishing House.

Hardt, Michael, and Antonio Negri. 2009. *Commonwealth*. Cambridge, MA: Belknap Press of Harvard University Press.

———. 2004. *Multitude*. New York: Penguin Books.

———. 2001. *Empire*. Cambridge, MA: Harvard University Press.

Hou Wailu 侯外庐. 2003. *Theorizing Ancient China's Social History* (中国古代社会史论). Shijiazhuang: Hebei Education Press.

Hu Huanyong 胡焕庸. 1935. "China's Population Line: Attaching Statistical Tables and Density Maps" (中国人口之分布——附统计表与密度图) in *Acta Geographica Sinica* (地理学报) 2.

Huang Huixian 黄惠贤. 1996. *Comprehensive History of Chinese Political Institutions*, vol. 4 (中国政治制度通史·第四卷). Edited by Bai Gang （白刚主编）. Beijing: People's Press.

Huntington, Samuel. 1996. *The Clash of Civilizations and the Remaking of World Order*. New York: Touchstone Books.

Hutton, Eric, trans. 2014. *Xunzi: The Complete Text*. Princeton, NJ: Princeton University Press.

Johnston, Ian. 2010. *The Mozi: A Complete Translation*. New York: Columbia University Press.

Kant, Immanuel. 1983. *Perpetual Peace: A Philosophical Sketch* (1795). In *Perpetual Peace and Other Essays*. Translated by Ted Humphrey. Indianapolis, IN: Hackett Publishing Company.

———. 1997. *Idea for a Universal History with a Cosmopolitan Intent* (1784) and *Perpetual Peace: A Philosophical Sketch* (1795). Chinese translation in *Critique of Historical Reason—Collected Writings* (历史理性批判文集). Beijing: Commercial Press.

Knoblock, John, and Jeffrey Riegel, trans. 2000. *The Annals of Lü Buwei*. Stanford, CA: Stanford University Press.

Legge, James, trans. 1967. *Li Chi Book of Rites: An Encyclopedia of Ancient*

Ceremonial Usages, Religious Creeds, and Social Institutions. Vols. 1 and 2, edited by Ch'u Chai and Winberg Chai. New York: University Books.

———. 1891. *The Sacred Books of China: The Texts of Taoism*, part 1. Oxford: Oxford University Press.

———. 1893. *The Chinese Classics with a Translation, Critical and Exegetical Notes, Prolegomena, and Copious Indexes*. Vol. 1. *Confucian Analects, The Great Learning, The Doctrine of the Mean*. Oxford: Clarendon Press.

———. 1882. *The Sacred Books of China: The Texts of Confucianism*, part 2. Oxford: Oxford University Press.

———. 1879. *The Sacred Books of China: The Texts of Confucianism*, part 1. Oxford: Clarendon Press.

———. 1875. *The Chinese Classics with a Translation, Critical and Exegetical Notes, Prolegomena, and Copious Indexes*. Vol. 2. *The Works of Mencius*. London: Trubner and Co.

———. 1865. *The Chinese Classics: With a Translation, Critical and Exegetical Notes, Prolegomena, and Copious Indexes*. Vol. 3. *The Shoo King* or *The Book of Historical Documents*. Hong Kong: London: Trubner and Co.

Lewis, Mark Edward, and Mei-yu Hsieh. 2017. "Tianxia and the Invention of Empire in East Asia." In Ban Wang ed. *Chinese Visions of World Order: Tianxia, Culture, and World Politics*. Durham, NC: Duke University Press.

Li Hongbing 李鸿宾. 2015. "Stag Hunting on the Central Plain: The Secret Behind the Expansion of the Northern Peoples into the South" (逐鹿中原：东北诸族南向拓展的秘密) in *Social Sciences Weekly* (中国社会科学报) January 29.

Li Qingshan 李庆善. 1996. *A New Theory of Chinese People: Viewing the People's Heart from Folk Sayings* (中国人新论：从民谚看民心). Beijing: China Academy of Social Sciences Press.

Li Xihou 李锡厚 and Bai Bing 白滨. 1996. *Comprehensive History of Chinese Political Institutions*, vol. 7 (中国政治制度通史·第七卷). Edited by Bai Gang (白刚主编). Beijing: People's Press.

Li Yunquan; 李云泉. 2014. *The Myriad States Come to Court: A History of Tributary Institutions* (万邦来朝：朝贡制度史论). Beijing: Xinhua Press.

Li Zehou 李泽厚. 2018. *The Origins of Chinese Thought: From Shamanism to Ritual Regulations and Humaneness*. Translated by Robert Carleo III. Leiden: Brill.

———. 2015. (由巫到礼，释礼归仁). Beijing: SDX Joint Publishing Company.

Liang Qichao 梁启超. 1936. "National Thinking of Transformation and Change: A Theory of Difference and Similarity" (国家思想变迁异同论). In *Ice Drinker's Studio: Collected Writings*. Vol. 1, Collection 6, "Treatise on the Great Power of Ethnic Conflicts" 饮冰室合集：文集 (论民族竞争之大势), in Vol. 2, Collection 10. Shanghai: Zhonghua shuju.

Liang Shuming 梁漱溟. 1949. *China's Modern Academic Classic—Liang Shuming Edition* (中国现代学术经典·梁漱溟卷). Shijiazhuang: Hebei Education Press.

Liang Sicheng 梁思成. 1998. *Chinese Architectural History.* (中国建筑史). Tianjin: Baihuawenyi Publishing.

Liu Qingzhu ed. 刘庆柱主编. 2010. *Chinese Archaeological Discoveries and Research, 1949–2009* (中国考古发现与研究 1949–2009). Beijing: People's Press.

Major, John, Sarah Queen, Andrew Meyer, Harold Roth, Michael Puett, and Judson Murray, trans. 2010. *The Huainanzi.* New York: Columbia University Press.

Man Zhimin 满志敏. 2009. *Climate Change Research in the History of China* (中国历史时期气候变化研究). Jinan: Shandong Education Press.

Meng Xiangcai 孟祥才. 1996. *Comprehensive History of Chinese Political Institutions*, vol. 3, (中国政治制度通史·第三卷). Edited by Bai Gang (白刚主编). Beijing: People's Press.

Milbourne, Olivia, trans. 2018. *The Spring and Autumn Annals of Master Yan.* Leiden: Brill.

Miller, Harry, trans. 2015. *The Gongyang Commentary on The Spring and Autumn Annals.* New York: Palgrave MacMillan.

Nienhauser, William H., et al., trans. 1994. *The Grand Scribe's Records.* Vols. 1 and 7, *The Basic Annals of Pre-Han China.* Bloomington: Indiana University Press.

"Nurhaci's Letter." 1984. In *Historical Materials from before the Qing Invasions* (清入关前史料选辑 1). Beijing: People's University of China Press.

Nye, Joseph. 2002. *The Paradox of American Power: Why the World's Only Superpower Can't Go It Alone.* London: Oxford University Press.

Olson, Mancur. 2000. *Power and Prosperity: Outgrowing Communist and Capitalist Dictatorships.* New York: Basic Books.

———. 1982. *The Rise and Decline of Nations: Economic Growth, Stagflation, and Social Rigidities.* New Haven, CT: Yale University Press.

———. 1965. *The Logic of Collective Action: Public Goods and the Theory of Groups.* Cambridge, MA: Harvard University Press.

Piketty, Thomas. 2013. *Le capital au XXI de siècle.* Paris: Edition du Seuil. *Capital in the 21st Century.* Cambridge, MA: Harvard University Press.

Pines, Yuri, ed. and trans. 2017. *The Book of Lord Shang.* New York: Columbia University Press.

Qian Mu. 1948. *A Guide to Chinese Cultural History* (中国文化史导论). Beijing: Commercial Press.

Qiao Liang 乔良. 2015. *Finance and War: Hegemony of American Currency and Sino-American Chess Games* (金融与战争：美元霸权与中美棋局), *National Defense Reference*, no. 11–12.

———. 2011. "Why Americans Go to War" (美国人为何而战). *China Youth Daily* (中国青年报) 02-25.

Qin Yaqing. 2018. *A Relational Theory of World Politics* (New York: Cambridge University Press).

Rao Zongyi 饶宗颐. 2015. *A Theory of Legitimacy in Chinese History* (中国史学上之正统论). Beijing: Zhonghua shuju.

Rawls, John. 1999. *The Law of Peoples*. Cambridge, MA: Harvard University Press. Chinese translation: Zhang Xiaohui et al. 张晓辉等译 . 罗尔斯：[万民法]. Changchun: Jilin People's Press.

———. 1971. *A Theory of Justice*. Cambridge, MA: Harvard University Press.

Rickett, W. Allyn. 1998. *Guanzi: Political Economic, and Philosophical Essays from Early China—A Study and Translation*. Vol. 2. Princeton, NJ: Princeton University Press.

———. 1985. *Guanzi: Political Economic, and Philosophical Essays from Early China—A Study and Translation*. Vol. 1. Princeton, NJ: Princeton University Press.

Santos, Theotônio dos. 1972. *Dependency and Social Change* [*Dependencia y cambio social*] . Santiago: Centro de Estudios Socio Económicos, Universidad de Chile. Chinese translation: 特奥托尼奥·多斯桑托斯：(帝国主义与依附). Beijing: Social Sciences Literature Press, 1999.

Sawyer, Ralph, and Mei-Chun Sawyer, trans. 1993. *The Seven Military Classics of Ancient China*. Boulder, CO: Westview Press.

Schelling, Thomas C. 1980. *The Strategy of Conflict*. Cambridge, MA: Harvard University Press. Chinese translation: 托马斯·谢林，赵华等译：(冲突的战略). Beijing: Huaxia Press, 2011.

Schmitt, Carl. 1996. *The Concept of the Political*. Chicago: University of Chicago Press.

Sima Qian 司马迁. 1982. *Records of the Grand Historian* (史记). Beijing: Zhonghua shuju.

Song Lian 宋濂. 1976. *Yuan History* (元史). (Beijing: Zhonghua shuju).

Su Qiqi 苏秉奇. 2013. *A New Exploration into the Origins of Chinese Civilization* (中国文明起源新探). Beijing: People's Press.

Taleb, Nassim Nicholas. 2012. *Antifragile: Things That Gain from Disorder*. New York: Penguin Random House.

Thompson, Kirill O. 1995. "When a 'White Horse' Is Not a 'Horse.'" *Philosophy East and West* 45, no. 4.

Voegelin, Eric. 1956. *Order and History*. Vol. 1, *Israel and Revelation*. Baton Rouge: Louisiana State University Press. Chinese translation: 埃里克·沃格林，霍伟岸、叶赢译 (秩序与历史·卷一·以色列与启示). Nanjing: Yilin Press, 2010.

Wallerstein, Immanuel. 2011. *The Modern World-System*. Vol. 1, *Capitalist Agriculture and the Origins of the European World-Economy in the Sixteenth*

Century. Berkeley: University of California Press. Chinese translation: 华勒斯坦, (现代世界体系·卷 1). Beijing: Higher Education Press, 1998.

Wang Fuzhi 王夫之. 2011. *Complete Works of Wang Fuzhi* (船山全书). Changxia: Yuelu Publishing House.

Wang Guowei 王国维. 2001. *Collected Writings—Discourse on Shang-Zhou Institutions* (观堂集林·殷周制度论). Shijiazhuang: Hebei Educational Press.

Wang Ke 王柯. 2001. *Ethnicities and States: A Comprehensive Overview of Thinking Chinese Multi-Ethnic National Unity* (民族与国家：中国多民族统一国家思想系谱). Beijing: Chinese Academy of Social Sciences Press.

Wang Mingming 王铭铭. 2012. "All Under Heaven (Tianxia): Cosmological Perspectives and Political Ontologies in Pre-Modern China." *HAU: Journal of Ethnographic Theory* 2, no. 1: 337–83

——. 2008. "China: Ethno-body or Civilization-body?" (中国：民族体还是文明体?). *Beijing Cultural Review* 文化纵横 12 .

Wang Tongling 王桐龄. 2010. *A History of Chinese Ethnicities* (中国民族史). Changchun: Jilin Publishing Group.

Watson, Burton, trans. 1993a. *Records of the Grand Historian: Han Dynasty I.* Columbia University Press.

——. 1993b. *Records of the Grand Historian: Qin Dynasty*. New York: Columbia University Press.

——. 1974. *Courtier and Commoner in Ancient China: Selections from the History of the Former Han by Pan Ku*. New York: Columbia University Press.

Wittgenstein, Ludwig. 1964. *Philosophical Investigations*. New York: Macmillan Company.

Xu Hong 许宏. 2014. *What Is China?* (何以中国). Beijing: SDX Joint Publishing Company.

——. 2009. *Earliest China* (最早的中国). Beijing: Science Publishing.

Xu Zhuoyun 许倬云. 2001. *History of the Western Zhou* (西周史). Beijing: SDX Joint Publishing Company.

Yan Mingshu 阎明恕. 2003. *A History of Marriage Alliances in Ancient China* (中国古代和亲史). Guiyang: Guizhouminzu Press.

Yan Xuetong. 2019. *Leadership and the Rise of Great Powers*. Princeton, NJ: Princeton University Press.

——. 2013. Edited by Daniel A. Bell and Sun Zhe. *Ancient Chinese Thought, Modern Chinese Power*. Translated by Edmund Ryden. Princeton, NJ: Princeton University Press.

Yang Kuan 杨宽. 2006. *An Institutional History of Ancient Chinese Cities* (中国古代都城制度史). Shanghai: Shanghai People's Press.

Yao Dali 姚大力. 2011. *Mongolian Yuan Institutions and Political Culture* (蒙元制度与政治文化). Beijing: Peking University Press.

Yu Lunian 俞鹿年. 1996. *Comprehensive History of Chinese Political Institutions*.

Vol. 5 (中国政治制度通史·第五卷). Edited by Bai Gang (白刚主编). Beijing: People's Press.

Zhang Guangzhi 张光直. See K. C. Chang.

Zhang Zhaosu 张兆裕. 2004. "The Chinese-Barbarian Distinction in the Ming Dynasty" (明代华夷之辨). In *Ancient Historical Documents: Ming and Qing dynasties* (古史文存·明清卷上). Edited by Chinese Academy of Social Sciences History Research Center (中国社会科学院历史研究所). Beijing: Social Sciences Literature Press.

Zhao Hui 赵辉. 2000. "The Formation of the Historical Trend of the Central Plain as Core" (以中原为中心的历史趋势的形成). *Wenwu* 文物 (*Cultural Relics*) 1.

Zhao Tingyang 赵汀阳. 2014. "The Forking Paths of Time—Contemporaneity as an Ontological Problem" (时间的分叉——作为存在论问题的当代性). *Philosophical Researches* (哲学研究) 6.

———. 2013. *The Fulcrum of First Philosophy* (第一哲学的支点). Beijing: Sanlian Press.

———. 2009. *Bad World Investigations* (坏世界研究). Beijing: People's University of China Press.

———. 2005. *Tianxia System* (天下体系). Nanjing: Jiangsu Education Press.

———. 2003. "Understanding and Acceptance." In *Les Assises de la Connaissance Reciproque*, edited by Alain Le Pichon. Paris: Le Robert.

Zhao Tingyang and Jules Régis Debray. 2014. *Words from Two Sides: A Correspondence Concerning the Problem of Revolution* (两面之词：关于革命问题的通信). Translated by Jean-Paul Tchang 张万申. Beijing: CITIC Press.

Zheng Youguo 郑有国. 2004. *Researching Traditional China's Institutes of Foreign Trade* (中国市舶制度研究). Fuzhou: Fujian Education Press.

Zhou Chenhe 周振鹤. 2013. *Sixteen Lectures on Chinese History and Political Geography* (中国历史政治地理十六讲). Beijing: Zhonghua shuju.

Index

Founded in 1893,
UNIVERSITY OF CALIFORNIA PRESS
publishes bold, progressive books and journals
on topics in the arts, humanities, social sciences,
and natural sciences—with a focus on social
justice issues—that inspire thought and action
among readers worldwide.

The UC PRESS FOUNDATION
raises funds to uphold the press's vital role
as an independent, nonprofit publisher, and
receives philanthropic support from a wide
range of individuals and institutions—and from
committed readers like you. To learn more, visit
ucpress.edu/supportus.